Direct Work
Social work with
children and young people
in care

Direct Work
Social work with children and young people in care

Edited by Barry Luckock
and Michelle Lefevre

BAAF
ADOPTION
& FOSTERING

Published by
British Association for Adoption & Fostering
(BAAF)
Saffron House
6–10 Kirby Street
London EC1N 8TS
www.baaf.org.uk

Charity registration 275689 (England and Wales) and SCO39337 (Scotland)

Reprinted 2009, 2010

British Library Cataloguing in Publication Data
A catalogue record for this book is available from the British Library

ISBN 978 1 905664 29 0

Project management by Shaila Shah, Director of Publications, BAAF
Designed by Andrew Haig & Associates
Typeset by Avon DataSet Ltd, Bidford on Avon
Printed in Great Britain by TJ International
Trade distribution by Turnaround Publisher Services, Unit 3, Olympia Trading Estate,
Coburg Road, London N22 6TZ

BAAF is the leading UK-wide membership organisation for all those concerned with adoption,
fostering and child care issues.

Contents

Acknowledgements

In preparing this book, we have been supported in various ways by a number of people in addition to our thoughtful and responsive chapter authors. In particular, we want to thank the following people for their support, kindness and generosity. Shelley Burdette-Dekin, Patrick Stevens, Jason Young and Jade took time to share their care experiences with us. Jenny Clifton, Karen Lawes and Emma Sutton made these connections for us and supported these discussions. Numerous other young people in and beyond care, whom we have known personally and professionally over the years, have also inspired us and taught us what good practice might mean. Clarissa Bergonzi and Martin Kay described their own experiences as effective practitioners. Lorraine Wallis and Julie Siddons provided the artwork for the book cover. Many thanks indeed to Amy, Claire and Kerry for allowing us to use their drawings. At BAAF, John Simmonds shared thoughts with us on the focus of the book and was as supportive as ever, whilst Shaila Shah was consistently positive and efficient as our editor. Jo Francis also helped in a patient way with the tying up of loose ends. Finally, we would like to thank Claire Lucius and Gillian Luckock, our partners, who have given us unfailing support as well as ever helpful advice and guidance.

Barry Luckock and Michelle Lefevre
November 2007

Direct work with children – delusion or reality?

John Simmonds

As this chapter is being written, I have two preoccupations. The first is concerned with the passage of time. It is 20 years since Jane Aldgate and myself worked together to edit our book, *Direct Work with Children* (Aldgate and Simmonds, 1988). That book arose out of the recognition by the teaching team responsible for the Diploma in Advanced Social Work course (Children and Families) at Goldsmiths College, University of London of the excellence of students' work in the direct work with children module. We wanted to bring that work to the attention of the profession given we were concerned to establish the importance of social workers undertaking direct work with children. The advanced course was the forerunner of what was to become a bigger framework of post-qualifying education for social workers. The course grew from a number of sources, Rowe and Lambert's seminal *Children Who Wait* (1973) Goldstein, Freud and Solnit's (1973) *Beyond the Best Interests of the Child* and the Department of Health's *Decisions in Child Care* (1985). All of these publications pointed to the precarious position of many children who had become the responsibility of the State but were suspended uneasily between their birth parents and wider family and their foster carers or residential establishments without having a sense of belonging, commitment or security from any of them. It was also a time where child abuse had forced its way into professional and public awareness and sadly social workers had become identified as part of the problem of child abuse, rather than its solution, by failing to recognise it or intervene to prevent it. The importance of high quality assessment skills, proactive decision making, planning and placement practice based on knowledge of child and family development were seen as core to addressing these issues and indeed to the course itself. The availability of the BAAF training pack, *In Touch with Children*, was also key in reinforcing the view that children were not just objects of any intervention but subjects with important views and feelings about what was happening to them. A team of very dedicated staff from the social work department at Goldsmiths, BAAF and other organisations ensured that the course developed and maintained its commitment to this important principle. It was core to the teaching programme and to required practice, the latter being particularly important as it involved a large number of local authorities and voluntary organisations who seconded their staff and provided them with high quality supervision and consultation.

Looking back at what was achieved through the Goldsmiths' programme is relevant to my second current preoccupation – the implications of the English White Paper, *Care Matters* (2006, 2007). The document is long and complex and is intended to make a significant improvement to the functioning of the care system and the lives of children who become its responsibility. One of the difficulties I had in formulating a response to the White Paper was knowing quite what to say when many of the issues *Care Matters* was concerned with were exactly the issues we were concerned about in the 1970s and 1980s – the very poor outcomes across a range of important dimensions of young people who have been "in care". *Care Matters* postdates a number of major English government initiatives – Quality Protects (1999) and Choice Protects (2002) and the Adoption Reforms initiated by the Prime Minister's Review of Adoption in 2000 (PIU, 2000) as well as the parallel reforms signalled by the Government's response to the Victoria Climbié Inquiry (DfES, 2003) and the Children Act 2004. However, if the reforms to the universal health and education systems have been slow to take effect, despite the investment of large sums of public money and significant upheaval, the reforms to the care system have shown only marginal improvement when measured against government set targets.

The current political concern with this discouraging state of affairs is not dissimilar to that of the late 70s and 80s when a wake up call sounded about the failings of the state care system with then a real sense of hope about what the social work profession might contribute to this, one critical part being by the development of sound continuing professional development and education that focused on advanced knowledge and skills. The general themes the Goldsmiths' course and our book were focusing on was summed up in the introduction to *Direct Work with Children* where we said:

> *The themes of the book are, we hope, explicit. They include the value of flexible perm-anency planning, the need for preparation, setting of boundaries and a sound knowledge base before work begins, and the valuing of the relationship between child and worker as an enabling part of the work and a recognition of its emotional content.*

We concluded the introduction by hoping that 'the central concern shown throughout the book is respect for the children themselves, whose experiences of sadness, loss and rejection led to the need for social work intervention in the first place. They too have a lot to teach us.'

As the chapters in this book demonstrate, the situation in 2007 is not the same as it was in the early 1980s. Some of the significant changes that stand out for me are as follows:

1. Human rights did not have an explicit legislative framework and the child as a "consumer" and the discourse of rights-based work did not exist.
2. Attachment theory was important, as it is now, but centred exclusively on Bowlby's exposition. The complementary evidence and framework of Mary Ainsworth (1978) was not then widely available. Bowlby and attachment theory was also controversial where it was seen to oppose feminist arguments for the independence and equality of women. Rutter (1972) had also raised questions about the over-reliance on the maternal deprivation hypothesis.

3. Child development theory had a significant place on the advanced course but there was controversy between the psychoanalytic and the behaviourist perspectives. This has now given way to a much more articulate and integrated perspective. Neglect, emotional abuse, trauma and brain development have been added to existing perspectives on the consequences of physical and sexual abuse. The introduction of the concept of "resilience" has been important in correcting what had become a too dominant picture of children being victims or the carrier of problematic issues.

4. Health, education and employability are now a more explicit part of the holistic picture of a child's needs and, as such, a part of care planning.

5. While the social work profession in England is now regulated by the General Social Care Council, other professions have become more established and provide more accessible and established routes for those wishing to work directly with children. The rise of competing providers and contracting out of services has changed the landscape of public services. In the 1980s, there was no independent sector of social work practice. Social workers stood in their own right as experts on their cases in care proceedings. Excessive reliance on competing evidence from "experts" to the exclusion of social workers views did not exist in the same way.

6. Permanency planning and stable placements continue to be as a significant a theme as ever they were and equally challenging to make a reality.

These are all significant changes but the one thing that has not changed is the importance of *listening to children*. This is highlighted in the introduction to *Direct Work with Children* and then again in *Care Matters* which sets out numerous proposals that children and young people should play a more significant role in the services provided for them. This should include general service monitoring and development as well as having a far more important voice in developing their own care plan. The White Paper and planned new Act in England proposes that each local authority should make a direct pledge to each child about service standards, that they should establish a Children in Care Council to monitor service provision, that every child should have access to advocates and independent representatives to ensure that they receive the care and services they need, and that they should be provided with health, education, leisure as well as social services to ensure that lack of opportunity is not an impediment to their development and participation in society. The role of the Independent Reviewing Officer is to be enhanced. So numerous are these proposals that the White Paper is promising to radically reform the care system. But my question now is how do these proposals compare to the kinds of issues being identified and in need of reform in the late 70s and 80s?

What follows are only examples of what was being written about during that time. It is not an exhaustive historical review. It is, however, illustrative of some very important themes. In one very influential study, Rowe *et al* (1984) said,

The verdict on long-term fostering is "not proven". In spite of many positive aspects, too many of the study placements had drifted from being short-term or indefinite into undeclared permanency . . . It was our very strong impression that, although many of the placements we studied were working well, they were doing so in spite of the system rather than because of it.

This message is recognisable today and is core to the findings of the York stability study (Sinclair *et al*, 2007). So to is one of the messages from the Government's 1976 publication, *Foster Care: A guide to practice* which warned that fostering practice was in danger of becoming 'arrangement dominated' rather than 'child orientated'. That Guide continued by recommending that social workers:

. . . train themselves in the discipline of observing and understanding the meaning of what they see and hear. To this end they must spend time with the child. (p 73)

However, 10 years after the publication of *Foster Care: A guide to practice* and perhaps sufficient time for its messages to have brought about real change, it was precisely the issue of 'spending time with the child' that formed the censure of the social worker in the Jasmine Beckford child abuse Inquiry (Blom-Cooper, 1985). In a particularly powerful passage, the Inquiry reports that:

Throughout the three years of social work with the Beckfords, Ms. Wahlstrom totally misconceived her role as the field worker enforcing Care Orders in respect of two very young children at risk. Her gaze was focused on Beverley Lorrington and Morris Beckford; she averted her eyes from the children to be aware of them only as and when they were with their parents, hardly ever to observe their development, and never to communicate with Jasmine on her own. The two children were treated as mere append-ages to their parents who were treated as clients, although Ms. Wahlstrom did tell the Magistrates in 1981 that her 'primary role is the welfare of the children'. In the meticulous record of nearly 100 pages of detailed notes kept by Ms. Wahlstrom and others in the social worker's report, there is not a single entry devoted exclusively to Jasmine and Louise.

Rowe *et al* (1984) report that in their study only two-thirds of social workers reported seeing the children for whom they were responsible in the previous year. The children's perception (supported by foster carers) was, however, quite different with a far smaller number reporting seeing their social worker alone. Rowe *et al* conclude:

The only explanation seemed to be that the "seeing alone" was often very brief and passed unnoticed by child and foster parent. It could still, of course, provide an opportunity for the child to speak confidentially to the social worker if he of she wished to do so, but it was evidently not something that the child could look forward to or count on. (p 159)

The Department of Health's 1991 *Patterns and Outcomes in Child Placement* takes a slightly different practice focus.

Often inadequate attention was paid to the history of the client's problems, to issues of discipline and authority within the home, to parents' expectations of the worker's intervention and establishing a knowledge base common to all participants. Too often, disagreements about the nature of problems and about methods of handling them remained unexplored undercurrents in exchanges between workers and clients. This approach was extremely unlikely to lead to substantial agreement over the purpose of care.

This is a troubling picture – social workers may appear to be very active in meeting and talking with their clients and even punctilious in recording notes of their meetings but it is often not clear what the objective of the work actually is because this has not been explicitly discussed. And without that discussion and thought being given to the nature of the issues facing the parents in relation to the care of their child, there could be no shared understanding of what needed to be done even if that meant disagreeing with one another.

More recently, the Joint Chief Inspector's Report on Safeguarding Children (Behan, 2005) says:

Having diagnosed what is required, social workers generally focus on co-ordinating services. We see a few examples of social workers who use their skills and relationships to work directly with children and their parents to alter the balance of behaviours in families and achieve changes to enable the child to stay with the family. But it has become exceptional for mainstream children's social services teams to provide these services for any length of time. (Para 6.36)

This suggests that the problem may have become even more pronounced so that after initial assessment work, the social work task becomes more explicitly high-level administrative work in commissioning from others whatever is required to sustain or improve parental functioning and children's safety and welfare. Is it the case that, despite repeated messages from research, from inspections and from serious case reviews, social workers need to focus their attention on children and directly engage with them and their parents in sustained, thoughtful and detailed work that the movement has been in the opposite direction and that it has now become "exceptional" for social workers to do this work themselves?

It is perplexing to hear an endless repetition of the messages that:

• it is core to the social worker's role that they work directly with children;

- that there can be serious and dangerous consequences when they do not do so;
- that there are positive benefits when they do;
- that children and young people want more contact with their social workers;
- and that social workers themselves see the advantages of doing direct work and would choose to do so if they were supported and had the time to do so.

But that there is:

- little evidence that social workers do very much direct work that children and young people are aware of;
- very limited evidence that it is effective when they do so;
- evidence that they are not trained to do so on social work training courses or are supported or encouraged to do so by their managers or agencies.

So after 30 or more years, what are we to make of this apparent movement in the opposite direction? *Care Matters* contains some very strong messages that children find it difficult to make contact with their social worker and cannot rely on what social workers say or what they promise, and that there are too frequent changes in social worker. *Care Matters* clearly takes this issue of social workers' lack of contact with children so seriously that it is proposing to re-model the social work profession to ensure that it can happen. But whatever this might come to mean, it is essential that we do not become seduced into an unrealistic picture of what this might mean in practice. The history of social work indicates that the issue of direct work has not lent itself to steady progression; if anything, the opposite. The fact is that the "problem" of direct work with children in social work has existed over a generation or more. It is a problem that has not found an easy solution and this engenders a great sense of dissatisfaction from children and young people and from many social workers. We need to ask ourselves: 'Is the failure to find a solution to this problem indicative of the fact that maybe we are functioning under some kind of collective delusion about the nature of the social work role or maybe a collective romantic illusion about what we would like the role of social workers to be?' And of course it may be, as has often been voiced in social work, that we fail to appreciate what good work does go on, that we only see the failures, and have great difficulty in acknowledging the commitment, determination and resourcefulness of the social work profession. Whatever the answer to this may be, it is no less important than it ever was that we more directly understand the nature of the problem in engaging in direct work that has resulted in a retreat from actually doing so. There are other issues which need to be understood and worked at and a good place to start is with some comments made by the author and journalist, Lionel Shriver (2007). She forcibly reminds us what can be at stake, when writing after the conviction of the parents of a child who had been abused after she was returned to them from local authority care.

These parents had 'scalded the girl's hands with boiling water, kicked her repeatedly in the groin, pulled out clumps of her hair, and locked her in the loo to sleep naked by the toilet . . . "Child B" was in so much pain that to be examined by a doctor she had to be put under general anaesthetic . . . "Child B" had been removed from parents suspected of being violent, and returning her was – easy to say now – a mistake. It does seem odd that social workers could have called on the family 20 times and not noticed anything amiss.

Shriver continues, commenting on the public perception of social workers:

Everybody hates you. You're employed to butt into a family's private business, and you're paid to be mistrustful. Because you're empowered to do dreadful things such as take children away from their parents, you're perceived as a threat. No one looks forward to you popping by. You routinely confront either raging hostility or artificial, brown nosing ingratiation, and either way it's hard to get straight answers in, what – 20 minutes? You can't spend long on a case, because you have a whole rota to get through in one day. How many of the people you are trying to help will not answer the door or treat you like rubbish? How many of these cases will be deeply depressing?

This perspective on social workers is a long way from the romantic illusion of direct work with children or adults because of the extent to which suspicion and hatred are stirred up in the course of the work. Whether it is the discovery of abuse, the dread of separation and potential loss of one's children, the humiliation or shame of being investigated for being a poor or dangerous parent, confrontation with one's alcohol, drug or mental health problem, or the memory of past experiences as a child, working with social workers can be deeply disturbing (AP, 2006). The problem, then, is how do social workers reconcile the wish to "do good" and being seen to be "doing good" with the client's fear or actual experience of actions that cause real distress and emotional harm? And how do social workers maintain that complex perspective when they also have a responsibility to give priority to one person's needs over another – the protection of a child from an abusive or neglectful parent? Human encounters work best on the basis of there being some sense of shared understanding and purpose between the people involved. Where fear, suspicion and hatred are active undercurrents in people's thoughts and feelings and threaten to break through to exert real force in the relationship, a volatile, unsafe state is created. For social workers whose primary task centres on working in such relationships, the powerfully unsafe feelings they engender are very disturbing. To actively keep in mind the possibility of these feelings working themselves out in the course of the work through 'raging hostility or artificial, brown nosing ingratiation' is very difficult. To maintain a realistic and hopeful state of mind which must be core to effective social work requires considerable emotional maturity. If Shriver's dynamic of suspicion is a part of what the social work role has to work with, then the full brunt of this dynamic will come into play in trying to resolve what appears to be the irreconcilable message: 'Trust me, I'm a force for good, believe me, I will do no harm' with an acknowledgement that 'I am a force that can and maybe will create disappointment, pain and suffering.' This is, of course, a fundamental dynamic at work at the heart of all parenting relationships although for the majority the force for good considerably outweighs the experience of pain.

If this dynamic is alive for adults it must also be alive for children. While the social worker needs to hold on to the belief that they are operating in the best interests of children, the child's thoughts and experience of this may be quite the opposite. At best there may be considerable relief about being removed from circumstances and people that are frightening, unpredictable or depriving and placed with a foster family or other placement that is warm, supportive and provides you with routine and meets your basic needs. But for many this will be compromised by the ache of missing the people and places the child knows, the uncertainty of what is and may be about to happen to them and unfamiliarity with and suspicion about the intention and behaviour of those now responsible for making plans for the future. And the system the child has now entered cannot readily be relied on to be more predictable, stable or child centred than existed before as inevitably it will have its own preoccupations, priorities and imperatives. For the social worker responsible for creating this, holding on to the belief that what they have arranged is better than the circumstances the child lived in before is important. But it is also likely that the social worker will be confronted with doubts about the robustness of the evidence that led to the child being removed, a recognition of the pain that they have caused the parents and the child, at the lack of control they have over what might now happen next or that they will be able to convince the child that 'it will work out for the best in the end'. Meeting the child face to face, with undercurrents of doubt and suspicion washing through the encounter, can be deeply distressing and depressing. Trying to find a safe place in one's mind where good thoughts and feelings come to the fore which make the child and social worker feel better both about each other as well the problems that need to be resolved can be a pressing concern but it may often just not be possible. Being left feeling upset, anxious or guilty at the end of such meetings when one has tried one's best can be intolerable.

Is it any wonder that social workers have opted out of positions that create such unbearable states of mind? Some have opted out of the role altogether into professions and organisations where there is some more ready acknowledgement by the client of the unsatisfactory or painful position that they are in and there is some means of putting into words the fear, anxiety and suspicion that are a part of helping relationships. The more pressing problem in social work itself are the defences that have been adopted by the profession and the organisations that employ social workers to prevent the kinds of feelings discussed above overwhelming the worker and the institution.

One form that has become commonplace is exemplified in the creation of rules or imperatives which often follow public or internal organisational scrutiny and humiliation: 'Do this and record that you have done it'. This is exemplified in the Westminster Serious Case review following the case discussed by Shriver. One of their recommendations is that 'Children must be seen alone to allow them to speak freely about their experience and their wishes and feelings'. And the second recommendation is that they must be 'recorded appropriately'. There is nothing wrong with this on the surface and indeed these kinds of imperatives can be helpful in giving structure to the work. The problem is that these imperatives have been made time and time again over many years. The issue is not that they are wrong but there is little acknowledgement of what statements like this actually mean in practice. It might be very reassuring to think that during each visit the social worker takes the child aside, asks the child whether daddy or mummy has been hurting them, and to feel confident that the child will give an unequivocal answer and that the parents will sit contentedly in the background while this happens, thanking the social worker for their care and concern as they leave. It is not that social workers do not or have not found ways of managing such difficult responsibilities and as a result discovered that something is amiss. But the excruciating pain of routinely negotiating such scenarios while retaining some sense of dignity and professionalism or indeed physical safety is just not recognised by 'learning the lessons' from case reviews and repeatedly making the same rules.

A second set of issues that is given some recognition in the same Westminster Review are the consequences when the system changes as different agencies and people become involved on the operation of active memory following the discovery of abuse. Memory is important in working with people – who they are, what they have said, who they have relationships with, what they are like and how this changes over time. Where the State takes some responsibility for this, memory will take the form of written and increasingly computerised records. However, important as these are, they cannot replace the living memory of people who have formed meaningful relationships and as a result can retain thoughts not only of the good things that have happened but are open to the painful and difficult things as well. Memory is important because it pulls together what has happened in the past with what is happening now to provide not only a sense of continuity but of meaning. When memories are too traumatic, as they often can be for clients and social workers, and can only be dealt with by denial or a wish to leave them behind, then it is important that somebody else, maybe a professional, can take responsibility for remembering. The fact that things may have been difficult and not have worked out well in the past can be placed in context through the strength and continuity of the relationship.

In the Westminster case, the children were placed with foster carers and the plan was to place them for adoption, such was the concern about the level of the father's violence. However, this plan was changed and the father undertook a programme to help him manage his violence. He did well on the programme although he was not then directly caring for his children and so the context was quite different. As a result of his completion of the programme, the original assessment of the risk that he posed to the children became more optimistic and a new plan was made to return them to him and his partner under supervision. The review comments that there was no active collective memory of the original seriousness of the risk that the father posed and this did not therefore play a significant part in the new plan. A collective mental state did not exist between the professionals which enabled them to struggle with the possibility of the past re-appearing in the present or the fact that the new plan was recreating the original violent family context. This presumably was the case not only for the professionals but for the parents themselves. Both the professional system and the family system seem to have convinced themselves that violent feelings brought on by hatred or jealousy had become a thing of the past. The new plan had not found a way of acknowledging that it was dealing with volatile "feeling states" generated by both the internal emotional world of the father and mother, including their own past experiences, and to the current realities of their external world. Feeling states do not operate according to bureaucratic rules. They ebb and flow, they are intense or calm, they can be denied or acknowledged, they can be clear or misleading. They move like the tides, channelled by the structure of the local environment and the historical forces that have created this, broadly predictable over time, but subject to variations because of particular local conditions. The nature of working in situations where feeling states are important requires an understanding that this is so. Bureaucratic thinking may helpfully shape some of the forces at work but they should not be identified as the only force that makes things happen. In some circumstances this can have very serious consequences as the injuries to child B demonstrated.

Thinking that captures the nature and particularly the dynamic nature of "mind states" is crucial to be able to work in situations where they are core. This is particularly so in social work where child development and human relationships are a central concern. The chapters in this book clearly demonstrate the wide range of tasks and purpose that make up direct work with children – assessors, planners, decision makers, change agents, advocates or representatives, quasi parental figures, therapists – within a range of settings, some formally constructed and others based on opportunity, all requiring high levels of practice and administrative skill as well as compliance with a complex legal framework. The value, knowledge and skill base that enables any of this is of a high order but again, as each of the chapters demonstrate, the essence is being able to communicate with a child in a way that is meaningful to them, sustain a relationship over time and create something that is purposeful and enables the child to move on. This may require following a set of professional or bureaucratic rules but above all, it requires sensitivity to both the child's mind states as well as the social worker paying attention to their own mind states and to the influence that one has on the other.

The history of social work demonstrates that the endless drive to create rules and imperatives has not served it well. Anxiety and public humiliation may have driven social work to this more defensive position but there is little evidence that the reponse has changed practice or improved confidence for the better. Legal and professional responsibilities undoubtedly continue to exist to a very high order but social work seems now to have moved to a position where the requirement to actually have any ongoing direct contact with clients has become "exceptional".

The fact is that the reality of a social worker's personal experience when faced with children and young people in vulnerable circumstances when their survival is threatened will make a direct impact on the social worker and will influence the way they think and feel about the work. The powerlessness of the child when their physical and emotional survival is threatened is often matched by the "felt" powerlessness of the adult. What children say in their words or through their behaviour or play can be not only difficult to hear and to make sense of but unbearable. This is particularly so when social workers have primary responsibility for creating the situation the child is currently in, separated from those that they know. Social workers must be able to process such feelings without either denying or being overwhelmed by them. In fact, feeling the powerlessness of the child may be an important part of understanding and making contact with the child's vulnerability.

The lack of a collective memory that can reflect with understanding on the struggles that social work has had with its core practice issues of working directly with people has had the effect of making it endlessly repeat that struggle. We are told or tell ourselves that we need a new beginning with bigger and better computer systems, organisational structures, systems of accountability, monitoring of achievement and a diverse market of service provision. But none of this can enhance or protect the children or adults that we work with when it is the complexity of struggling with the dynamics of "mind states" that are core to practice. The development of the kinds of professional thinking and sensitive emotional responsiveness that helpfully puts difficult feelings and dilemmas into words and enables relationships to develop cannot be addressed by such approaches. If anything, the reliance on such solutions has pushed core practice issues even further into the background, yet there is surprise when poor practice emerges once again.

Conclusion

The chapters that follow are really important in demonstrating what can be achieved when well-trained, reflective, insightful and committed social workers undertake direct work. The effort or issues involved for all of the contributors in doing the work that they did should not be underestimated. In different ways they all point to a way forward. So, it is with some hesitation that I conclude this chapter with what seems like a set of recommendations.

- That direct work with children needs to be identified as a practice issue and that the specific requirements of practice must drive training, professional development, supervision and management of the work, not the other way around.

- That social workers need to be trained through substantial direct observation and contact with children during training and subsequently. This should always include opportunities to reflect on the significance of what is observed and felt to the observer.
- That meaningful contact with children, whatever the explicit purpose or remit of the social worker, requires the development of a relationship that will have emotional content and require time to develop.
- Social workers need to be trained to understand the ways that the child's feelings, particularly those that are troubling or distressing will have an impact on them. These feelings can create a powerful set of forces that influence the development of the work in ways that are helpful when they are understood and unhelpful when they are not. These forces can extend beyond the direct contact that the child has with the social worker to influence the system as a whole and the dangerous defensive consequences that this can have on consistency and active memory. It is essential that supervisors and trainers understand this and that training and supervision enable these issues to be discussed, reflected, learnt and acted upon.
- That the pressure to identify with the child's distress, anxiety or predicament can be great and needs to be properly understood to enable a helpful position to be taken throughout the work, as also the pressure to identify with the predicament of the child's parents or with other carers, particularly the guilt that results from the pain the actions of the social worker has caused in separating the child from the parents. The process and force of identifications can be great but they need to be understood and resisted in order to maintain a helpful and responsible position in relation to the child.
- That the training, assessment and validation of direct work with children requires more than what has become the dominant determination of thinking – the competency framework. Work that depends on the dynamic interplay of the emotional states of the child and worker over time needs its own language sensitive to these states. The static descriptors of the competency framework deaden the process driven aspects of the work.
- That there needs to be sufficient critical mass in the workforce to drive and sustain the expertise and conditions that promote direct work. Without the availability of routine senior positions in the social work profession and social work organisations that provide a focus for this expertise, direct work will be confined to either something that "trainees do" or is commissioned out to other organsiations. Similarly, these senior roles must not just be confined to providing consultancy to others, although this is critical to developing and sustaining the discipline, but in delivering a "direct work" service in the same way that those in senior roles in other professions directly deliver their services to clients.
- It is critical that the workforce is not otherwise preoccupied with its survival because

of excessive instability or change, the lack of a meaningful or valued identity or identification with hopelessness and despair about the possibility of undertaking satisfying or constructive work. Parents who are similarly preoccupied do not provide the best conditions for the development of their children. It is critical that social work does not become overly identified with these processes.

- Structural and organisational arrangements need to be in place so that the thinking and emotional responsiveness required to undertake direct work are supported. In particular that there is organisational tolerance of and support for the uncertainty and anxiety that are commonly created during direct work which become and are important sources of learning and development in the development of the work. Organisational arrangements need to focus on creating the conditions that promote this alongside other priority, resource and timescale issues.

It should be clear that I think the important issues to reflect on and learn from are the messages from the past and the ways that these need to be incorporated into the present to influence the future. When we have been told over 30 years or so that we are not properly listening to children, we need to understand why. Promising that we will find more time and be more effective in the future without understanding just why this has been so very difficult will not produce any effective change unless we understand not only the forces that attract us to the work but those that make us avoid it. The current picture is not good and it will take a more insightful and in-depth understanding as well as determined effort to change this. The points above result from what I have learnt and reflected on from past experience in the context of reading this book. They will serve little purpose unless they are discussed, reflected upon and, perhaps, challenged. Social work and social workers need to actively engage in the development of its core ideas, not just mouth that we will learn the lessons from our mistakes only to repeat them over and over again. It means facing up to things that most professions don't usually have to face up to, certainly not in as direct a way as social work continually finds itself doing.

References

Ainsworth M. (1978) *Patterns of Attachment: A psychological study of the Strange Situation*, Hillsdale, NJ: Lawrence Erlbaum Associates

Aldgate J. and Simmonds J. (1988) *Direct Work with Children*, London: BAAF/Batsford

A. P. (2006) 'A father's experience of care proceedings', in Thorpe M. and Budden R. (eds) *Durable Solutions*, Bristol: Jordan Publishing, pp 23–28

Behan D., Bell D., Bloomfield E., Bridges A., Flanagan R. and Owers A. (2005) *Safeguarding Children*, London: CSCI

Blom-Cooper L. (1985) *A Child in Trust*, Wembley: London Borough of Brent

Bowlby J., Fry M., Ainsworth M. and Salter D. (1965) *Child Care and the Growth of Love*, Harmondsworth: Penguin

British Agencies for Adoption and Fostering (1984) *In Touch with Children*, London: BAAF

Department for Education and Skills (2002) *Choice Protects*. Retrieved November 2007, from Every Child Matters, http://www.everychildmatters.gov.uk/deliveringservices/multiagency working/glossary/?asset=glossary&id=22371

Department of Education and Skills (2003) *Keeping Children Safe: Government response to the Victoria Climbié Inquiry – Report*, Command Paper, London: DfES

Department of Health (1991) *Patterns and Outcomes of Child Placement*, London: HMSO

Department of Health (1999) *The Government's Objectives for Children's Social Services*, Crown Copyright, London: The Stationery Office

Department of Health and Social Security (1976) *Foster Care: A Guide to Practice*, London: HMSO

Department of Health and Social Security (1985) *Social Work Decisions in Child Care: Recent research findings and their implications*, London: HMSO

Freud A., Solnit A. and Goldstein H. (1973) *Beyond the Best Interests of the Child*, London: Andre Deutsch

Performance and Innovations Unit (2000) *Prime Minister's Review of Adoption*, London: Cabinet Office

Rowe J., Cain H., Hundleby M. and Keane A. (1984) *Long Term Foster Care*, London: BAAF/Batsford

Rowe J. and Lambert L. (1973) *Children who Wait: A study of children needing substitute families*, London: Association of British Adoption Agencies

Rutter M. (1972) *Maternal Deprivation Reassessed*, Harmondsworth: Penguin

Secretary of State for Education and Skills (2006) *Care Matters: Transforming the Lives of Children and Young People in Care*, London: DfES

Secretary of State for Education and Skills (2007) *Care Matters: Time for Change*, London: DfES

Shriver L. (2007, February 11) 'Have you ever read a headline that praised a social worker?', *Independant on Sunday*

Sinclair I., Baker C., Lee J. and Gibbs I. (2007) *The Pursuit of Permanence*, London: Jessica Kingsley

Introduction

Barry Luckock and Michelle Lefevre

It's not rocket science! Kids just want to be wanted because when you're in care you feel like no one wants you. You just want people to listen, understand and be there on a regular basis so you know that you've always got something to hang on to. It's not too much to ask! (Unnamed child in care, cited in Morgan, 2006, p 28)

This book is for social workers with responsibility for children and young people[1] in public care. It is about that commitment and skill involved in listening to, understanding and being there on a regular basis that, time and again, is demanded by young people of all ages living away from home in foster, adoptive and residential care. Their experiences and perspectives are reported throughout the various chapters collected together here, providing a constant reminder of the nature of the "direct work" task in social work.

We have approached our editorial role in a spirit of optimism. Social work has been re-confirmed as the 'lead profession' for children and young people in care (Scottish Office 2006, Department for Education and Skills, 2007). In England there is now official recognition that 'The day-to-day experience of the corporate parent is embodied for children in care by the *work* of practitioners' (p 11, our emphasis). It is clear that this "work" must once again include the committed and skilled face-to-face engagement with "their" social worker demanded by young people as well as those enhanced care planning procedures that produce the stability and permanence needed for a happy childhood and successful future. Indeed, the *Care Matters* White Paper not only supported the view of young people that what was needed was 'social workers to listen to them and have more time for them' (p 11), it also set out proposals for 'remodelling the workforce' to help achieve this aim. The 'lack of a continuous personal relationship' with their social worker has now been identified as a 'key problem' for children (Le Grand, 2007, p 5). Firmly on the agenda, as a result, are arrangements for improved training and skills for social workers (Luckock *et al*, 2006; Children's Workforce Development Council, 2007), better support for newly-qualified practitioners and new models of social work practice that will 'result in more time being spent by social workers on relationship-building with children' (Department for Education and Skills, 2007, p 130).

---

[1] We refer to "children and young people" in our title because this is the most common phrase to describe whom we are talking about. In general, in the text, "children" and "young people" are used inter-changeably and not as terms to denote either developmental or rights perspectives on childhood.

.ese are promising developments, although it remains to be seen how successfully , renewed commitment to restoring continuity of social work relationships with .nildren and young people at the heart of the care system will be translated into change on the ground. There is a history of ambivalence in policy about the actual nature of the "direct work" task in social work, and continued uncertainty in day-to-day practice about what counts as appropriate engagement and communication with children. This has undermined the development of effective direct practice with children in care. Social workers seem to have lost confidence and belief in their "direct work" role and task (Commission for Social Care Inspection, 2005). Agencies and managers have found it difficult to support the development of models of practice and supervision that value personal capability, commitment and skill in building and sustaining relationships with vulnerable and disadvantaged young people. In discussions with social work practitioners, it is common for the tension between the demands of desk-based and direct work to be identified. It is almost invariably said that there is simply too little time left, after the assessment, planning, reviewing and the rest is done, to be spent with children.

We too think the lack of time for children has become a major constraint. However, the way time is used is equally important and the way distinctions are often made between "indirect" and "direct" work is not always helpful. Many practitioners now refer to their (relatively brief) direct engagements with children as "doing a piece of work", as if the bureaucratic culture of task completion at the desk or in the meeting has become the only way to think about and undertake "direct work". The process of explaining to children what is being planned with and for them, ascertaining their wishes and feelings about their circumstances and helping them manage feelings of expectation, sadness, anger and confusion has too often become detached from the personal relationship that would enable the kind of communication needed for direct work to be really effective. As an experienced practitioner said to one of us recently, 'Direct work has become associated with getting something down on paper with felt tips, doing an eco-map or worksheet, something physical that is *produced* and which illustrates that "direct work" has been done.'

This book takes a rather different approach. Instead of separating "direct work" off, as if it were one of a number of *tasks* to be juggled under pressure of too little time, our aim is to see it reintegrated and restored to the centre of social work, understood as a set of *relationships*. In reconnecting the professional task to the personal relationship, the centre of gravity of practice is changed and it becomes possible to see how social work really can be "child-centred". Different metaphors are used throughout the book for this core idea, that effective communication is based less in the episodic use of a set of "direct work" practice skills and tools and much more in the establishment and sustaining of a facilitative relationship. Some people use the language of developmental psychology and therapy to describe what it is that makes this relationship facilitative, describing it as "containing" and providing a "secure base" for a child. Others see things first in terms of rights, voice and choice, indicating the need for the social worker to be a "consultant" and "advocate". These perspectives are sometimes set against each other in academic texts and in practice too. We think there is no need for social work as a profession to do this. Whether practitioners start with the image of a childhood in care as being compromising either to welfare or to rights, the common requirement is to make oneself available as a personal resource for a child. In this respect, the idea that effective direct practice is akin to a shared journey of understanding and accomplishment is also found here. "Being there" certainly, but being there with a purpose or a set of related purposes, that have to do with opening up and not diminishing life chances for children in and beyond care.

None of this is to say that effectiveness in direct practice does not require the development of professional skill and technique. It has been said that there are a 'hundred languages of childhood' (Edwards *et al*, 1993) and we include chapters that present a diversity of communicative approaches that connect to the different capabilities and aspirations of young people. Effective relationships for practice clearly require an adequate measure of technical competence and confidence as well as a large degree of personal commitment. However, we have avoided a "cookbook" approach because our primary concern here is to encourage reconsideration of *how and why* relationships with young people might be established and sustained and not just *what* practice tools can be employed in the process. As several of our contributors remind us, it is *who* the practitioner is as a person that matters most for many young people in care.

In turn, though, many social workers have told us just how difficult it is to be that kind of person for the child, how demanding to maintain the proper boundaries between personal commitment and primary professional task. Social work with children can be enlivening and enjoyable. It is especially rewarding when things work out well, as they often do. But managing the expectations and emotions of children in family and other transitions in a context of constrained resources can also be an unnerving experience. So it is equally important to appreciate the personal experience of the social worker to consider what support might be necessary for direct work to be approached in a positive and hopeful rather than a fearful and avoidant frame of mind. We have included chapters that explore the nature of this challenge because without supervision and support individual practitioners should indeed ask whether expectations of them are too great and the risks on both sides significant.

Equally, our emphasis on the nature of the *social work* relationship with the child should also not be read to suggest that we think the work with children in care of other professionals is redundant. Nor is any assumption being made that the restoration of the personal social work relationship to the heart of practice should diminish the direct role of parental and other carers in supporting children to make sense of and manage their care experiences and realise their hopes for their own lives. Social work is one role amongst several and we have included chapters that explore the direct work approaches of therapists, advocates, pedagogues and other residential workers. And many of the contributions remind us that it is to the child's permanent carers that social work must ultimately look to meet the primary "direct work" task. To this extent the social work relationship, and the direct practice role and task, is both facilitative of other relationships and transitory. But "ultimately" is often a long time coming for a child in care, and certainly seems so even when the best-laid plans are in hand or the separation from home relatively brief. The social worker is always a 'transitional participant' (Kanter, 2004, p 86) in the life of the child. However, the nature of the transitions involved and the particular responsibility of the profession mean that the direct social work role is both emotionally and socially pivotal. This book seeks to stimulate thinking and provide encouragement, especially to those practitioners who carry that large responsibility for the rest of us.

We have organised the various contributions to this book with these intentions specifically in mind. The collection is arranged in five self-standing but linked sections. These can be read sequentially in order to gain a fairly comprehensive and definitive account of the theory and practice of contemporary direct practice in social work with children in care. Alternatively, specific sections and individual chapters can be selected according to need and interest. The sections are arranged as follows.

Section 1: Rethinking direct work with children and young people living in care
This initial section includes two chapters in which the nature and experience of direct social work practice are considered in some detail. The first chapter (Barry Luckock) provides a practical framework for thinking about relationship-based practice with children. In doing this, it explores the nature of transitions for children separated from their family of origin and describes the parameters of the direct practice role in care, permanence and opportunity planning. The second chapter (Michelle Lefevre) sets out the core personal qualities, values and commitments which underpin the social work relationship with children and describes key skills and approaches indicated by research and practice experience to be necessary for effective practice. These chapters are intended to provide a practice foundation for what follows.

Section 2: Differing perspectives on the care experience
The three chapters in this section present contrasting perspectives on the experience of being looked after away from home with consequent implications for direct practice. The first presents the view from attachment theory (Gillian Schofield). The second draws on a psychodynamic perspective to make sense of the connections between children's internal and external worlds (Margaret Smallbone). The third employs a sociological perspective on the experience of care (Sally Holland, Emma Renold, Nicola Ross and

Alex Hillman). These chapters will help in the development of an integrative perspective on childhood and family and social life.

Section 3: Approaches to communication and engagement
The six chapters in this section set out different stances or approaches to the direct work which will be more or less appropriate, depending on the social work role and context and the needs of the particular child or young person. There are accounts of consultation and advocacy (Nigel Thomas), observation (Danielle Turney), the use of play, symbolic, and creative methods (Michelle Lefevre), augmentive and assistive modes of communication especially useful with disabled children (Ruth Marchant), and the potential offered by interactive media in direct practice (Afshan Ahmad, Bridget Betts and Les Cowan). Finally, Adrian Ward's chapter on "opportunity-led" work considers how every encounter presents possibilities for engagement and intervention in the moment.

Section 4: Direct work in context
In the fourth section, the focus shifts to specific practice contexts within which direct work is undertaken. The eight shorter chapters included here present accounts of, and/or arguments for, the employment of distinctive approaches with a diversity of children and young people. Accounts of work within a particular role include ascertaining wishes and feelings as a children's guardian in care proceedings (Anna Gupta), direct work in care planning in the lead professional role (Andy Cook), undertaking "life story" work (Alan Burnell and Jay Vaughan), and communication in residential work (Adrian Ward). Work with particular groups of children include unaccompanied asylum-seeking children (Ravi Kohli), lesbian, gay and bisexual teenagers (Ane Freed-Kernis and Richard McKendrick) and groupwork with adopted children (Lorraine Wallis). Pat Petrie's chapter considers the European approach to social pedagogy and what might be learned from this.

Section 5: Supporting the practitioner
The final section of the book focuses on the type of organisational and policy context necessary for confident and effective work with children. These concluding chapters are concerned with the role of external consultation in helping social workers and carers sustain relationships with children (Leslie Ironside) and issues in organisation and supervision of direct practice (Gillian Ruch).

References

Children's Workforce Development Council (2007) *Roles and Tasks of Social Work Project*, http://www.cwdcouncil.org.uk/projects/roleandtasks.htm

Commission for Social Care Inspection (2005) *Making Every Child Matter: Messages from inspections of children's social services*, London: Commission for Social Care Inspection

Department for Education and Skills (2007) *Care Matters: Time for change*, Cm 7137, London: DfES

Edwards C., Gandini L. and Forman G. (1993) *The Hundred Languages of Childhood: The Reggio Emilia approach to early childhood education*, Norwood, NJ: Ablex

Kanter J. (ed) (2004) *Face to Face with Children: The life and work of Clare Winnicott*, London: Karnac Books

Le Grand J. (2007) *Consistent Care Matters: Exploring the potential of social work practices*, The Stationery Office, Nottingham

Luckock B., Lefevre M. and Orr D. with Tanner K., Jones M. and Marchant R. (2006) *Knowledge Review: Teaching, learning and assessing communication skills with children in social work education*, London: Social Care Institute for Excellence

Morgan R. (2006) *About Social Workers: A children's view report*, London: Commission for Social Care Inspection

Scottish Executive (2006) *Report of the 21st Century Social Work Review: Changing lives*, Edinburgh: Scottish Executive

Section 1

Rethinking direct work with children and young people in care

1   Living through the experience: the social worker as the trusted ally and champion of young people in care

Barry Luckock with Patrick Stevens and Jason Young

Introduction

In policy and practice alike it has been easy to lose sight of children in care and neglect their needs. The history of child welfare in the UK is punctuated by official reports that testify to this fact (Curtis, 1946; Utting, 1997; Waterhouse, 2000; Social Exclusion Unit, 2003). Research findings continue to confirm that being in care is no guarantee, in itself, of stable and loving family relationships or enhanced social opportunities (Sinclair, 2005; Selwyn *et al*, 2005; Skuse and Ward, 2007). Not only has it taken too long for needs to be assessed, plans put in place and the placement to be found (Cabinet Office, 2000) but also it has not been consistently possible to ensure that the quality of the family and friends, foster, residential or adoptive care available will be good enough in any case for the child in question. In the absence of family stability it is unsurprising that educational and other outcomes have remained so disappointing (HM Government, 2006a).

Yet, despite the longstanding recognition that 'Corporate parenting is not "good enough" on its own' (Department of Health, 1990, p 11), it has been the procedural performance of children's services agencies rather than the relationships formed by skilled practitioners working directly with children and young people that has been the primary focus of interest. At its lowest point this approach resulted in the idea that there was a 'stock of looked after children' (Cabinet Office, 2000, p 86) that needed shifting through care to adoption as if they were goods in transit with a limited shelf-life. Only latterly, with the confirmation that it is indeed the social worker who should be the 'lead professional' for children in care (HM Government, 2006a; Scottish Executive, 2006), has attention turned again to the question of what counts as effective direct practice on a day-to-day basis.

The *Care Matters: Time for Change* White Paper argued that the responsibility for children and young people was corporate and that the 'difficulties faced by those in care cannot be overcome by any individual or part of the system acting alone' (Department for Education and Skills, 2007, p 6). However, it also recognised that 'the day-to-day experience of the corporate parent is embodied for children in care by the *work* of the practitioner' (p 11, italics added). This was a welcome return to the idea that direct social work practice with children and young people was the lynchpin in both the organisational system and network of relationships that constitute public care. It came at a time in the UK where we had become accustomed to expressing regret for what has been lost in the engagement between the social worker and the child in care, but had been far less able to say exactly what it was that we expected of that relationship. The White Paper argued that appropriate arrangements should be put in place 'to enable social workers to spend more time with the child' (p 124). It is now possible to think more clearly once again about how that time ought to be spent and what is the personal contribution of the social worker to the corporate process of providing "good enough" parenting or better where a childhood is lived in and out of care.

This chapter considers the distinctive nature of such a childhood and what is necessary to ensure that corporate parenting is 'personalised and given a human face' (BASW, 2003, p 3) as it sets about the task of helping young people in care not only to survive but also to realise their ambitions in life.

Care journeys

Along with others (see Kohli, Smallbone, this volume), the chapter will assume that a childhood in and out of care is perhaps best seen as a journey. However, the emphasis here is on the integration of the two distinctive aspects of this journey that are usually considered separately. Whether or not care is a means of supporting or replacing existing parenting and family life, children and young people have to be helped in finding ways of:

- *re-establishing a sense of self and belonging and family and social relationships* following trauma, separation and loss – this is the journey to stable and permanent family and social life in childhood and beyond;
- *re-negotiating professional and other support services and wider social opportunities* designed to maximise their overall well-being – this is the journey to adulthood in its own right.

These care journeys involve navigating new sets of relationships in both the family and service systems and beyond. At the heart of these networks is the young person's relationship with their social worker. And the main task of *their* social worker is to be a constant guide and companion, acting as a trusted ally en route through unfamiliar and often scary terrain towards intended but often elusive destinations. The nature of this alliance is explored in this chapter in some detail.

In taking this approach, the ultimate aim is to redefine what has become known as "direct work" with children. In particular, it will be argued that there is a need to reconnect the *sets of tasks* ("needs assessment", "wishes and feelings work", "life story work" and the like), which have come to characterise what is thought to be "direct" about practice

(Fahlberg, 1994; Ryan and Walker, 2007), with the *core relationship* between the young person and their social worker that has become so difficult to think about and describe. The intention is to release social work practice from a paradox, whereby the more that "direct work" gets narrowed down to a series of "pieces of work" the less possible it seems for social workers to find time or confidence to do it. Instead of the old distinction between (face-to-face) "direct work" done *with* children and (bureaucratic) "indirect work" done *for* them (Statham *et al*, 2006), what is envisaged here is a far more committed joint project.

Social work with children in and out of care: a bridge or a tour operator?

The idea that care can be seen as a journey is not new. In her influential practice text, Vera Fahlberg (1994) describes the child's 'journey through placement', from the family of origin to a permanent substitute home. From this perspective, the social worker plays a bridging role for the child in family transition. Clare Winnicott used this image when reflecting on her work as a child care officer in post-war England (Winnicott, 1963, in Kanter, 2004), using it to show the importance in social work of 'bridging gaps' (p 171) between fact and fantasy, within the separated child's mind, as well as those created between them and their parents when they lived away from home. The image retained influence in practice in the UK (and US) into the 1980s (see for example Horne, 1983), although it was the concern with connections between people in the *external* world, rather than the integration of feelings and thoughts in the child's *internal* world, that soon came to dominate day-to-day social work practice (see also Smallbone, this volume). It is also important to note that the nature of these family connections has changed over time. In the 1980s the emphasis in foster care and adoption was on what Fahlberg later called 'disengagement work' (1994, p 325), whereby the child's journey involved leaving previous family relationships behind on the way to a substitute home. In due course, with the growing recognition that children in care had to be helped to 'hold multiple families in mind' (Rustin, 1999), the bridging role once again had to include the maintenance and management of contact and links between a constellation of ongoing familial affiliations and relationships (Hart and Luckock, 2004; Neil and Howe, 2004).

More recently, policy-makers in the UK have also begun to use the metaphor of travel to understand the care process. In this case, the idea is that children do not simply need support in moving between families but also require help in steering a course through services more generally as they set out on the pathway to adulthood. The care system is now required to provide not only a route to secure attachments and permanent or stable family lives but also access to enhanced life-chance opportunities as a whole. In this way the full potential of disadvantaged children can be achieved (HM Treasury/Department for Education and Skills, 2007). Here the role of the social worker is to be less a bridge between family lives and more a co-ordinator of professionals (and parental carers) in 'a team around the child' (HM Government 2006b, p 32). The aim is to ensure that 'children's needs are met smoothly instead of (them) having to struggle to navigate a complex system' on their own (p 32).

In the first approach, children in care are seen primarily as *members of families* who need care to safeguard and promote their welfare. In the second case, they become *consumers of services* who should be given better access to opportunities which support active citizenship and increased say about services that facilitate them. In this shift of focus, the social worker begins to look less like an emotional bridge or link between children and their divided feelings and families and more like a travel agent or tour operator, acting as 'a single point of contact for the child' and engaging them in 'making choices' as they navigate their way through the complex maze of children's services (HM Government, 2006b, p 3).

Family and personal journeys: the social worker as companion and ally

The approach taken in this chapter is rather different because it seeks a more rounded and robust approach to social work with children. The bridging role of social work is powerful because it conveys an image of firm footing and connectedness, internally and externally, for a child embarked on the transition to permanence and belonging within an uncertain and changing network of family relationships. Its foundations in psycho-social casework (Winnicott, 1963, in Kanter, 2004), psychodynamic (see Smallbone, this volume) and attachment theory (see Schofield, this volume) give it sound practice, theoretical and empirical grounding. Also compelling, though, is the idea that corporate parenting involves signposting and support in the effective transition of children in their own right, and increasingly under their own steam, from disadvantage to full adulthood opportunities and citizenship. The research on the risks to well-being posed by a childhood in care (Sinclair, 2005), and on the importance of access to good (mental) health care (Meltzer *et al*, 2003; Chambers *et al*, 2002), education (Harker *et al*, 2004) and social participation (see Holland *et al*, this volume) in ensuring potential is achieved and life enjoyed, supports the renewed policy emphasis on the focal position of social worker in "corporate parenting" (HM Government, 2006a). This activist stance is an aspect of social work valued and increasingly demanded by young people themselves (see Thomas this volume). And the idea that the social worker in either role should see themselves as part of a team, that includes family members as well as professionals, provides a powerful vision of collaborative working and shared responsibility.

What is missing, though, is the recognition of just how powerful the dynamics of discontinuity and disadvantage are on these respective journeys through placement and childhood. Similar recognition is needed of how important it is that social workers commit themselves as companions to be relied on, and allies to help in the struggle, especially when the going gets tough and confidence is low. It is this *continuously engaged relationship* that is the essence of effective social work with young people and one which has proved increasingly hard to sustain in practice. At its heart are three core elements:

- an *emotional capacity* to get in touch with and contain the feelings, thoughts and behaviours stirred up for children in care and the people with parenting and family responsibilities for them;
- an *ethical commitment* to championing the rights of young people to participation in decisions, access to services, and support and social justice more generally through childhood and beyond;
- an *expertise and authority* which are demonstrated through the continued exercise of organisational position and influence as well as by personal and professional skill and confidence in face-to-face work with young people.

These are principles for practice that have increasing backing from research, especially the personal accounts of young people themselves (Morgan, 2006; Skuse and Ward, 2007; Holland *et al*, this volume). They underpin a model of "direct work" that confronts the tendency for the fragmentation in the child's life to be mirrored, or 're-enacted' (Britton, 1981, cited in Emanuel, 2006), in fragmentation in the service response. In this model, therapeutic communication with children and championing their interests are together integral to the core direct social work role. They are not aspects of the relationship and task that can be separated and hived off as a substitute for committed personal engagement. And although talk of professional authority and expertise provokes unease in some quarters, there is no shortage of evidence that practitioners are most valued when they are comfortable in their role and confident in their knowledge and skills (Sinclair, 2005). Denial of the authority of the social work role at the heart of "corporate parenting" is no more helpful than is its over-officious use. Arguably, it is the undermining and lack of support of professional autonomy and authority that has contributed to the loss of confidence in practice so often reported over recent years in UK social work (Cooper and Lousada, 2005).

In summary, children need trusted social work allies who have personal and professional confidence to work with them to map out and manage their journeys through care and childhood. A working alliance has to be established and developed. The focus of the relationship at the heart of this alliance has two main aspects:

- helping the child express, understand, contain and integrate their *emotional experience* of separation and loss, in order to re-establish family relationships;
- collaborating with the young person in identifying, mobilising and co-ordinating the *social resources* necessary to confront social disadvantage and achieve social justice and well as personal care.

We look first at what counts as an effective *emotional engagement* between a young person in care and their social worker before turning next to a discussion of the *social action* which constitutes the other half of direct practice. The central importance for effective social work of the establishment of a 'therapeutic relationship', as the basis of a 'working alliance' in practice, is once again attracting research (McNeil *et al*, 2005, p 4) and policy attention more generally (Scottish Executive, 2006).

What then is the nature of an appropriate "caring" and "therapeutic" relationship in these circumstances?

Living through the experience: working with feelings and facilitating the personal and family narrative

This is how Patrick, who has had 'quite a few social workers during my time in care', sees the social work relationship with young people in care:

I think at the time you (Patrick means the social worker) build up stronger relationships and you come to new levels of understanding with people and you know more about them and their circumstances. You grow up through their case. You may not start at the beginning knowing everything, at the time you have to look back at the past and you come to know them as well as if you were their social worker then. (emphasis added)

Patrick's suggestion, that an effective social worker is one who 'grows up' through the child's case, is worth thinking about carefully. This striking inversion of the developmental account of a childhood in care is captivating and instructive. It reminds us from the outset that direct work involves a shared journey of discovery and progress and one that takes time and careful attention. This what Clare Winnicott meant when she said working 'with' children needed social workers 'to live through the experience with the child as fully as possible, without denying the pain, and accepting the sadness, anger and depression' (1986, p 40) of the situation. In this way children would feel 'understood and accepted right down to the painful sad bit in the middle' (p 41). Winnicott contrasted this direct, unwavering and personally engaged communication of concern and support with a more avoidant and hence deceitful kind of practice, in which children were offered 'distractions of one kind or another' (p 41). By enabling children to name and face, rather than deny and avoid, their feelings, the social worker was helping them make sense of their separation and develop resilient responses. It is this capability that lies at the heart of the assessment and decision-making process in care and permanence planning.

Working with feelings

In Patrick's case it was his social worker's avoidance of his feelings, at one of those 'crisis situations' (Winnicott, 1986, p 39) that characterise separation and care, that got their relationship off to such a bad start:

I wanted contact with my sister, who was going up to be adopted . . . we talked about what type of contact I would like. I wanted to be able to still see my sister face to face. The social worker went away and said, yes you can still see her when she has been adopted, that will be fine. And then I wasn't allowed to see her face to face and I didn't get an explanation at the time of why that was. I did later on because I got an advocate and they helped me find out why. At the time I was told I couldn't see her face to face when she was adopted. The social worker found the best way to speak to me wasn't to sit down and speak to me herself and discuss why I wouldn't be able to, she put me into counselling and gave me a psychologist. I don't think that helped our relationship much. (Patrick's emphasis)

Patrick's account of his experience confirms the personal importance of the social work relationship ('*our* relationship'), for a young person in care. What matters to Patrick is that the social worker let him down personally as well as professionally when he needed her to be there for him. At this stage, as a result, she remains 'the' social worker rather than 'my' social worker. In Patrick's words, 'I detached myself from what I'd said and my mind automatically moved her aside'. The account reminds us how important it is for a young person to be fully involved in the assessment and decision-making process, in this case about the contact plan (see Thomas and Freed-Kernis and McKendrick, this volume). It also illuminates the potential for divisions and splits to become established in the 'team around the child' when emotions are not engaged and contained within that relationship (see Smallbone and Ruch, this volume).

Arguably, seen from a purely organisational perspective, things might not look too bad here, with the social worker as "lead professional" apparently getting Patrick prioritised on the CAMHS list and then ensuring he had his own advocate. From Patrick's perspective, this is missing the point. It may be that the *service* appears reasonably comprehensive and well integrated, the social worker having made the assessment of need and the therapist dealing with Patrick's feelings whilst the advocate handles his rights, but his *experience* is far from it. For him the social worker's 'retreat from engagement' (Cooper and Lousada, 2005, p 27) at a crucial moment, not finding a way to 'sit down and speak to me *herself* and discuss why . . .', left him feeling deserted within the professional system ('put me into counselling'), not cared for by it.

We do not know the causes of this desertion in Patrick's case. It may be that, as he suggests, the social worker had not been able to release herself from a trap she was caught in, having first assured him that he would be able to see his sister and then having to explain subsequently why this was not possible. Perhaps the initial reassurance resulted from a need in the social worker herself to cope with Patrick's upset about his loss and commitments were made that were inappropriate and unrealistic (see Lefevre and Smallbone and Ironside, this volume). Or it might have been the case that initial plans had to be changed, or that Patrick himself had misunderstood and "not heard" in the first place a more nuanced and unwelcome message about contact. Perhaps Patrick's social worker felt attacked by his anger at the time, although he himself can only recall his upset. Perhaps she herself had nowhere safe to take her feelings of impotence in the face of his requirements and needs and the limited time and space she had available to respond to them. These considerations remind us of the demands to be borne by the "corporate parenting" relationship.

Facilitating the personal and family narrative

Nonetheless, situations like this can leave young people bewildered and upset in the moment. For Patrick it also deepens his sense of personal displacement and family disruption and further undermines his capacity to make sense of his troubling childhood experiences and put them in their place. This reminds us that the goal of social work is not only to form a containing relationship that helps those children settle feelings and thoughts. It is also to use that relationship to help them restore a sense of order and pattern to their lives. This capacity to develop a *coherent narrative of oneself in relationships and over time* normally develops within and strengthens the attachment process in the family of origin (see Schofield and Ironside, this volume). When young people come into care, the social work role is to help them maintain or restore their capacity to retain, retrieve and reassemble their personal and family story (Hart and Luckock, 2004). However, instead of this being seen as a core aspect of the continuously engaged relationship outlined here, the process is all too often derailed.

In this respect, Caroline Lindsey talks about the dangers of the 'failure to bear the child and his story in mind in a coherent and informed way' when social workers keep changing due to agency practices and staff retention problems. This fractured response can then be 'reflected by the child's own sense of confusion about the representation of himself' (2006, p 8). This replicates earlier experiences of not being attended to carefully or thought about. Children are left, with 'little or no experience of a containing mind with any continuity in their lives, to help mediate the impact on them of traumatic experience' (Kenrick, 2006, p 70). Similarly, Hamish Canham describes how important time is for children in care whose lives have been marked by unpredictability and discontinuity rather than order and routine (1999, p 161). In this way they are effectively 'abandoned' and 'left feeling that no-one has time for them' (p 162). This results in a 'piling up of unresolved anxieties and preoccupations (which) gives rise to much confusion in terms of order and sequence and, consequently, of time itself' (p 162). Thus, when Patrick was left without an explanation of why he could not see his sister an opportunity was lost. This would have helped him manage continued feelings of grief through separation and loss and, on the basis of this, to help him make better sense of, and introduce some measure of planning into, his unfolding family life and relationships in time and space.

Of course Patrick's account shows how the continued estrangement of young people from their family story, as well as from their family members, can happen where the social worker is a consistent but not an emotionally available figure. In this case, it is important to recognise that contemporary social work understanding of what constitutes effective life story work, and current methods and practices (see, for example, Ryan and Walker, 2007), might be contributing to rather than ameliorating this problem. Conclusive research evidence is awaited (McKeown *et al*, 2006). However, as attachment theory would suggest, when life story work is detached from the emotionally containing relationships that would enable a child or young person to reintegrate fragmented and painful experiences, it can maintain or reinforce that split between the 'feeling of what happens' (Damasio, 1999) and the official account. In particular, the temptation to separate out life story work from a containing and therapeutic relationship should be very carefully considered (see Burnell and Vaughan, this volume). Patrick himself retains strong feelings about his own experience of being expected to do life story work:

> *Being in care felt like my whole life was an open diary. Nothing was for me or who I was. It felt like Big Brother (television programme). The whole idea of having to do a life story book is rubbish. In a strong relationship with a social worker when the child or young person wants to find things out they will seek advice and help to do this. You can't simply push everyone into the same mould.* (Patrick's emphasis)

Patrick is reminding us here of the fine line to be managed in practice between intrusion that, in his words, 'drives people further apart' and enablement that respects the fact that young people are already trying to make sense of their lives. For him, it is the 'strong relationship' that allows him to 'suss things out and piece them together by myself' before using the social worker to get them to 'gel'.

In theoretical terms, this life-story process is understood as the facilitation and development of a *narrative capability* in young people. In practice, this means taking good care to provide attachment and other containing relationships which will enable young people to:

- get in touch safely with the feelings evoked by their experiences;
- reconnect those feelings with events in time and space;
- reconstruct, on a continuous basis, an authentic 'family story' as they move through care and beyond (Byng-Hall, 1999; Hart and Luckock, 2004).

It is essential not to attempt any short cuts here. In recent years social work has been influenced by solution-focused (O'Hanlon and Weiner-Davis, 2003) and narrative (Hall *et al*, 2006) approaches. These have contributed to the development of a hopeful and encouraging professional mindset and stance during a potentially dispiriting period, in which defensive and procedural modes of practice have tended to dominate. Of particular value have been theories and methods that emphasise the way in which solutions are co-constructed through a joint narrative process (Parton and O'Byrne, 2000). The idea that social workers should enable people to give voice to their own stories is at the heart of the renewed focus on advocacy as a task for social work and a professional role in its own right (see Thomas, this volume).

Nonetheless, this "narrative turn" has its problems too, especially where the assumption prevails that problems are solved simply by changing the ways people talk about them. Language alone can certainly change the way problems are defined, understood and acted upon (Hall *et al*, 2006), but a secure sense of self in space and time can only be achieved when the feelings experienced are connected to and contained by the words used to describe and explain them. This is what is meant by the idea of an 'autobiographical self' (Damasio, 1999). Young people in care may be faced with a variety of contrasting, perhaps conflicting, representations of themselves and their history and the task of constructing an agreed narrative or story involves choosing the best words. This was once known as providing the child with a "cover story", the intention being to help prepare them to face expected embarrassment and stigma (e.g. 'My mum was too ill to look after me safely at home').

Many life story books read in this way, as justifications by others for the difference and difficulty implied by a childhood in and out of care. Learning to tell the "care" story in this way might help as a temporary defence strategy, and might make it easier for adults to bear the emotional impact of the real story, but the ultimate objective of life story work is much more important than this. This is because the words or representations used have to be congruent with the memories and feelings evoked by the experience if they are to be truly autobiographical. Achieving an autobiographical stance means being able emotionally and mentally to situate oneself positively in time and place – even when faced by continued conflicting accounts of who you really are. The lack of this capacity means always being caught up with the emotions of the moment or having no feelings at all. Enacting this failure to deal with feelings through difficult behaviour can follow. There follows the experience of being lost for the kind of words and phrases that would help you make your own sense of where those feelings and behaviours came from and how they could be put back in place.

Living through the experience

Jason is a few years older than Patrick. He left care a while ago now, after spending his teenage years mainly in children's homes. When he tries to look back and make sense of it all he realises he is 'lost for words', as if the care experience itself has separated him off from who is and what he can say about himself:

> *I just feel like it wasn't my life, that time wasn't my life, being in a children's home, it just didn't feel like I was really there . . . I've never felt settled so getting settled is like a really scary thing as well . . . I'm trying to live my life now but I'll never forget I was in care . . . its really difficult to put into words, to put the story together.*

Jason finds it particularly tricky to talk about the people who looked after him during these years. This is partly because when you are in care, as others have said, it is safer not to allow yourself to get too attached:

> *. . . there are so many people in and out of your life . . . it's very hard to kind of build up relationships and sort of know how long people are going to be around.*

But he also thinks his amnesia might be protecting others from painful reality too, a rather different cover story to the one discussed earlier:

> *Maybe, possibly, because I don't understand my time in care, that keeps other people safe – from ever knowing what really needed to happen, like a cover up – keeps people comfortable.*

Like Patrick, Jason had a social worker who stuck around in the background, and who is still occasionally in touch by card or phone, years later. This is important to Jason because these contacts help him in the task of reconnecting with, and reconciling the difference between, the person who was in care then and the person he is trying to be now:

> *. . . it's always nice to have someone who knew you way back, some time ago, and you can talk to them about what you are doing now and they can actually see the difference . . . it kind of helps you confirm it in your own mind . . . I used to feel parts of me were still sort of somewhere else, like in the kid's home I was in . . .*

These 'interesting conversations' reassure Jason that being in care is something that does not have to define him for life. But they also remind him that, as a result of that experience, 'I don't feel fully formed'. So far as his "case" is concerned, 'the book's not completely shut, it's still kind of open and all the papers are sort of all over the place'. They should remind us too that the way social work relationships are ended is as important a professional consideration as the way they are established in the first place.

Indeed, the two are directly related. In many of the accounts of young people who have left care there are references, such as the one made by Jason, to continued contact with social workers long after professional responsibilities have ended. Sometimes the professional relationship has been substituted by friendship and another caring adult has joined the network of relationships around a young person. Perhaps this has happened for Jason. Often, though, the status of the enduring contact is not apparent and this raises the question about why it has been difficult for the worker to let go. This seems to involve neither ending a transitional professional relationship effectively nor transforming it into a very different kind of commitment. Jason's account seems to suggest that the contact helps him temporarily reconnect with himself and his history. It certainly gave him the experience of mattering to someone else over time. Nonetheless, it ultimately reminds him that the necessary work could not be completed at the time. The papers, and the relationships described in them, remain 'sort of all over the place'.

Jason continues to work hard, in his words, to 'get to know myself again' and 'find my place in the world'. He is determined to resist any tendency to blame anyone for leaving him feeling pretty much on his own in facing these tasks. Yet he also knows that in care 'feelings get neglected', as Clare Winnicott understood, and that he needs to talk about that a good deal more now because that did not happen earlier.

Things seem to be working out rather more happily for Patrick at the moment, even though, like Jason, being in care left him without a permanent family home. The relationship between him and his social worker took an important turn, as can be seen from his account of arranging contact subsequently with his mum:

I wanted to go and see my mum, who was living in Liverpool. My social worker really respected the fact that I was going to travel all the way up to Liverpool on my own and she was helping me make the arrangements to get the travel warrant, and arranging where I had to change. I respect her a lot for that. Also, she was very truthful to me by saying it is a long way, things might not go well while you are staying up there. You are staying there for two months, it's a long time. It hurt me to hear and she knew it hurt me to hear, but she still said it to me, and that made me respect her a lot.

Patrick does not say much about how his ('my') social worker helped him prepare for (further) difficulty and disappointment in his disrupted and distanced relationship with his mum. But it is clear that what he valued was both her frankness and, crucially, her capacity to convey understanding and acceptance of the hurt this caused. It was on this basis that she now could become an effective companion and ally for Patrick, 'growing up through his case' alongside him, and helping him come to terms with what he had lost in the past (a family life with his sister and mother) and what he could expect in the future. As Patrick says, 'I did a lot of it by myself, being by myself and sussing it out, piecing everything together in my head and then speaking to my social worker. Getting the final construction was both of us together.' As a result, Patrick finds it much easier than Jason to talk coherently about his care story, connecting emotion and narrative, feelings and words, as he situates himself in his own life story.

The continuity of engagement between Patrick and his social worker became rooted in an authentic emotional relationship but it also required her to be a reliable source of practical support. This is the second core element of the working alliance, where a collaborative approach to identifying, mobilising and co-ordinating resources provides social opportunities, and enables a young person to develop increasing confidence and capability to take advantage of them.

Confronting disadvantage: relationships, resourcefulness and social justice

Patrick respects his social worker because she committed herself to 'helping me make the arrangements' that would lead to a safe arrival in Liverpool to stay with his mum. It is just this combination, of listening to what young people say they want to do and seeing the possibility of achieving that ambition, making the case on their behalf with others who have power, sorting out the finances or other resources as promised and including them in the process throughout, that feature in many reports of valued social work (Sinclair, 2005; Edwards, 2006; Morgan, 2006; Skuse and Ward, 2007). If a childhood in care is to be understood as a journey taken to successful citizenship into adulthood, as well as to stable family membership and identity, the social worker must be a *respectful and resourceful* companion and guide. This means recognising the barriers faced by young people. It requires reliability in bringing organisational resources and authority to bear to help young people confront and overcome their socially disadvantaged position.

There are two distinct aspects to this *resourceful practice*: the process of linking the ambitions of young people to the resources needed for their achievement. This first is to facilitate participation in assessment and decision-making and increase the control young people have over the journey they plan for themselves and the services and opportunities that will help them achieve their ambitions, as defined by themselves. This objective is arguably best understood as a matter of respect and rights (see Holland *et al*, and Thomas, this volume). However, it is also at the heart of the rather different approach in government policy in England, which increasingly positions young people as 'consumers' and emphasises the need for professionals to put their voice at the centre of plans designed to personalise services and maximise choice (Department for Education and Skills, 2007). The second aspect is to ensure that those services and opportunities are actually available and made accessible for young people. Confirming the lead professional role of the social worker, requiring a 'team around the child' to be co-ordinated by that lead professional and giving discretion back to the social worker over the control of small amounts of money are all intended to support service enhancement and access. At the same time, additional duties have been placed on local authorities (and schools) in England to prioritise opportunities for children in care (HM Government, 2005). Other proposals have also been made, intended to enhanced access to leisure and health. These changes are designed to 'close the gap in outcomes' (HM Government, 2006a, p 10) between all young people and those leaving care. Similar developments are now in hand in Scotland (Scottish Executive, 2007).

In fact, research evidence and practice experience indicate that closing this gap will require the kind of active and sustained 'corporate parenting' that talk of 'co-ordination', 'navigation' and facilitating 'choice' does not fully convey. Children discriminated against by virtue of class, ethnicity, gender and disability find it difficult enough to catch up with their more socially privileged peers in an increasingly competitive and divided society (Schoon and Bynner, 2003). Those who have also lived a childhood in and out of care without finding a secure or permanent family base are doubly disadvantaged. As the research of Mike Stein and others has repeatedly shown, the dynamics of social exclusion for care leavers are extraordinarily powerful unless stable and continuous supportive and caring relationships have been formed (Stein, 2006). These family and other relationships work best not only when they provide a secure emotional base, but also where they encourage ambition and aspiration and support the establishment and development of wider social networks. In these ways, young people gain access to and make confident use of valued social resources, such as education (Jackson, 2007), health care, housing, employment and leisure (Gilligan, 2007). This is what is meant by the idea of 'social capital' (Ferguson, 2006) and young people moving through care without a secure family base are particularly vulnerable to ending up in adulthood with very little of it.

Where stable and enduring family relationships and actively enabling parenting have not been secured, young people might be expected to draw more directly and continuously on the containing, bridging and networking capabilities and commitments of their social worker. Of course there is evidence that the 'self-reliance and self-advocacy' (Cameron, 2007, p 48) of some young people will carry them through to success, for example, in education, notwithstanding the absence of a stable family home or an effective social worker. This research supports the argument that practitioners need to take into account the strengths and resilience of young people and their desire to have control over their lives, even though this poses difficulties for professionals. Patrick reminded us of this. The developmental concept of resilience sits comfortably alongside the ethical commitment to ensuring the active participation of young people in the crucial decision-making processes en route. These ideas are very important, not only because they remind us that young people's *rights* as citizens are easily trampled on (see Thomas, this volume) but also because they encourage practitioners to be hopeful about, and respectful of, their *capabilities* too (see Lefevre, Chapter 2 and Holland *et al*, this volume).

However, the frustration of young people with the lack of social work and other support in these cases also reminds us that self-reliance is something to be recognised and respected when it is demonstrated rather than prescribed by default. There is a danger, otherwise, that the emphasis on choice and resilience might provide a smokescreen for negligence. Young people can get left stranded, competing on their own with peers who have far better access to social capital and resources by virtue of family and social support. Enabling young people to gain control over their lives is not a simple process of handing over power and responsibility, as if it were a baton, and setting them off on the next lap on their own, however well signposted the course has been.

Rather than assume self-reliance, the research on transitions through young adulthood shows that resilience is best seen less as an individual attribute or expectation and more as 'a dynamic process of positive adaptation in the face of significant adversity or trauma' (Schoon and Bynner, 2003, p 22; see also Hart and Blincow, 2007). The dynamism comes from a combination of child characteristics, including a reflective capacity underpinned by early secure attachment (Fonagy et al, 1994). Also involved are family characteristics, involving stability and support, and wider social factors, including specific support in using opportunities available from people like teachers. These aspects get linked together effectively when high aspirations are set and arrangements for what Schoon and Bynner call 'continuing protective support' (2003, p 28) in the face of persisting adversity are put in place. Positive plans and achievements then result.

Furthermore, this research shows that transitions are rarely experienced as smooth journeys along clearly marked pathways to predicted destinations as notions of "pathway planning" suggest. Instead of embarking on a sequential and purposeful process from childhood to adulthood, care to independence, the evidence is that care leavers often move on via a series of false starts and wrong turns (Biehel et al, 1995; Cameron, 2007). In this they are no different from those young people generally who 'backtrack along the transition path' (Jones, 1995, cited in Horrocks, 2002, p 332) and return home before setting out again. In this way the journey to adulthood is perhaps best seen as an expedition requiring a well-resourced base camp, from which directions can be given and supplies provided when the terrain gets scary and the destination is unclear. However, for many young people moving through and beyond care, the availability and commitment of the back-up team is in serious doubt. This is where the resourcefulness of the social worker should come to the fore. This means getting actively involved in ensuring that young people in care are as equally well equipped as any others and staying around for as long as possible to be there for them. It means being prepared to take up the journey alongside the young person when the going gets particularly tough and being tenacious and persistent in helping them back onto the right track where necessary.

A good example of how this works in practice is provided by the experience of care leavers who have gone on to study at university. Despite the distinctive nature of this 'exceptionally resilient' (Ajayi and Quigley, 2006, p 80) group, the strong and consistent commitment of their foster carers and/or their social workers was crucial, in most cases, in determining their ultimate success. The research finding, that 'consistent financial and personal support from the local authority is as important as the stability of the care placement' (p 80), should remind social workers how important they are in equalising life chances and confronting discrimination for the disadvantaged children in their care. As the research team insists, 'the basic principle is that social workers and carers should offer the same level of support and guidance that well-informed and adequately resourced parents would give to their own children' (p 81). Without powerful professionals working alongside them, taking responsibility for confronting the structural dynamics of exclusion and discrimination, disadvantaged young people are left fighting their cause on their own.

Conclusion

In setting out the principles of good direct practice at the time of the introduction of the Children Act 1989, Jane Rowe said, 'Every child and young person needs at least one individual to whom s/he is "special", who retains responsibility over time, who is involved in plans and decisions and who has ambitions for the child's achievement and full development' (Department of Health, 1990, p 11). This combination of 'personal investment' (Mallon, 2007, p 108) and professional authority and resourcefulness still constitutes the essence of an effective direct work role in social work. This is not to confuse the social worker, as the embodiment of the "corporate parent", with those direct carers (birth, relative, adoptive or foster) who ultimately provide the renewed sense of emotional security and family belonging required for a successful childhood in care. Nor is it to suggest that the rounded and robust picture of direct social work presented here should make redundant the roles of therapist (see Smallbone, this volume), advocate (see Thomas and Freed-Kernis and McKendrick, this volume) or pedagogue (see Petrie, this volume), or indeed the family centre worker or any other practitioner who shares responsibility for keeping a young person on track. Social work is not a substitute for the permanent care and commitment of parents, friends and partners. In this respect it should be remembered that the social worker is always a 'transitional participant' (Kanter, 2004, p 86) in the life of a young person. Furthermore, the social worker is only one amongst several members of the professional 'team around the child'. Nonetheless, it is only the social worker who occupies the 'strategic position', identified so clearly and so long ago by Clare Winnicott (1963, in Kanter, 2004, p 171).

As we have seen, a 'collapse of strategy' (Britton, 1981, cited in Emanuel, 2006) is always a risk, given the emotional and social dynamics of discontinuity and disadvantage inherent in journeys through care. The persisting tendency of organisations and their practitioners to mirror the fractured experience of young people, by avoiding engagement and referring on responsibilities and tasks, has been recognised in policy and law on integrated working. The talk of making a public pledge of support to young people in care

(Department for Education and Skills, 2007), to ensure their social inclusion, is a further important step towards backing them on the pathway to adulthood. The challenge for the social work profession now is to renew its own commitment to the development of a more effective direct work role. This is one that sees the social worker as a support not a signpost and puts relationships and resourcefulness rather than tasks and procedures at the heart of the work.

References

Ajayi S. and Quigley M. (2006) 'By degrees: care leavers in higher education', in Chase E., Simon A. and Jackson S. (eds) *In Care and After: A positive perspective*, London: Routledge

BASW (2003) *Looking after children: Be my social worker – the role of the child's social worker*, Birmingham: BASW

Biehal N., Clayden J., Stein M. and Biehek M. (1995) *Moving on: Young people and leaving care schemes*, London: The Stationery Office

Britton R. (1981) 'Re-enactment as an unwitting professional response to family dynamics', in Box S., Copley B., Magnana J. and Moustaki E. (eds) *Psychotherapy with Families: An analytic approach*, London: Routledge and Kegan Paul

Byng-Hall J. (1999) 'Creating a coherent story in family therapy', in Roberts G. and Holmes J. (eds) *Healing Stories*, New York: Oxford University Press, pp 49–66

Cabinet Office (2000) *Adoption: Prime Minister's Review, issued for consultation – a Performance and Innovation Unit report*, July 2000

Cameron C. (2007) 'Education and self-reliance among care leavers', *Adoption & Fostering*, 31:1, pp 39–49

Canham H. (1999) 'The development of the concept of time in fostered and adopted children', *Psychoanalytical Enquiry*, 19, pp 160–171

Chambers H. with Howell S., Madge N. and Olle H. (2002) *Building an Evidence Base for Promoting the Health and Well-being of Looked After Children and Young People*, London: National Children's Bureau

Cooper A. and Lousada J. (2005) *Borderline Welfare: Feeling and fear of feeling in modern welfare*, London: Karnac Books

Curtis M. (1946) *Report of the Care of Children Committee*, Cmnd. 6922, London: HMSO

Damasio A. (1999) *The Feeling of What Happens: Body, emotion and the making of consciousness*, London: Heinemann

Department for Education and Skills (2007) *Care Matters: Time for change*, Cm 7137, London: The Stationery Office

Department of Health (1990) *The Care of Children: Principles and practice in regulations and guidance*, London: HMSO

Edwards A. (2006) 'Relational agency: learning to be a resourceful practitioner', *International Journal of Educational Research*, 43, pp 168–182

Emanuel L. (2006) 'The contribution of organizational dynamics to the triple deprivation of looked-after children', in Kenrick J., Lindsey C. and Tollemache L. (eds) *Creating New Families: Therapeutic approaches to fostering, adoption, and kinship care*, London: Karnac Books

Fahlberg V. (1994) *A Child's Journey Through Placement*, London: BAAF

Ferguson K. (2006) 'Social capital and children's wellbeing: a critical synthesis of the international social capital literature', *International Journal of Social Welfare*, 15, pp 2–18

Fonagy P., Steel M., Steele H., Higgitt A. and Target M. (1994) 'The Emanuel Miller Memorial Lecture 1992: the theory and practice of resilience', *Journal of Child Psychology and Psychiatry*, 35:2, pp 231–257

Gilligan R. (2007) 'Spare time activities for young people in care: what can they contribute to educational progress?', *Adoption & Fostering*, 31:1, pp 92–99

Hall C., Slembrouck S. and Sarangi S. (2006) *Language Practices in Social Work*, London: Routledge

Harker R. M., Dobel-Ober D., Berridge D. and Sinclair R. (2004) 'More than the sum of its parts? Inter-professional working in the education of looked after children', *Children & Society*, 18:3, pp 179–193

Hart A. and Blincow D. with Thomas H. (2007) *Resilient Therapy with Children and Families*, London: Routledge

Hart A. and Luckock B. (2004) *Developing Adoption Support and Therapy: New approaches for practice*, London: Jessica Kingsley

HM Government (2005) *Statutory Guidance on the Duty on Local Authorities to Promote the Educational Achievement of Looked After Children under Section 52 of the Children Act 2004: Statutory Guidance*, Nottingham: DfES Publications

HM Government (2006a) *Care Matters: Transforming the lives of children and young people in care*, London: HMSO

HM Government (2006b) *The Lead Professional: Practitioner's guide*, London: HMSO

HM Treasury/Department for Education and Skills (2007) *Policy Review of Children and Young People: A discussion paper*, London: HMSO

Horne J. (1983) 'When the social worker is a bridge', in Sawbridge P. (ed) *Parents for Children*, London: BAAF

Horrocks C. (2002) 'Using life course theory to explore the social and developmental pathways of young people leaving care', *Journal of Youth Studies*, 5:3, pp 325–335

Jackson S. (2007) 'Progress at last?', *Adoption & Fostering*, 31:1, pp 3–5

Jones C. (1995) *Leaving Home*, Buckingham: Open University Press

Kanter J. (ed) (2004) *Face to Face with Children: The life and work of Clare Winnicott*, London: Karnac Books

Kenrick J. (2006) 'Work with children in transition', in Kenrick J., Lindsey C. and Tollemache L. (eds) *Creating New Families: Therapeutic approaches to fostering, adoption and kinship care*, London: Karnac Books

Lindsey C. (2006) 'Introduction', in Kenrick J., Lindsey C. and Tollemache L. (eds) *Creating New Families: Therapeutic approaches to fostering, adoption and kinship care*, London: Karnac Books

Mallon J. (2007) 'Returning to education after care: protective factors in the development of resilience', *Adoption & Fostering*, 31:1, pp 106–117

McKeown J., Clarke A. and Repper J. (2006) 'Life story work in health and social care: systematic literature review', *Journal of Advanced Nursing*, 55:2, pp 237–247

McNeil F., Batchelor S., Burnett R. and Knox J. (2005) *Reducing Re-offending: Key practice skills*, Edinburgh: SWIA and Glasgow School of Social Work

Meltzer H., Gatward R., Corbin T., Goodman R. and Ford T. (2003) *The Mental Health of Young People Looked After by Local Authorities in England: The report of a survey carried out in 2002 by Social Survey Division of the Office for National Statistics on behalf of the Department of Health*, London: The Stationery Office

Morgan R. (2006) *About Social Workers: A children's views report*, London: CSCI

Neil E. and Howe D. (eds) (2004) *Contact in Adoption and Permanent Foster Care*, London: BAAF

O'Hanlon W. and Weiner-Davis M. (2003) *In Search of Solutions: A new direction in psychotherapy*, New York, New York: WW Norton & Co

Parton N. and O'Byrne P. (2000) *Constructive Social Work: Towards a new practice*, London: Macmillan

Rustin M. (1999) 'Multiple families in mind', *Clinical Child Psychology and Psychiatry*, 4:1, pp 51–62

Ryan T. and Walker R. (2007) *Life Story Work* (3rd edn), London: BAAF

Schoon I. and Bynner J. (2003) 'Risk and resilience in the life course: implications for interventions and social policies', *Journal of Youth Studies*, 6:1, pp 21–31

Scottish Executive (2006) *Report of the 21st Century Social Work Review, Changing lives*, Edinburgh: Scottish Executive

Scottish Executive (2007) *Looked After Children and Young People: We can and must do better*, Edinburgh: Ministerial Working Group Report

Selwyn J., Sturgess W., Quinton D. and Baxter C. (2005) *Costs and Outcomes of Non-Infant Adoptions*, London: BAAF

Sinclair I. (2005) *Fostering Now: Messages from research*, London: Jessica Kingsley

Skuse T. and Ward H. (2007) *Children's Views of Care and Accommodation*, London: Jessica Kingsley

Social Exclusion Unit (2003) *A Better Education for Children in Care*, London: Social Exclusion Unit Report, Office of the Deputy Prime Minister

Statham J., Cameron C. and Mooney A. (2006) *The Tasks and Roles of Social Workers: A focused overview of research evidence*, London: Thomas Coram Research Unit

Stein M. (2006) 'Research review: young people leaving care', *Child and Family Social Work*, 11:3, pp 273–279

Utting W. (1997) *People Like Us: The report of the review of the safeguards for children living away from home*, London: Department of Health/The Welsh Office

Waterhouse R. (2000) *Lost in Care: The report of the tribunal of inquiry into the abuse of children in care in the former county council areas of Gwynedd and Clwyd since 1974*, HC 201, London: The Stationery Office

Winnicott C. (1963) 'Face to face with children', in Kanter J. (ed.) (2004) *Face to Face with Children: The life and work of Clare Winnicott*, London: Karnac Books

Winnicott C. (1986) 'Face to face with children', in *Working with Children*, Practice series: 13, London: BAAF

2 Knowing, being and doing: core qualities and skills for working with children and young people in care

Michelle Lefevre

Introduction

Adults communicate with children and young people[1] within a wide range of relationships and contexts and for a variety of purposes. Consider the mother who is attempting to work out whether the cries of her newborn infant mean he is hungry, scared, frightened or suffering a wet nappy; the youth advisory worker seeking to inform teenage girls about safer sexual health practices; and the schoolteacher attempting to impress a group of bored and restless 11-year-olds with the beauty and timelessness of Shakespeare.

In each of these scenarios it can be seen how communication is often *two-way* in nature (Triangle, 2001), even when this is not immediately apparent, and is guided by the *purpose and context* of that communication. So, the mother is attempting to make sense of cries of distress which are not yet understood by the infant. The accuracy and nature of her response conveys to the child either that his distress is understood, and so meaningful and important, or not. This is mediated through the *relationship* forming between them and how this single response fits into the overall pattern of responses, attuned or not (Stern, 1985). The youth advisory workers know their health-care messages must acknowledge and counter the *cultural* norms, beliefs and pressures which influence young women to discount the information they are attempting to impart. The teacher is attempting to communicate knowledge and aesthetic awareness to the pupils but he may also convey his *feelings*, deliberately or not, towards the pupils, towards the subject and towards teaching, so that they might pick up his enthusiasm, boredom, or irritation. Their negative behavioural responses are likely to influence what he does next. He might, for example, become angry and sarcastic, or feel useless and give up. Of course, this would be unlikely to depend solely on their impact upon him but additionally draw upon other factors such as his *personality, self-esteem*, and *feelings about his role* and profession borne out of his *experience* of teaching. Consequently, he may just shrug and write it off as a bad day.

It can be seen, then, that communication can entail the exchange of many kinds of information, both directly and indirectly, incidentally as well as purposefully. Unconscious, denied or private as well as intended and overt expressions of feelings,

---

[1] For the sake of brevity, the term "children" will be used from here on to refer to children and young people.

ideas and experiences may be transmitted. Individual, interpersonal, social, structural and cultural influences enter the frame, affecting both what is conveyed and what is understood. Many or all of these dynamics will come into play when social workers and children interact, ensuring that communication between them is rarely a straightforward process of information exchange (Luckock *et al*, 2006).

Some of these complexities will be explored through considering the kind of planning around communication that might be needed when a social worker needs to move a child to a different placement. A semi-fictional example of the case of Ben, who is based on a composite of children I have worked with through the years, is used as the backdrop. Key concepts for practice are highlighted and illustrated with the words of Jade and Shelley. Jade is an 11-year-old white British girl in foster carer who has recently described to me the ways in which her social workers have communicated and worked with her. Shelley was in care for much of her childhood and is now aged 21 with a child of her own. They hope that their ideas about what constitutes good practice will be useful for helping other social workers think about how to communicate and engage with children and young people. Their thoughts are very much in tune with those identified by recent research studies which have sought the views of children and young people in care directly (e.g. Biehal *et al*, 1995; Selwyn, 1996; Thomas *et al*, 1999; Bourton and McCausland, 2001; Morgan, 2006; Skuse and Ward, 2008, forthcoming; Holland *et al*, this volume).

Planning a placement move

Ben, aged eight, came into foster care three months ago following a long history of neglect in his family. His mother has had periodic depression and a long-term alcohol misuse problem. Her relationship with Ben's stepfather is volatile and mutually violent. This is Ben's third placement. The first was on an emergency basis over the weekend when Ben was removed from home because of risks to his safety from the escalating violence at home. The second was intended to be longer-term but he needed to move after one month due to his foster mother becoming seriously ill. Care proceedings have been instituted and a range of professionals have been engaged in assessment and intervention with Ben's birth family to see if matters in the home can improve and Ben can return home safely. This care plan has been discussed with Ben.

It had been intended for Ben to remain in this placement until the court had made a final decision regarding Ben's future. However, there is now the need for a further placement change. Ben's carers have been finding his behaviour increasingly difficult to manage, e.g. he has been bullying towards their own children who are younger than him. Following Ben hitting and bruising their six-year-old son, they have given an ultimatum that he must move in the next week.

Ben has seen numerous social workers both before and during his time in care. His last social worker, Gail, left six weeks ago, moving to another job elsewhere, and the case has been held on duty in the interim due to staff shortages and staff sickness. Lucy has now been allocated as Ben's long-term social worker and is about to make her first visit to Ben. She needs to think about both her overall role as a key social worker for a child in care and the legal, policy and practice objectives to be promoted, as this context will frame all subsequent communication. She can then consider the particular tasks which derive from these. The one which dominates the agenda is explaining to Ben about his impending placement move.

Giving children information and explanations

Jade and Shelley emphasised to us how important it was for them that they received clear information and explanations about why they were moving so that they could understand what was to happen and the reasons for it. Jade's social worker had 'said it in a very nice and clear way' that she could no longer live with her aunt but had to move into foster care. Shelley's had tried to put things in terms that she could make sense of:

> *I do think it is good to have a lot of explaining about what is going to happen and what is going to take place . . . She would make it more simple for me to have a conversation. Not a simple conversation but whereas some social workers do talk very authority like . . . she would translate it.*

Social workers don't always feel confident that they are the best person to undertake this. Shelley told us how she had been sent some distance away to a specialist clinic so that someone separate from her situation could help her understand matters.

> *I had to go up to [—] every Monday for two years to go and see – I am not sure if it was a psychiatrist or a therapist – but it was to help understand why I had gone into care. I didn't think they did a bit of good for me. The only thing was it ruined my maths because I missed maths every Monday. When I went to take my exams I wasn't too good with it.*

As Burnell and Vaughan (this volume) point out, it is essential for practitioners to have read case files and to know the real details of what has happened to children. However, children themselves already have lots of information and mis-information about their lives from their own experience and from what others have told them. Practitioners need to sensitively and carefully help children make sense of the different kinds of information, allowing the information-sharing and understanding process to be two-way. For Shelley, this did not happen at the specialist clinic:

I felt like she didn't know anything about my life. I felt she was just reading it out of a book, well not a book . . . a file. I felt like she was not even trying to understand me. I felt she was just trying to make me realise something that I already knew that she wasn't touching on very well.

Whereas non-directive and creative methods for exploration may be useful, even crucial, at other times (see below and Lefevre, this volume), they are not a substitute for direct, unequivocal communication when it is necessary:

I mean, if she understood me and had spoken to me about it, talked to me as a person instead of getting me to write things down and play with play dough and do finger painting and things like that . . . I really didn't feel it was appropriate in trying to help me understand why I had first gone into care. Apparently it was supposed to make me understand . . . I don't see how or how they expected it to, really.

What ultimately had been most useful for Shelley had been her own social worker taking the time to explain things carefully in an age-appropriate way yet treating her with respect as a "person":

I felt my social worker helped me more to understand why I was in care because she sat down and spoke to me like a person and made me understand in a way that a child does understand.

For both Jade and Shelley it had been essential that, when being given difficult inform-ation about moves, the social worker was sensitive and understanding about the impact on them of the information. They felt their social workers understood how they were feeling. Jade remembered:

Yeah, I was upset . . . I was actually. She kind of explained why [my aunt] didn't have enough money. She was very calm and explained things . . . she was gentle.

Shelley wanted social workers to give children who are to move placements:

. . . lots of reassurance that everything would be OK and the promise that there is going to be somebody there that they know and would help them if there are problems . . . I think that to know there is going to be somebody on the end of the phone you are more likely to ring up and say you have got a problem, whereas if you don't know who you are going to get at the other end of the phone, I think that is also very . . . deterring really. I think to help settle in there needs to be a great deal of talk about it really . . . not just 'This is where you are going to go and I will call you next week'. I don't think that is appropriate. I think a good couple

of days checking to see if they have or are settling in, I think that would be appropriate.

Finding out what children think, feel and want

Both Jade and Shelley remind us, though, that giving information and explanations are not enough in preparing children like Ben for a move. They describe how frustrated and powerless they have felt when a social worker merely tells them what is going to happen and expects they will go along with it. Ideally, it should be more of a consultative process, as Shelley suggests, more of a:

'Is this what you would like, is it or isn't it?' kind of thing, rather than 'This is what is best for you and this is how it is going to be'.

This follows the ethical principle of *inclusive* practice. Children like Jade, Shelley and Ben have the *right* to participation in decision-making about issues of concern to them. The research studies noted above have highlighted the importance to young people of being enabled to express their views and have them listened to and taken into account. The extent to which social workers actively follow this principle, though, will be influenced by their perception and expectations of children. Many social workers have very low expectations of children with physical and learning disabilities, for example. This disables them further, because 'if adults expect to get little or nothing from communicating with [disabled] children, that is probably exactly what they will get' (Stalker and Connors 2003, p 33; Marchant, this volume).

Ben's last worker, Gail, had lowered expectations of the competence of all children, perceiving them to be not yet fully formed or developed – human 'becomings' rather than human 'beings' (Qvortrup, 1987). Whereas Gail felt this meant she was attuned to Ben's vulnerability and need to be looked after, arguably she treated him as 'incompetent, unreliable and developmentally incomplete' (Mayall, 2000, p 121). As we saw above, this was how Shelley had been left feeling. Gail was able to think about Ben's needs for support, protection and guidance but thought that this meant many decisions should be made on his behalf rather than in consultation with him. This left Ben feeling that what he thought was of no importance.

This has been confirmed by Ben's experience. He had no choice in the ending of either the first or the second placement – they were dictated by circumstances, for example, the foster mother falling ill. Whether or not he returns home depends mainly on the recommendations of professionals following the completion of assessments and the decision of the court. This has left Ben feeling scared, powerless, disregarded and angry. These *feelings need to be recognised and contained* by the adults around him as this is crucial both for Ben's emotional well-being and for maximising the possible success of the move (Applegate, 1997; Donovan, 2002; Ruch, this volume).

Lucy (Ben's recently allocated social worker) must, then, not only help Ben to express his feelings about the move but must also mitigate his feelings of being powerless and always being let down by others. Providing emotional reassurance is not enough. Ben will also need to feel involved, informed and consulted, and that he has an influence over *how* the move takes place and (depending on available resources) the kind of placement he is to move to. This is his legal entitlement. By providing him with information and explanations, seeking his views and ensuring that they are taken into account in decision making, Lucy can give Ben a clear message that his views and feelings are important both to her and the professional system and will be attended to.

This approach begins to allow Ben to feel more empowered (see below) but it does not mean that he should be left feeling like he is the only one in control of the situation. Whilst he has competence in certain aspects of his life, his stage of maturation means he often needs adults to act competently and authoritatively on his behalf (Uprichard, 2007). Most children recognise and (mainly) welcome this.

Jade:	*I'd tell them I'm not happy with that unless it's for my best, for my benefit, so they know that it's the right thing to do. Then they know that and I can trust them and they can do that.*
Michelle:	*So you know that sometimes actually the adults around you might . . .*
Jade:	*Be right!*
Michelle:	*Yeah, be right.*
Jade:	*I don't always like that!*
Michelle:	*But you know you can trust people sometimes to make those decisions.*

Unlike Jade, Ben has not learned that he can trust the adults around him to make good and safe decisions about his life. It will be crucial for Lucy to keep explaining to, consulting with, and advocating and intervening appropriately on behalf of Ben in order to begin to impact on this internalised world view.

Being child-centred

In order to both help Ben understand what is to happen and learn from him what his views and feelings are, Lucy will aim to ensure that her practice is as child-centred as possible. This will mean Lucy putting Ben's needs and rights at the centre, adapting her way of communicating to his, and going at his pace, rather than at the pace of work.

Ben's competence in communication is not fixed but can be enhanced or diminished by the skill in facilitation which Lucy demonstrates in understanding and working with him (Thomas and O'Kane, 2000). Gail was not very confident or experienced in working with children and tended to see their age and stage of development as limiting their communicative ability. This was reinforced for her when she sat Ben down to ask him direct, often closed, questions about his views and didn't get many answers. Many children find this kind of questioning rather alienating, suspecting, often accurately, that it contains a hidden agenda (Thomas and O'Kane, 2000). Ben would just grunt, shrug, look away or start playing with his games console. This would make Gail feel frustrated and useless and she would find herself doing most of the talking to try to keep the conversation going (Corcoran, 1997). When her supervisor suggested she might need to get to know Ben better in order for them to feel comfortable with each other, Gail pointed out how her busy caseload had many other priorities. She reported to the review that Ben had been unable to express any views about his situation and reassured herself that she was making decisions in Ben's best interests.

This dissatisfied Lucy when she read the file. She is very committed to the principle of children's participation and believes that Ben has a right to his views being heard and taken into account. For her, it is a crucial part of her role and task that she understands what Ben is thinking, feeling and experiencing. She recognises she must maximise her skills and techniques to succeed in her role and tasks with Ben. Lucy considers the kind of *vocabulary and concepts* she will need to use to ensure that she and Ben understand each other. These will need to be in tune with Ben's cognitive and intellectual capacity. It will be helpful for Lucy to have some *underpinning knowledge* about child development norms (e.g. Sheridan, 1997) which will give her some pointers about a child of Ben's age, but it will be important that she does not make too many assumptions, as there is a potential for discrimination and cultural bias where abstract norms are rigidly applied (Robinson, 2001; Goldstein, 2002). Instead, Lucy should learn about what Ben understands as an individual. This can best be done by getting to know Ben, observing him (see Turney, this volume) and interacting with him. Playing games or doing other activities together are an ideal way of doing this (Thomas and O'Kane, 2000; see also Cook, Lefevre and Ahmad *et al*, this volume). Lucy can also get additional information from the people who know Ben well, e.g. his family, foster carers or teachers. In these ways, she will understand more about Ben's *stage of development* and the extent to which his neglectful earlier experiences have delayed this (Jones, 2003).

Consequently, Lucy learns that Ben's vocabulary and conceptual understanding are less than she might have expected for an eight-year-old boy and she adjusts the words and terms she uses accordingly. With other children, Lucy might have additionally needed to think about what is understood when English is a second language, using interpreters for deaf children and learning alternative ways of communicating with children with learning disabilities (see Marchant, this volume).

Lucy knows that children of Ben's age and stage do not communicate only through verbal and written language. Much of their thoughts, feelings and experiences are unprocessed, even unconscious, and are held in *symbolic* forms (Winnicott, 1996). This means that they are not readily accessible to the child and, even if they are, they may well not have the language, conceptual understanding or emotional or reflective capacity to verbalise them to another. If Lucy wants to understand what Ben really thinks and feels, she will need to attend to what is communicated more obliquely. She might draw on a range of *play-based and creative techniques* to do so (see Lefevre, this volume). This might include using free drawing or sandplay with figurines to give Ben the freedom to 'express the world in his own terms' (Thomas and O'Kane, 2000, p 61). More structured exercises can also be very useful in giving children an effective voice in their care planning, such as rating scales with a happy face at one end and a sad or angry one at the other (McGoldrick and Gerson in Mattaini, 1995) or ecomaps and genograms either on paper (Walton and Smith, 1999; Altshuler, 1999) or as part of computer programmes (Mattaini, 1995).

Much is also communicated through children's *behaviour and relational style* (see Schofield and Smallbone, this volume). We know that Ben's current placement has already broken down because Ben is experienced as having "difficult" and aggressive behaviour. Lucy starts from the position of assuming that this behaviour is at least in part a response to Ben's feelings of being powerless and disregarded in placement decisions. She speculates that his shrugs and withdrawal could signify both anger and his perception that it is pointless to say what he feels directly as his views and feelings are irrelevant to others. In this way, Ben's behaviour is purposeful; it can convey how he feels inside and how he perceives others and his situation.

By taking this perspective, Lucy does not feel pushed away by Ben. Instead, she views his grunts and shrugs as forms of communication that are about him rather than her. She believes them to be meaningful and as she does not yet understand them, sees it as her responsibility that she learns to do so.

Engaging and forming a relationship with children

Lucy believes that she will not be able to make sense of Ben's indirect communications unless she understands him better, and that he is unlikely to cope with discussions about difficult matters and confide in her unless he trusts her (Munro, 2001; Bell, 2002). She is not surprised when Ben demonstrates by his behaviour that he does not yet feel ready to talk to her. They do not know each other and she anticipates that his previous experiences will make him wary of her and less likely to share sensitive information – other social workers and carers have come and gone, why should he trust her or invest in her? She decides then that her first priority on her initial visit must be to begin to engage Ben in a relationship where some initial working *trust* can be established.

Like Gail, she too has a busy caseload and the administrative demands of working with a child in care make prioritising such direct work with children very difficult (Schofield and Brown, 1999; Leveridge, 2002; Garrett, 2003). However, Lucy recognises that her objectives will simply not be achieved without attention to this, as relationships are the conduit through which successful communication occurs (Schofield, 1998; Roth *et al*, 2005). The norm for children like Ben is that people are unpredictable and unsafe. Lucy must convey to Ben that she is consistent, emotionally available and dependable, if his trust is to develop (Cleaver, 1996; Schofield and Brown, 1999).

Lucy recognises Ben has had too many changes of social worker (and placement) and intends to commit to remaining with him for as long as possible. Of course, social workers have personal life circumstances which might impact upon this, necessitating moves away, periods of maternity leave, etc. Whilst these might be unavoidable, it is important that workers consider the impact of these on the children with whom they are working rather than defending against this. Gail's feelings were, 'I have to look after myself and I can't afford to let Ben's concerns affect me'. This made her emotionally unavailable for Ben and meant no one attended to the effect on him of this change. It compounded the traumatic loss for him of his family and confirmed his views about the unreliability of others.

Similarly, social workers cannot always control service reorganisations, etc, which lead to changes of worker but, again, it is important for them to consider what this might mean for children. Jade told me the longest she'd had a social worker for was one year:

Yes, not for very long because apparently every year they change, because the boss moves them around and everything. So you change social workers, get to know them and then they move again, just like that.

I asked her if she thought that was a good idea.

Not really . . . because once you get to know them they're moving away and you have to work hard with the other one to get to know them again.

Such changes are clearly unacceptable and should be addressed head-on by the *Care Matters* (Department for Education and Skills, 2006) agenda to ensure continuity of relationship between children and their social workers.

In order for her and Ben to get to know each other better and build up a relationship, Lucy negotiates with her manager for some *uninterrupted time* with Ben away from other work pressures to give her time to *prepare* for the work, *establish a safe and relaxed environment*, and reflect afterwards in order to make sense of Ben's communications (see Ruch, this volume). She knows that the relationship will take some time to build up but that she needs to establish with Ben early on who she is and what can be relied upon.

Lucy will be drawing on her own *personal qualities* to build up this relationship (Farnfield and Kaszap, 1998; Bell, 2002). Children tend to trust practitioners who seem sincere and genuine, who can show real feelings and behave in an ordinary human way.

They want someone who can be enthusiastic and humorous, 'fun, not just boring' (Prior *et al*, 1999, p 134). Jade had valued this in her foster carer's support worker, S.:

Sometimes he's very humorous and funny. He makes things fun . . . He's really, really nice . . . and kind and everything. He always makes up jokes and everything and – it's hard to put it – he's always happy, he's never grumpy. He helps me when I'm stuck and everything. If we're, like, in a bad mood or something with my sister or something he cheers us up and he makes things a laugh. It's really good.

Children want someone who genuinely cares about them as an individual, and shows this by being friendly, warm and demonstrating personal touches like remembering their birthday (Prior *et al*, 1999). Jade appreciated how S. was friendly with her despite her carers being his main priority:

Yeah, it's like it's not just to do with his work, what he has to do.

By comparison, it seemed clear to her that, for a previous worker:

It was like her job, basically.

Shelley had had one social worker through much of her childhood and this relationship had become of particular importance to her because no stable or permanent home was found for her:

Yes, there was almost a friendship there.

Social workers sometimes worry that being friendly and caring in this way oversteps the boundaries and could confuse children. Shelley speculated that this could happen if social workers allowed children to cross too far over into their personal lives, for example, by inviting them into their homes.

I don't think it would be appropriate for the sheer fact it is the social worker's life of her own and then there could become problems with obsessed children . . . They can cause problems which are not necessary. Keep work and your home life separate. But then it is always nice if a social worker will sit there and have a conversation about her family as well as yours. Not in great detail, but like if she explains 'I have got two children and they are growing up', that is a kind of reasonable conversation, not 'come home and meet my children'. I don't think it was because she wanted to show her children off.

Clearly, it is not ideal that Shelley's most important relationship was with her social worker. It should have been with a permanent family or substitute carer. The social worker should normally remain a more transitional figure focused on care and permanence planning rather than the kind of substitute parent that Shelley's became (see Luckock, this volume). However, placements do fail for a variety of reasons and the social worker then often takes on much more importance, perhaps being the only consistent figure in some children's lives. This sharing of herself in this way allowed the relationship between Shelley and her social worker to develop and gave Shelley an experience of mattering to someone else, which she might not have got elsewhere:

> *I do think we had a close 11 years. I did say to her I wished she was my mum. I hated every single foster family I went to and she understood me, which I found excellent and very reassuring – that there was somebody that understood me and it wasn't just me that wasn't being understood.*

Working with therapeutic processes

Lucy's main role with Ben is focused around particular tasks rather than being a therapist for him. However, "depth" and unconscious processes more associated with therapeutic work will arise between children and their social workers when this is not anticipated, even unwelcomed (Ruch, 1998). It will be essential for Lucy to attend to these if she is to promote their relationship and begin to make sense of what Ben is feeling and experiencing. This requires Lucy to have a degree of *emotional capacity* and capability:

> *To understand a child's fear, sadness, loss, trauma, joy for instance, workers have to be able to understand how they themselves experience these emotions so they can understand how their feelings influence their understanding of and contribute to their interactions with children.* (Krueger, 1997, p 155)

Using the self in this purposeful way requires Lucy to have previously *reflected* on personal experiences and relationships so that she knows herself well and can distinguish the feelings and responses which she brings to the encounter as a result of her own personality and experience (proactive counter-transference) from those evoked by Ben's strong feelings and transference towards her (her reactive counter-transference) (Mackewn, 1997; see also Smallbone, this volume).

Gail had not been as prepared to look into herself and question her own responses. She had struggled to form a relationship with Ben and their communication remained stilted. She did not really want to face up to the way he made her feel useless, which had re-evoked feelings from her childhood of not being good enough, and preferred to defend herself by projecting their difficulties in relating solely onto Ben – it was his problem, not hers. When she moved him from his first to his second placement, she guessed that he did not want to move and that it would be disruptive to him. This worried her but, as she didn't feel comfortable with Ben or know how to respond to him, she remained rather withdrawn and ill at ease. Gail did not know what reason to give him for the move as she thought it might be worrying for him to be told the carer was so ill. She also worried that it would contravene the carer's privacy for Ben to be told this. Gail's discomfort about these matters and inability to articulate them or work through them interfered with her capacity to explain things in a way which made sense to Ben, so that he ended up rather unclear about what was going on. This compounded Ben's sense that the adults were not in proper control of his life. He felt confused and rejected and that the move was a punishment for being bad. To Ben, Gail seemed matter-of-fact, uninvolved, even brusque, when discussing such monumental matters as where he was to live and helping him pack, so Ben received the impression that she didn't understand the significance of the move and that he was being abandoned once again.

His perceptions affected Ben's capacity to settle in the new placement. He seemed to want to test out the new carers by being difficult so that if they were not going to keep him, he would know sooner rather than later; in this way he would protect himself from future disappointment. He resented the safety and security the birth children of the foster carers experienced and this made him want to attack them. Of course, these feelings were barely conscious as far as Ben was concerned. He could not have articulated them to himself, let alone to anyone else. He would have needed Gail to be attuned to the subtleties of his behaviour for her to begin to make sense of this with him. She could not and it became a self-fulfilling prophecy – the placement broke down.

Lucy has needed to recognise this pattern very quickly and must immediately begin to work this through with Ben in order for it not to immediately dictate the progress of the next placement. She speculates how his feelings about adults, social workers, moves and this placement are likely to not only influence how he experiences and makes sense of the information she gives him but also shape the kind of overt reaction he displays. Ben's history is of adults generally failing to think about him and his life or consider his feelings, and reacting negatively when he shows distress as a result. This makes him unable and afraid to tell or show Lucy about feelings such as pain and loss. Instead, he appears not bothered or "cut-off". Trauma, misattunements, lack of containment and insecurity of attachment (see Schofield, this volume) cause him to feel emotionally dysregulated in stressful situations, so he is unable to hear or comprehend what is said to him. It will be essential for Lucy to provide a holding or containing environment for Ben, a space where his feelings can emerge safely with someone who can bear them, think about them and help him understand them. Lucy will use skills such as mirroring, empathy and attunement to achieve this (Winnicott, 1996).

How might Gail have increased her emotional capability so she could use herself more effectively in the work? She might have been helped to recognise how her own unresolved life experiences (such as her rather punitive childhood) had affected her by being encouraged into self-reflection through a training course, supervision on a particular case, peer discussion, or even from watching a film or reading a book. Self-reflection and ongoing supervision might have then been sufficient for her to begin to make sense of how the personal impacted upon the professional, although it would be essential for the supervisor to ensure the boundary between supervision and therapy was not crossed:

> *The basic boundary in this area is that supervision sessions should always start from exploring issues from work and should end with looking at where the supervisee goes next with the work that has been explored.* (Hawkins and Shohet, 2000, p 45)

If it then transpired that more in-depth work was required to resolve particular issues, Gail might have then referred herself for individual or group counselling or therapy. Such self-work is often considered as the foundation stone of effective therapeutic encounters with others.

Issues of power

Despite their mandated authority to plan for children in care, social workers like Lucy and Gail do not always feel powerful or in control in their difficult role. Resource constraints and angry or defensive reactions, such as Ben's shrugs and withdrawals, can make them feel de-skilled and that they have little agency. They can then forget quite how powerful they appear to others. When they do not consult with children or do not explain why certain things occur or why they make particular decisions, children like Ben often feel very powerless. As we have seen above they may become fearful, suspicious or hostile or just give up. Ben has come to feel that expressing his views and feelings is pointless and that social workers merely pay lip-service to the principles of inclusion and participation. Lucy will need to work hard to convince Ben differently. Otherwise he will feel as Shelley did with the worker from the specialist clinic, like:

> . . . *an undermined child. I just felt there is authority there and I don't think somebody needs to feel that. I think they need to feel they are on the same level. If they are not then it is a waste of time, really, I think. You are just not ever going to be getting anywhere.*

Workers like Gail sometimes take a position where they see themselves as the "expert" who should make all decisions on behalf of children (Holland and Scourfield, 2004). At the age of eight, Ben cannot and should not make all his own decisions. However, Gail ignored the unique knowledge and understanding Ben had about himself which would have been crucial for her to take into account in her planning. Lucy is alert to the possibility that Ben will convey his thoughts and feeling through his play, behaviour and relational style. She will need, though, to guard against over-interpretation of this and aim, wherever possible, to allow information from Ben to emerge non-directively and negotiate possible meanings with him (Ryan *et al*, 1995). Sharing of power in these ways certainly does not mean Lucy passing all her power over to Ben. Ben needs her to retain her adult professional authority in the way that she works with him and the system. This not only provides the containment and boundaries which enable a child of Ben's age to feel safe but also reassures him that he can rely on her to work competently *for* him (Winnicott, 1996).

Another power issue important to children is that of *confidentiality*. Many children in the care system have complained about lax professional standards regarding this (Munro, 2001). They want to be able to fully confide in someone about their concerns but may become reluctant to share thoughts and feelings because it all gets written down in the file and shared with strangers (Ryan *et al*, 1995). Of course, social workers would argue that they share information with other relevant professionals as needed in order to promote children's welfare and keep them safe. It will be important, though, to question whether all the times that this occurs are strictly necessary if children's rights are to be respected. The boundaries and limits to confidentiality should always be spelled out in advance to children and, wherever possible, their informed consent to breaches in confidentiality should be sought (Applewhite and Joseph, 1994). Even quite young children are able to understand why workers might need to pass on information about them (Carroll, 2002).

Both Ben and Lucy are white; however, Ben's feelings of powerlessness or oppression might have increased if, for example, he was black or from a minority ethnic group (Graham, 2007). He might feel Lucy does not understand the cultural backdrop to what he feels and says and be unequal to the task of conveying such complexities. A whole shading of meaning might be lost. This would be intensified if English were not Ben's first language (see Kohli and Gupta, this volume). In this situation, Lucy might need to enhance her *cultural competence*, increasing her knowledge of Ben's cultural background and norms to avoid tensions and misunderstandings arising due to any differences in communicative and relational styles (Caple *et al*, 1995; Hodge, 2002). It would be important for her, though, not to make assumptions or over-simplifications about this, but to learn from Ben and his family (Ahmed, 1986).

Additionally, Lucy should commit to an *anti-racist* approach. If Ben were black, dual heritage or from a minority ethnic community, his emotional well-being and identity development are likely to have already been affected by the age of eight by growing up in a racist society. He might feel uncomfortable with, fearful of, or further disempowered by a white worker. Lucy would need to consider the possible impact on Ben's communicative capacity of these dynamics, acknowledging these with Ben and working to mediate them (Modi *et al*, 1995; Robinson, 2001).

Knowing, being and doing – the three domains of skilled social work communication

What this chapter has attempted to show is how communications between children and their social workers are likely to be complex, even problematic, due to the impact of the feelings and perceptions of each on the situation. The context of their interaction, the worker's role and tasks and the previous experiences of them both, in particular the child's experience of loss, uncertainty, insecurity of attachment, powerlessness, trauma and abuse, can inhibit, interrupt, even derail intended communications. Many of the factors which muddy the waters for children such as Ben cannot be changed, at least not in the short term. It will be essential for workers to understand and take these dynamics into account as broadly as possible in order to minimise their impact and facilitate clearer communication.

A number of pointers for good practice have been drawn out of the vignette above. They can be mapped onto a tripartite model which represents three domains within which the skills, knowledge and capabilities of social workers can be positioned (Lefevre *et al*, in press):

Being

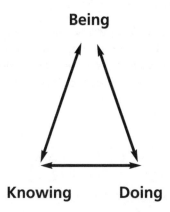

Knowing   **Doing**

- The domain of "knowing" represents the kinds of knowledge and understanding that workers need in order to make sense of the complex range of contexts and dynamics which underpin their communication with children. This might include knowledge about the impact on children's development of adverse life circumstances such as discontinuity of care and clarity about the social work role and task.
- "Being" reflects personal aspects of the individual. It can include both their emotional capacities and capabilities (to form relationships, be warm and caring, be self-aware, work with strong feelings) and their value base, the ethical commitments they make to children (attending to their rights as well as their needs, sharing power appropriately).

- "Doing" relates to the kind of techniques and micro-skills which workers might need, such as using age-appropriate language to give information, listening to children, and using play and activities to engage and communicate with children.

The bi-directional arrows of this triangular model reflects my view that none of these domains operate in isolation but are co-dependent. So a task such as Lucy seeking Ben's views and feelings about his impending move has been seen to require comprehensive "knowing" (e.g. making sense of how Ben's experiences have affected his conceptual and perceptual understanding), appropriate ways of "being" (including Lucy using her self and emotions to form a relationship and having a commitment to children's participation) as well as the "doing" skills of clear and child-centred information-giving and effective listening techniques. This model can be used as a framework to structure and promote the professional development, reflection and planning of practitioners like Lucy and Gail.

Final words

The final words go to Jade. These are the three most important things she believes practitioners need to think about when they're working with children:

One would be 'listen to them and let them have their say'. The second one would be 'help them', 'be there for them'. And the last one would be 'communicate well with them and explain things; explain if they don't understand and explain it again and again and again till they do, even though you'd probably get a sore throat, but make sure the boy or girl knows what's going on'.

References

Ahmed S. (1986) 'Cultural racism in work with Asian women and girls', in Ahmed S., Cheetham J. and Small J. (eds) *Social Work with Black Children and their Families*, London: BAAF/BT Batsford

Altshuler S. J. (1999) 'Constructing genograms with children in care: implications for casework practice', *Child Welfare*, 78:6, pp 777–90

Applegate J. S. (1997) 'The holding environment: an organizing metaphor for social work theory and practice', *Smith College Studies in Social Work*, 68:1, pp 7–29

Applewhite L. W. and Joseph M. V. (1994) 'Confidentiality: issues in working with self-harming adolescents', *Child and Adolescent Social Work*, 11:4, pp 279–94

Bell M. (2002) 'Promoting children's rights through the use of relationship', *Child and Family Social Work*, 7:1, pp 1–11

Biehal N., Clayden J., Stein M. and Wade J. (1995) *Moving On: Young people and leaving care schemes*, London: HMSO

Bourton A. and McCausland J. (2001) 'A service for children and a service for the courts: the contribution of guardians ad litem in public law proceedings', *Adoption & Fostering*, 25:3, pp 59–66

Caple F. S., Salcido R. M. and di Cecco J. (1995) 'Engaging effectively with culturally diverse families and children', *Social Work in Education*, 17:3, pp 159–70

Carroll J. (2002) 'Play therapy: the children's views', *Child & Family Social Work*, 7:3, pp 177–187

Cleaver H. (1996) *Focus on Teenagers*, London: HMSO

Corcoran J. (1997) 'A solution-oriented approach to working with juvenile offenders', *Child and Adolescent Social Work*, 14:4, pp 277–88

Department for Education and Skills (2006) *Care Matters: Transforming the lives of children and young people in care*, London: The Stationery Office

Donovan M. (2002) 'Social work and therapy: reclaiming a generic therapeutic space in child and family work', *Journal of Social Work Practice*, 16:2, pp 113–123

Farnfield S. and Kaszap M. (1998) 'What makes a helpful grown up? Children's views of professionals in the mental health services', *Health Informatics Journal*, 4:1, pp 3–14

Garrett P. M. (2003) 'Swimming with dolphins: the assessment framework, New Labour and new tools for social work with children and families', *British Journal of Social Work*, 33:4, pp 441–463

Goldstein B. P. (2002) 'Black children with a white parent – social work education', *Social Work Education*, 21:5, pp 551–563

Graham M. (2007) *Black Issues in Social Work and Social Care*, Bristol: The Policy Press

Hawkins P. and Shohet R. (2000) *Supervision in the Helping Professions* (2nd edition), Buckingham: Open University Press

Hodge D. R. (2002) 'Working with Muslim youths: understanding the values and beliefs of Islamic discourse', *Children and Schools*, 24:1, pp 6–20

Holland S. and Scourfield J. (2004) 'Liberty and respect in child protection', *British Journal of Social Work*, 34:1, pp 21–36

Jones D. (2003) *Communicating with Vulnerable Children: A guide for practitioners*, London: Gaskell

Krueger M. (1997) 'Using self, story, and intuition to understand child and youth care work, *Child and Youth Care Forum*, 26:3, pp 153–61

Lefevre M., Tanner K. and Luckock B. (in press) 'Developing social work students' communication skills with children and young people: A model for the qualifying level curriculum', *Child and Family Social Work*

Leveridge M. (2002) 'Mac-social work: the routinisation of professional activity', *Maatskaplike Werk/Social Work*, 38:4, pp 354–362

Luckock B., Lefevre M. and Orr D. with Tanner K., Jones M. and Marchant R. (2006) *Knowledge Review: Teaching, learning and assessing communication skills with children in social work education*, London: Social Care Institute for Excellence

Mackewn J. (1997) *Developing Gestalt Counselling*, London: Sage

Mattaini M. A. (1995) 'Visualizing practice with children and families', *Early Child Development and Care*, 106, pp 59–74

Mayall B. (2000) 'Conversations with children: working with generational issues', in Christensen P. and James A. (eds) *Research with Children: Perspectives and practices*, London: Falmer Press, pp 98–119

Modi P., Marks C. and Watley R. (1995) 'From the margin to the centre: empowering the black child', in Cloke C. and Davies M. (eds) *Participation and Empowerment in Child Protection*, London: Pitman, pp 80–103

Morgan R. (2006) *About Social Workers: A children's views report*, Newcastle upon Tyne: Office of the Children's Rights Director

Munro E. (2001) 'Empowering looked-after children', *Child and Family Social Work*, 6:2, pp 129–137

Prior V., Lynch M. and Glaser D. (1999) 'Responding to child sexual abuse: an evaluation of social work by children and their carers', *Child and Family Social Work*, 4:2, pp 131–143

Qvortrup J. (1987) 'Introduction: the sociology of childhood', *International Journal of Sociology*, 17:3, pp 3–37

Robinson L. (2001) 'A conceptual framework for social work practice with black children and adolescents in the United Kingdom', *Journal of Social Work*, 1:2, pp 165–185

Roth A., Fonagy P., Target M., Phillips J. and Kurtz Z. (2005) *What Works for Whom? A critical review of treatments for children and adolescents* (2nd edn), London: Guilford Publications

Ruch G. (1998) 'Direct work with children: the practitioner's perspective', *Practice*, 10:1, pp 37–44

Ryan V., Wilson K. and Fisher T. (1995) 'Developing partnerships in therapeutic work with children', *Journal of Social Work Practice*, 9:2, pp 131–40

Schofield G. (1998) 'Inner and outer worlds: a psychosocial framework for child and family social work', *Child and Family Social Work*, 3:1, pp 57–67

Schofield G and Brown K (1999) 'Being there: a family centre worker's role as a secure base for adolescent girls in crisis', *Child and Family Social Work*, 4:1, pp 21–31

Selwyn J. (1996) 'Ascertaining children's wishes and feelings in relation to adoption', *Adoption & Fostering*, 20:3, pp 14–20

Sheridan M. (1997) *From Birth to Five Years: Children's developmental progress*, revised and updated by Frost M. and Sharma A., London: Routledge

Skuse T. and Ward H. (2008, forthcoming) *Listening to Children's Views of Care and Accommodation*, London: Jessica Kingsley

Stalker K. and Connors C. (2003) 'Communicating with disabled children', *Adoption & Fostering*, 27:1, pp 26–35

Stern D. (1985) *The Interpersonal World of the Infant: A view from psychoanalysis and developmental psychology*, New York, New York: Basic Books

Thomas C., Lowe N. V., Beckford V., Lowe N. and Murch N. (1999) *Adopted Children Speaking*, London: BAAF

Thomas N. and O'Kane C. (2000) 'Discovering what children think: connections between research and practice', *British Journal of Social Work*, 30:6, pp 819–35

Triangle (2001) *Two-Way Street: Communicating with disabled children and young people – communication handbook*, Leicester: NSPCC

Uprichard E. (2007) 'Children as "beings and becomings": children, childhood and temporality', *Children and Society*, published online, advance access, 29 June 2007

Walton E. and Smith C. (1999) 'The genogram: a tool for assessment and intervention in child welfare', *Journal of Family Social Work*, 3:3 pp 3–20

Winnicott C. (1996) 'Communicating with children', *Smith College Studies in Social Work*, 66:2, pp 117–28

Section 2

Differing perspectives on the care experience

3   Providing a secure base – an attachment perspective

Gillian Schofield

Family relationships are the first and most significant context in which the child's sense of self develops. From birth, children will be looking to people in their family circle to help them manage their world and to make sense of who they are and how they fit in. The newborn baby gazes into the human faces which come into view, looking for recognition and reassurance. From that point on, the child's mind is actively engaged in processing the information they receive from these interpersonal encounters in order to answer some very challenging questions. Who am I? Who are you? What will happen if I am hungry or lonely or start to cry? These questions, in different forms, stay with us all our lives, but the questions children ask and the answers they find in the context of family relationships are going to have a major impact on all areas of current and future functioning and happiness.

Where children have been separated from their families of origin as a result of harmful or absent parental care and are growing up in foster care, adoption or residential care, the self develops in a context of loss combined with fresh opportunities for loving and being loved, healing and growth (Howe, 1998; Wilson *et al*, 2003; Beek and Schofield, 2004; Schofield and Beek, 2006). For these children, though, the universal questions of 'Am I lovable?' and 'Who will look after me?' take on particular meanings which need to be understood in the context of their previous experiences in relationships. Social work with children from troubled backgrounds in such complex psychosocial contexts requires a good understanding of risk and protective processes in children's development. Attachment theory can be invaluable in aiding that understanding, but also in understanding the role that social workers themselves can play in providing a secure base for children through their relationships with them. This chapter uses the core concepts of attachment theory to explore both the experience of children and young people growing up in foster, adoptive or residential care, and the implications of keeping attachment theory in mind when working with children.

A secure base

The majority of children come into public care from families characterised by adversity, poor parenting, neglect and abuse (Sellick *et al*, 2004; Sinclair, 2005). They will generally have lacked the experience of caregivers who were available and responsive to their needs.

From infancy, the child is biologically programmed to seek proximity to one or more caregivers who offer reliable care and protection (Bowlby, 1969). The significance of the availability of this secure base (Bowlby, 1988) is that it reduces the child's anxiety and enables the child to explore, confident in the knowledge that support and help are there when needed. Exploration in infancy will begin simply with the infant's interest and pleasure in exploring the face of the caregiver and gradually move on to exploration and enjoyment of other aspects of the sensory world – looking with interest at bright colours, enjoying the taste of new foods, listening to the sound of the rattle, smelling their mother's scent, touching a velvet teddy bear. In contrast, where infants who come into care have lacked trust in the availability of a parent as a secure base, the most striking aspect of their behaviour is the lack of awareness, interest, pleasure and exploration in both their interpersonal and physical environments.

> *Tammy came into care at 10 months old, having experienced consistent physical and emotional neglect from birth. She had been shut away in her bedroom for much of the time or left strapped in her buggy. She was not picked up for feeding. Admitted first to hospital, Tammy was entirely limp with no muscle tone, laying completely flat and going floppy when picked up. She did not respond to light, sound, toys, her mother's face or voice. She also did not respond to the nurses. Her only faint response was to her two-year-old sister's voice. Once in foster care, she was at first very passive and unresponsive and then became very resistant to care.* (abridged from Schofield and Beek, 2006, pp 163–164)

Tammy had learned not to trust in the availability of adults and combined with the impact of separation and loss of familiar people and environments, this led to her lack of trust, even in a new environment which offered her available and responsive care.

Older children will similarly show signs of their lack of trust in a new environment by their reluctance to seek or accept or truly believe in care and comfort when it is offered. One foster carer described how Luke, a four-year-old child, newly placed with her, was very reluctant to accept a good-night kiss. It was only after she had placed Barney the dinosaur, a soft toy, on his bed and given Barney a good-night kiss for some months that Luke asked if he could have a kiss before Barney. For Luke, as for many children, lack of trust was linked to feelings of powerlessness which this carer was addressing through letting him be the one to choose when he felt enough trust in her as a secure base to ask for a good-night kiss. Luke went on to gain increased pleasure and confidence in play and exploration.

School-aged children and adolescents will also show their lack of trust through their lack of interest and capacity to explore and learn. Caregivers and social workers need to think in terms of not only providing care and reassurance, but also simultaneously promoting activity and exploration. The child's experience of competence and safe exploration reinforces trust, just as the experience of reliable support promotes exploration. Frequently, assessment of a child's attachment security in a placement focuses on the warmth or specificity of relationships, when it is often the child's capacity to enjoy new types of food or Brownies or football or school which is the first sign that the child is feeling more secure in relationships.

Exploration in this context also means the capacity to explore difficult thoughts, feelings and memories, since this too requires a secure base provided by the caregiver, the social worker or, preferably, both. These links between security, exploration of difficult issues and pleasure in activity are some of the key elements in promoting *resilience* (Gilligan, 2001), enabling children to manage the challenges of the home, school and community environments in spite of past experiences of trauma and adversity.

The importance of mind-mindedness

Reliable and available secure base care that reduces anxiety can only be truly effective if the caregiver has been able to think of the infant or child or adolescent as a whole person with a mind which contains a range of thoughts and feelings that need to be understood. Tuning in to the thoughts and feelings of this particular child in this particular context, what Miens (1997) has called *mind-mindedness*, is essential if the caregiver's or social worker's response to the child's needs is going to be timely and accurate. Many children who come into care have not experienced being understood and having their ideas and feelings actively and accurately thought about or taken into account in this way. This lack has a number of consequences for children's capacity to regulate or manage their own feelings or to take into account the feelings of others, even when placed in more responsive and caring environments.

When children come into care and are separated from familiar places and people, there is inevitably a rush of extreme anxiety. Whether the experience is interpreted by the child as one of being kidnapped, being given away or being taken away as a result of their own bad behaviour (Fahlberg, 1994), the child is likely to be highly stressed. This experience of raised anxiety will also be true for some children who move placements without enough time for thought or preparation, or after experiencing a difficult placement breakdown following a period of conflict and uncertainty.

Such moves of family, home and, often, school and community would be a challenge for any child to manage emotionally and cognitively. But for children who have often felt overwhelmed by anxiety in the past and have few resources for thinking about or managing their feelings – and little trust in other people to help them – it is likely that perplexing thoughts and difficult behaviours will continue to trouble them. It is essential for social workers helping children with moves and their consequences to be aware of both the range of stories/explanations and the range of feelings that individual children may hold in their minds as they work to manage the complexity of their experiences. Mind-mindedness in social workers needs to be accompanied by knowledge of the developmental stage of each child and the implications of different explanations. As Fahlberg suggests, children who believe they have been given away experience low self-esteem and depression, while children who believe they have been kidnapped experience a lack of trust and raised anxiety.

For many children, however, planned placement moves may provoke some anxiety but are still experienced as a very positive step. Some children remember experiencing a clear sense that the move to their foster or adoptive home was a good thing. As one teenager looking back to her first day in a permanent placement at the age of six put it, 'I came here and there were teddies all on the bed . . . I was very happy – it was a sigh of relief' (Schofield, 2003, p 105). So although it is important to work with feelings of grief and loss, it is equally important not to assume that a move is a negative experience and to listen to and observe each child closely.

Most children will have some degree of mixed feelings about moves and separation and may miss familiar people and places, while also feeling guilty when they discover that they are enjoying a clean bed or realise that they are beginning to love their new family. For children who have not had help to understand or manage their feelings in the past, facing both raised anxiety and mixed feelings is particularly hard. For caregivers and social workers, the task then of tuning into the child's thoughts and feelings has a most significant role. This task is not only about understanding the child, but also about helping the child to move towards the knowledge that mixed feelings are a normal part of all relationships, that strong feelings can be thought about, understood and managed by others and, gradually, by the child, and that even extreme anxiety and anger need not overwhelm them.

In this context, secure base availability and mind-minded responsiveness go hand in hand. In direct work with children, the explicit physical and psychological secure base availability of the social worker needs to be linked to a thoughtful, though often tentative, commentary that names feelings and helps the child to start to understand what happens when they become anxious or angry, or indeed loving, and to find ways of expressing the full range of feelings without becoming overwhelmed or overwhelming others. This will help the child to make sense of their feelings about their history as far as is developmentally possible – although for all children the subject needs to be revisited at each developmental stage, so that children can take a story into adulthood that helps them maintain a sense of self as valued and valuable.

Internal working models

Where children's difficulties with trust, with regulating emotions and with troubled behaviours persist, even in the context of caring new families and residential settings, this can best be understood by thinking about the powerful lessons that have been learned when children needed to *adapt* their behaviour in order to survive in difficult previous family environments. Here the concept of *internal working models* (Bowlby, 1969) can be helpful.

During the first year of life, infants will be starting to form mental representations, beliefs and expectations of themselves and other people, based on the quality of the care they have received. These mental representations are necessary aids for *all* infants and children in predicting how other people are likely to act, and therefore help each child to behave in ways that maximise the care and protection they experience in their particular environment. Over time, these mental representations form internal working models which reflect the quality of the child's experiences in relationships. Where a child is receiving sensitive, reliable care, the lessons learned and the expectations formed will be that adults are available and to be trusted and that the self is valued, valuable and competent to get their needs met. Where the child experiences rejecting, unpredictable or frightening care, the child will develop internal working models of the self as unlovable and other people as hostile or withholding of care and affection.

The power of these internal working models is that they will dictate not just what the infant or child or adolescent is thinking, but how they behave and how they communicate their feelings. The child's positive or negative beliefs and expectations will affect not just their thoughts and feelings but also the expression on their face and the way they show their confidence or their anxiety and expectation of welcome or rejection. Aggressive or anxious facial expressions and behaviours that result from anticipating rejection give negative messages to adults and other children, who are likely to react by avoiding closeness to the child or by more active forms of rejection, including disciplinary action. Thus, troubled children provoke reactions which confirm and reinforce their existing negative beliefs about themselves and about what they will experience when they get involved in relationships with other people.

For children engaging in direct work with a social worker, it is likely that very similar processes will occur. In direct work with a child who has expectations of hostility and shows it in their face and behaviour, there is always a risk that just as foster carers, adoptive parents and residential workers may get drawn into repeating the child's experience of rejection, so even in a therapeutic setting the social worker may start to feel overwhelmed by or rejecting towards a child who adopts survival strategies that are hostile or controlling.

The major difficulty for maltreated and troubled children in entering new families or engaging in therapeutic work and forming a relationship with a social worker is not only a profound lack of trust, but the fact that previous adaptations to aid survival make them highly resistant to accepting or learning from new and different experiences of caregiving or relationships with social workers. Maltreated children often find it especially difficult to process new information about relationships and so see good care as a "trick". As Crittenden (1995, p 401) puts it,

The individual may so distrust both affect and cognition that even discrepant information may not trigger the mind to re-explore reality. Instead the mind may determine that this too is trickery and deception or that the risk of mistakenly responding as though it were true is too great to be tolerated. In such cases, the representation of reality is like a false, inverted mirror image in which good and bad, true and false are reversed.

Thus, caregivers and social workers who attempt to provide sensitive care and a secure base may be viewed with distrust and suspicion, as people to be controlled and as sources of anxiety rather than sources of security.

Although children coming into foster, adoptive and residential placements will, to varying degrees, share similar feelings of anxiety, loss and a lack of trust, there will also be a number of important differences in the way in which they attempt to manage their anxieties. Their different *strategies* need to be understood because they indicate not only different ways of thinking and behaving, but also different ways of communicating or avoiding communicating their thoughts and feelings in relationships, including relationships with social workers. It is here that an understanding of *secure and insecure patterns of attachment* in children of different ages may help social workers to be alert to these differences and to use their understanding to increase their own capacity to tune in to the mind of the child.

Secure and insecure attachment patterns

Patterns of secure and insecure attachment provide us with models of the ways in which children, and indeed adults, think about and manage their close relationships. Building on the core concepts of attachment and the Strange Situation procedure, researchers identified one secure and three types of insecure attachment patterns (Ainsworth *et al*, 1971, 1978; Main and Solomon, 1986). Understanding these patterns can help to make sense of the behaviours and relationship, the strengths and difficulties that children may bring into placement and into their relationships with caregivers and with social workers (Steele *et al*, 2003; Schofield and Beek, 2006).

Secure attachment patterns
It is important to think clearly first about the characteristics of secure attachment patterns. This is, in part, because there will be some children who come into new placements with secure attachment patterns, but also because it is necessary to understand the gaps in the

experience of insecure children *and* to be able to identify signs of progress in children once they start to feel more secure in new relationships.

Where a birth parent has been consistently responsive to the child's needs and care has been reliable, the child is likely to have developed a secure attachment pattern that is reflected in an internal working model of the self as loved and lovable and of others as available and protective. The secure child is more likely to seek help when necessary, but also to be confident in exploring the world, safe in the knowledge that the caregiver can be trusted to be there if needed. For these children, perhaps coming into care because a parent is too ill to care for them, the experience will mean a profound sense of loss. The strengths that they have developed will be threatened by discontinuity and feelings of bereavement, such as denial, anger and despair, and they will find it hard to accept the care and availability of caregivers or of social workers. Although infants and older children may be able to draw to some extent on their experience of trust and their previous strategies for seeking comfort and for exploration, this separation event will not make sense in the context of their previous experiences and they will have few strategies to deal with unfamiliar feelings of helplessness and powerlessness, anger and depression. Paradoxically, their lack of previous experiences of stress and separation (and therefore strategies for dealing with them) may make it particularly difficult for them to manage their grief. In infancy in particular, internal working models of adults as caring and available have developed in relation to very specific people and will be threatened by the loss of those figures.

Although the experience of loss should never be underestimated for children moving from a relationship in which they have felt secure, it is apparent from the experiences of infants and children who very successfully move from secure attachment relationships in bridge foster placements into adoption and long-term foster care that careful preparation of the child and close co-operation between bridge carers and new parents can facilitate a successful placement. Secure attachment cannot be "transferred" or gifted from bridge carers to new parents, it has to be earned by the new parents. But it is possible to think about ways in which the child's recovery from appropriate grief for the loss of the bridge carers and growing capacity to form an attachment to the new parents can proceed alongside each other. The secure child is likely to have some capacity to express, think about and manage feelings and this can be the focus of both verbal commentary and simple verbal and non-verbal messages of acceptance, care and concern from all of the adults involved. Continuity of different kinds – whether it be food, clothes or a familiar teddy – can help in this process, but continuity of social worker through this period of transition can also hold the child's anxiety and offer a secure base for the child to explore their feelings about the loss of the foster carers and the foster home and the experience of new caregivers.

Avoidant attachment patterns

Where a birth parent has been consistently *rejecting* of the child's emotional demands, *intrusive* and *insensitive* to the child's emotional needs, the child is likely to have learned to shut down on any displays of emotion, avoid making a fuss and be self-reliant. This *avoidant* attachment pattern is based on lack of trust and anxiety about rejection and intrusion. However, the behaviour is organised and adaptive, in that it is the most likely way for the child to achieve some physical proximity, if not emotional closeness, to this particular parent. It is therefore important to remember that the child is not indifferent to or attempting to avoid a relationship. The child's strategy of avoiding making emotional demands is designed to achieve the best relationship that might be available when a parent finds the child's emotional demands too difficult to manage or accept. When an avoidant infant is assessed at 12–18 months in the Strange Situation (Ainsworth *et al*, 1971), for example, the infant will show little if any emotion when the mother leaves the room or at the subsequent reunion. The infant has learned that shows of emotion risk provoking a rejection, so not making a fuss and focusing on the toys may preserve the relationship. However, physiological tests of heart rate and skin response show that the child is highly aroused and anxious during the separation (Spangler and Grossman, 1993). Thus, even a young child has already learned to control displays of anxiety and emotion, which can make it difficult for social workers undertaking assessments.

Older children with this strategy for coping will often persist in being self-reliant in their behaviour, but will still be longing for a relationship. The anxiety they experience about rejection and the need to manage their repressed anger can also sometimes have other consequences; for example, leading to children becoming bossy or even bullying other children. Having learned to dismiss the importance of their own feelings, they often lack empathy and consideration for the feelings of others. Regulating their feelings has become a task of first repressing the display of emotions and then denying that feelings exist or matter; for example saying, 'I don't care if my mum doesn't come for contact' or 'He shouldn't cry like that – I didn't really hit him hard'. Sadness and anger can burst out in ways that may, over time and for some children, become associated with the development of conduct disorders and anti-social behaviour.

From the avoidant infant or child's point of view, the situation of moving into a new or different care or adoptive environment is highly stressful. But the more anxious they feel, the more likely they are to shut down on their feelings, since familiar coping strategies are most apparent when children are stressed. Because their internal working model of self and relationships suggests that they need to be anxious about the care they will get from adults, their learned response of shutting down on attachment behaviours is felt to at least protect them from abandonment and get the best that is available from relationships. However, having developed a survival strategy of keeping feelings under wraps and looking after themselves, they are now in a family situation where there may be reasonable expectations that emotions are shared and that retreat into yourself or into your bedroom is not the way family relationships are conducted.

The behaviour of children with avoidant strategies in a new foster or adoptive home or residential placement may seem easy to manage at first, as the child is likely to be rather quiet and self-reliant. However, it is not long before the child's lack of emotional engagement, often accompanied by active rejection of or apparent indifference to the care which is offered can provoke the rejection that the child fears. The child's behaviour may provoke responses which confirm their expectations and reinforce their internal working model. This cycle can be apparent from as young as 12 weeks old, when foster carers report finding an unresponsive baby difficult to care for (Dozier *et al*, 2002), right through childhood and into adolescence.

Carers, whether of infants, primary school-age children or teenagers, can often feel resentful, in spite of themselves, that they are caring for a "lodger", so will need support from social workers to work gently towards helping the child in a non-intrusive way to begin to communicate about and value emotions, and to join the family. In the beginning, for example, young infants may feel more comfortable feeding themselves their bottle while the carer or adopter sits nearby, speaking gently to the child and only gradually over some days moving closer and obtaining the child's "permission" to offer a cuddle. Older children also may be more comfortable with gradually shared family activities, such as feeding the goldfish, building a castle, making a cake – even simply watching a video together, when the carer and the child can be side by side and the focus is practical and indirect rather than direct and emotionally laden.

Social workers in their work with children, therefore, need to be similarly aware of the anxiety about intrusion and the reluctance to engage in dialogue about emotions that are particularly characteristic of these children. Although the goal may be ultimately to help the child towards naming and valuing feelings, the pace will have to be the child's. Getting alongside a child and appealing to their reason – perhaps their satisfaction in constructing things or even the practical task of gluing photographs in a life story book – and only very gradually working towards some signs of the emotions that have been repressed and denied is more likely to build trust. This issue of pace is a particular challenge where the work with the child is expected to fit into a timescale imposed from outside – such as the court requiring some indications of the child's "wishes and feelings". The inevitable paradox here is that the more the child feels rushed the more likely he or she is to shut down or say 'I don't care'. And of course, until decisions are made about return home or permanent placement, the protective shield they have placed around themselves may continue to feel necessary (Schofield, 2005). Progress needs to be incremental, and more open communication with the social worker is only likely to occur when the child feels some level of trust in their whole environment.

Ambivalent/resistant patterns

Where a birth parent has been *insensitive* to the child's needs while being *inconsistently or unpredictably* available and responsive, the child will have learned to increase displays of emotion and demands for attention. This *ambivalent* pattern too can be seen to be an organised and adaptive strategy, in that constant demands will eventually produce a reaction from the parent, even if it is a negative reaction. This reaction indicates that the parent is at least physically available, even if the emotional quality of that availability is not wholly reassuring and the response is one of anger.

This pattern is often referred to as *resistant*, because infants and children lack trust that the caregiver will be reliable and so resist care even when it is offered, as they fear that it may not last. In the Strange Situation, for example, infants will be particularly distressed during the separation and when the mother returns will cling, continue to show distress and not settle back to play.

From the toddler years onwards, displays of emotion start to alternate between being rather *coy*: 'Mummy, please can I have some sweets – I'm really, really hungry and I've been a good boy' and, if this does not work, *coercive*: 'Give me some sweets or I'll scream.' The child thus tries to attract the caregiver's interest and concern by displays of neediness, but then becomes angry and demanding when that concern is not forthcoming or does not match up to the child's hopes. This is not an unusual strategy for a toddler or pre-school child to adopt at times, but it is the intensity and the persistence as they grow into middle childhood, that makes the behaviour a problem and specific to this pattern.

Children with this pattern in the pre-school years, through middle childhood and into adolescence will show continuing preoccupation with the availability of relationships. Some children may become increasingly coercive, while for other children the experience of unpredictability leaves them feeling completely helpless and dependent. These patterns of behaviour also affect relationships with teachers, with social workers and with friends, who may be inclined to offer care initially, but in different ways may withdraw when the child becomes too needy or excessively demanding.

For foster carers, adoptive parents, residential workers and social workers, these more emotionally responsive children may at first meeting appear open, lively and keen to make a relationship. But difficulties emerge when any boundaries are set or constant availability is not provided. The swings of mood may then become extreme, with anger expressed in intense distress or rage, breaking toys or windows and so on. Alternatively, very helpless, clingy children may simply follow the caregiver around, being too preoccupied with and distrusting in relationships to accept reassurance and often, therefore, being unable to use the caregiver as a secure base for fully engaging in play or learning.

For social workers, managing their own responses to the child's alternately needy/angry but always demanding behaviour is a challenge. But so also is managing the child's tendency to split the world into perfect best friends and unforgivable worst enemies. Very often children will try to build an alliance with the latest person in their network – which could be the new social worker – and invite them to criticise either the former social worker or the caregiver. Open and straight communication with the child is important, but so also are carefully built partnerships to provide a consistent circle around the child to increase the child's sense of trust and security.

Disorganised and controlling attachment patterns

For children who experienced caregivers in their birth family who were frightening or frightened (due to unresolved trauma in their own past or perhaps current fear and trauma through domestic violence), the dilemma would have been that any approach by the infant or child in search of proximity and care would have increased rather than reduced anxiety. The caregiver thus became a source of anxiety rather than the source of care and protection. This is what Main and Hesse (1990) have called, 'fear without solution'. Infants cannot resolve this situation and, having a limited behavioural repertoire, they will only be able to cry helplessly at first, but then are likely to give up and shut down physically and emotionally – as described earlier in the case of Tammy. In the Strange Situation, disorganised infants, by the age of 12 months, will show their dilemma in a confusing mixture of approach and avoidance, such as crawling towards but then away from the parent at reunion, or walking backwards towards the parent crying. At other times the behaviour is more chaotic and disoriented, with unusual behaviours, such as hitting the parent and then falling flat on the floor.

Over time, toddlers will learn some strategies to cope and avoid harm – such as pretending to feel positive emotions in order not to upset the caregiver, a behaviour evident in maltreated children from 18 months onwards (Crittenden and DiLalla, 1988). Overwhelmed by feelings at times, however, the toddler may become chaotic, withdrawn or may dissociate and cut off entirely (Liotti, 1999). In the pre-school years, children who have lacked an organised strategy to cope with their caregivers as disorganised infants and toddlers, begin to develop strategies for coping. These strategies tend to be focused on controlling the fearful environment and often include an element of *role-reversal*. Thus, the four-year-old who is frightened and confused starts to become punitive and aggressive, often trying to boss or taunt the parent, even when this leads to an aggressive response towards the child. In contrast, some children develop role-reversing strategies of compulsive caregiving or compulsive self-reliance, both of which in different ways deny the parent's role of caring for the child, either by showing concern for the parent's welfare or not letting the parent care for the child.

When children with histories of adapting to their environments in this way come into care, they often show a range of behaviours that are controlling but also worrying, exasperating and difficult for carers to manage and social workers to resolve. Behaviours such as stealing and lying, or more obviously disturbed behaviours such as smearing of faeces or aggression against younger children or family pets, cannot only cause distress in the family but may lead to placement breakdown. Particularly difficult to live with is a child's controlling, contemptuous facial expression or tone of voice. It is not easy to bear in mind the child's difficult history when a three- or four-year-old laughs and jeers at a parent who is trying to pick up the mess from the floor after the child's dinner has been thrown from the table. From the child's perspective, desperate times when control has eluded them now require desperate measures to assert themselves and survive.

However, it is essential for social workers to bear in mind that such strategies are not operating at a conscious level and that the child would certainly be unable to say "why" they behave in extreme ways that upset others so much and provoke further rejection. The child's blank expression when challenged is not entirely a contrived response. For the children too it can seem as if they must be "mad" to behave in ways that are so apparently irrational and pointless. Traumatised children seem to move from victim to persecutor to rescuer in their relationship with caregivers (Liotti, 1999), a pattern that is often reflected in the feelings of the caregiver – and indeed the social worker may also feel at times like a victim, a persecutor or a rescuer in relation to the child. The role of supervision – a secure base provided for the social workers – is particularly important when working with children who are both so needy and so controlling.

It is necessary to bear in mind that not by any means all children who have disorganised attachment patterns have experienced maltreatment or will show extremes of disturbed behaviour. But it is the *combination* of a disorganised attachment and experiences of abuse and neglect that creates the most risk for relationship and developmental problems, risks that persist when children are placed in new families or residential care. It is also important to bear in mind that children from apparently similar backgrounds of abuse and neglect may have reacted very differently and so it is necessary to be informed by theory and research, but also to be open minded about the impact of adverse early environments on the individual child. Although some children with a history of physical or emotional abuse and neglect will show extremes of behaviour and great trouble with attachment relationships, other children with apparently similar histories will behave in relatively straightforward ways, responding to care in the new placement, attending school, joining the football team and making friends.

Concerns that the latter group are "too good to be true" and that disturbed behaviour may emerge later will be valid for some children, and it is essential not to assume that an apparent lack of problems means the child should be labelled "resilient". But there will be children who are genuinely thriving, for whom there have been some protective factors which have helped them to develop strengths in spite of what appears to be overwhelming odds. This may be traceable from the history – perhaps a period cared for by grandparents or good foster carers at a key point in their development. Or it may be that current caregivers have been very effective at meeting the child's needs for security.

The notion of *resilience* is a helpful one, but only if resilience is understood to be 'relative resistance to psychosocial risk experiences' (Rutter, 1999), rather than the child being immune to all harm or adversity. It is also important to bear in mind that, for most children, resilience characteristics are likely to include some genetic factors, such as intelligence or an easy sociable temperament, but include much more that is derived from their environment, such as self-esteem and self-efficacy. From this perspective it is therefore preferable to focus on how the caregiving environment and the therapeutic work with a child can promote and increase security and resilience (Gilligan, 2000, 2001; Schofield and Beek, 2005).

Keeping attachment in mind

For infants, children and adolescents the experience of adverse care followed by separation and the development of new relationships in substitute care is always going to be challenging. But, as David Howe has put it, because the problems which children face have developed in the context of close relationships, it is only in the context of close relationships that the therapeutic change that is needed can be provided (Howe *et al*, 1999; Howe, 2005).

Keeping attachment in mind means holding the child's experience in mind. This applies equally to the social worker responsible for helping the child manage their past and present lives as it does to the parents and carers who provide the day-to-day care. In particular, it means reflecting constantly on the meanings that lie behind behaviour and on what is in the mind of the child when the child looks around and appraises the risks and opportunities that they face.

Attachment provides a useful framework both in terms of the core concepts, such as a secure base and internal working models, and in the explanation of how attachment patterns emerge as strategies for adapting to different environments. It provides explanations of why difficulties in behaviour and relationships persist, but it also holds within it the prospect of transforming children's lives through the provision of care and new relationships.

For the social worker who is providing a secure base in their work with the child and who is enabling the child to make use of the secure base on offer in a foster/adoptive family or residential placement, the prospect of assisting the child to shift their developmental trajectory towards security and resilience is of major significance for the child's future health and happiness. However, they need to know that they are supported by colleagues and managers who provide a secure base for them, to reduce anxiety and to facilitate their own creativity and exploration.

References

Ainsworth M. D. S., Bell S. and Stayton D. (1971) 'Individual differences in strange-situation behaviour of one-year-olds', in Schaffer H (ed.) *The Origins of Human Social Relations*, New York, NY: Academic Press, pp 17–52

Ainsworth M. D. S., Blehar M., Waters E. and Wall S. (1978) *Patterns of Attachment: A psychological study of the strange situation*, Hillsdale, NJ: Lawrence Erlbaum

Beek M. and Schofield G. (2004) *Providing a Secure Base in Long-Term Foster Care*, London: BAAF

Bowlby J. (1969) *Attachment and Loss: Vol 1 Attachment*, London: Hogarth Press

Bowlby J. (1988) *A Secure Base: Clinical applications of attachment theory*, London: Routledge

Crittenden P. M. (1995) 'Attachment and psychopathology', in Goldberg S., Muir R. and Kerr J. (eds) *Attachment Theory: Social, developmental and clinical perspectives*, Hillsdale, NJ: Analytical Press, pp 367–406

Crittenden P. and DiLalla D. (1988) 'Compulsive compliance: the development of an inhibitory coping strategy in infancy', *Journal of Abnormal Child Psychology*, 16:5, pp 585–99

Dozier M., Higley E., Albus K. and Nutter A. (2002) 'Intervening with foster infants' caregivers', *Infant Mental Health Journal*, 23:5, pp 541–54

Fahlberg V. (1994) *A Child's Journey through Placement* (2nd edn), London: BAAF

Gilligan R. (2000) 'Promoting resilience in children in foster care', in Kelly G. and Gilligan R. (eds) *Issues in Foster Care Policy, Practice and Research*, London: Jessica Kingsley, pp 107–126

Gilligan R. (2001) *Promoting Resilience: A resource guide on working with children in the care system*, London: BAAF

Howe D. (1998) *Patterns of Adoption: Nature, nurture and psychosocial development*, Oxford: Blackwell Science

Howe D. (2005) *Child Abuse and Neglect: Attachment, development and intervention*, Basingstoke: Palgrave Macmillan

Howe D., Brandon M., Hinings D. and Schofield G. (1999) *Attachment Theory, Child Maltreatment and Family Support*, Basingstoke: Macmillan

Liotti G. (1999) 'Disorganisation of attachment as a model for understanding dissociative psychopathology', in Solomon J. and George C. (eds) *Attachment Disorganisation*, New York, NY: Guilford Press, pp 291–31

Main M. and Hesse E. (1990) 'Parents' unresolved traumatic experiences are related to infant disorganised attachment status: is frightened and/or frightening the linking mechanism?', in Greenberg M. T. and Cummings E. M. (eds) *Attachment in the Preschool Years: Theory, research and intervention*, Chicago IL: University of Chicago Press, pp 161–182

Main M. and Solomon J. (1986) 'Discovery of an insecure-disorganised/disoriented attachment pattern', in Brazelton T. B. and Yogman M. W. (eds) *Affective Development in Infancy*, Norwood, NJ: Ablex, pp 95–124

Miens E. (1997) *Security of Attachment and the Social Development of Cognition*, Hove: Psychology Press

Rutter M. (1999) 'Resilience concepts and findings: implications for family therapy', *Journal of Family Therapy*, 21:2, pp 119–144

Schofield G. (2003) *Part of the Family: Pathways through foster care*, London: BAAF

Schofield G. (2005) 'The voice of the child in family placement decision making', *Adoption & Fostering*, 29:1, pp 29–44

Schofield G. and Beek M. (2005) 'Risk and resilience in long-term foster care', *British Journal of Social Work*, 35:8, pp 1283–1301

Schofield G. and Beek M. (2006) *Attachment Handbook for Foster Care and Adoption*, London: BAAF

Sellick C., Thoburn J. and Philpot T. (2004) *What Works in Adoption and Foster Care?*, London: BAAF

Sinclair I. (2005) *Fostering Now*, London: Jessica Kingsley

Spangler G. and Grossman K. (1993) 'Biobehavioural organization in securely and insecurely attached infants', *Child Development*, 64:5, pp 1439–1450

Steele M., Hodges J., Kaniuk J., Hillman S. and Henderson K. (2003) 'Attachment representations and adoption: associations between maternal states of mind and emotion narratives in previously maltreated children', *Journal of Child Psychotherapy*, 29:1, pp 187–205

Wilson K., Sinclair I. and Petrie S. (2003) 'A kind of loving: a model of effective foster care', *British Journal of Social Work*, 33:8, pp 991–1003

4 Making sense of the experience of transition: psychotherapeutic insights for young people and their social workers

Margaret Hunter Smallbone

Introduction

We can be in transit for only a little while – as long as we can hold in our minds two places: our journey's beginning and our journey's end. When we know ourselves to be passing through, we think differently. Maybe we will allow strange customs and practices to be imposed on us without too much protest, and we hold back on opinions and our assertion of our rights. In someone else's home the smells are different, they eat at the wrong time and they act as if it is normal to wait until the last slow eater has finished dinner before serving the pudding. We can put up with it for a little while, it is not going to last. We do not invest in friendships that are to be fleeting, we remind ourselves that these are not our people and we cling to home in our thoughts.

> *They were all so quiet – the first family I stayed with. They practically whispered and there was no music on, no one made any noise. It made me feel so strange – I could hear myself swallowing – I could hear myself breathing! I wanted someone to shout, to put the telly on loud – and that was another thing, hardly any telly. I couldn't wait to get out of there.*[1]

This was how 14-year-old Cathy explained to me how she could not bear being in a foster home.

We sometimes describe children as being in transition because their care plan says their current situation is not permanent. However, I learned from Susie, one of my first child clients, that you cannot be in transition indefinitely, in her case for six years, from age four to ten. The adults were talking of a future which never came and meanwhile Susie had to live with people whom she was told she would soon be leaving. I remember discussions of whether she could make a secure attachment in a family. If you are never given the opportunity, how can anyone know? As the years went by, what did she make of all this future talk? Susie found it confusing and frightening to be told that the present was not really to count and her hidden worry was that she would never be claimed because she

---

[1] All names have been changed and details removed that could identify individuals.

was not really good enough. At the same time, she feared moving at all as she felt settled in the residential home.

Young people in transition, journeying from traumatic experiences with those known, to new experiences, new places with those unknown, are glad of a reliable guide. The social worker is well placed to fulfil that role. Social workers meet the child's family and take the child to a place of safety. Or they move the young person between the placement that has ended and the placement that is beginning. They know why the journey has been made; they know the destination and the possibilities of return. They are the human face of difficult decisions and discontinuities. They are also a human bridge between the two worlds the child will now inhabit. If the social worker has been involved with the child over some time, they become an invaluable source of memories, someone who knows the past and present. There is an absence in many accommodated children's lives of people in this position; sometimes the social worker is the only one.

It is hard, therefore, to credit the belief of some social workers that they are personally unimportant. This is certainly not the child's view. Of course, this does not mean the social worker will necessarily be liked. They may be feared or hated, at least on the surface. Many young people have strong ambivalent feelings towards their social workers and a close relationship with them can directly help the young person work through their anger, grief, mourning and gratitude. But every child I have encountered in the care system understands the importance of their social worker. Many young people will have a grudging respect for the protective stance of the social worker, even if they disagree with decisions made. In my experience, however, young people in care criticise not so much their social workers' actions but their inaction. Accommodated young people express the wish that their social worker was more available, more on hand for questions and responses. Many young people feel that they would like to be known by their social worker and kept in contact, kept in mind. Especially when links to the family of origin are frail or problematic, when powerlessness is keenly felt, the link to this powerful social work adult is important. Perhaps the most important idea that psychoanalysis has for social workers is that of ambivalence (Kerr, 1995).

I am not criticising individual social workers when I emphasise this social work responsibility. There was a policy shift away from direct work by social workers. There was a move to make them brokers of services, in the mistaken belief that other professionals – CAMHS, for example – could better do this important work. But the work done by other professionals is different to the unique contribution a social worker can make. This contribution can be about balancing hopes and fears with what is likely to happen. Few therapists will be as well placed to have an overview of the looked after child's life. And whilst work with the internal world of the child is important, so too is the child's external world (see Luckock, this volume). The constant changes and events in the families of looked after children contribute directly to their sense of well-being, as well as to their sense of loss, of chaos and ineffectuality. Social workers who are allowed time to get to know accommodated young people can be of enormous help to the child's sense of safety and continuity on their journey through care.

In this chapter, I use examples of my own therapeutic work with young people in foster care and adoption to help in the process of thinking about the experience of transition, with the hope that social workers will find that psycho-dynamic insights can be useful and encouraging to their work with young people. Neville Symington (1986), in his inspiring book, *The Analytic Experience: Lectures from the Tavistock*, reminds us: 'If we remember that psychoanalysis is the servant of the truth, we rub shoulders with all those who seek truth in other disciplines and walks of life' (p 24). I also want to encourage social workers to feel that they can contribute therapeutically to children's lives, not just in meetings and behind the scenes, but in partnership with their young charges, getting to know them and understand them directly.

Despite my training as a long-term child psychotherapist, I have often met with children in care who are "passing through" because they or I will not be available for longer-term work, because I have been asked to meet them just to give an opinion, or they have agreed to meet me because they need some short-term help. In effect, I have found these brief meetings can be useful to the young person and to the care team planning for their future. They can focus us on the views and needs of the young person and allow us to listen more carefully to what they have to say. My role in brief interventions is as much to the network as it is to the child. I try to inform the child's social worker, who will play a much longer and key role, about the preoccupations and needs of this child in transition.

Daniel: in long-term placement at last

'Those swords look good – are they play-swords?', Daniel asked me, looking around my room at our first meeting. 'I like play-fighting. I don't do real fighting now. You've got good toys in your room.'

He looked with longing at the swords but resisted his wish to touch them. He answered my questions with good grace about his life and family. His mum lived a very long way away, very long and it takes two hours in the car to get there. He gets sick in the car sometimes. His nine-year-old face clouded with worry and he fell silent.

'I've been in four foster families,' he continued. 'The first one didn't like me,' and again he stumbled to a halt.

'Did you like them?' I asked.

'No, I didn't!' and he grinned. 'They were horrible! Then the next one was alright but they had their own boy and he tied me up. He kept locking me out of rooms and that – locking me in the hallway. In the next place they were kind but I was naughty all the time. I've got a really bad temper. If someone calls me names I will punch them in the face. But I've improved now and Shirley says I am much better than I used to be. I've got a good school report now. I like it at Shirley's and I can stay there until I am 18.'

He looked seriously and directly at me now for the first time as if trying to gauge my power to influence these events.

'I do want to stay with Shirley now,' he said.

I re-explained my role as a therapist who was going to meet with him three times to see if therapy every week would be something he would want to do or if it would help him. Therapy would be about having someone to talk to privately, but I would be telling people about our discussions, and helping his foster carers and social worker consider whether therapy was a good idea. I would also be thinking about which therapist would suit him, if we decided on one. I explained that it would not be me as I did not visit this centre every week. (Later on, I would explain to him about confidentiality within the limits of safety and that he could talk about therapy with whoever he wants but the therapist must respect confidentiality unless he would be in danger of harm.)

He took this in gravely.

'Therapy is about thinking and sharing worries and difficulties,' I said.

'I have got worries,' he volunteered immediately. He told me that his little sisters, two of them aged seven and five, were to be adopted. 'I am not allowed to see them,' he said incredulously, 'only once to say goodbye.' His face was pale as he struggled to repeat words said to him. 'There is going to be a letter-box. They will use a letter-box . . . I can send them letters and draw pictures. I'm no good at drawing! They are not allowed to see me.' He stared bitterly.

Silence filled the room and I could think of nothing to say. But he was not looking at me, his head was bowed and he muttered, 'Too much shouting. It was too much shouting. I think they knew but I couldn't stand all that shouting.'

'Who knew?' I asked. 'Who was "they"?'

'My mum and dad. They were always shouting and that. Because my sisters kept on being naughty.'

At our next meeting, Dan made clear that he would like to meet regularly with a therapist. He also took me to task with my assertion that I would not be his therapist. Within minutes of being in the room he asked me, 'What therapist am I going to have then?', and followed this up with close questioning of my movements and why I was not available.

At the same time he was industriously mixing sand and water in the sand-pit to make "concrete". He told me his dad had made concrete once. That was in a different house – his family have lived in lots of different houses. His family had to keep moving because people kept making trouble and throwing stones at their windows so they had to move. And it happened again! People threw rocks at them and made more trouble so – move to another house. He reflected that if this was cement it would set rock-hard and if he tipped it up on the floor it would make a hole in the floor and we would trip over it and get hurt.

Towards the end of our third and final meeting, Dan made two caves in the sand, fashioning them carefully to accommodate a lion and a lioness. He kept reinforcing a boundary between the two caves, then arranged fences between and around the two caves. Finally he put a man "standing guard" by the dividing fences.

'He can see if they are fighting and stop them. They can't hurt this man because he is the keeper. He keeps them from fighting.' He paused and seemed unconvinced. 'We will put this wall around him,' he said, 'and we'll give him a weapon. I know, a sword.'

This is the construction he left with me when we parted, telling me, 'Don't let other boys muck it up'.

Reflections

An encounter with a boy like Daniel lasts a lot longer than the three hours we were together. He conveyed his feelings forcefully so that I could attend care planning meetings about him with a strong sense of his needs and his feelings. This tiny piece of time has very small resource and cost implications in relation to the thousands of pounds that will be spent accommodating and caring for him over the following ten or more years.

What we gain is not just a snapshot of what Dan says but of his internal world, his thoughts and feelings that he will carry with him through these years of public care. "Internal world" is a term from the *object relations* school of thinking, which, following Melanie Klein (1932), emphasises early relationships as a defining feature of child development. Klein emphasised the reality to the child, and to the unconscious, of a mental space where people and events are felt to really exist, interact and have feelings.[2] The space to listen and then reflect on what has been communicated is critical to this process. Wilfred Bion (1962) called this reverie, linking it to a mother's attunement to her

---

[2] The reader is directed to *The Handbook of Child and Adolescent Psychotherapy* (Lanyado and Horne, 1999) for an accessible introduction to these ideas.

baby, and reminded us that, although we give it a special label, millions of mothers and fathers do it every day.

This is the sine qua non of therapeutic work. There has to be time and care to think about what has been communicated, that is, receiving the child's *transferences*. Transference can be defined as 'the experiencing of feelings, drives, attitudes, fantasies and defences towards a person in the present which do not befit that person but are a repetition of reactions originating in regard to significant persons of early childhood, unconsciously displaced on to figures in the present' (Mattinson, 1992, p 33). The worker must then engage in a process of thinking and feeling about what has been stirred up in him or herself as a result of the child's transference. These reactions can be defined as *counter-transference* and, when reflected upon critically, may provide useful information about the child's internal world and relational style (Hunter, 2001). All of this is necessary to emotional understanding and containment, and certainly necessary before *interpretation* can begin.

Firstly, we can see that Daniel is a boy with some generosity and appreciation for what he is given – he begins our meeting with a compliment. He is a boy worried by his own capacity for aggression – for what he might do with the play-sword, for hitting name-callers. These traits of self-criticism and concern for others will be useful motivators for Dan to change his behaviour, and we can observe this capacity already beginning in his school reports and his wish to please Shirley, his foster carer. His tendency to self-blame may also make him vulnerable to depression and sensitive to rejection, which we see several times in my meeting with him: he says the first foster family did not like him; he cross-examines why I will not be his therapist; he fears the rejection of neighbours; and is desperate to be good enough for Shirley. This is a boy, then, who needs his efforts to be appreciated because the risk to his anger management is whether he can sustain belief in his own control. Dan is the kind of boy whose behaviour could deteriorate if he becomes disheartened. We can see from the many fences and barriers he needs to erect to contain the fighting lions that he is worried by the need for very strong controls to limit aggression.

Daniel's internal world is expressed here as a place where warring parties must be kept apart. In object relations terms (Klein, 1932), this does not simply mean his external parents but a situation which characterises his thoughts and feelings, his internal parental images, eternally at war.

Dan's communications of feelings about his mother and then his sisters reveal a boy who wears his heart on his sleeve. His pain and hurt are very near the surface and, on reflection, I thought of the desperate quality, almost skin-less aspect of this (Bick, 1964). This is likely to be evidence of indiscriminate attachment rather than my skill at eliciting his feelings. Dan probably cannot guard his emotions and they pour out of him without restraint. He immediately wants me, with little judgement of whether I am what he needs. Charming though this may appear, and moving, it is not particularly healthy for a nine-year-old in a brief acquaintance – it will make him vulnerable as a victim and links to his low self-esteem. However, it is a better prospect for development, unlike the tough, hardened children, of which there are too many in the looked after population and who make themselves "doubly deprived" (Henry, 1974). Dan's talk of the painful, sometimes sick-making gap between his mother and himself indicates an area that he will have to gradually mourn as he tries to adjust to this loss. He is a boy in mourning – wracked with guilt and anguish for the things that went wrong in his family. These feelings of loss are forcefully conveyed.

Loss is such a huge part of transition. It is what makes thoughtfulness so hard to bear. For we have to be able to bear the sadness, the helplessness, the rage, the despair. We serve as witnesses to the cruelty within these children's lives. And how do we understand and balance our responses if we get close enough to feel the losses? This is not work for the faint-hearted and it is unlikely to be done well without support. Child psychotherapists have our own analysis, we are a part of teams and we have regular clinical supervision. Social workers who want to get close to their children in transition need equivalent supports (see Ironside, this volume).

Compounding the loss of his parents, the proposed loss of his little sisters is a bitter blow to Daniel. I felt that the cruelty of this decision was laid bare and my discomfort in witnessing this filled me with anger.

These are difficult issues. I could conclude that my anger is a failure in my capacity to contain, and that it is absorbed from Daniel's. It is unlikely to be of help to Daniel to change tack within the session to an advocacy role. Such issues must be taken away and reviewed as counter-transference, that is, as feelings evoked in the therapist but originating in the child. The difference is also that between feelings and judgement; no reason is likely to remove Daniel's pain but there might be rational considerations which make suspending contact a prudent move. The therapist may ask questions of the network to understand the dilemmas faced by the decision-makers, as well as the pain of the child. It is difficult in these circumstances not to identify with the child's view and accuse each other of heartlessness. We witness this often enough in our work in the care system; often it is acted out in inter-agency hostility.

Nevertheless, the role of advocacy for the child's point of view can be an important part of working with children in transition. Decisions do sometimes need to be challenged. I have never been convinced that our current policies around sibling contacts have been given the weight they deserve; not all are defensible.

So there are occupational hazards in this intimate work: one may find oneself uncomfortably at odds with decisions made on behalf of children. One may feel ready to fight their cause and be unsure how much we are acting out their anger and rejection. We may need to find out about siblings and their best interests, and social workers may have to fight for causes which they lose and then comply with what they cannot change. But social workers often have enormous impact in these decisions and I have witnessed colleagues who go that extra mile to arrange contact visits, or who make it their job to accompany their charges at contact. Who else will speak to the losses that are compounded when we separate children from siblings? A social worker who knows the reasons, or who keeps the departments' promises with regard to contacts is invaluable to a young person in transition.

Setting aside Daniel's external situation, it is worth revisiting his internal one, his less conscious communications. Whilst Dan tells of his bad temper and his naughtiness, which lost him one foster family whom he thought kind, we can see other triggers for his angry outbursts. He cites being called names as something he cannot bear. This is a red rag to many of our bullish young people, linking to their sense of vulnerability in self-esteem. To be in a family which is breaking up, to come into foster care, these are serious blows to self-esteem. It is unbearable for this boy with his fragile sense of self-worth to be pulled down lower. He punches out, he becomes an aggressor when he cannot tolerate being a victim. Self-respect is crucial here: Dan needs a way of believing in himself securely so that he can withstand the names he is called. We know from research into children's resilience that acknowledgement of loss (Fraiberg *et al*, 1980), reflective self-functioning (Fonagy *et al*, 1992), and being able to tell a coherent life story (Main *et al*, 1985) all build emotional strength in children (see Luckock, this volume).

In the context of my telling Dan I am not available to see him, his immediate association is with the rejections his family have had in trying to find a stable home. He repeats the belief of his family that it is other people who spoil things and reject them, *other* people who throw rocks at them. Because he says this immediately after he showed his feeling of rejection at me, I am arguing that they are linked.

His next actions follow quite a different version of events. He is making cement and remembers his father doing this. He tells me in the session that his play-cement can become rock-hard and destructive and harm us both. Is it his internal belief that it is father's hardness and Daniel's tendency to copy him that brings harm? The tone in which he spoke to me was one of warning, perhaps of threat. Implicit in the sequence is the idea of revenge for rejection, of rocks on both sides of the interaction.

But the main protagonists of violence in Daniel's play are the shouting parents and their representation as lion and lioness that need to be kept apart. So we have a representation of Dan's experience as the witness who cannot tolerate the shouting, transmuted to the keeper who stands between the lions. Dan's conscious identification is with this peacekeeper – he seems to act as if he were the keeper in the room, keeping the lions apart. But I was concerned when I saw him resort to the sword for this purpose. I wondered whether he thought it was alright to use violence if it was in a good cause. I wondered if he justified in this sort of way some of the violent outbursts I was told he had in school. That would be the unconscious intent of mixing concrete and using weapons – his own wish to be violent, hidden in an identification with dad or wild lions.

Although Dan may be unaware of these motives, other people may read them correctly. Unconscious does not necessarily mean invisible to others. So the class teacher may tell me angrily, 'Dan is always getting into fights that do not really concern him – I think he just uses them to excuse his own anger. And he simply will not take responsibility for his own actions. It is always someone else's fault!'

This scenario will need further untangling for Dan to own and control the feelings embedded in it. Will he allow his own aggression as necessary because its means are justified by its end? Will he be able to notice the parts of him waging an angry war? When a nine-year-old has to be larger than his parents, when they have no moral authority over him, this does not lead to easy acceptance of the authority of teachers or foster carers or therapists. The easily given trust and compliments are not the whole story but are coloured by mistrust of adult motives and adult control (why am I really not seeing him every week? How can he control what I do with other children?). So Dan has a struggle ahead of him to give up his own grand peace-keeping role and allow himself to be ruled. Hidden in the pain of warring parents, there is an over-valuation of his own power and, therefore, more culpability for his rejection. Dan will need to disentangle these beliefs before he can put his guilt into its proper context. He is set to worry for many years to come that it is his own aggression and anger that caused all this loss and wreckage. In order to be relieved of these beliefs he will have to accept the less palatable truth that he is just a young boy without the power to rule the grown-ups. At that point he may finally believe his social worker's kind words that it is not his fault.

Taylor: In the shadow of the past

By contrast, let us meet another nine-year-old boy who, like Dan, had been in foster care for two years when we met. Taylor had been living in a "short-term" foster home with his brother and both were planned to be placed separately. The situation had dragged on for this length of time evidently due to discontinuities in social workers and the inability of the local authority to cope with staff shortages. Taylor was not simply in transition but in a hiatus where he and his brother were drifting in care. Children in this situation cannot securely plan for the future in a focused way; even a dental appointment brings up the question of where they will be by the next six-month check up.

Taylor had a worn, resigned air when he met me and his restlessness and resistance in the room was shown by his several times opening the door, checking the corridors and scanning through the windows for anyone leaving or entering the building. Taylor was on alert all of the time and not keen to let down his guard with this unknown woman. Nevertheless, it had been his choice that he meet with me on his own and without his foster carers. In between these checking behaviours, he began to diffidently play with a large toy helicopter.

He played silently, muttering to himself, and excluding me. The policemen had a gun and arrested people, then shot them and pushed them over a cliff. I gently made sure he saw I was interested and was trying to follow what he did.

'This lady says "Stop! You are mad!"' and he made the policeman push her over the cliff.

'Do you think that lady is like me?' I asked him.

'Well, you do see mad people. Isn't that your job?'

'I see all kinds of young people who may have worries and problems. My job is to see if we can work together and if I can help them.'

He moved the policeman to the dollhouse. 'He isn't a policeman he is a robber.' He made the robber systematically turn over every item in the dollhouse, pushing furniture down the stairs, pulling drawers out of wardrobes, mattresses from beds, covers from chairs, up-ending tables and sinks.

'Is he stealing or spoiling?' I ask.

'He don't care. He's robbing it all.' He cleared a space in the debris for the robber to hide in.

'He has got everything but it all seems wrecked,' I said.

He did not answer. Then he picked up one of the dolls from a carry-cot on the other side of the room. From this greater distance, and whilst systematically stripping off her clothes, he said, conversationally, 'I used to rob. It was for no reason.'

'Perhaps you were angry.'

'No.' He pulled a baby doll from her cot and dropped her on the floor.
'You are not having a soft bed. I am having it! Naw! It's babyish.' And he tossed it aside. He looked for a gun telling me he was going to shoot her.

'You are showing me that there is nowhere safe for a baby to sleep whilst an angry robber is about.'

He looked around the devastated room and suddenly opened the door. He told me he wanted to leave and I did not prevent him but walked with him along the corridor. He suddenly dived into a toilet and I waited. When he emerged he said defiantly, 'I ain't coming back'.

I let him know that it was up to him but I felt it was a shame because we just had 15 more minutes. He walked back into the room and I felt his despair as he looked about. I was careful to let him be close to the door and I pointed out some craft supplies lying untouched on a side table. He was soon cutting and sticking in a surprisingly competent way, making a mask. I tried to help him unobtrusively and described what he was doing in a positive way.

After some easier minutes he said, 'I've got a problem – it's of a hurting kind. There's a boy at school who is a hurting kind of boy.'

'Is he bullying you?'

'Sort of.'

We discussed what he could do about this boy who he said was sometimes his friend. I tried to ascertain if other boys helped him, whether the teacher knew, if his foster carers would help. He curled his lip derisively. 'The teachers are all sacked – there's no more teachers. And John and Susie they don't care about me – they never believe me!'

We had reached the end of our time and I told him I would think about what he had told me. I asked if he wanted to come back next week. I forgot at that moment that the question was putting him too much on the spot and I added, 'I would like to see you next week. Will you come?'

'Alright,' he shrugged.

The following week, he was easier in the room but he played an intense game where a "ghost robber" kidnapped and corrupted captured boys. The boys were said to be bad and their mother did not want them. They shared the robbers' loot, fought, killed each other, came back from the dead, robbed and ruined houses. Again, he seemed to get grim pleasure from the pursuits of the aggressors. The baby doll was stuffed 'into a smelly sock where she can't breathe much'.

He denied being bullied at school and said that the boy he had mentioned previously was "alright". Despite the apparent discomfort of the session, he was not eager to leave and I was left with the feeling that he yearned for more.

Reflections

One reels away from an encounter like this, filled with alarm. There seems little enough time to help Taylor to amend his fierce internal landscape. This is a world where malevolence triumphs and where identification with an abuser is the only route to a semblance of safety or control.

Initially, Taylor was hypervigilant and had to keep checking that he could remove himself from me should he need to. The concern with exits and entrances, with escape routes, is typical of traumatised and abused children who have been held against their will during abuse (Hunter, 2001). I have seen these patterns in girls who have been sexually abused and in children who have suffered severe injury. Taylor's history included beatings from a sadistic father and sexual knowledge beyond his years. He had told his teacher that he had seen his parents having sex but neither he nor his siblings made specific allegations about sexual abuse. The fact that they acted out sexually together was indicative of unrevealed activities in their home and their highly sexualised activity was one of the governing reasons for the plan to place them separately. Despite this, they were still sharing a bedroom and a home together and my guess was that sexual and sadistic activities continued to be part of their interaction. The danger for his younger brother, from a boy as disturbed as Taylor, should not be taken lightly. Farmer and Pollock (1998) put the risk at 50 per cent that sexually abused children in care abuse others. Watkins and Bentovim (1992) also warned of the high risk of abused boys becoming abusers, and seminal work undertaken at Great Ormond Street Hospital by Skuse *et al* (1998) has gone some way to identifying risk factors for abused boys becoming abusers. Taylor would score highly on these factors, which include the experience of violence and poor maternal care.

Taylor showed me destruction, with a mixture of provocation – from which he gained pleasure – and revelation – from which he gained some relief. He was largely identified with an abuser, who in the second meeting seemed to be an adult male, possibly his father. When an abused boy shows an identification with an abuser, we understand the process as one of *traumatisation*, what was called the Stockholm syndrome after hostages were found to develop an identification with their captors as a way of surviving terror and threat of death (see also Hodges *et al*, 1994).

Cruelty was portrayed as contagious and endless. Haunted by ghosts, Taylor was showing me that he felt he was still in the grip of a despoiler. There seemed no refuge for Taylor in the destructive play he showed me. In effect, it became persecuting to him and at the point where he looked around to see chaos, he suddenly became a victim, feared to stay with this mess and wanted to leave.

This flipping from the stance of persecutor to victim is a version of the *paranoid-schizoid* state that object relation theorists describe as prior to psychic integration in the *depressive* position (Klein, 1932). The paranoid-schizoid is a primitive state of mind which Klein posited as part of normative development during the first six months of life when experience is overwhelming and ambivalence and conflict cannot be tolerated. The infant would split all experience (including himself and others) into two polarised categories – good and bad – and push them outside of himself (project). The "good" provided by others such as the mother can be selected to be introjected (taken inside) and the child can then experience himself as "good" also. The "bad" can be attacked as it is external. However, it then becomes powerful and terrifying in its own right and provokes intense fear (or paranoia) for the child. Klein suggested that if the mother can contain the infant's terror and attacks, integrating them alongside his love, desire and gratitude, it is possible for the infant to attain the depressive position which enables him to tolerate conflict, fear, ambivalence and the mixture of positive and negative traits in himself and others. Without this, Klein suggests, the child may grow on into adulthood with a tendency towards such splitting and projection.[3]

Here, I would suggest that, for Taylor, the world is divided into bullies and victims. Taylor does not want to be a victim or to accept his feelings of fear. Instead, he tries to be a bully, which would lodge the unwanted feelings of fear into the baby doll or into me. It is a sign of hopefulness for his good development that he could not completely convince himself of this. I think I helped at this point by saying, 'You are showing me that there is nowhere safe for a baby to sleep with an angry robber about.' My remark does not condone or blame, it does not take sides against Taylor but describes the scene as relational. It gives him, or seeks to give him, a therapeutic alliance from which the play in the room can be followed.

But disconnected for a moment from the safety of the abuser's role, Taylor was overwhelmed and wanted to leave. Because I grasped his despair, I helped by my acceptance of him having a short break. I then invited him to return.

In working with a very edgy, persecuted boy like this, one has to rely on instinct, on lightness of touch and on the *unconscious communication* of the boy's need for help (see Lefevre, this volume). This is a boy who thinks I will condemn him, say 'You are mad!' rather than try to help. This is a boy who creates an atmosphere where to say I want to help him sounds weak and sentimental. I have to bear in mind that he may be showing me how his father bullied them all. There is a message in his telling me 'I used to rob'; the past tense may indicate what he has had to bear. At any rate I must not overlook the baby thrown out of bed. It is instructive to see that upon re-entering the room Taylor used my help constructively and then put before me a dilemma which is about being bullied. I took this up literally although it became clear he does not; 'The teachers are all sacked,' he said.

At our second meeting, Taylor was, throughout, in identification with an abusive man. In his play, he showed how he and his brother became corrupted. Although I saw his identification was with the robber, the baby put into a smelly sock may also be an infantile part of Taylor who could find little safe space for his own smallness and dependency. Taylor made me a witness to abuse and I could use an invitation to therapeutic alliance ultimately to offer him a way to consider and confront abuse without being either victim or perpetrator.

---

[3] See Hinshelwood, 1994, Chapter 7, for a fuller discussion.

This is one of the difficulties for the abused: how to communicate without repeating the whole abusive scenario. So I held onto hope that Taylor may not simply be gratified by my audience to his nastiness but may yet want a way to escape.

The needs of a boy like Taylor in transition are immense. Unless we get enough right, we will be watching as his cynicism and rage harden him into the sadist that was his father. Taylor's world is one where perverse pleasure can be gained from the ruin of hope, from the disruption of a baby's need for warmth and care. Taylor will need skilled help and supported foster care. He is not likely to get by without because, unlike Daniel, his inner resources are twisted and impoverished. Henry (1974) called this "doubly deprived" to underline the inner deprivation which prevents external help getting through.

Taylor is likely to perplex and frustrate his carers as he tortures the dog and resists their affection. He is an excluded and unclaimed boy who will need to be challenged and channelled into more healthy relationships.

Social work practice with young people in transition

Boys like Daniel and Taylor need good social work support alongside individual psychotherapy, support to gain access to therapy and to keep them coming to it despite their ambivalence. Of course, this does not mean ignoring children if they have negative views about attending therapy and taking appropriate action where therapy is abusive, damaging or harmful for children. But it is essential for social workers to be aware that many children (or indeed adults) will feel negatively about their therapy or therapist at some point. Consequently, the situation should be reviewed with therapeutic insights such as these in mind rather than automatically assuming that there is something wrong or even that the work should stop. Instead, in cases like these the social worker, psychotherapist and foster carers need to become a supportive team around the child to support the therapy. Fortunately, I can report that Taylor's social worker, his therapist, his foster carers and I worked together over several years to achieve a good outcome. His social worker was an important moderator of the foster carers' desire to "let him forget", as was my argument that during the two years before he began psychotherapy, he had not forgotten but was in constant trouble for bullying. This piece of work was achievable because we met regularly, discussed our differences, listened to each other's points of view and acted as a secure network around Taylor. We gave him the rare experience of a child looked after, that the adults all worked together to help and contain him.

Perhaps we do not want to consider the cost implications of effectively helping someone like Taylor? The work was done within a not-for-profit specialist foster care agency. I see no reason why it should not have been carried out between CAMHS and the local authority, as are many of my cases. What I cannot accept is what is sometimes claimed, that 'We do not know how to help him'. We do know, and the cost is only marginally more than accommodating him without fully helping. The cost of not doing so is grim as well as expensive. The worst of it for me would be that, at nine years of age, boys like Taylor are still willing to change, and we owe them the chance.

If we can bring to bear on our planning for young people a real attempt to comprehend their view of the world, their issues and needs, we stand much more chance of advocating for them effectively (see Thomas, this volume). Regular meetings between young people and their social workers are integral to this process.

What has to be carefully understood are the practical parameters of containment and the need for transparency in the motives of the meetings. So, a meeting place must be adequate to the emotions likely to be aroused and exchanged. The adult involved in direct work must be receptive and that includes being calm, orderly, clear of purpose, and emotionally attuned to the young person. The young person must be told what the social worker is trying to do and must agree to the endeavour. It is practical burdens which more usually derail the therapeutic nature of a meeting rather than the absence of psychoanalytic concepts, though the latter are more than useful. The social worker whose diary or managers constrain her to being late, breathless, hassled by traffic and running to her next appointment is communicating a barrage of messages which tell a child to not bother her. A timetable that must continuously be changed at the last minute is not adequate for the task.

Similarly, a social worker engaged in getting to know a child and steering them through life changes will have to set aside personal modesty in favour of the powerful role they will play for the child, in the real world and as a *transference object*. Young people in care express enormous hurt and rejection when they fail to get in touch with their social worker and receive messages of cancelled meetings as a comment on their personal worth to that worker. Being aware of the extreme sensitivity to rejection felt by accommodated children is crucial. Being aware of ambivalence in their feelings towards us helps us survive. Being aware of acting out and the tendency to reject us before they feel themselves rejected, all of this is necessary to work effectively with young people in transition.

Within my therapeutic setting, therapeutic meetings with children and young people are assisted by me having a predictable timetable and others having a low expectation of my availability. The social worker who sets aside time to get to know her charges has to be aware of and construct her own suitable framework for the task. It is important to start as you mean to proceed – not lengthening availability from a rush of compassion, but standing up to the fact that what one gives is never compensation for harm suffered. It is always better to be conservative and clear about promises rather than optimistic and unsuccessful. I see good social workers giving a framework of predictability to their meetings, even one that can be time-adjusted: 'I will see you three times in the next six weeks and then we will review and plan from there.' This sort of framework is a stock in trade for mental health practitioners who are trained that this kind of arrangement will hold anxiety far better than even more frequent meetings on an ad-hoc basis. To be held in mind over time is a powerful communication to a young person whose world is shifting. Knowing what you can expect from the other person and having predictable time with them keeps at bay fears of being forgotten and dropped as well as unrealistic hopes for contact. Being trustworthy, keeping to what you say demonstrates respect and enhances trust more than words.

Medina: a failed adoption

Medina, who was placed for adoption at the age of ten, was not thought to be in transition but in a permanent home. However, she found that she could not adjust to this. At first things went fairly well but as it dawned on Medina that she was being asked to belong solely to this family, 'to be their girl,' as she expressed it, she found that she had really been in transition all along, with a buried hope of reunification with her birth mother.

When I met Medina for the second time, she could not believe that I had remembered what she had said to me two weeks before. Partly this was because she rarely listened herself and was much better at giving out than taking in. However, she had noticed that I listened intently to her and this kept her coming to see me for a while.

Medina, then, was a 14-year-old in transition. She told me she was determined to be relocated back in her home town a hundred miles away: 'I've told them, a max of six weeks or I start running away.' Unlike many of the young people I meet who are trying to hold still whilst plans are made above their heads, Medina was at an age where she was filled with her own agency.

A striking aspect of Medina's case was a long-standing and reliable contact between her and her social worker. Of course, it is devastating for a social worker to succeed in placing a child successfully, only to have the placement break down years later. But I heard from Medina how grateful she was that the same social worker helped her through this nightmare time. Perhaps this human link served to keep Medina from the depression or violent acting out of many of her contemporaries, for it was evident to me that Medina was not a young woman who had given up. Of course, it was not the whole story but I appreciated her attempt at toughness; perhaps she appealed to the delinquent in me and I liked her from our first meeting. It is not necessary to like someone to help them, but it can help. Medina expected me to be a "con artist" and to fill her with psycho-babble. I sometimes obliged and our discussions were good humoured with lots of indignation on her side. She had been in an adoptive family for four years, her longest period of stability in a long care history. She had been cut off from contact with her impossibly alcoholic mother at Dan and Taylor's age, nine. She told me she deliberately broke down her placement because:

I agreed I wouldn't see my mum and my older sister and it was alright at the beginning. But I got to hating it, being adopted because it sort of meant that I was their girl – only

I wasn't. They were sort of brain-washing me to be like them, but in the end I wasn't having it.

Medina had used her powerful weapon of running away to force a move to another home. As she predicted, her mother was brought back into her life and contact of a precarious sort reinstated. Too late Medina found that 'I should wait until I am a bit older to cope with my mum'.

In the few weeks that we were to meet we had a number of discussions about success and failure. Medina was in danger of characterising her life to date as a series of failures whilst I was at pains to point out to her that she had been in school more than out of it, co-operative more than destructive, a family member more than a loner, and successful for long stretches of time. It was galling to think that she would look only at her failures and believe that they negated her achievements. These conversations helped her and she became less provocative and destructive. She was less keen on my attempts to get her to realise that she projected onto others what she thought of herself. She was very fond of words that were there to trick and confuse, so it was not surprising that she expected this from me. Her worries about being brain-washed were connected to her need for identification with her mother and her birth family.

Sadly, it was not true that she disliked her adoptive parents. Tempted as she was to hate her own mother and to betray her with this new family, she could not resolve her need for these massively rejecting scenes where her poor adoptive parents reaped a harvest they did not plant nor deserve. In a less boisterous mood with me one day she admitted, 'I was too old to be adopted. I couldn't forget enough and just go on as if I was their kid. But sometimes I wished I could.' Young people like Medina are caught up in the throes of mourning, revisiting their early attachments as adolescence dawns. Sadly, too much of adoption requires them to choose either/or when their emotional well-being is dependent on their finding a way to integrate these identifications, which are felt to be parts of the self.

With Medina and her social worker, we had many discussions of how to continue to support her through this process. It had not gone as anticipated when she was adopted. However, she had experienced some important stability and care in her life and these were gains worth acknowledging. Medina's social worker reclaimed her own optimism when she saw that Medina's story was not one only of failure. Along with the difficulties there had been gains. The hope for the future was that just as the social worker had continued to care for and work with Medina, there was hope to integrate her life experiences and to remember that there had been many positive aspects to the adoptive care. Moving on to a foster home where less emotional attachment was asked of her, Medina used her social worker to link her to this new family as well as to look back with less scorn on the past. This sort of life story work is not necessarily done at set times or on paper, but is part of the ongoing relationship that a constant social worker can provide. It is the social worker's holding of ambivalence that is crucial here. It makes a huge difference to the valuing of one's past if the facts are not distorted entirely by current emotions and allegiances. Saying goodbye to Medina after a brief acquaintance, I thought how fortunate she was to have a social worker who knew her so well, who had accompanied her so far and who continued to be a steadying force for good in her turbulent life.

Conclusion

I have tried to show that children in transition can be in very different places inside themselves. Daniel who had settled in his foster home after two years, was still having to navigate the difficult business of mourning for his lost brother even as he attached to his current carers. Taylor was in grave trouble in his identification with an abuser, and his drifting care plan contributed to his detachment. Medina needed to come to better terms with her journey through care. All three of these young people could be helped by good supportive social work, enhanced sometimes by direct work or life story work according to the skill of the social worker. The attempt to get to know their clients better, to understand their viewpoint, to link past and present, inside and outside realities was real social work that had enormous gains for these children in transition.

References

Bick E. (1964) 'Notes on infant observation in psychoanalytic training', *International Journal of Psychoanalysis*, 45, pp 558–66

Bion W. (1962) *Learning From Experience*, London: Heinemann

Farmer M. and Pollock S. (1998) 'Sexually abused and abusing children in substitute care', in Department of Health (ed.) *Caring For Children Away from Home: Messages from research*, Chichester: Wiley, Department of Health

Fonagy P., Steele M., Steele H., Higgitt A. and Target M. (1992) 'The theory and practice of resilience', *Journal of Child Psychology and Psychiatry*, 37:2, pp 231–257

Fraiberg S., Adelson E. and Shapiro V. (1980) 'Ghosts in the nursery: a psychoanalytical approach', in Fraiberg S. (ed.) *Clinical Studies in Infant Mental Health*, London: Tavistock

Henry G. (1974) 'Doubly deprived', *Journal of Child Psychotherapy*, 4:2, pp 29–43

Hinshelwood R. D. (1994) *Clinical Klein*, London: Free Association Books

Hodges J., Lanyado M. and Andreou C. (1994) 'Sexuality and violence: preliminary clinical hypotheses from psychotherapeutic assessment in a research program of young sexual offenders', *Journal of Child Psychotherapy*, 20:3, pp 283–308

Hunter M. (2001) *Psychotherapy with Young People in Care*, Hove: Brunner-Routledge

Kerr A. (1995) 'A psychoanalytic approach to the work of the guardian ad litem' in Trowell J. and Bower M. (eds) *The Emotional Needs of Children and Their Families*, London: Routledge

Klein M. (1932) 'The significance of early anxiety situations in the development of the ego', in Klein M., *The Psychoanalysis of Children*, London: Hogarth Press and Institute of Psychoanalysis

Lanyado M. and Horne A. (1999) *The Handbook of Child and Adolescent Psychotherapy: Psychoanalytical approaches*, London: Routledge

Main M., Kaplan N. and Cassidy J. (1985) 'Security in childhood, infancy and adulthood: a move to the level of representation', in Bretherton I. and Waters E. (eds) *Growing Pains of Attachment Theory and Research: Monographs for Society for Research in Child Development*, 50

Mattinson J. (1992) *The Reflection Process in Casework Supervision* (2nd edn), London: Tavistock

Skuse D., Bentovim A., Hodges J., Stevenson S., Andreou C., Lanyado M., New M. and McMillan D. (1998) 'Risk factors for the development of sexually abusive behaviour in sexually victimised adolescent males: cross-sectional study', *British Medical Journal*, 317, pp 175–9

Symington N. (1986) *The Analytic Experience: Lectures from the Tavistock*, London: Free Association Books

Watkins B. and Bentovim A. (1992) 'The sexual abuse of male children and adolescents', *Journal of Child Psychology and Psychiatry*, 33:1, pp 197–218

5 The everyday lives of children in care: using a sociological perspective to inform social work practice

Sally Holland, Emma Renold, Nicola Ross and Alex Hillman

Introduction

This chapter has three main aims. Firstly, it describes how contemporary sociological approaches to the study of childhood can enable us to make sense of the social worlds of children and young people. Secondly, the chapter reports on how we are drawing on such approaches to inform the establishment of an ongoing research project with looked after children, (Extra)ordinary Lives, and some findings from the research are presented. Thirdly, the chapter explores the relevance of sociological approaches to the study of childhood for direct practice, drawing out implications of both the research methods and some of the research findings for those who work with children and young people.

Exploring children's worlds using sociological perspectives

In the late 1990s, the Economic and Social Research Council funded a large programme of research called *Children 5–16: Growing into the 21st Century*. This was a response to a shift in the way that academics, policy makers, legislators and practitioners were coming to understand children and young people and their place in society. It was stated that:

> *The Programme will consolidate and build on this work through a focus on children as social actors. This will be achieved by examining children as active agents, influencing as well as being influenced by the worlds they live in, and/or through research which treats children as the primary unit of analysis (rather than subsuming them under, for example, the household) ... The Programme will attempt to illuminate the middle period of childhood and the nature and quality of children's family and social lives, children's sense of belonging and their contribution to society, together with their understandings, expectations and aspirations for the future.*[1]

This summary is a useful starting point for this chapter. It signals a marked shift in the social sciences from viewing children as passive objects of research and policy making to research participants whose perspectives are not only important in their own right but

---

[1] http://www.hull.ac.uk/children5to16programme/intro.htm, Economic and Social Research Council (undated).

whose accounts are taken as competent portrayals of their experiences (Qvortrup *et al*, 1994). It has long been recognised that "childhood" is fundamentally a social construction, in that there is no universal norm of what the experiences of childhood are or should be and when childhood begins and ends (James *et al*, 1998). Notions of what it is to be "a child" vary within and between cultures, over time and across generations (James and James, 2004). Nevertheless, dominant discourses endure in research, in policy and in popular culture about children and childhood (Valentine, 1996; James *et al*, 1998). These include early concepts of children as inherently evil, requiring discipline and correction, or as innocent, requiring nurturance and protection. Both can be understood in terms of risk anxiety, as fear of children and fear for children (Scott *et al*, 1998). Discourses about looked after children in the media and in social work literature, for example, can tend to polarise children as either "innocent victims" at risk from abusive parents or "out-of-control" and in need of restraint (Stainton-Rogers and Stainton-Rogers, 1992). Whether "at risk" or "creating risk", most children and young people who are looked after are represented in terms of their futures – these being bleak futures with poor outcomes. More complex and more upbeat understandings of looked after children are somewhat thinner on the ground (Chase *et al*, 2006; Winter, 2006).

The emphasis on futures and outcomes also has a long history. Traditional theories of childhood, both early developmental psychology and early socialisation theories, viewed childhood primarily as a preparation for adulthood and considered children only in terms of their future becomings, rather than "somebody" in their own right (Walkerdine, 2004). Social policies with children as the object of their enquiry have focused on, and been justified as, producing adult citizens. Prioritising futures and "outcomes", however, neglects children's everyday, "now" experiences and the complex relationship between their past, present and future. Developments within contemporary social science research, however, are beginning to emphasise not only children as "beings", rather than solely "becomings", but how children are constituted as both being and becoming (Lee, 2001; Prout, 2005).

Early socialisation theories which viewed children as passive recipients of social processes and relationships have been widely critiqued (Jenks, 1992). Locating children as "social actors", active in the construction and determination of their social lives, the lives of those around them and the societies in which they live, has led to more complex explorations of the ways in which children exercise agency (James and James, 2004). This also involves recognising a range of social and cultural norms that heavily regulate children's ability to make choices in numerous contexts from the family to the wider community which continue to construct children as relatively passive and powerless (Christensen and O'Brien, 2003).

The social and cultural contexts in which children are located are thus key influ-ences in making sense of the social world of the child. Significant to this are developments within sociology regarding notions of space and place, that link in with geographical literature. Recent years have witnessed a surge of interest in and research into the geographies of children and childhood (Holloway and Valentine, 2000). Here, the ways in which children give meaning to their everyday environments, be they rural, suburban, inner-city, near or far from networks of relatives, and how children engage in and with these local environments form a significant part of how children's lives are negotiated. Structural relations between children and adults are important, however, children do not form a homogenous group. Socio-cultural factors like class, gender, ethnicity and nationality all have social and material effects on their everyday experiences (Connolly, 1998; Renold, 2005; Scourfield et al, 2006). Societal expectations of children from particular socio-economic and cultural backgrounds will strongly affect how people respond to children and how these children develop their own sense of self.

Sociological approaches exploring social identities, relationships and cultures have developed significantly in the field of childhood studies. In particular, poststructuralist perspectives have challenged the notion that individual identity categories (e.g. girl, boy, sister, brother) or collective identity categories (e.g. family) can be known in any straightforward or fixed way (Hadfield et al, 2006). For example, rather than trying to define the concept of "family", many sociologists would be interested in finding out what a family does, the family practices that make people feel that they belong to each other (Morgan, 1991). Who we are, then, is not something fixed or singular or easily known. Rather, identity is always evolving, always in-process. It is something that is experienced, expressed, managed and continuously performed differently according to context and over time (Goffman, 1959; Butler, 1993). While the concept of identity is big business in social theory, it is a concept that has filtered down to the level of practice. For example, materials such as the Looking After Children guidance (Department of Health, 1995) and the Assessment Framework (Department of Health, 2000) tend to encourage a semi-public labelling of children specifically using the concept of "identity" in arenas such as statutory reviews and court reports. Although these materials have important and worthy intentions of encouraging holistic attention to the child's life, practices such as reproducing phrases from textbooks and pasting phrases from form to form encourage fixed and deterministic notions of children's lives and expected futures (Holland, 2004).

Lastly, contemporary sociological research on children's lives has been drawn to qualitative methodologies that pay attention to and draw out children's own perspectives, rather than learning about their lives through the eyes of others (Christensen and James, 2000; see Greig et al, 2007) and in more direct ways than is possible through experimental or survey-style research. This shift, which views children as active participants rather than passive objects in the research process, is again related to the desire to recognise children as active meaning makers in their own right and thus experts on their own lives. This is especially important given that children's views have historically been (and in some research practices continue to be) marginalised (Woodhead and Faulkner, 2000). Contemporary research studies which prioritise children's voices and experiences, (i.e. how children understand and express themselves) are often drawn to ethnographic and, in the case of our own longitudinal research, narrative approaches (James and Prout, 1998). By using a narrative approach to explore and understand children's accounts, we pay less attention to verifying the "facts" or "truth" of a story, and instead focus on the meaning that the story has for the child and what it might tell us about how they understand themselves and their relationships with others. Narrative approaches, which are used in research, in social work and in therapeutic practice, recognise 'the ways in which we make and use knowledge to create and preserve our social worlds and places within them' (Fook, 2002, p 132).

The next section of this chapter explains how some of these developments, particularly the focus on the "everyday", on "voice" and on method have underpinned and informed our own sociologically driven research study at Cardiff University: "(Extra)ordinary Lives: Children's everyday relationships in public care".

The (Extra)ordinary Lives project

Children who are looked after are often called upon to reflect on their lives. For example, they are routinely asked to express their opinions about themselves in reviews, and occasionally about the looked after system more generally in consultations about policies and practices. However, these questions are often only directed at aspects of their lives that relate to professional, and thus adult-centred, areas and interests and are usually framed within discourses of protection (e.g. health, self-care skills, etc) or rights (e.g. education). Much of what we "know" about the social world of children who are looked after is restricted to aspects of their life or experiences as they relate to the looked after system. While aware that both their experience of the looked-after system and the care they receive more widely are important, we have designed a research project that foregrounds children's everyday lives, allowing children and young people the freedom to choose what aspects of their lives to explore and how to represent these. We were also aware that young people who are looked after often complain that consultations are one-off occasions and that they have no knowledge of what happens to their opinions and sometimes view practitioners as only visiting and asking about their lives when a statutory review is due. We therefore wished to conduct a piece of research that built relationships over a longer period of time, and where the ethos was one of reciprocity.

Following consultations with Tros Gynnal, a children's charity specialising in advocacy, and some young care leavers, we set up a fortnightly project for looked after children and care leavers, which we called 'Me, myself and I'.[2] Nine young people aged 10–20 living in foster care, kinship care or independently as care leavers in one local authority took part in the study over a school year (2006–7). The young people (seven girls and two boys) were invited to explore any aspect of their everyday lives that they chose, using any of the materials we made available. These included video and still digital cameras, scrapbooks, art and writing materials and music mixing on laptops. Most young people also used the space (in a comfortable building owned by the children's charity) as a place to relax after school or work, to eat, socialise and play. Some wished to do life history interviews, chose to keep diaries or took us on guided walks of their current or former neighbourhoods. Indeed, some of our most productive conversations took place in the car or when walking. At the same time as running this project, we as researchers observed the processes and tape-recorded many of our interactions with the young people. The young people were constantly reminded that this was a research study and that they had control over what was recorded and could decide what they wished to share with us from the materials they had produced. One girl only participated briefly in the project. The other eight participants took part for the full school year and have expressed a wish to maintain ongoing contact with the research team, which will be fulfilled by occasional "catch-up" meetings and reunions.

The reciprocal nature of the research included an aim to provide young people with opportunities for fun and for learning new skills. We employed the oldest participant ("Jolene") as a youth support worker with the younger participants. The participative ethos was promoted by regularly discussing the aims and methods of the research with the young people, getting their ideas on how to understand their lives better, and feeding back to them what we felt we had found out and understood about their lives. We will be returning to each participant in the near and far future (if they continue to wish to keep in touch) to involve them further in analysis and dissemination of results, and to avoid the common phenomenon of adults making connections and then losing touch with young people who are looked after.

Our research questions examine the notion of children's participation, a common claim in both current practice and research studies. We have tried to critically examine our own and others' claims to be enabling children to be full participants in a process. To this end, we are mindful not to evade the issue of adults' retention of power of resources, process and agenda. In our research, we informed the young people that we were interested in their relationships (e.g. with friends, families, carers, local communities and professionals), in

---

[2] The overall research study is called Extra(ordinary) Lives: Children's everyday relationship cultures in public care. It is one of the demonstrator projects from the Qualiti node (Qualitative Research Methods in the Social Sciences: Innovation, Integration and Impact) of the ESRC National Centre for Research Methods (see: http://www.cardiff.ac.uk/socsi/qualiti/).

places of importance to them and their negotiation of their localities, in their identities, and any other aspects of how they live their everyday lives or how they understand who they are. More formally, some of our research questions include:

- In what ways do "looked after" children experience belonging to, or dislocation from, their local communities, "family", friends and other social networks over time and across social contexts?
- What does it mean to identify and be identified as "looked after" across different "public" and "private" spaces?
- What are the conditions within which "looked after" children create and maintain "safe" spaces to manage their relations/hips and "identity-work" in the ways that they want?
- What structures, cultures, settings and spaces do children identify that support more positive identities of children in public care?

Many of the sociological developments within the field of childhood studies mentioned earlier in the chapter inform this research, such as: taking an interest in children's lives as they are lived in the "here and now", not just in relation to the future adults they will become; an awareness that much of what we understand about children's lives is socially constructed by the dominant discourses that are embedded in our society; and a desire to critically listen to children's own stories and representations of their lives.

The next section gives some examples from the data we generated with the young people in the research study, and has two aims. Firstly, this section illustrates the ways in which our approach (a sociology of everyday lives) facilitates the generation of rich and complex personal accounts from the perspective of children living and negotiating those everyday lives. Secondly, we wish to give space for young people's voices to be reported directly in this chapter. The data included here relate to one theme: schooling. The theme was chosen for this chapter to illustrate the research approach adopted and because it was a strong theme to emerge from these young people's accounts of their everyday lives. Schooling was not a theme we researched directly with the young people, but we would suggest that our approach enabled the young people to talk in more depth about their experiences of schooling, as they did about many other social spaces they inhabit. We believe this approach allowed the young people to contribute more about their lives than a more structured style of interviewing might have produced. In keeping with a narrative approach, the data have not been neatly compartmentalised into neatened, short quotations. Instead, we report longer extracts from these young people's narratives in an attempt to foreground their voices rather than our "findings".[3]

---

[3] A series of dots (. . .) denotes that a word or phrase has been cut (usually just a single word or phrase from the researcher). A slash (/) denotes interruption or overlapping speech.

(Extra)ordinary Lives data examples: young people's interactions in and with the school environment

Nevaeh

In the course of a long, taped discussion with one of the researchers, Nevaeh[4] (aged 17), tells the story of all the places she has lived since leaving her family home at 14 and eventually coming into care after a period of homelessness. Throughout this conversation she regularly referred to school and education. During the discussion she mentions the changes of school associated with her regular changes of address, the long periods of missed schooling when her life was more unstable, how important education is to her and how, when she finally was placed successfully with an experienced carer, she was able to feel that she was in a "proper family", linking this to her carer's positive attitude to schooling. The following is a series of extracts about schooling from the hour-long discussion.

> *(Whilst living at home): Cause I used to get bullied at home and at school. But it was like I used to go to school just to get away from there.*

> *(When homeless): I moved in with (friend), and I heard nothing, I had to wash my clothes every day just so I could wear them, cause that was all I had, I had nothing else, you know. I wasn't in school for ages and ages and ages. And education has always been a big part. Sorry, but I've always wanted to have a good education, because once you've got a good education I think anyway, you're sorted.*

> *(Whilst with recent foster carers): It's great, it's like a proper family life…That's how it is. You know, when I used to come home from school, 'How was your day?' She did that and asked, how was my day? She's like, (inaudible) she was there for me for my School Prom and then when I got my GCSE results . . . And since I was with her, ah I did brilliantly at school, really really well in school, because I had no confidence to go to school before. I mean it was like, I was being bullied in my first school, and then in my second school, I was friends with everybody. I liked, it went from being, I was miserable, overweight, I was getting bullied, I was just so much always crying until I moved onto (carer) a couple of months later I was a totally different person, just totally different. It was wicked.*

Nevaeh is able, in retrospect, to tell a narrative of her education with an ending, as she has now left school, is living independently and is in paid employment. She uses the story of her schooling to illustrate how, when she was homeless and moving between various family members and friends, she was not living the sort of life she felt was a proper life

---

[4] All young people chose their own pseudonymns. Nevaeh is "heaven" spelt backwards.

for a child, in terms of prioritising education and living with people who cared about education, and therefore showing their care for Nevaeh. Through the story of her schooling, we are able to obtain a glimpse of Nevaeh's interpretation of her life story, what that means to her current identity and expectations regarding childhood and family life.

Keely

Keely (aged 13), on the other hand, is still experiencing her schooling. She is currently fostered, but she has had many different care experiences, including residential care. Every time we meet Keely, she relates another episode of her interactions with teachers and with peers in school. Through these, it is possible to gain a sense of how Keely negotiates her everyday identities as "looked after", academically able and with a keen sense of injustice at the administration of the school regime. The following extracts are taken from a tape recording of a car journey when a researcher collected Keely from school. Brief interjections from the researcher have been omitted.

> *What he (senior school teacher) did, he goes, he goes, 'I know your family life and I know your brothers have just gone into care and all that'. I went, 'Three people in the class knew that, I didn't want everyone knowing, they all gonna come up to me now, right, and do my head in'. And then he went, 'Keely, calm down'. I went, 'Screw you, you just like, blatantly just told everyone'. And he went, 'Keely, there's no reason to get upset about it'. I went, 'I'm not upset, I'm just mad at you for doing it, like'. (further conversation took place on other topics) . . . And I do not like holidays at all . . . I hate 'em...I love my school, I just don't like the teachers. I can do all the work . . . The work's too easy though. It's just like – oh, do something different . . . (in the holidays I) miss my friends, you know, don't – cause, like, I'm in care I'm not allowed to give out my phone number so I can't use that.*

Keely expresses here her fury at her teacher referring to her care status in front of her peers. She has only been in this school for a year and has established herself as 'the hardest girl in the school' (as she herself puts it) through physical fighting. She appears, and feels, vulnerable through reference to her family problems. However, as well as the negative brushes with authority, it also appears that school holds many positives for her, in terms of academic achievement and friendships. Yet, here again, her care "status" intervenes, in that (in her case) she is not allowed to give out her foster carers' number to her friends.

On another occasion, Keely and Nevaeh happened to be having a lift in the car together. Keely mentioned that she has been having problems with some of her friends in school because she has been moved up two sets.

Nevaeh: *I had friends like that who wouldn't speak to me because I was higher than them in school . . . So I used to lie a lot and tell them that I was thick and . . .*

Keely: *I did that.*

Nevaeh: *Yeah.*

Keely: *And then I moved up and then . . . When she kicks off, she goes, 'Keely, you're not that intelligent', well I'm more intelligent than you, now go away . . . If my homework was done in school they would all think that I was guinea (goody goody) . . . I would be, like, 'Shut up'.*

Research in the sociology of education points to struggles for socially and economically marginalised girls and young women to seek out and maintain educationally successful identities in school (Lucey *et al*, 2003). It is perhaps the case that these young women who are in care have even more of a challenge in terms of negotiating social identity with their peers and teachers. Both had moved schools on a number of occasions and had to form new friendships in mid-adolescence in fairly challenging school environments. Societal expectations are for these young women, from challenging social backgrounds and now in care, to underachieve academically (Berridge, 2006). For each of them, the formal and informal worlds of school frequently collide; academic achievement forms part of their identity, but so does maintaining a "hard" image (Renold, forthcoming).

Jolene

Jolene (aged 20) offered to do a life history interview as part of the project. Afterwards she read the transcript, reflected on it and further discussed her understanding of her life and the significance of her history to her current identity. Like Nevaeh, the narrative of her schooling has a conclusion as she has left school and is now working, whilst waiting to go to university. Also like Nevaeh, her narrative describes her foster carers' attitudes as important in enabling her to succeed academically. Earlier in the interview she (rather affectionately) recalls how her birth family would let her miss school on her birthday, something that would never have been allowed in her foster home. She goes on to describe her educational progress after coming into care in late primary school. Brief interjections from the interviewer have been omitted.

So I've been able to change those things (the culture of her birth family) with me. Do you know what I mean? So if I realise the things, I do the same things as them and I don't like it then I can change it because I've seen what it does . . . I think I've definitely broken that (she is describing a family culture of low achievement). I mean I'm 20; I've got no kids so that is a starter. Em, I, I've been to college and I'm planning to go to university and no one in my family's ever been to sixth form college . . . Em, I came out of school with good results, em, when it wasn't easy. I didn't just work and then just get these grades. I had to work for them because I'm not, em, I'm not like very academic . . . so, you know, em, (pause) one thing is like I've learned is that if you want something you've got to work for it, in different aspects. If you want something, like, and you need money, then you need to work for it and save that money and you can't just spend money on these random crap that people do which honestly sometimes I do. Now I did for years. It took me a while to break that, that one, em, but also if you want something, like I want to go to university, you have to work for it. I knew when I was in school that I would need my maths GCSEs and I was only 15 when I did my exams and I knew I would need it and I worked my hardest on it and I came out with a D and I need a C, so I went to college and I did maths again and I still got a D, so I did it again and I just kept going until I got my C . . . I got it my third time, but out of all my exams, all my exams were C to B except my maths and the reason that I wasn't good at that was because I missed so much schooling as a kid, but I knew that that, that is what I would need so I kept working at it, and working at it and working until I got there. Whereas my family, like my cousin he went to sixth form, he was doing sport, he was offered a scholarship (abroad) to do sport. Did he take it? No. I mean, are you kidding me? [laughter] I would be well gone by now.

Kate

Kate (aged 15), who attends a special unit for students with learning difficulties within a comprehensive school, and lives in kinship care, talked on numerous occasions about her interactions with peers and teachers at school. By getting to know her over a year, we were able to piece together an understanding of her sense of identity and relationship cultures, out of what were at times rather confusing stories. Here are extracts from a taped conversation on the fourteenth project session. The researcher and Kate are looking at a slideshow of photographs she has taken of her family, bedroom and local community. As they look at the slideshow, Kate chats about the photos, but also about her relationships with her family and a great deal about school (interestingly, since none of her photos related to school). A little of this narrative is reproduced below. It can take several readings to make sense of. The researcher's words are in regular text.

I can't wait until I leave school. And school goes, 'What you doing now, Kate? Stop doing that.' Oh my god, you should have seen them though. Miss Brown does my head in.

Does she? What does she do?

Like in maths, I goes, 'Miss, I'm stuck.' She goes, 'Wait a minute then Kate.' So what do I do? Rush on ahead. I goes, 'I'm okay now Miss.' 'No you're not.' 'Listen.' 'No, I want to do this now'. She goes, 'No listen.' So I kept on doing it and then of course I throw my book, she didn't like it. I threw it straight across the classroom and she won't like it. The pages will be pulling out and I ripped the pages out of my book.

Oh dear.

I'm going wrong, rip em, I don't care . . . I don't care about my book . . . my boyfriend said you can (inaudible)

What do you think you'll do when you leave school?

Go to college.

Yeah? What would you like to study there?

Don't know. You could go to pubs, you could go anywhere then.

Yes.

I'd be happy then, away from that school. I won't – and I won't be visiting it.

Won't you? Do some people come back?

They'll come back and goes, 'I wish, I wish I was up in your year Kate'. I goes, 'Yeah, I wish I left school.' . . . God you should see, you should see half of them. 'I want to come back into school.' 'No you don't. School's rubbish. I hate school.'

But the only thing I can't read after the words. So I'm up in special needs; I've got difficulties reading and everything. I try and goes, 'Miss, I can't read this. Can't read that.' And what do I go off and do? Read it. 'Now spell it out, Kate.' Oh my god, driving me mad. Teacher – half of them have left school anyway, hates them . . . I hates the teachers, was it. I refused to do PE . . .

I ran out of a classroom before. My teachers dragged me . . . 'Get out Kate.' What was it? Every time I had a pen in my hand my teachers turn round and goes, 'Get out now'. Me and my friend were marking each other with felt tips. He's got a mark straight across there with blue. I marked him up on the back of his neck and my teacher went mad with me. He never goes mad with him, does he? . . .

So I got – Ruth (cousin) hasn't got no problems, I have?

Right.

Not, not with people I don't mean.

No, I know.

With reading and that . . .

I gave the teacher a look then I'm gone. If she'd asked me I would have been gone and I would have been gone home. I can walk out of school no problem.

Yeah.

And then all they've got to do is just phone my Nan. Yeah. I'm not scared to do that.

And then what happens?

Then I'm grounded.

In these extracts Kate lets us know that she does not like school. It appears that the rules do not make sense to her and the teachers behave irrationally and unfairly without listening to her. She also tells us something of her relationships with her classmates, and introduces her cousin Ruth and her Nan (both of whom she lives with) into the narrative. Towards the end of the extract, Nan is brought in as an alternative authority figure by the teachers, but Kate lets us know that she is not scared of her Nan as she knows the consequences of her Nan's involvement. To Kate, the predictability of her Nan's response to bad behaviour can be seen to contrast with the perceived unpredictability of the teachers in the school. Her cousin's academic ability (this is also mentioned later in the conversation) is contrasted to her own difficulties with reading and writing. But she is careful to assert her identity as someone who can get on with people, and indeed as someone who can stand up to the irrational (to her) rules and methods of the school and the teachers.

By understanding Kate, Keely, Jolene and Nevaeh's talk about school as a series of narratives about themselves and their relationships within the social space of the school, with their carers and with their futures, we escape being boxed in by concerns as to whether their stories about school are accurate or truthful. Our constructions of our identities and life stories are not fixed, but will change over time and according to our audience. Jolene and Nevaeh might have told dramatic stories of everyday school life, like Keely and Ruth, if they were still in the throes of school attendance. Indeed, both remarked at times on how much some of the young participants reminded them of their younger selves. Instead, both of the young adult participants were able to tell more completed and redemptive narratives of schooling that eventually went well and led to better things. Whilst Nevaeh's measurable outcomes do not look totally successful on paper (teenage motherhood, currently unemployed), by looking at how she understands the trajectory of her life we can see a more nuanced picture that includes a sense of having triumphed over adversity. In the next section, we discuss how, in addition to reaching a broader understanding of these young people through their narratives, we can use these narratives to enable the young people to plan for positive change in their lives.

This section has only produced a snapshot of a few of the findings from the study. This small group of participants gave us privileged insights into their narratives of their everyday lives, producing hundreds of photographs, several filmed sequences, and hours of conversation. The final section makes links between this small-scale research study, and everyday practice with looked after young people.

Relevance to practice

There are some excellent larger scale studies that enable us to know something about the general patterns of looked after children's lives (see, for example, Sinclair *et al*, 2007). What small sample, participative, in-depth research studies, such as (Extra)ordinary Lives, do is to explore the individuality of children's lives behind the statistics and generalisations allowing us to take forward the sociological approaches to childhood outlined at the start of this chapter. In this sense, this research is closely aligned to practice, and we believe that there are some implications for practice from the study. Four areas are noted in this conclusion.

- Firstly, that by paying attention to young people's narratives about their lives, we can understand their identities in all their messy complexity and avoid narrow or stereotypical constructions of young people in care.
- Secondly, that by enabling young people to choose how they wish to communicate with us, we recognise them as social actors and begin to move our practice away from adult-centric procedures.
- Thirdly, it is argued that sustained relationships are needed in order to communicate successfully with children and young people in care.
- Lastly, it is suggested that as practitioners we can work with young people's narratives to enable them to plan and achieve positive change in their lives.

The young people in our study, like young people everywhere, are impossible to stereotype. In one sentence they can tell a narrative of hatred for school, and a fierce desire to achieve academically. Their feelings towards their birth families are often a complex mixture of love, loyalty, disdain, anger and indifference. They may present as strong, often tough, in their brushes with authority figures, but at the same time feel confused and upset by rules that appear unfair and arbitrary. By paying attention to the narratives told by young people, we listen to what they choose to tell us, and how they frame themselves and others within the story. This gives some insight into how they see themselves, or at least the "face" they wish to present to the person they are talking to. It gives some indication of their priorities and how they respond to, replicate or perhaps challenge dominant discourses about, for example, childhoods, gendered identities, performing family, being in care, etc. By researching with these young people over a period of time, we have been able to see narratives about their lives unfold, shift and be revised. This approach in communicating with young people, shifts the emphasis away from "truths" about their experiences, or "what they really think" about themselves. It recognises that we do not possess a single static identity or history. It prioritises instead self-perception and understandings of past, present and future as constantly being performed and revised. By applying this approach to practice we can avoid deterministic or narrow descriptions of young people's identities in assessments and reviews, and perhaps avoid alienating those young people who do not recognise themselves in such reviews, and even stop them becoming self-fulfilling.

Many practitioners working with looked after young people are skilled communicators who are able to facilitate in-depth conversations with young people about their everyday lives, needs and aspirations. However, in the context of high case loads and a rapid turnover of staff, interactions between young people and practitioners such as social workers are at risk of becoming formulaic. Pressurised professionals can become overly focused on completing the correct paperwork, such as statutory review or assessment and action forms. Young people can feel that questions are being asked about their lives because of a bureaucratic routine, rather than because the questioner is genuinely curious about how they are. A key aspect of the (Extra)ordinary Lives project was that young people were enabled to choose their own methods to communicate with the researchers about their lives. Whilst not all practitioners have expensive equipment such as digital camcorders to hand, any adult can start a relationship by asking a young person how, where and what they prefer to communicate and, wherever possible, giving the young person some editorial control over how and where personal information is reported. Such an approach embraces the conceptualisation of children as active members of society. It also enables a focus on the young person's everyday life in the present rather than just focusing on outcomes – the adult they will become.

With young people who are looked after, we need to acknowledge that their identities and feelings about their life situation, relationship with their birth families, aspirations and understanding of their history will be constantly shifting over time and in different social settings. Therefore, relationships with young people need to be sustained on an ongoing basis. Brief interventions for assessments, or sporadic visits by social workers, are likely to produce a narrow understanding of young people's lives. McLeod (2007) gives a reflective account of some of the difficulties she encountered when conducting one-off research interviews with looked after young people. These included a reluctance to talk at all, giving very brief responses, a tendency to change the subject and giving responses that appeared to be untrue. She found that these same young people's social workers had similar communication patterns with the young people. One of her conclusions is that relationships need to be ongoing and positive before young people will be prepared to talk to an adult about issues that concern them:

Clearly, achieving a constructive relationship with some teenagers is the work of many months, or even years, and will not easily be achieved in a regime where brief interventions are the norm. (McLeod, 2007, p 285)

At the beginning of our research fieldwork, most of the young people answered our questions briefly and politely. After a period of time they talked in much more depth about their everyday experiences. They were also much less polite! In order to make some sense of young people's social worlds, we must build relationships that are sustained and move beyond the constraints of one-off research interviews or sporadic professional interventions.

Whilst research such as that reported in this chapter has a principal aim of reflecting the narratives of young people, and analysing these in their social and cultural contexts, practitioners need to do more than analyse: they must also provide support and therapeutic and practical help. It has been argued that, by paying attention to people's narratives about their lives, and by viewing these narratives as unfixed and multi-faceted, we can enable people to interrogate, evaluate, disrupt or even overturn their narratives in order to promote positive and creative change (Parton, 2002). By enabling young people to talk about their lives we can allow them to 'control, reframe and move on' (Parton, 2002, p 243). This approach has been developed in the field in the form of solution-focused interventions, narrative therapy and the strengths perspective. These take a collaborative style of working, rather than an 'expert-centric style' (Healy, 2005). The practitioner works alongside the young person to acknowledge their narratives of their lives. Sometimes, by simply listening to and validating their narrative, they may help an individual's (or group or community's) sense of self in the face of negative labelling by other individuals, systems or institutions. At other times, narratives are negative or destructive and the practitioner should attempt to enable a young person to deconstruct their own narratives and re-construct a narrative that opens up a possibility of change (Fook, 2002). Parton and O'Byrne (2000) and Fook (2002, pp 132–141) give many practical examples of how people may be enabled to "restory" their lives, which may involve more than just talk and understanding but also provide a framework for practical action to tackle negative behaviours, material deprivation and social injustices.

Conclusion

This chapter has focused on how recent sociological understandings of children and childhood have relevance to how we understand and communicate with young people who are looked after. It has suggested that "childhood" is socially constructed, that identities are performative and contextual, and that children can be regarded as social actors whose perspectives are important. We should be as interested in children's lives in their own right as in the adults they will become and pay attention to the narratives that young people tell in order to gain a more holistic understanding of their perspectives. These understandings of children and young people enable us to frame our communication with young people in terms of active participation by the young person, a willingness by the adult to listen over a sustained timespan and a broad conceptualisation of what the young person is communicating to us. Where necessary, we can also work with the young people's narratives to enable them to "restory" their lives and plan for positive and practical change.

References

Berridge D. (2006) 'Theory and explanation in child welfare: education and looked-after children', *Child and Family Social Work*, 12:1, pp 1–10

Butler J. (1993) *Bodies That Matter: On the discursive limits of "sex"*, London: Routledge

Chase E., Simon A. and Jackson S. (eds) (2006) *In Care and After: A positive perspective*, London: Routledge

Christensen P. and James A. (eds) (2000) *Research with Children: Perspectives and practices*, London: The Falmer Press

Christensen P. and O'Brien M. (eds) (2003) *Children in the City: Home, neighbourhood and community*, London: Routledge/Falmer

Connolly P. (1998) *Racism, Gender Identities and Young Children*, London: Routledge

Department of Health (1995) *Looking After Children: Planning and review forms and assessment and action records (Revised)*, London: HMSO

Department of Health (2000) *Framework for the Assessment of Children in Need and their Families*, London: Department of Health

Economic and Social Research Council (undated) *An ESRC Research Programme an Children 5–16: Growing into the 21st century* http://www.hull.ac.uk/children5to16programme/intro.htm

Fook J. (2002) *Social Work: Critical theory and practice*, London: Sage

Goffman E. (1959) *The Presentation of Self in Everyday Life*, London: Penguin

Greig A., Taylor J. and Mackay T. (eds)(2007) *Doing Research with Children*, London: Sage

Hadfield L., Lucey H., Mauthner M. and Edwards R. (2006) *Sibling Identity and Relationships (Relationships and Resources)*, London: Routledge

Healey K. (2005) *Social Work Theories in Context*, Basingstoke: Palgrave

Holland S. (2004) *Child and Family Assessment in Social Work Practice*, London: Sage

Holloway S. L. and Valentine G. (2000) *Children's Geographies: Playing, living and learning*, London: Routledge

James A. and James A. L. (2004) *Constructing Childhood*, Basingstoke: Palgrave

James A., Jenks C. and Prout A. (1998) *Theorising Childhood*, Cambridge: Polity

James A. and Prout A. (eds) (1998) *Constructing and Reconstructing Childhood: Contemporary issues in the sociological study of childhood* (2nd edn), London: The Falmer Press

Jenks C. (1992) *The Sociology of Childhood*, Aldershot: Gregg Revivals

Lee N. (2001) *Childhood and Society: Growing up in an age of uncertainty*, Buckingham: Open University Press

Lucey H., Melody J. and Walkerdine V. (2003) 'Uneasy hybrids: psychosocial aspects of becoming educationally successful for working class young women', *Gender and Education*, 15:3, pp 285–300

McLeod A. (2007) 'Whose agenda? Issues of power and relationship when listening to looked-after young people', *Child and Family Social Work*, 12, pp 278–286

Morgan D. (1991) 'Ideologies of marriage and family life', in Clark D (ed) *Marriage, Domestic Life and Social Change*, London: Routledge, pp 114–38

Parton N. (2002) 'Postmodern and constructionist approaches to social work', in Adams R., Dominelli L. and Payne M. (eds) *Social Work: Themes, issues and critical debates*, Basingstoke: Palgrave, pp 237–246

Parton N. and O'Byrne P. (2000) *Constructive Social Work*, Basingstoke: Palgrave

Prout A. (2005) *The Future of Childhood*, London: Routledge/Falmer

Qvortrup J., Brady M., Sgritto G. and Winterberger H. (1994) *Childhood Matters: Social theory, practice and politics*, Aldershot: Avebury Publishing

Renold E. (2005) *Girls, Boys and Junior Sexualities*, London: Routledge/Falmer

Renold E. (forthcoming) '"Marks" of achievement: schooling un/intelligible femininities', in Jackson C., Paechter C. and Renold E. (eds) *Girls and Education 3–16: Continuing concerns, new agendas*, Buckingham: Open University Press

Scott S., Jackson S., and Backett-Milburn K. (1998) 'Swings and roundabouts: risk anxiety and the everyday worlds of children', *Sociology: The Journal of the British Sociological Association*, 32:4, pp 689–705

Scourfield J., Dicks B. Drakeford M. and Davies A. (2006) *Children, Place and Identity: Nation and locality in middle childhood*, London, Routledge

Sinclair I., Baker C., Lee J., Gibbs I. and Stein M. (2007) *The Pursuit of Permanence: A study of the English child care system*, London: Jessica Kingsley

Stainton-Rogers R. and Stainton-Rogers W. (1992) *Stories of Childhood: Shifting agendas for child concern*, Hertfordshire: Harvester-Wheatsheaf

Valentine G. (1996) 'Angel and devils: moral landscapes of childhood', *Environment and Planning D: Society and Space*, 14, pp 581–599

Walkerdine V. (2004) 'Developmental psychology and the study of childhood', in Kehily M. J. (ed) *An Introduction to Childhood Studies*, Buckingham: Open University Press

Winter K. (2006) 'Widening our knowledge concerning young looked after children: the case for research using sociological models of childhood', *Child and Family Social Work*, 11, pp 55–64

Woodhead M. and Faulkner D. (2000) 'Subjects, objects or participants? Dilemmas of psychological research with children', in Christensen P. and James A. (eds) *Research with Children: Perspectives and practices*, London: Falmer, pp 9–35

Section 3

Approaches to communication and engagement

6 Consultation and advocacy

Nigel Thomas

Introduction – children as consumers, children as citizens

The focus of this chapter is on ways in which social workers can enable children and young people to participate effectively in decisions about their lives in care, both informally and formally, as individuals and also in groups.

The approach one takes to this work is strongly influenced by how one sees children and young people. If we see them primarily as needy or problematic, then we are likely to work with them in ways that reinforce their dependence and powerlessness. If, on the other hand, we see children as resourceful, then we are more likely to be open to the different ways in which they can contribute to the working relationship we have with them. Moss *et al* (2000) counterpose the 'child in need' to the 'rich child', using the example of early years services developed in Reggio Emilia, Northern Italy, where a conception of the child as rich and resourceful is fundamental to practice.

In terms of their relationship to the care system, there are, I suggest, three distinct ways of seeing children and young people. The first is as *recipients of care*. From this viewpoint, children are the objects of our intervention, and the aim is to care for them, to meet their needs as we assess those needs, and to ensure their optimal development. The second is as *consumers of a service*. From this viewpoint, children are our customers, and we are accountable to them (along with their parents) for the quality of the service we provide. The third is as *citizens*. From this viewpoint, children are participants in the care system and in their living situation, with corresponding rights.

All three viewpoints are valid, and need to form part of our overall perspective. Children and young people do have needs which must be properly assessed and met, in order to assure their welfare in the present and to maximise their life chances in the future. They are indeed consumers of a service, entitled to proper choice, good value and a mechanism for making complaints and suggestions. However, we must never forget that they are also citizens with rights, both in general as members of a democratic community (although currently without the right to vote) and in particular as the people who are actually living in foster homes and children's homes, with the right to participate in decisions about their lives. These rights are clearly set out in the United Nations Convention on the Rights of the Child, and also in the Universal Declaration of Human Rights, which applies to children as much as to anyone else. The approach we take to issues of consultation and advocacy must therefore recognise children and young people as citizens, not only as consumers of services and recipients of care.

There is a wide range of contexts in which children and young people may participate in decisions about their lives in care. There is the everyday decision-making that takes place in children's daily lives in the home and elsewhere – from what to wear, what to eat, or what time to go to bed, to decisions about after-school activities, going on holiday or moving house. There is the decision-making that takes place in formal planning meetings or care reviews, and in and around the courts. There are also formal and informal processes for complaints and representations. Finally, there are wider processes of decision-making – collective decision-making in group care, and more general processes of policy making and service planning. My aim in this chapter is to consider what makes for effective consultation and advocacy in each of these different contexts.

There is also a range of different ways in which children and young people may be consulted or included in processes of decision-making. These include various kinds of *informal engagement* through conversation, play or shared activity, as well as inclusion in *formal processes* either directly or through an intermediary. Children and young people may also be offered informal support with the formal processes. *Advocacy* may be provided either by professional advocates or by other people working with children. Finally, children and young people may be included on an *organised* basis through groups or representatives.

In this chapter, I try to set out some helpful ways of thinking about these different methods and contexts of consultation and advocacy, by looking in turn at informal engagement, formal decision-making processes, advocacy, complaints and representation, collective decision-making, and policy and service planning. In each case I try to identify what constitutes good practice in this area, drawing on research and on direct experience of different kinds of work with children and young people in the care system. In the process I also look at some issues that can be challenging for practitioners in this aspect of work with children and young people.

The examples given later in this chapter are based on actual cases worked with by an advocacy organisation in Wales. They are chosen to illustrate some of the situations in which an independent advocate can help to move things forward for a child.

Informal engagement – establishing a dialogue

Informal engagement is the bedrock of consultation and advocacy practice with children and young people in care. However important rights-based approaches and formal systems may be, in the end the child's experience of consultation and advocacy depends crucially on the quality of communication that takes place in their relationships with social workers, carers and other adults directly involved with them. Other chapters in this book offer a wealth of insights into how to make these informal relationships work well for children and young people. My purpose here is to show some of the ways in which good practice in using relationships and in communicating effectively with children and young people can support their rights to consultation and advocacy.

That all children and young people are different is a truism. Children in care come from a wide variety of backgrounds and have very different personalities. In addition, of course, they bring with them a variety of experiences, some very exceptional and often distressing for themselves and those working with them. All these factors will have an impact on the relationships they make, on how they communicate, and on their expectations and preferences.

Children and young people may have varying attitudes to the issue of participation in decision-making. Some may be very keen to be involved, whilst others are more diffident or reluctant. Research has identified the following distinct positions:

- "Assertive" – expecting to have a say in decisions;
- "Dissatisfied" – believing that children should have more say than they do;
- "Submissive" – taking the line that adults know best;
- "Reasonable" – expect to be heard, but think adults should make decisions;
- "Avoidant" – children who find decision-making with adults difficult.

(Thomas and O'Kane, 1999; Thomas, 2002)

Some children may find it easier to engage in everyday decisions than to be involved in the more formal processes of decision-making that children in care are subject to, but there is evidence that successful engagement in everyday decisions can be a good foundation for taking part in the more formal processes. Of course, children looked after are usually living in a family home where there may already be established routines, or in a residential establishment with existing rules and rotas. These situations demand a degree of flexibility on the part of adult carers, in order to maximise the opportunities children have for exerting some control over their lives.

Adults' attitudes vary too, and this can be crucially important to children's opportunities to participate. In research these have been characterised in the following terms:

- "Clinical" – this approach focuses on the child as in need of treatment, and children may be excluded on the basis that they are not emotionally "ready" or might make a bad decision; on the other hand, sensitive work to engage children can also come from this approach.
- "Bureaucratic" – this approach centres on fulfilling organisational and procedural requirements in relation to decision-making, which may leave little space for effective children's participation or sensitive communication with children.
- "Value-based" – this approach regards children's involvement in decisions as a positive good in itself, either because it is a right or because it leads to better decisions.

- "Cynical" – this approach assumes that children have too much say and are irresponsible or manipulative.

(Welsby, 1996; Thomas and O'Kane, 1999)

Butler and Williamson (1994) suggest that the ability of adults to engage with children and enable them to talk about sensitive matters depends on a number of factors, including aspects of personal style. The most important factors they identified in their research with children were *willingness to listen, availability*, a *non-judgemental and non-directive* approach, *humour, straight talking* and *trust and confidentiality*. They also found that children tended to talk to friends when they wanted to "unload" and to trusted adults when they wanted advice, information or action. However, many children said that they didn't really confide in anyone, perhaps illustrating that one cannot take communication for granted.

Who one is may sometimes matter as much as *what* one does. Depending on the experiences and the expectations they bring to an encounter, some children may only feel comfortable in opening up to a worker of a particular gender or ethnic background. Children and young people may also latch onto a particular person for all kinds of reasons, some of which may not be immediately apparent. The trusted adult referred to by Butler and Williamson would typically be a particular person – most often "Mum", but it could be someone else. A particular foster carer, teacher or youth worker may elicit a response where others fail. The most important thing is that someone should be communicating with the child or young person about their wishes and feelings, and that the responsible social worker should – whether directly or indirectly – be linked into this process.

In the end, the responsibility of the social worker, and of all those working with a child or young person, is to establish a dialogue so that the child can play a full part in all important decisions in her or his life – both the little ones and the big ones. For different children the starting point of this process will be different, and so also may be the destination; but the journey is broadly the same. The skills needed are at bottom the skills of open and empathic communication needed for all social work practice, and a willingness to adapt to different needs and communicative styles in order to facilitate this. For example, when working with some disabled children where there are significant barriers to communication, a starting point of asking: 'How am I going to communicate with this young person in order to establish her wishes and feelings?' is clearly more productive than assuming that: 'This person cannot communicate with her wishes and feelings effectively'.

The following list, based on research with children in care, offers one way to remember some of the key points about communicating with children and young people.

"TRANSACTS"

- *Time* – it is essential to have enough time to spend with a child; they do not necessarily want to talk by appointment. Time also means working at the child's pace, allowing them to stay in control.
- *Relationship, trust and honesty* – children communicate best with people with whom they have relationships of warmth and trust. It is important to be friendly and open, empathic and above all "straight" with children.
- *Active listening* – the skills of "active listening" developed in counselling can be helpful in work with children. This means responding to cues, restating and drawing out the meaning of what the child is saying, combined with the expression of warmth, empathy and acceptance.
- *Non-verbal communication* – an adult's tone of voice, facial expression, body language and even style of dress can affect how children communicate.
- *Support and encouragement* – children need support and active encouragement to speak up, especially when they have something difficult or negative to express. An adult may sometimes need to offer to express a child's views for them. Children don't like it when they feel they are being judged or criticised, and they don't like to be put "on the spot".
- *Activities* – many children find it very boring to "just sit and talk". Games, writing, drawing and other activities can be used to make the process more interesting. Life story work can be an excellent way to involve children in reflecting on their situation.
- *Choice, information and preparation* – children must have a choice about whether and how they participate in a decision-making process. They are more able to have their say if they have been prepared for the discussion and given time to think about things beforehand.
- *The child's agenda* – it is important to give children space to talk about issues that concern them, rather than just having to respond to adults' questions.
- *Serious fun!* – the fact that serious matters are being discussed doesn't mean that everyone has to be po-faced. Most children find this alienating; some find it threatening. If decision-making processes can be made more enjoyable, children are more likely to get involved.

(Thomas, 2005a, based on Thomas and O'Kane, 1998a)

Formal decision-making – ensuring a real and effective say

I like meetings because I get to say what I want to say and they get to know what my views are. (Thomas, 2002, p 148)

We want to change the way reviews are done. I mean it's your home, you don't want a load of random strangers sitting in your front room. (Voice for the Child in Care, 2004, p 51)

It is now well established in law and good practice that children must be consulted about the arrangements for their care and, implicitly if not explicitly, that they have a *right* to a say. In England and Wales this expectation began with the Children Act 1975, which gave local authorities the duty to consider the wishes and feelings of a child provided with care by them. The duty was substantially extended by the Children Act 1989, so that it applied to local authority and court decision-making processes both before and after a child came into care or accommodation. Subsequent regulations and guidance have emphasised further the importance of including children in the planning and review of their care, and under section 53 of the Children Act 2004 the duty to consider a child's wishes and feelings has been extended both to the provision of services for children in need and to the investigation of harm. As for children facing adoption proceedings, a requirement to consider the child's wishes and feelings was included in the Adoption Act 1976 and further extended in the Adoption and Children Act 2002. Similar legislation applies in Scotland and Northern Ireland.

These requirements mean that there is a significant difference in the status of children who are looked after when compared to the rest of the child population. In general, children in England and Wales do not have the legal right to a say in decisions made by their parents, nor do their parents have a duty to consider their wishes and feelings, unlike Scotland, where parents do have a limited legal obligation to consider children's views. Other salient differences in the situation of looked after children are that there are likely to be more adults involved in decisions about their lives, and that many of the decision-making processes are relatively formal, for instance, meetings with agendas, minutes and rules of procedure. The challenge is to include children in these decision-making processes in a way that does not overawe, alienate or bore them, and that at the same time protects their right to make a real and effective contribution to decisions.

Research some years ago showed that growing numbers of children were attending meetings to discuss their care, and in some cases taking an active part in discussions, but that they found the meetings often boring and sometimes intrusive or uncomfortable (Grimshaw and Sinclair, 1997; Thomas, 2002). Several factors appear to affect the quality of children's participation, in particular:

- how well prepared they are to take part in the process;
- how much information they have about the context in which decisions are to be made;
- how well supported they are in voicing their opinions.

The latter support might come from a social worker, key worker or foster carer who is involved in the meeting as a participant. In many cases the child will be entirely comfortable with this. On the other hand, it can be difficult for both parties if they have different views, and an independent source of support should be offered to any child who is likely to need it. This may include advocacy, which I discuss further in the next section. Guidance originally issued under the Children Act 1989 urged that 'The possibility of a child being accompanied to a review meeting by a person who is able to provide friendly support should be considered' (Department of Health, 1991, p 83).

A comparison of child care managers' perceptions of children's participation in decision-making in care, conducted in 1997 and repeated in 2004, suggested that there had been a degree of change in the culture, with more creative thinking about how to include children (Thomas, 2005b). However, the report of the Blueprint Project showed that children's dissatisfaction with review meetings was largely unchanged from the research conducted a decade earlier:

> *Children and young people have said that they feel they are not involved in the conversation at reviews, it goes on around them, and is about them but it doesn't engage them. They often feel they are talked about in a negative way. They hear things they are unprepared for from people who they had previously trusted. There are too many people in the room and they don't have enough of a say about who attends.*
> (Voice for the Child in Care, 2004, p 51)

For children to be fully involved in the process, it has to be one with which they feel comfortable. This has implications for what happens before and after decision-making meetings; it is arguable that, when looked at in terms of the quality of the child's experience of participation, any meeting is only as good as the work that precedes it. The "TRANSACTS" list above of key points for communication with children and young people applies equally to these formal processes as it does to informal engagement. Making children comfortable also has implications for how the meetings themselves are organised. Here, *flexibility* is the watchword – participants and managers must be prepared to adapt the process to make it responsive to the ways in which children like to communicate, and in particular to the needs of individual children. One social worker, searching for a more natural setting in which to make decisions, something closer to ordinary family life, suggested to a researcher: 'Have the meeting around the kitchen table . . . at ten past eight in the morning over dippy eggs and orange juice!' (Thomas, 2002, p 162)

Suppose that all goes well, and that a child is well prepared to participate in a key decision-making meeting, has the information she or he needs and feels comfortable and supported in expressing their views. The critical questions then are:

- what kind of dialogue is able to take place?
- who has the final say if decisions are contested?
- how much weight is to be given to the child's views, especially if they do not accord with those of key adults?

Clearly, the aim of including children in important decisions about their lives, in partnership with the adults who have responsibility for their welfare, should be to create space for a dialogue in which all those involved, including the child, have the opportunity to express their own views and hear the views of others, before coming to a conclusion which ideally is one that everyone can agree with, or at least that everyone can understand and support. Hoggan (1991, p 31) suggests that 'we need to ensure that our motive is to open up real dialogue between adults and children, rather than to persuade children to accept our adult decisions'. Roche (1995, pp 286–7) argues that dialogue depends in part on 'no longer seeing the relationships that children have with significant adults as naturally and necessarily hierarchic'. If discussions are approached in this spirit, then in many cases differences of opinion can be overcome.

As Schofield and Thoburn (1996) have shown, good practice does not seek to "balance" the child's wishes and feelings against her or his best interests, so much as to bring the two together. For one thing, it is in a child's interests to have his or her wishes and feelings considered. For another, a decision based on considering a child's wishes and feelings is likely to be a better decision, both because the child will probably be more committed to it, and because the child may well have a very sound sense of what is likely to work out.

Nevertheless, however well the process is managed, and however open participants are to genuine dialogue, there will be occasions when they differ on important issues. In practice, this often arises over issues to do with return home or contact with parents, where a child's desire to be with her or his family clashes with a social worker's concern that this may involve risk or distress, or impede alternative planning (see Thomas and O'Kane, 1998b; also Munro, 2001). Sometimes, it is necessary for adults with responsibility for a child's long-term welfare to be quite firm in saying how things have to be. On other occasions, however, good practice consists of trusting the child's judgement, even if this means taking a risk. There are few decisions in child care planning that offer total certainty of a desirable outcome – more often it is a matter of weighing up different kinds of uncertainty.

It is also important to have clear arrangements for monitoring decisions and actions. Often it is not possible to be sure that a plan is the right one until it has been tried and tested. A clear, open and accessible review process, in which the child remains fully involved, is of critical importance here.

Example 1: Dawn

Dawn is nine years old and lives at home with her mother and older sibling. Dawn contacts Voices From Care for advice and support as she fears that social services are planning to take her into care. Social services are saying that Dawn's mother is emotionally and psychologically harming Dawn, by making Dawn think she is unwell when she is not and by exaggerating any minor illness that Dawn has. Dawn has missed several months of school. It is difficult for Dawn's mother to work with social services, and Dawn will not engage with the social worker because of her fears of being removed from home. Voices From Care are able to work with Dawn to explain social services' concerns, to explain to Dawn what is going on and the jargon being used. Voices From Care listen to Dawn's views on life at home and convey these to the social worker, encourage Dawn to speak directly to the social worker, and inform her of her rights. Social services undertake an assessment of Dawn and her family, to which Dawn is able to contribute with support from Voices From Care. Dawn is not registered on the child protection register, but social services offer time-limited services to Dawn and her family. Voices From Care maintain contact with Dawn.

Advocacy – speaking up and getting people to listen

Advocacy is about enabling a child or young person to speak for her/himself, or speaking for a child or young person. The term advocacy is commonly used to refer to the practice of representing a child or young person, of providing them with advice and support, and of conveying their needs and wishes to the appropriate local authority. The majority of children and young people we spoke to understood advocacy to mean, or involve, speaking up for someone, understanding, talking and making other people listen and consider their views. It was frequently described as helping, and the words "important" and "powerful" were used often. (Children's Commissioner for Wales, 2003, p 69)

As Oliver (2003) points out in her review of advocacy for children and young people, advocacy can also be for groups of children and young people – indeed, collective advocacy is central to the role of someone like the Children's Commissioner for Wales. However, in recent years there has been a growing emphasis on the role of advocates in supporting individual service users – not just children, but adults with learning disabilities too – to express their views and have them considered.

Although there appears to be a degree of shared understanding of what advocacy means, in general terms at least, it can take a number of distinct forms. Oliver found four principal models of advocacy in theory and practice:

- *professional advocacy* by someone paid and trained for the purpose;
- *citizen advocacy* by a volunteer;

- *self-advocacy* where someone is enabled to speak up for themselves; and
- *peer advocacy* by someone who shares a similar experience.

Of course, we should all be advocates for children and young people with whom we are working, with a responsibility to speak up for their interests and help them to give voice to their wishes. It is arguable that this is, in fact, one of the most important tasks for a social worker with a child in care. However, children also may need someone who is there solely for this purpose, with no other responsibilities. This may be a friend, or it may be an advocate provided by an advocacy service, sometimes in conjunction with an independent visitor service. Comments by Armstrong (2006) suggest that the Government regards independent visitors as equivalent to advocates, although others would argue that there are important differences. Such services exist in most parts of the UK, most often commissioned by local authorities from the voluntary sector. Although there is no statutory requirement to provide advocacy services, government policy in England and Wales since at least 2002 has been to encourage all local authorities to ensure that every child who is looked after or in need has access to an independent advocate, and national standards make clear what is expected of an advocacy service (Department of Health, 2002; Welsh Assembly Government, 2003). These include the following core principles.

- Advocates should work for children and young people and no one else.
- Advocates should value and respect children and young people as individuals and challenge all types of unlawful discrimination.
- Advocates should work to make sure that children and young people in care can understand what is happening to them, can make their views known and, where possible, exercise choice when decisions about them are being made.
- Advocates should help children and young people to raise issues and concerns about things they are unhappy about. This includes making informal and formal complaints under section 26 of the Children Act 1989.

(Department of Health, 2002, p 2)

Example 2: Bethan and Richard

Bethan, aged 10, and Richard, aged 11, are siblings and have lived with the same foster carer for five years. The local authority has concerns over the care the foster carer is able to provide, especially as Bethan and Richard are approaching their teenage years.

The local authority undertakes an assessment of the foster placement, which causes Bethan and Richard to feel highly anxious. Voices From Care provides advice and support to reassure Bethan and Richard and to explain to them procedures which will need to be gone through before any decisions regarding the placement can be made.

Voices From Care supports Bethan and Richard to express their views as part of the assessment and explains what further actions they may be able to take if they are dissatisfied with the outcome of the assessment. Voices From Care offers consistent, general befriending at this uncertain time.

For a social worker, working with an independent advocate can be challenging, especially if the advocate asserts on behalf of the child a point of view that is at odds with the social worker's view of what is in the child's best interests. The advocate is not there to make life comfortable for the social worker or for the local authority, but to ensure that the child's own views are articulated effectively and to help the child engage in dialogue with the authority and those responsible for providing care. As Dalrymple (1995, p 111) puts it, an advocate does not work from a *best interests* perspective but from a *rights* perspective, and 'from the young person's definition of the problem'. She also argues forcefully that for advocates to be trusted by children and young people, and to be able to empower them in a world dominated by adults, they must be able to ensure children of confidentiality – which may also present a problem for social workers and agencies where child protection policies and concerns tend to discount children's right to keep things confidential (Dalrymple, 2001).

Dalrymple's research has shown that, for most children and young people, their advocate is at the same time a friend – 'someone who knows you and your problems', 'she'll always be a friend for me' – and a source of strength – 'having an advocate in the room meant I felt I could [influence things] and I wasn't taking the whole lot on my own' (2005, pp 7–8). However, far from seeing the advocate as the only person who is speaking up for the child, Dalrymple argues that we should 'promote a culture of advocacy', so that all adults involved in the lives of young people understand and are committed to the ideas and values which underlie the practice of advocacy (2005, p 12). The role of being a friend and support for the child, and helping her to speak up for herself, should not be a strange one for a social worker or for a carer – rather, these are key elements in any helping relationship.

On the other hand, experience in practice shows that there can be real limits on the ability of a social worker – or a foster carer, or a birth parent – to offer genuine advocacy to a child in many situations. For Dawn (Example 1), the social worker could not be an advocate because of Dawn's anxiety about working with social services. It often appears, for instance, with issues around placement moves, contact with birth family, or a move into independent accommodation, that the child's view may clash directly with the views of key adults about what is in the child's best interests. Young people often understand this, and may be reluctant to rely on a social worker to be their advocate for these reasons.

In other cases adults may, whether intentionally or not, influence the views the child is able to express unless there is real independent support. Additional difficulties can arise where more than one child is involved in a decision. In the case of Bethan and Richard

(Example 2), there might well be conflict between the interests of brother and sister, and it could be difficult for a family social worker to represent both fairly. In such a situation the contribution of one or more independent advocates may be vital.

Example 3: Alem

Alem is 11 and has lived in a children's home for eight months. He would really like to return home to live with his mother. This is not possible at the moment because of his mother's mental health problems and Alem's recent aggressive behaviour. Voices From Care helps Alem to attend a review meeting to express his wishes and to take part in the discussion about the changes that need to be made before Alem can return home.

As Alem is only 11 years old, it is generally considered unacceptable for him to remain indefinitely in residential care. It is decided that Alem should move into foster care, once a suitable placement is found.

Voices From Care supports Alem to express his views about what kind of foster placement he needs. Advice and support workers help Alem to make sure social workers understand how important it is to him to have frequent, regular contact with his mother. Voices From Care will attend future meetings with Alem and discuss with him his move into foster care and ensure his views are taken into consideration.

Complaints and representations – encouraging feedback and being ready to "blow the whistle"

One measure of the way in which children are increasingly accepted as consumers with rights, if not as citizens, is that children in receipt of services under legislation such as the Children Act 1989 are entitled to make complaints and representations, and to have them heard and responded to. The case of Alem (Example 3) is a good example of one where a complaint or representation might easily arise.

Despite this legal right, it is not easy for a child in care, who may feel very powerless, to bring a complaint, and this is one situation where an advocate is likely to be needed. As well as helping the child to speak up, an advocate may also need to assist the child through complex bureaucratic processes – to write letters, follow up responses, and so on.

A formal complaint can also be challenging for the social worker working with a child, especially if the complaint is about the service for which they are responsible or even about them personally. One naturally feels defensive, and this can make it difficult to respond constructively. Support from colleagues and managers is helpful, but not in a way that means "closing ranks" and denying the validity of the child's viewpoint.

There are two views of complaints in an organisation. One is that any complaint is a failure, and that in a well-run organisation formal complaints do not arise. The other, more productive view, is that complaints are an important part of the feedback process. Taking this view, a certain level of complaints is an indicator of health, while an absence of complaints probably indicates that clients are insufficiently aware of their rights. This view is implicit in the Children Act 1989 and in regulations under the Children (Scotland) Act 1995, both of which refer to "representations" as well as complaints. In other words, children may not only complain about things that are wrong, but ask for things to be done better – or differently.

When children do not have an effective and accessible outlet for complaints and concerns, the consequences can be appalling. The report into the abuse of children in care in North Wales concluded that the lack of complaints procedures, and the institutional discouragement of complaints not only by children but also by staff, were foremost among the failures in practice that allowed sexual and physical abuse to continue for year after year (Waterhouse, 2000). It was this report that provided the political impetus for creating the post of Children's Commissioner for Wales in 2000; by 2005, all five countries in the British Isles had similar appointments. The findings of Waterhouse and similar reports also have profound implications for practitioners. The most important implication is the need to remain open to what the child is saying, either verbally or in other ways, not to dismiss or overlook it, even when it is inconvenient or difficult to address, and to share concerns with colleagues and with managers. If a "culture of advocacy" means anything, it must include a readiness to "blow the whistle".

Policy and service planning – enabling a collective voice for children

Most of our attention so far in this chapter (and indeed in most of the book) has been focused on individual decision-making. If children and young people are citizens, then they also have rights to take part in collective decision-making processes, in relation to the services provided to them currently and planned for the future.

In recent years, a great deal of work has been done to create opportunities for children to be consulted about service policy and planning. Statutory arrangements for joint planning of services to children and families increasingly require that consultation with service users, or potential service users, is part of the process. For example, the Children and Young People's Plan (England) Regulations 2005 require the local authority to consult 'such children, relevant young persons and families . . . as the authority consider appropriate' and 'such persons or bodies representing children, relevant young persons or families as the authority consider appropriate' (regulation 7). Many local authorities have taken initiatives to bring young citizens together to engage in dialogue about their needs and how they can be met effectively. Striking examples include the work of the "Investing in Children" initiative in County Durham, which works to engage different groups of children, including looked after children and care leavers, in dialogue with decision-makers (Cairns and Brannen, 2005). For organisations wishing to engage more fully in participation, the "pathways to participation" model offered by Shier (2001) can be useful.

Some agencies have tried to create groups or networks of young people in care and to support them in meeting on a regular basis. This work has its own challenges, some of them practical. For children in group care, meeting together happens naturally and it may not be too difficult to share ideas and contribute to collective decision-making, especially if adults are receptive to this. For the majority of children in foster families, however, this kind of network can be more difficult to initiate and to sustain. However, there are instances of good practice in this area (see Examples 4 and 5).

Example 4: The Blueprint forum

The forum is a group of young people who have experience of being in care. The forum is our chance to have a say about what it's like to be in care and what can be done to make things better. The forum is a chance to learn about your rights and campaign on the issues that affect your lives. The forum gives young people an opportunity to have YOUR SAY. There is no set plan – the forum members decide what the agenda should be.

This is the mission statement of a group organised by the NSPCC in the local authority of Rhondda Cynon Taff. The forum started in the late 1990s, and works with young people aged 14–21 from residential and foster homes. Up to 15 attend each monthly meeting. Numbers have to be limited because of rules about staff ratios and the problem of transport, but the organisers would like to extend the service to younger children. Young people hear about the forum from their social workers.

The project aims to:

- empower young people by developing their capacity to participate;
- be a point of support for young people who have experience of the care system;
- provide a relaxed and social environment with a good dose of fun;
- provide an opportunity to discuss and share experiences;
- inform and influence policy and practice, locally and nationally.

Examples of the work of the forum include:

- contributing to a review of residential care;
- helping in recruitment of social work students;
- developing policies on bullying;
- advising other areas on setting up similar groups.

Example 5: The FCA Young People's Forum

This forum is run by the South Wales branch of Foster Care Associates, an independent agency providing foster care across the UK. It meets in each school holiday, currently attracts about 18 children and young people to each meeting, and is growing.

The forum is open to all children over nine placed with the agency, who are individually invited by letter to join the group, with follow-up from social workers. The group mixes work with fun, and has had a measurable impact on agency policy. For example, a workshop identifying issues of concern within the group led to a meeting with the director and a change in policy for respite care. Each year the group sends delegates to a UK-wide conference of children placed with the agency.

In bureaucratic organisations, the results of children and young people's participation in service planning may not be seen immediately. Changes may take time to implement, and the process may not be straightforward. This means that it is important to engage children throughout the process, to give feedback on their proposals, and to develop cyclical processes of dialogue rather than one-off or one-way consultations. When this is done well, young people's input can have a real impact. For instance, for years most, if not all, local authorities insisted on police checks for any overnight stay by a young person in care with their friends. Now, largely as a result of the dissatisfaction expressed by young people with this policy, it is common to allow short sleepovers to take place at the carers' discretion (Thomas and O'Kane, 1998c).

In Wales, the National Standards of Participation, developed by a consortium of children's organisations and endorsed by the Welsh Assembly Government, provide a clear and accessible statement of the principles on which this kind of work should be based if it is to command the confidence of children and young people (Children and Young People's Participation Consortium for Wales, 2006).

Conclusion – ideas for practice

In all these areas of practice, the challenge ultimately is to create and facilitate spaces where children and young people can engage in thinking about their care, and where necessary assert their views with confidence, both in respect of their individual lives and on a collective basis in relation to wider issues of service provision. Children are experts on their own lives; decisions and plans that make use of their knowledge, experience and judgement are better informed and more likely to be successful. Children are also citizens with rights, and when we provide them with care we should do so in a way that respects their rights and gives them real opportunities to challenge our policy and practice. This is not always easy, especially when we also have obligations to protect them and when we work in organisations that are not always good at supporting direct work with children or at empowering social workers to work creatively.

Help and ideas are available from a number of organisations with a growing experience of working with looked after children and care leavers in a rights-based way – such as Voice (formerly Voice for the Child in Care), Voices from Care Cymru, and The Who Cares? Trust (see below for addresses). For those interested in reading further, a very useful summary of research evidence in relation to young people's participation was produced by Research in Practice as part of the *Quality Protects* initiative (Sinclair and Franklin, 2000). The two volumes produced by Kirby and colleagues (2003) for the DfES are a very helpful resource. For international developments in children's participation, there is a good recent review in Lansdown (2006).

Acknowledgements
Many thanks to Carol Floris of Voices from Care Cymru for her ideas and suggestions and for the three case examples. Thanks also to Fiona Stevens of NSPCC/Blueprint and Helen Burt of Foster Care Associates.

Websites

Voice	www.voiceyp.org
Voices from Care Cymru	www.voicesfromcarecymru.org.uk
The Who Cares? Trust	www.thewhocarestrust.org.uk

References

Armstrong H. (2006) *Speech by Minister for the Cabinet Office and Social Exclusion at Conference on Advocacy for Looked After Children and Children in Need* (www.cabinetoffice.gov.uk/about_ the_cabinet_office/speeches/armstrong/pdf/advocacy.pdf, accessed 11/03/2007)

Butler I. and Williamson H. (1994) *Children Speak: Children, trauma and social Work*, Harlow: Longman

Cairns L. and Brannen M. (2005) 'Promoting the human rights of children and young people: the "Investing in Children" experience', *Adoption & Fostering*, 29:1, pp 78–87

Children and Young People's Participation Consortium for Wales (2006) *'Do we meet your standards?' National Children and Young People's Participation Standards*, new.wales.gov.uk/ docrepos/40382/4038232/403829/403829/1295328/nat-standards-young-people-1.pdf?lang=en (accessed 15/4/07)

Children's Commissioner for Wales (2003) *Telling Concerns: Report of the Children's Commissioner for Wales' review of the operation of complaints and representations and whistleblowing procedures and arrangements for the provision of Children's Advocacy Services*, Swansea: Children's Commissioner for Wales

Dalrymple J. (1995) 'It's not as easy as you think! Dilemmas and advocacy', in Dalrymple J. and Hough J. (eds) *Having a Voice: An exploration of children's rights and advocacy*, Birmingham: Venture Press

Dalrymple J. (2001) 'Safeguarding young people through confidential advocacy services', *Child & Family Social Work*, 6:2, pp 149–160

Dalrymple J. (2005) 'Constructions of child and youth advocacy: emerging issues in advocacy practice', *Children & Society*, 19:1, pp 3–15

Department of Health (1991) *The Children Act 1989 Guidance and Regulations Volume 3: Family Placements*, London: HMSO

Department of Health (2002) *National Standards for the Provision of Children's Advocacy Services*, London: Department of Health

Grimshaw R. and Sinclair R. (1997) *Planning to Care: Regulation, procedure and practice under the Children Act 1989*, London: National Children's Bureau

Hoggan P. (1991) 'The role of children in permanency planning', *Adoption & Fostering*, 14:4, pp 31–34

Kirby P., Lanyon C., Cronin K. and Sinclair R. (2003) *Building a Culture of Participation: Involving children and young people in policy, service planning, delivery and evaluation (Handbook)*, London: Department for Education and Skills

Kirby P., Lanyon C., Cronin K. and Sinclair R. (2003) *Building a Culture of Participation: Involving children and young people in policy, service planning, delivery and evaluation (Research Report)*, London: Department for Education and Skills

Lansdown G. (2006) 'International developments in children's participation: lessons and challenges', in Tisdall K., Davis J., Hill M. and Prout A. (eds) *Children, Young People and Social Exclusion*, Bristol: Policy Press

Moss P., Dillon J. and Statham J. (2000) 'The "child in need" and the "rich child": discourses, constructions and practice', *Critical Social Policy*, 20:2, pp 233–254

Munro E. (2001) 'Empowering looked after children', *Child and Family Social Work*, 6:2, pp 129–138

Oliver C. (2003) *Advocacy for Children and Young People: A review*, London: Institute of Education

Roche J. (1995) 'Children's rights: in the name of the child', *Journal of Social Welfare and Family Law*, 17:3, pp 281–300

Schofield G. and Thoburn J. (1996) *Child Protection: The voice of the child in decision making*, London: IPPR

Shier H. (2001) 'Pathways to participation: openings, opportunities and obligations', *Children & Society*, 15:2, pp 107–117

Sinclair R. and Franklin A. (2000) *Quality Protects Research Briefing No 3: Young People's Participation*, Dartington: Research in Practice (available at www.rip.org.uk/publications/documents/QPB/QPRB3.asp)

Thomas N. (2002) *Children, Family and the State: Decision-making and child participation*, Bristol: Policy Press

Thomas N. (2005a) *Social Work with Young People in Care: Looking after children in theory and practice*, Basingstoke: Palgrave Macmillan

Thomas N. (2005b) 'Has anything really changed? Managers' views of looked after children's participation in 1997 and 2004', *Adoption & Fostering*, 29:1, pp 67–77

Thomas N. and O'Kane C. (1998a) *Children and Decision Making: A summary report*, Swansea: University of Wales Swansea, International Centre for Childhood Studies

Thomas N. and O'Kane C. (1998b) 'When children's wishes and feelings clash with their "best interests"', *International Journal of Children's Rights*, 6:2, pp 137–154

Thomas N. and O'Kane C. (1998c) 'Why can't I stay with my friends?', *Community Care*, 19 December

Thomas N. and O'Kane C. (1999) 'Children's experiences of decision making in middle childhood', *Childhood*, 6:3, pp 369–387

Voice for the Child in Care (2004) *Start with the Child, Stay with the Child: A blueprint for a child-centred approach to children and young people in public care*, London: Voice for the Child in Care

Waterhouse R. (2000) *Lost in Care: Report of the Tribunal of Inquiry into the abuse of children in care in the former county council areas of Gwynedd and Clwyd since 1974*, London: The Stationery Office

Welsby J. (1996) 'A voice in their own lives', in De Boer W. (ed.) *Children's Rights in Residential Care in International Perspective*, Amsterdam: Defence for Children International

Welsh Assembly Government (2003) *National Standards for the Provision of Children's Advocacy Services*, Cardiff: Welsh Assembly Government (www.childrenfirst.wales.gov.uk/documents/advocacy-standards-e.pdf)

7 The power of the gaze: observation and its role in direct practice with children in care

Danielle Turney

Introduction

The exploration of underpinning capabilities and skills for direct practice in fostering, adoption and residential care has been the theme of this section of the book. This chapter focuses on *observation* and considers what it can contribute to effective and empowering work with children and young people in care. Allocating a chapter to the meaning and use of observation suggests that what is being considered here is something more than just a commonsense idea of looking and seeing. So the first part of the chapter gives an account of the particular approach to observation that is being discussed here before going on, in the second part, to pose the basic question: why observe children?

The third part considers how the skills and understanding that observation promotes can be used to enhance everyday practice in fostering, adoption and residential care; the focus is on the nature and importance of the "observer stance" as a basis for communication and direct work with children and young people who are living away from their families of origin and as a framework for reflective practice. The final section looks at the relationship between observation and anti-oppressive practice, paying particular attention to issues of power and diversity and how they manifest themselves in the context of observation.

What is observation and how do you do it?

Pioneered by Esther Bick, infant observation was introduced into the training of child psychotherapists at the Tavistock Clinic in 1948 and has remained an integral part of the preparation for psychoanalytic practice. A modified approach to infant and child observation (ICO), drawing on Bick's model, has more recently been used outside the context of clinical training to support the professional development of other groups, notably social workers (Briggs, 1992; Wilson, 1992; Trowell and Miles, 1991). Indeed, ICO has become a recognised component of many training courses at both qualifying and post-qualifying levels.

Observation can take many different forms, depending on the context and immediate purpose, but in the Tavistock approach, the observer starts the process of observation without an agenda or list of things to look for, and with no tick sheets or grids to complete. Instead, she observes the same child for one hour per week, for an agreed period of time. In psychotherapy training, the observation typically extends across one or two years. Social work courses, working to a very different professional agenda, have adapted the approach to fit a much reduced timeframe and may ask students to observe for a period of between six and ten weeks. Particular attention is paid to the students' ability to adopt an "observational stance", something I discuss in greater detail in the third part of this chapter.

The observer does not try to play with the child or talk to the parent/carer but instead adopts an attitude of "detached engagement": she is a friendly and attentive presence but does not actively "do" anything other than observe. A common first reaction to this form of observation is to ask: 'Well, what do I actually do then? What am I expected to look for?' It can be quite difficult to answer this question, because this approach to observation does not specify in advance what the observation is "for", beyond providing an opportunity to observe the child in his or her environment, interacting with carers, siblings or peers. Regular observation over a period of time allows the observer/observed relationship to settle down, thus minimising the possible distortions of the "observer effect", i.e. that the participants behave differently because the observer is present.

The observer does not take notes during the observation, but afterwards writes up a detailed narrative account of what has just taken place. A key element of this method is a regular, facilitated seminar group where members take it in turns to present an observation for discussion. The observer only includes observation data in her write-up, but would be encouraged to reflect on the feeling and emotional content of the observation in the seminar group, where different interpretations of the material could be discussed (Wilson, 1992). Some social work courses have further modified the Tavistock method and encourage observers to write as full an account as possible, taking account of their own reactions, thoughts and feelings whilst involved in the observation.

On many courses, observation has remained focused on pre-school age children or babies and has been a valuable source of learning about early child development and attachment issues. John Simmonds (1998, p 91) notes that:

> We have limited knowledge of what is learnt when the method of observation is used beyond its original frame. Similarly, while the argument for the use of the method of observation as an important tool in the development of social workers has been well made, the use of what is learnt from observation in practice settings where social workers are engaged in routine activities related to their role and responsibilities is not well documented.

However, this may be changing as training courses have broadened the use of this kind of narrative approach to observation (for example, see Hughes and Heycox, 2005; Le Riche, 2006) and in addition, practitioners have increasingly taken the model into different settings and explored its use with different groups (see, for example, Le Riche and Tanner, 1998; Hindle and Easton, 1999; Mack, 1999; Trowell, 1999; Tanner and Turney, 2000; Fleming, 2004; Green, 2005; and Rustin 2006). This chapter continues that exploration and offers some thoughts on what observation, and the learning it gives rise to, might contribute to everyday practice with children who are separated from their parents and family of origin, both within and beyond the context of the training course.

Why observe children?

Focused observation of the sort described offers an important source of knowledge about child development and a site for developing understanding of attachment theory. The *National Framework for the Assessment of Children in Need and their Families* emphasises that a 'thorough understanding of child development is critical to work with children and their families' (Department of Health (DH), 2000, pp 10–11) and has identified that the principles underpinning the whole framework are "rooted" in child development. The *Common Core of Skills and Knowledge for the Children's Workforce* Guidance (Department for Education and Skills (DfES), 2005) confirmed this emphasis and the *Care Matters* White Paper (DfES, 2007) has led to a review of social education and training to ensure that specialist knowledge and skills underpin practice. Through close and continuing observation in a non-clinical setting – the child's home, a daycare centre, the childminder's – students build up their knowledge of "ordinary" child development and "the world of the child".

A range of questions about cognitive, physical, social and emotional development can be prompted by observing quite a simple piece of behaviour, for example, seeing the child playing in the sandbox at the children's centre or with play-dough: what is the child doing? How do children play and communicate and, particularly, how does *this* child communicate? Does he or she play alone or with others? Is this the kind of interaction you would expect to find with children of around that age? These are all relevant questions and ones that help to build up a broad understanding of the range of "normal" development.

Observing babies or younger children interacting with their parent or carer sheds light on different styles of parenting/caring and of family and peer interaction. It also allows insight into the nature of the attachment relationships the child is forming and the degree of "emotional fit" (Sinclair *et al*, 2005, p 86) between them and their carer(s). An understanding of attachment theory and different patterns of attachment relationship is likely to be particularly important in working with children and young people in the care system, many of whom will have had very disrupted experiences of relationship and little opportunity to establish secure attachments (see Schofield, this volume).

Where practitioners have built up their understanding of child development and attachment relationships through observation, they can then draw on this to help them make sense of behaviours in children and young people with whom they work in a range of settings and circumstances on placement and beyond. This can be an important part of the assessment process, for example, when making decisions about where and with whom a child should live, or what kind of therapeutic support might be needed. And once a child is placed, observation can deepen and inform the assessment needed to make a permanence plan.

> Carolyn is a three-and-a-half-year-old girl of white British descent. She was left alone or unsupervised for extended periods of time and was often caught in the middle of domestic violence between her parents. At the age of two, she was made the subject of a care order and placed with a foster carer, Mandy, with whom she has remained for the last 18 months. Observations during this period have shown that she still has no clear attachment to the foster carer or, indeed, to members of her family of origin. Carolyn does not engage readily with Mandy and shows no distress when left. Although she uses names – for example, "mummy" or "Mandy" – appropriately, these "labels" seem to have little emotional significance for her. The social worker has been struck by Carolyn's lack of affect and is concerned about her long-term ability to form positive attachments. Drawing on the observation data, he has successfully argued the case for focused therapeutic work with Carolyn to address attachment issues. In addition, the insights into Carolyn's behaviour and relationships afforded by these observations have provided valuable material for the Child Permanence Report.

In this case, using observation as part of the ongoing assessment helped establish a deeper understanding of Carolyn's needs and contributed to the planning process. And it is clear that such an approach could have wide application – for example, in helping the practitioner understand the meaning and significance of contact visits with a parent for a looked after child. A very clear message is coming through from a range of sources (including the DH (2000), via the Assessment Framework, and the DfES (2007), via *Care Matters*) that observation has a crucial role to play in assessment of children and families and the systematic approach discussed in this chapter helps to keep the child very much at the heart of the process. At the same time, it is perhaps worth noting that while observation can provide a particular perspective, it is clearly not the *only* source of information about that child or young person. As Baldwin (1994) remarks, the voice of the observed also needs to be heard, both to corroborate observational data and also as a valid source of information in its own right (see Thomas, this volume).

Development does not happen in a vacuum and it is important that students and practitioners have a good understanding of the broader context within which it takes place. This reflects the ecological approach underpinning the Assessment Framework and involves an understanding of factors such as "race" or ethnicity, class, gender, disability, sexuality and how they impact on, or are experienced by, the child and his or her family. Observation provides an opportunity to understand the child in context and can highlight a number of significant issues around, for example, gender, care and caring, and identity.

In addition to supporting and contextualising learning about child development, this approach to observation offers the opportunity to develop and practise skills in recording

– critical in all areas of social work and social care practice. One of the things that students typically really worry about when they start an observation is whether or not they will be able to remember anything afterwards, if they are not "allowed" to take notes. In practice, this is rarely, if ever, a problem! If anything, the reverse is true and students may feel overwhelmed by the amount they *could* write, in trying to capture an observation as fully as possible.

If practitioners have a sound understanding of patterns of child development and attachment and the ability to record accurately and in detail, then this is likely to contribute to better (and indeed better *evidenced*) assessment, which in turn is a necessary precursor to more effective intervention. But observation has more to offer than the opportunity to develop these skills, essential though they undoubtedly are for competent practice. In bringing infant and child observation into social work education and training, '[the] link was made . . . between knowledge of human growth and development, observational skills and effective social work communication with children' (Luckock *et al*, 2006, p 39; see also Schofield, 2005).

A recent study by Ward and colleagues (2005) into young people's views of care and accommodation highlighted the importance to children and young people of having a good relationship with their social worker, and one of the things that defined a good working relationship was the worker's ability to 'communicate well with them and understand their feelings' (Ward *et al*, 2005, p 13). Spending time with a child in care, seeing what they do, with whom they interact and the nature or quality of those interactions, becoming aware of their likes and dislikes, learning how they display emotions – at one level, it is clear that observation can help to provide a foundation for effective communication, based on a genuine attempt to understand that child's view of the world. And in so doing, observation provides an opportunity to think about the child's unintended or unconscious communications as these are expressed, for example, through behaviours in the placement or relationships with foster and other carers (see Smallbone and Lefevre, this volume). I will return to this point in the next section.

The observer stance: managing emotions and building reflective practice

One of the challenges of observing is keeping the child/young person in view. At a practical level, observing in a busy nursery, for example, can involve quite a lot of effort on the part of the observer as the child darts off to the other side of the room to play with a friend, goes off on a bike or decides to go and hide in the playhouse. When there is a lot of activity, keeping a focus on one child can be difficult – and the observer may find their attention caught by other children, particularly if they are doing something apparently more interesting than "their" child. But in practice, the ability to maintain that focus may be critical.

Time and again, inquiry reports into child deaths draw attention to the way in which vulnerable children have slipped from sight. They describe situations where social workers were focused on the often very needy parents rather than the child (Blom Cooper, 1985); where workers were intimidated (Newham Area Child Protection Committee, 2002) or otherwise prevented from seeing the child properly (London Borough of Greenwich, 1987); and other instances where, for whatever reason, professionals simply did not seem to acknowledge the child's presence – to the extent that one inquiry report, into the death by neglect of a baby, noted that it was 'almost as if he did not exist' (Bridge Child Care Consultancy, 1995).

The cases referred to above – relating to Jasmine Beckford, Ainlee Labonte, Kimberley Carlile, and "Paul" respectively – all involved children who died "at home". While the death of a child in care is rare, there are numerous examples where failure on the part of relevant professionals to "see" what was going on allowed abuse and neglect of vulnerable children, who were living away from their families of origin, to continue over an extended period (Levy and Kahan, 1991; Kirkwood, 1993; Waterhouse, 2000). And it should be remembered that Victoria Climbié, whose death in 2000 was the subject of one of the most significant inquiries in recent years, was a child who had been privately fostered. Such children have been among the most vulnerable; indeed, shortly after Victoria's death, Philpot (2001) noted that privately fostered children often remained 'hidden from public scrutiny', with little protection in law and often scant attention in practice. In Victoria's case, it was not so much that she was "hidden", but rather that the signs of her distress were repeatedly either misunderstood or simply "not seen" by an extensive array of professionals. In his opening speech to the Laming Inquiry, Neil Garnham QC commented as follows:

Victoria's death was not simply an isolated act of madness by two sick individuals. Her ill-treatment was prolonged. It was not hidden away, out of sight of the authorities. As we shall discover, the signs were there. In fact, it seems as if the signs were on display time and time again, but they went unheeded. (http://www.victoria-climbie-inquiry.org.uk/)

As the different inquiry reports referred to above show very starkly, the importance of keeping the child/young person "in the picture" cannot be over-estimated; while there are certainly occasions when it is extremely difficult, the ability to observe, maintain focus and attend to detail may be critical to the well-being, or even the survival, of a vulnerable child.

So what is the "observer stance" and how can it be used? Put briefly, the observer or observational stance refers to the attitude of "detached engagement" mentioned in Section 1. In taking on the role of observer, the practitioner is given the opportunity to stand away from what Simmonds (1998) calls the 'me in role' and concentrate on the 'observer me' – and this may be quite a challenging task. Judith Trowell and Gillian Miles (1991, p 53) offer the following view:

The observational stance requires them [the observer] to be aware of the environment, the verbal and non-verbal interaction; to be aware of their own responses as a source of invaluable data, providing they are aware of what comes from them and what from their clients; and to develop the capacity to integrate these and give themselves time to think before arriving at a judgement or making a decision.

As this quote highlights, observation is potentially quite a complex process and involves the observer holding on to a number of threads at the same time: for example, being aware of the surroundings, and the different ways in which people convey information, including non-verbal or unspoken communication. In addition, there are issues around the management of emotions generated by observation. Trowell and Miles identify that the observer's affective responses – their thoughts, reactions and feelings – provide important information and therefore need to be attended to; as they put it, the observer needs to be aware of what comes from them and what from the client (sic). (See also Rustin's (1989) reflections on observation and understanding, and Wilson 1992.)

When a practitioner observes a family, there is an opportunity to be in the situation in a qualitatively different way. Rather than being preoccupied with interviewing or other related activities, the practitioner can pay close attention to the events and processes taking place. The absence of active participation can give the practitioner the opportunity to think about and digest what is both seen and felt. This can enable the practitioner to notice some of the subtle and frequently complex dynamics of family relationships. Such dynamics can go unnoticed when an active participant, particularly when involved with a family for a long period of time . . . (Tanner and Turney, 2000, p 344)

Attending to or being sensitive to feelings is not always comfortable:

In an observation seminar, a practitioner, David, described a young child he was observing at a playgroup. The little girl, Lisa, had been sitting at a table with other children but was not joining in with their activity; instead, she was sitting very still and sucking both her thumbs. As David focused on Lisa's stance, his manner changed and became less animated; there was a strong feeling of sadness which permeated the group.

Stopping to think about the feeling of sadness evoked by the observation, to work out where it "belonged", David talked quite emotionally about the way that Lisa presented – how sad she seemed, how little attention she got from the staff, and how hard he, the observer, found it to see Lisa being overlooked . . . what emerged was a picture of a child almost literally "holding herself together" in an environment which was not emotionally supportive and where adult help and engagement seemed to be lacking.

The idea of "mirroring" in the observation process has been explored by Gillian Ruch (2007) and helps to make sense of the observer's reactions here: David's (unconscious) emotional response could be seen as a reflection of Lisa's own emotions in this situation, which he conveyed very eloquently – though unintentionally – to the group.

> On another occasion, an observer described, in some detail, what appeared to be a very close and affectionate interaction between a mother and her young baby. Everything the observer, Jan, recounted pointed to a warm and satisfying relationship between the two. But Jan herself was quite ambivalent, even negative, in her response to the mother, and could not get beyond the feeling that the situation was "too perfect" and that there must be something wrong. Again, this was discussed in great detail in the seminar group and nothing concrete could be identified to support this response. In the safety of the seminar group, Jan was able to acknowledge that this reaction was perhaps more about her than about this particular mother and baby and that she felt quite jealous of the mother who appeared to have had a choice that Jan had not had herself – to stay at home with her new baby. Jan became quite upset thinking about how difficult she had found the first weeks back at work, when she had wanted to spend more time at home with her son. Seeing this mother so happily absorbed in her baby stirred up strong feelings of jealousy, sadness and guilt, making her doubt the rightness of her decision to go back to work when she did. To protect herself, she needed to find fault with the relationship and could not "allow" it to be as it appeared.

Both these examples are clearly open to a range of interpretations, but the point I want to draw out is that, by attending to the feelings evoked by the observation, it was possible to come to very different conclusions. In the first example, the emotion appeared to "belong" to the child and what the group picked up reflected something of her emotional experience. In the second situation, the feeling of there being something wrong seemed to belong more squarely with the observer and reflected *her* current preoccupations and perspectives. Clearly, it is important for childcare workers to be open to the possibility that relationships are not as they appear on the surface, but at the same time, there is also a need to be able to see and accept genuine warmth and affection where they exist.

If the observer's own feelings are not acknowledged and examined, it can have significant consequences for action. For example, in a practice context, failing to address the feelings evoked for her could lead Jan to over-emphasise any perceived risk and to respond in a punitive way towards this mother. For David, though, an unwillingness to pay attention to the feelings of discomfort or dis-ease that the observation left him with could lead him to minimise any risk to Lisa and leave her exposed to a situation where her needs were not being met.

Using the observer stance of "being rather than doing" creates a reflective space within which the observer can attend to their emotional responses. When observation is carried out as part of a training programme, students are encouraged to reflect on, analyse and evaluate observation material and use this to construct meaning. As I have suggested, treating the observer's reactions as significant and working out "what belongs where" opens up the possibility that the child's unconscious communications can be "picked up" and thought about. Briggs (1992, p 60) observes:

The experience of observation can have a crucial impact on developing social workers' sensitivity to the needs of children and clients in general, to the impact of emotion in clients, their relationships and in the workers themselves.

The examples with David and Jan show that observation can generate difficult feelings for the observer, and these can be particularly hard to bear when they are a reflection of a child's pain or anxiety. The seminar group provides a safe space within which the observer can articulate and process their own feelings, and consider the emotional dynamics of the observation. Modelling emotional attunement and containment (Luckock *et al*, 2006, p 39; Ruch, 2007) in the seminar group provides a framework that the student may then be able to transfer to practice and use in their own direct work with children and young people.

For practitioners in residential or fieldwork settings who are working with emotionally challenging situations on a daily basis, the need for an equivalent space in which to reflect is critical. But this kind of thinking space, or experience of containment (Bion, 1962), is not always available. It is perhaps possible to consider the abusive situations that occurred in children's homes in Staffordshire ("pin down") and in North Wales (Waterhouse, 2000) in the light of these comments about containment. As noted previously, inquiries into child deaths and examples of "programme abuse" (Kendrick, 1998) remind us that, in situations which are complex and emotionally fraught, time and again workers seem to have simply stopped seeing or to have looked elsewhere and to have been unable to recognise or acknowledge a child's pain or fear. I raise this not to blame individual workers for failing to see what was happening but to acknowledge the difficulty of maintaining a level of emotional openness and engagement in the absence of appropriate containment, in Bion's sense of the term. Allowing oneself to become properly aware of the child's unconscious communications would, in turn, generate a need to take action which may itself appear impossible for an inexperienced, over-stretched and possibly frightened worker. How much easier then just to disengage, to minimise contact with the child and to distance oneself from the emotional and practical costs of truly seeing.

Without an effective and reliable space in which to think about and process what they have observed, there is then a serious risk that workers will be unable to bear the feelings evoked and may simply "switch off". However, where such reflection is supported and adequately contained – through individual or group supervision, for example – much can be learned and practitioners may be facilitated to take effective action (see Smallbone and Ironside, this volume).

Reflection offers the worker "thinking time" and discourages premature judgement by allowing them to explore different aspects of an observation before coming to any decisions (Mack, 1999). Adopting the observer stance invites the practitioner to take an attitude of "respectful uncertainty" (Taylor and White, 2006, p 948) and to manage the anxiety that goes with "not knowing". Natasha Quitak (2004, p 250), reflecting on her student experience of child observation, identifies the value of being able to 'stay with' uncertainty – a position she neatly summarises as 'don't just do something, sit there!' – and notes how easily the capacity to reflect is undermined 'precisely when it is most needed: at times of heightened emotion' (p 250). Observation through time enables the observer to build a much more rounded picture of the child and their context of care. But the information gained is always going to be partial and subjective (which is not the same as "not evidenced"!), a point I will return to.

The previous discussion has highlighted some of the possibilities and difficulties of adopting the observer stance. In the final part, I move on to consider what observation can contribute to an understanding of issues of power and diversity in direct work with children.

Observation, power and diversity

There are tensions in the process of observation and potential ambiguities in relation to anti-oppressive practice. In the first place, the experience of observing/being observed without interaction contradicts everyday social norms and can feel uncomfortable for all those involved, especially in the early stages. Part of this discomfort perhaps is an acknowledgement of the power of the gaze – the power of the looker in relation to the "looked at". And critically, when observation is used in a formal practice context (that is, rather than as part of a training/learning programme), there is a danger that the asymmetry in the observation relationship will simply reflect and reinforce the power imbalances which characterise the "everyday" relationship between professional and service user.

Baldwin (1994) considers how observation can be used to contribute to a practice that takes account of power differences and imbalances by making sure that marginalised or socially excluded groups and individuals are kept "in the picture". He notes a tendency for those with less power (for example, children, people from black and other minority ethnic groups, disabled people, older people) to become invisible, for their voices and opinions to be ignored. But as he points out: 'Seen and heard should apply to all children, as it should to other marginalised groups. It would seem a worthy value position to underpin good practice in observation' (p 79).

Research has repeatedly shown that children and young people in the care system are often heavily disadvantaged and likely to experience social exclusion (DfES, 2006), so an approach that ensures that they are kept more obviously "in sight" would seem beneficial. But a lot of thought needs to go in to setting up an observation – deciding who needs to be informed, who gets to give or withhold permission, what the terms of the observation will be, and so on. Much can be done at this stage to acknowledge the rights, dignity and sensitivities of the person being observed (Hindle and Klauber, 2006) and to treat them as an active subject rather than an object of concern or scrutiny.

Observation provides a context for learning about difference and diversity; as Ellis (1997, p 56) notes:

One of the features of the observational experience is that it brings us into close contact not only with the common elements of human growth and development but also with the rich and infinitely variable differences which make up each individual human being.

But those differences are not neutral: some aspects of identity are viewed positively by the majority society (for example, being white, male, heterosexual, able-bodied), while others (being black, lesbian or gay, disabled) are not, and these views are reinforced by powerful social norms, structures and institutions. So just recognising difference, while important, is not enough; rather, 'a theoretical framework that considers power and oppression and not just cultural difference is essential' (Baldwin, 1994, p 80). Observation can provide opportunities for the observer to use this knowledge to reflect on the impact these factors have on an individual's development and family circumstances.

A thoughtful awareness of both commonality and difference gives the observer space to reflect on 'the ways in which socio-cultural frameworks shape and give meaning to our interpretations' (Ellis, 1997, p 57; see also Hsu and Arnold, 2006). Narrative approaches to observation make use, or take account, of the subjectivity of the observer and with this, the assumptions and prejudices they bring to the observation experience. Working with individual subjectivity is critical – observation is, after all, always 'filtered through someone' (Miller and Klauber, 2006, p 196) – and challenges what Baldwin (1994) sees as the 'myth of objectivity'. His argument is that the observer should not try to be "objective", if that is taken to mean assuming that they are starting with no preconceptions or prejudices. Arguably, there is no value-free vantage point from which to start so the need is, rather, for the observer to be as aware as possible about the beliefs, assumptions and values they hold, as these underpin the judgements they make about others.

The issue of subjectivity arises explicitly in relation to the recording process. Given the almost infinite number of things that could be noted, it is clear that an element of selection must be involved in producing the narrative account which follows an observation – and this operates not just at the level of choosing *what* gets recorded, but also *how*, i.e. the language used to describe different experiences or behaviour. Much has been written about the power of language to define and construct "reality" (e.g. Potter, 1996; Fairclough, 2001; Cameron, 2006) and this is particularly apparent in recording. Discussing a narrative account in the seminar group, there is the opportunity to consider the choice of words the observer has used to record their experience and to reflect on the significance, the meaning they convey. Does it matter, for example, that a five-year-old girl is described as "bossy"? This particular question arose in one seminar group and led to quite a heated discussion of the gendered connotations of the word and an exploration of why the observer had chosen it in preference, for example, to "assertive". A small example, perhaps, but indicative of the power of language to construct and "fix" individuals within particular discourses.

Children and young people in care are the subject (or perhaps rather too often, the objects) of a lot of other people's writing – case notes, court and panel reports, Child Permanence Reports, residential care workers' notes, and so on. Even where their views and opinions are properly canvassed and reported, children and young people may still find themselves in situations where the words of the (adult) professional carry more weight. It is clear, then, that the power to define – people, events, behaviours – and make one's definition stick is not evenly distributed. Reflecting on language use is perhaps one way of addressing this imbalance of power. This is not to say that practitioners either can or should avoid writing things about young people, or even that their accounts should necessarily have less influence. But what it does mean is that practitioners need to take responsibility for the language they use and be prepared to justify it.

In this section, I have considered some of the ways in which observation can contribute to an understanding of diversity and power, and the issues it raises in relation to anti-oppressive practice with children and young people in the care system. While there are some contexts within which observation can be disempowering or oppressive, there are also significant ways in which it can be used to promote anti-oppressive practice. As I suggested earlier, observation allows the observer to see the child in context, and an anti-oppressive approach will ensure that factors such as "race", class, poverty, and gender, as well as other aspects of "difference" remain visible and central. So the complexities and ambiguities of the process need to be balanced against the nature and quality of the information that can be generated through observation and the impact this can have on practice. In short, observation needs to be linked to the development of an "equality model" (Tanner, 1998) as part of a commitment to a broader anti-oppressive practice.

If observers are willing to engage with a reflective process, there is the potential for observation to be developed as a tool for recognising, thinking about and responding to power relationships. (Tanner, 1998, p 59)

Conclusion

Observation is not a substitute for direct work with a child or young person in care but supports the development of the necessary knowledge, skills and values for such work. A sound understanding of child development and attachment relationships, together with the ability to "stay with" the child and to focus on their inner emotional world provides the foundations for effective and authentic communication. And good communication, in turn, is a prerequisite for the kind of empathic and empowering relationship within which direct work can take place to bring about better outcomes for vulnerable children and young people. This chapter has sought to show that observation offers a distinctive way of thinking about the child's overall experience by allowing consideration of both their inner and external worlds – and that a grounded awareness of both is essential for effective and anti-oppressive practice.

Acknowledgement
Thanks to Kulbant McLaughlin and Trevor Evans for their comments on an earlier draft of this chapter.

References

Baldwin M. (1994) 'Why observe children?', *Social Work Education*, 13:2, pp 74–85

Bion W. (1962) *Learning from Experience*, London: Heinemann

Blom Cooper L. (1985) *A Child in Trust: The report of the Panel of Inquiry into the circumstances surrounding the death of Jasmine Beckford*, London: London Borough of Brent

Bridge Child Care Consultancy (1995) *Paul: Death Through Neglect*, London: The Bridge Consultancy Service

Briggs S. (1992) 'Child observation and social work training', *Journal of Social Work Practice*, 6:1, pp 49–61

Cameron D. (2006) *On Language and Sexual Politics*, London: Routledge

Department for Education and Skills (2005) *Common Core of Skills and Knowledge for the Children's Workforce. Non-statutory Guidance*, London: DfES

Department for Education and Skills (2006) *Care Matters: Transforming the Lives of Children and Young People in Care*, Cm 6932, London: DfES

Department for Education and Skills (2007) *Care Matters: Time for Change*, Cm 7137, London: The Stationery Office

Department of Health (2000) *Framework for the Assessment of Children in Need and their Families*, London: The Stationery Office

Ellis L. (1997) 'The meaning of difference: race, culture and context in infant observation', in Reid S. (ed.) *Developments in Infant Observation: The Tavistock model*, London: Routledge, pp 56–80

Fairclough N. (2001) *Language and Power*, (2nd edn) London: Longman

Fleming S. (2004) 'The contribution of psychoanalytical observation in child protection assessments', *Journal of Social Work Practice*, 18:2, pp 223–238

Green K. (2005) 'From birth to adoption: Jenny's story', *Infant Observation*, 8:2, pp 157–167

Hindle D. and Easton J. (1999) 'The use of observation in supervised contact in child care cases', *International Journal of Infant Observation*, 2:2, pp 33–50

Hindle D. and Klauber T. (2006) 'Ethical issues in infant observation: preliminary thoughts on establishing an observation', *Infant Observation*, 9:1, pp 7–19

Hsu H.-W. and Arnold K. (2006) '"Being left out" and "being alone in the presence of someone" – what is the difference?', *Infant Observation*, 9:3, pp 269–279

Hughes M. and Heycox K. (2005) 'Promoting reflective practice with older people: learning and teaching strategies', *Australian Social Work*, 58:4, pp 344–356

Kendrick A. (1998) '"Who do we trust?": the abuse of children living away from home in the United Kingdom. Paper presented to the 12th International Congress on Child Abuse and Neglect', *Protecting Children: Innovation and Inspiration*, ISPCAN, Auckland, 6–9 September 1998

Kirkwood A. (1993) *The Leicestershire Inquiry 1992*, Leicester: Leicestershire County Council

Le Riche P. (2006) 'Practising observation in shadowing: curriculum innovation and learning outcomes in the BA Social Work', *Social Work Education*, 25:8, pp 771–784

Le Riche P. and Tanner K. (eds) (1998) *Observation and its Application to Social Work: Rather like breathing*, London and Philadelphia: Jessica Kingsley Publishers

Levy A. and Kahan B. (1991) *The Pindown Experience and the Protection of Children*, Stafford: Staffordshire County Council

London Borough of Greenwich (1987) *A Child in Mind: Protection of Children in a Responsible Society. The Report of the Commission of Inquiry into the Circumstances Surrounding the Death of Kimberley Carlile*, London: London Borough of Greenwich

Luckock B., Lefevre M., Orr D., Jones M., Marchant R. and Tanner K. (2006) *Teaching, Learning and Assessing Communication Skills with Children and Young People in Social Work Education*, Social Work Education Knowledge Review 12, London: SCIE

Mack B. (1999) 'The contribution of infant observation to therapeutic social work with a child in need', *International Journal of Infant Observation*, 2:2, pp 102–115

Miller B. and Klauber T. (2006) 'Using the video *Observation Observed* in teaching: a discussion', *Infant Observation*, 9:2, pp 191–197

Newham Area Child Protection Committee (2002) *Ainlee*, London: London Borough of Newham

Philpot T. (2001) *A Very Private Practice: A report into private fostering*, London: BAAF

Potter T. (1996) *Representing Reality: Discourse, rhetoric and social construction*, London and Thousand Oaks, CA: Sage

Quitak N. (2004) 'Difficulties in holding the role of the observer, *Journal of Social Work Practice*, 18:2, pp 247–253

Ruch G. (2007) '"Knowing", mirroring and containing: experiences of facilitating child observation seminars on a post-qualifying child care programme', *Social Work Education*, 26:2, pp 169–184

Rustin M. (1989) 'Encountering primitive anxieties', in Miller L., Rustin M. and Shuttleworth J. (eds) *Closely Observed Infants*, London: Duckworth

Rustin M. (2006) 'Infant observation research: What have we learned so far?', *Infant Observation*, 9:1, pp 35–52

Schofield G. (2005) 'The voice of the child in family placement decision-making', *Adoption & Fostering*, 29:1, pp 29–44

Simmonds J. (1998) 'Observing the unthinkable in residential care for children', in Le Riche P and Tanner K (eds) *Observation and its Application to Social Work: Rather like breathing*, London and Philadelphia: Jessica Kingsley Publishers, pp 91–110

Sinclair I., Wilson K. and Gibbs I. (2005) *Foster Placements: Why they succeed and why they fail*, London and Philadelphia: Jessica Kingsley Publishers

Tanner K. (1998) 'Towards an equality model: observation through a power lens', in Le Riche P. and Tanner K. (eds) *Observation and its Application to Social Work: Rather like breathing*, London and Philadelphia: Jessica Kingsley Publishers

Tanner K. and Turney D. (2000) 'The role of observation in the assessment of child neglect', *Child Abuse Review*, 9:5, pp 337–348

Taylor C. and White S. (2006) 'Knowledge and reasoning in social work: educating for humane judgement', *British Journal of Social Work*, 36:6, pp 937–954

Trowell J. (1999) 'Assessments and court work: the place of observation', *International Journal of Infant Observation*, 2:2, pp 91–101

Trowell J. and Miles G. (1991) 'The contribution of observation training to professional development in social work', *Journal of Social Work Practice*, 5:1, pp 51–60

Ward H., Skuse T. and Munro E. R. (2005) '"The best of times, the worst of times": young people's views of care and accommodation', *Adoption & Fostering*, 29:1, pp 8–17

Waterhouse Sir R. (2000) *Lost in Care: Report of the Tribunal of Inquiry into the abuse of children in care in the former county council areas of Gwynedd and Clwyd since 1974, HC201*, London: The Stationery Office

Wilson K. (1992) 'The place of child observation in social work training', *Journal of Social Work Practice*, 6:1, pp 37–47

8 Communicating and engaging with children and young people in care through play and the creative arts

Michelle Lefevre

Introduction

In my earlier chapter (this volume) I drew attention to how social workers need to be able to draw on much more than just direct and explicit methods of communication when they are working with children and young people.[1] Games and activities were seen to be essential to engaging, getting to know, and building a trusting relationship with children of all ages. Verbal and written language were observed to be not always the best way to find out what children and young people are thinking and feeling, how they understand the world, or the impact upon them of their life experiences. Instead, it was noted how more child-centred approaches, which might include play or the creative arts, are needed to facilitate children in care to express themselves more freely, in their own ways, and on their own terms.

This chapter explores in more depth why this might be so. It begins with considering children's spontaneous use of play and creative, artistic or symbolic imagery to explore and express their inner worlds. It then focuses on the role of games and activities in engaging and building relationships with children, and the use of play and arts-based methods to enhance information-sharing, assessment and decision-making with children. Normally these approaches will be supplementary to other more direct language-based ways of communicating with children and helping them to express themselves.

Where social workers have undertaken additional training, they might use these skills and techniques in more therapeutically oriented interventions (see Burnell and Vaughan, this volume). However, it is important that workers do not step outside the boundaries of their skill and experience. There should be no expectation that social workers using symbolic and creative modes of communication would function at the level of art or play therapists, who use these forms as primary therapeutic tools and should be formally trained and experienced in their use (Wickham and West, 2002). Instead, the art forms should be seen as bridges to open up communication with children who are finding it hard to express themselves and engage with others at a direct or verbal level. This can be as

---

[1] For the sake of brevity, the term "children" will be used from here on to refer to children and young people, unless teenagers specifically are being discussed.

straightforward as Cook's description of singing with a child on a car journey (see this volume).

Where the social worker intends to carry out a more focused therapeutic intervention using the creative arts or play, the child's need and readiness for the intervention should be determined by a suitably qualified, skilled and experienced practitioner. It would be important to consider, for example, whether the child might benefit more or additionally from some direct verbal contact about issues of concern to her (see the views of Shelley in Chapter 2 – she was looking for information and explanations rather than an opportunity to express herself through play). The worker's capability to carry out therapeutic work must also be assessed. The line manager/usual supervisor may not always be the most appropriate person to determine this and a specialist practitioner may need to be consulted. Such an assessment will take into account the social worker's training, qualifications and experience and whether they have a suitable environment in which to meet with the child, ring-fenced time to ensure they can make a reliable commitment, and access to skilled clinical supervision (Doyle, 2005).

Why direct talking is often not enough

The symbolic representation of experience

Before infants and toddlers develop language they do not have chronological memories of events to shape their perceptions of the world, themselves and others in a logical or coherent form. Instead, their thoughts, feelings and experiences are believed to be represented in *symbolic* form within what may be called their internal world (Winnicott, 1971; Klein, 1989). This inner realm is deeply subjective; the figures which inhabit it are not literally the same as the physical people, places or objects the infant has experienced. Instead, they are mental and emotional representations, formed from these subjective perceptions – 'an amalgam of actual experience and perception' (Horner, 1991, p 8). This internal world will manifest itself in symbolic form through the infant's spontaneous play and can be communicated to others in this way. So simple games such as peekaboo, which develop between infants and their parents/carers, can represent a child's awareness of and feelings about what is there and then not there, such as the parent leaving them and returning (Bruner and Sherwook, 1979, quoted in Dubowski, 1990). Children's earliest scribbles can be understood as 'a symbolic substratum upon which representation develops' (McGregor, 1990, p 51). Such play is, then, a significant part of a child's developing understanding of and comfort with themselves, others and the environment (Mahler *et al*, 1975).

Well beyond infancy children continue to need opportunities for spontaneous play and creative image-making, either on their own or with peers or carers, in order to be able to explore and process their experiences, thoughts and feelings. Just as with infants, simple images (such as a drawing of a house) and games (like hide-and-seek), as well as being fun, often have a deep metaphorical meaning and purpose (Lewis, 1993; Peleg-Oren, 2002; Scarlett *et al*, 2005). Gradually, as intellect develops and language forms, the ability of most children to recognise, name and communicate their thoughts and feelings in more direct ways increases.

However, for some children much of their internal life will remain unprocessed and in symbolic form for much longer than might be expected according to developmental norms. This is because this developmental stage is not just predicated on age and intellectual inheritance but also influenced by external experience – factors such as abuse, trauma and insecurity of attachment. Some children reach adolescence still with neither the language to name their experiences nor the conceptual and affective frameworks through which to interpret and process them (Winnicott, 1996). Where earlier emotions, feelings and experiences have been pushed away or repressed, perhaps because they felt unbearable or were not contained and regulated by the parent or attachment figure, they remain unprocessed and can rarely be brought back simply in the same form (Bion, 1962; Schore, 1994; Howe, 2005). Instead, the internal world offers them back later as 'seemingly irrelevant bits and bobs, like jigsaw pieces of a window, or in code as play, metaphor and image' (Bolton, 1999, p 62).

This is particularly so with pre-verbal trauma which cannot usually be accessed consciously through language. Feelings tend not to be connected to event memories, as they would be if the child were older. Instead, what happened to them is "remembered" by the body, with the child remaining unclear as to why they are frightened, angry, distressed, etc. Such experiences can really only be processed and communicated through symbolic forms (McMahon, 1992; Levinge, 1993). These difficult and damaging experiences can be further compounded as a result of children's separation from their birth family and where the substitute placement experience is unstable and unsettling. Children's current experience then joins this rather jumbled backdrop and they struggle to form a coherent ongoing narrative (see Luckock, this volume).

This will be the case for many children in care who have been removed from their birth families as a result of abuse, neglect and insecurity of attachment. Readers will recognise this picture of children who find it hard to interpret their bodily sensations, explain their motivations, describe their emotions or give opinions. Just as we saw with Ben in Chapter 2, the following direct questions might provoke a 'don't know', shrug, blank look, or the child turning away:

- How do you feel about not living at home with your mum?
- Why did you hurt X?
- Who do you want to live with?

Social workers want, and have, to understand what is going on for children and consult with them about care planning. But they often struggle when they attempt to do so head on because some of these children will have simply no frame of reference for this conversation. Their experience is locked inside at a symbolic level. Consequently, additional ways of communicating, which are less direct and verbal, must be found if we are to listen to the "music" as well as the words of what young people communicate (Malekoff, 1994).

Engaging children who don't want to talk

Some children, even when they do have the ability to process, frame and communicate issues of importance to them, still do not do so. Many children in care will be unused to adults really listening to, understanding and validating them. This may not just be as a result of earlier inadequate parenting but through the impact on children of discontinuity of placements and inadequate consultation and inclusion by the adults around them. Children may feel it is pointless to tell their social workers what they are thinking and feeling because they don't expect them to be interested in what they say or to act on it (Fahlberg, 1994).

As we learned with Ben in Chapter 2, a relationship of trust must first be built up if the social worker is to be able to carry out the tasks of their role. Activity- or arts-based interventions, playing games and having fun together are an ideal way of promoting this (Dillenburger, 1992; Thomas and O'Kane, 2000). The use of activities as a 'third object' or 'third thing' (Winnicott, 1964), something for the worker and young person to focus on together which takes them away from the uncomfortable intensity of their interaction, can defuse matters (Bell, 2002). These could include playing with toys like dolls or building bricks (McMahon, 1992), engaging in board or computer games (Pardeck and Murphy, 1986; Ahmad *et al*, this volume), talking about or playing with pets or animals (Gonski, 1985; Hoelscher and Garfat, 1993; Mallon, 1994) or chatting about the child's hobbies or any shared interests to help establish a connection.

Such activities are not just important for engaging younger children but can be very helpful with teenagers (Mishne, 1996). Many young people do go through an uncommunicative stage (Corcoran, 1997). A face-to-face situation where the worker is attempting to verbally interact with a silent teenager who glares or averts eye contact can reduce the confidence of even the most experienced worker to rock bottom. A conversation about football, a wander around the shops together or being prepared to learn about a young person's favourite band can shift this dynamic and gives the message that the social worker is interested in him or her as a person.

Workers must involve themselves fully as individuals in an engaged relationship if this is to work; a distanced "professionalism" will not suffice. This will call upon personal qualities such as a capacity to be playful, creative, fun, real and emotionally warm in their interactions (Bow, 1988; Prior *et al*, 1999; Ringel, 2003). Arguably, if a practitioner does not have these qualities, or is not prepared to draw on them in their professional role, then they should reconsider whether they should be working with children at all.

When talking can be unsettling

Whereas some children feel supported, reassured and respected by direct conversations about difficult circumstances, such as a placement move (Prior *et al*, 1999), others can also be disturbed and destabilised by talking directly about painful experiences (Holoday and Maher, 1996; Moroz, 1996).

> When Ben[2] first came into care he was in an emergency foster placement over the weekend and then in another placement for a month with foster carers Karen and Dave. He needed to move suddenly from that placement when Karen became seriously ill. This gave little possibility of preparation time. His social worker at the time, Gail, visited him after school to explain to him that he was to move placement the next day. She wanted to find out what he thought and felt about the move but had limited time with him so her focus was on practicalities, e.g. telling him about where he was going, explaining when she would pick him up, sorting out who would help him to pack. Ben gave no verbal response to the news about the move, putting on his 'I'm not bothered' face. He had no questions for Gail. Karen's illness and Dave's concern about Karen meant they were unavailable to talk with Gail about how Ben might react to the news of the move.

> When Gail came to collect Ben the next day, she learned from Dave that Ben had urinated under his bed and smeared faeces in the bathroom. Although Ben had formed a good engagement with Karen and Dave, when he moved to his subsequent placement he was experienced as difficult from day one, bullying Diane and Jim's own children who are younger than him. This culminated in them insisting Ben moved on from them after only a couple of months.

Children like Ben certainly do need to be given information and explanations about moves and to be consulted with directly. But workers like Gail need to be aware that this is not a straightforward conversational process and it potentially has a powerful impact on children. Gail's visit met some of her statutory obligations but in word not spirit. She does not acknowledge or contain Ben's feelings or enable him to process what has occurred. She does not find out what all this means to him. Consequently, it is Ben's behaviour both that night and in the subsequent placement that indicates the strength and complexity of his responses.

> Ben now has a new social worker, Lucy, who is responsible for preparing him for the move from Diane and Jim to live with Gina, a single female carer. Lucy knows Ben

---

[2] See Chapter 2 for an introduction to Ben's situation. Ben is aged eight and in care. His previous social worker is Gail and his current worker is Lucy.

likes drawing and colouring and begins to think about how she might use artwork as a way of engaging and forming a relationship with him, giving him information about the move and exploring his thoughts and feelings about it.

Lucy has the opportunity to learn from Gail's mistakes here and will need to consider what creative, play-based and symbolic methods and techniques might assist her with this.

Using play, symbolic and creative approaches in social work with children

Beginning to work more playfully and creatively

The Italian educationalist Malaguzzi (in Edwards *et al*, 1993) suggested that there were a 'hundred languages of childhood', an abundance of possible modes of communication with children. Social workers will need to feel confident and capable in understanding and using as many of these as possible if they are to speak the language of a particular child. Ideally, a worker's choice of medium with a particular child (e.g. drawing, playing with dolls or figurines, using web-based or electronic media) would be based on that child's response to what is available in the environment and whether the social worker thinks that certain tools or approaches might help the child express or work through a specific issue (Webb, 2003). However, workers are likely to be drawn to what they have been trained to use, what they have read about and the modes of communication and expression most familiar or comfortable to them. As a social worker with a musical background, for example, I instinctively sang songs with children as part of building a relationship and encouraged them to use keyboard and percussion to express their feelings (Lefevre, 2004).

Working with what you are familiar can offer many creative possibilities but it can also be limiting. The more approaches you feel confident in using, the more likely it is that you and the child will find a mode of communication which works between you. This means moving out of your comfort zone and into the child's. To learn what this is, it is best to begin with a period of non-directive play and activity where you follow rather than lead. Aim to spend some time with the child and find out what he or she enjoys or feels comfortable doing. For some children this will be dolls, others puppets, bricks, football or painting. The list is endless. You can generally take your lead from children as most tend to "know" unconsciously what they need if the space and the tools are available. Your role can then be to follow, mirror and amplify the child's play (Oaklander, 1978). The philosophy of non-directive play therapy defines this as an individual's self-regulating, self-healing capacity, believing it is often sufficient for workers to provide a safe space for children in which their play is supported and facilitated without interference or interpretation (Wilson and Ryan, 1994).

Sometimes, busy social workers do not feel they have time for such doings in their task-driven environments. But non-directive play should be re-defined as purposeful activity. It informs assessment – learning about how the child functions, relates and communicates. Children feel met, appreciated and contained. A safe and trusting relationship has the space to develop in an environment in which children 'feel comfortable and understood and [able] to express and process their feelings' (Webb, 2003, p 405). Non-directive activities such as these also enable areas of feeling that children 'may not be able to put into words or would deny in conversation' to be opened up (Thomas and O'Kane, 2000, p 59). Children, too, tend to feel more relaxed and likely to engage with the process than they might with direct questioning where they might be suspicious of the worker's agenda and the consequences of what they convey (ibid).

Working with visual art

As adults, many of us become under-confident or uncomfortable about the idea of drawing or painting. Perhaps this came about as a result of humiliating art classes at school where we were told our images didn't look like they were supposed to and we forget how natural, artless and uncontrived drawing once was for us:

All children draw spontaneously. In its most basic form making marks is as natural as making sounds, gestures and movements. Given a surface and a means of making a mark, any child will leave a trace of its drawing activity, a visual record of its contact with that surface. This is true of children regardless of their cognitive, social, visual, or even physical abilities. (McGregor, 1990, p 39)

Younger children tend not to have yet internalised notions of what "proper" art should be. They don't usually constrain themselves by trying to characterise "real" images of objects and people per se, but are satisfied with representing their 'understanding of the way objects operate in the world, the way they behave in space and time' (ibid). Encouraging children in care to begin free-painting, modelling or drawing in a safe and trusting environment harnesses this innate creativity and enables feelings and symbolic thought to be expressed (Case and Dalley, 1990). The complexities of their experience can be processed and children may convey what is important to them and/or significant in their internal world (Bannister, 2003). This enables a picture shaped in children's own terms to emerge, often a richer one than that acquired when children are constricted by the conceptions and assumptions underpinning social workers' suggestions about what to draw (Thomas and O'Kane, 2000).

As with other forms of play, supporting and tracking the child's artwork is often a sufficient intervention, providing a transitional space (Winnicott, 1971) in which the worker–child relationship can form and unconscious processing can take place (Wilson and Ryan, 1994). It is crucial that untrained workers do not rush to explore more deeply than the child, or they themselves, are prepared for. They should also beware of defining and interpreting what has been drawn and assuming what children's artwork means to them. Children's arts images are not literal statements, providing definitive evidence of what has happened to a child. Instead, in drawing and painting, children are overlapping both their inner and outer worlds, 'a mixture of reality and fantasy' (Case and Dalley, 1990, p 3). It may be far more likely, for example, that children would communicate abusive experiences through 'making a mess . . . rather than through a drawing depicting who did what to whom, on a particular occasion' (ibid, p 4).

Instead, workers should seek to provide a safe and unconditional space, encouraging children to work at their own pace and in their own way. Much useful work can be done by simply staying with the art image created (McNiff, 1992). Rather than discussing the general significance of aspects of the image, the worker should comment neutrally on the visual qualities of the specific tree, animal, colour or shape that has been drawn (Oaklander, 1978). This enables the child and worker to stay connected and supports the child in what they are doing so that they do not feel led or criticised. Within this process it is important to allow whatever colours and shapes the child wants to emerge, not just to look for aesthetically pleasing images. Comments such as 'I can see lots of red lines' can also indicate attention and enthusiasm (see Oaklander, op cit, for suggestions). Very open questions are often safest, such as 'Maybe you'd like to tell me about your picture – I'm really interested in it'. If, by contrast, workers jump too readily to questions and comments like 'Is that your house?', 'Is that the boy's mother?', they are already constraining the possibilities of associations and meanings.

There is, of course, also a place for more structured and directive exercises using visual imagery to elicit children's views and feelings regarding their circumstances. Simple, low-tech focused imagery may be very successful if presented in an engaging and age-appropriate way. For younger children this could include rating scales using a happy face at one end and a sad or angry one at the other (McGoldrick and Gerson in Mattaini, 1995). Ecomaps and genograms are an effective way of engaging collaboratively and dynamically with children to enable them to convey their understanding and experience of family dynamics, social relationships and community networks (Walton and Smith, 1999). They have been found to give children in care an effective voice in their care planning (Altshuler, 1999). They can be designed simply with pens and paper using words and pictures, with small figurines to denote individuals which can be moved around, or with pre-designed computer programmes (McMahon, 1992; Mattaini, 1995). Imaginative and projective exercises such as magic castles and life rivers are designed to provoke children's imagination and enable them to give a vivid picture of their thoughts and feelings (see, for example, Striker and Kimmel, 1978; Sunderland and Engelheart, 1993).

These tools can be helpful where the worker has a clearer sense of what needs to be worked on or needs to cover particular areas during assessment. For some children, they can be used more successfully after a short period of non-directive work has enabled the direction to be established and an engaged relationship between child and worker has already formed. With other children, they may be a helpful engagement tool, as the 'third object' (Winnicott, 1964). Again, the important guide will be to go at the child's pace wherever possible. Children who are very young, are disorganised in their attachments, have certain learning difficulties and/or are still very traumatised by their experiences will struggle most with engaging in and concentrating on a structured activity, and workers will need to re-assess and reconsider more non-directive work if this occurs.

Working with stories

Stories and fairy tales provide rich metaphors for many universal aspects of human experience. Fairy tales can help children learn about themselves, experiment with aspects of their personality, and expand their opportunities for making sense of the world and the behaviour of others at many different levels (Bettelheim, 1977). These stories speak to children's unconscious and enable them to sense the commonality of their experience and develop ways of adapting and managing their world. Polarised archetypal characters (e.g. hero/villain, fairy godmother/witch) allow children to consciously or unconsciously identify with certain qualities, allocate traits to others, understand motivations, learn about different kinds of choices and play with new ways of looking at things (Barker, 1985, p 13).

Working with the metaphor of fairy stories such as Cinderella or Hansel and Gretel can be particularly useful with children who are wary of verbalising or even making conscious negative feelings regarding the way they have been treated by a parent or carer.

Mary had experienced years of abuse and neglect prior to coming into care. As a result she had internalised a self-view of being worthless and was unable to provide herself with rudimentary self-care. She stooped, with head facing the floor, avoiding eye contact, chewing her knuckles anxiously and mumbling. She was very taken with a double-ended doll in my therapy room which seemed to symbolise Cinderella's story: one end was dressed in rags; when the doll was turned upside down she wore a ball gown.

Over many weeks Mary used the dressing up clothes to act out Cinderella being transformed from a position of ignominy, neglect and abuse to being the "belle of the ball". She experimented with standing regally, looking out on the world, taking care over and pride in her appearance. She exerted control over her environment. Over time, it became apparent that Mary was transforming this behaviour more into her daily life. Her posture changed noticeably to become more like the "belle" character. Her self-care gradually improved. My sense is that, through enacting this metaphorical character, Mary was able to experience life in a different way to ever before. She was able to taste a different way of being. At first it was unfamiliar, but as it became more habitual she could incorporate it into a newly developing sense of self.

Unless they have therapeutic training, social workers should do no more than follow children's leads and support their play by providing a safe space and attuned responses, "tracking" what the child is doing, rather than setting out to work through these issues. Therapists can work more dynamically with the symbolic and metaphorical material.

Stories can be a way of giving information and explanations to children who are too young or distressed to make sense of what has been said. Hendry (1988) turned the account of why two very young children had to move placements into a story. This was presented as a book which could be read to the children. It was illustrated with drawings and pictures to make it more appealing visually. Telling the story to them in the third person meant the children could engage with it gradually and make their own connections; consequently it was less threatening. The use of the story book was later supplemented with play materials, such as small figures and dolls house furniture, to illustrate what would be happening when they moved placement. The mobile nature of these also enabled the children to be actively involved in the story and for changes to be incorporated as they occurred.

Guided reading with pre-existing books (also called bibliotherapy) is another way of helping children to verbalise their thoughts and feelings (Pardeck and Pardeck, 1987; Sunderland and Armstrong, 2001), although there is a lack of research evidence about the effectiveness of this technique (Pardeck and Markward, 1995). There are now available a wide range of story books written about specific issues which carers and workers can use with children. Some have additional sections or supplementary publications to alert carers and/or professionals to issues to be aware of and how to further open up areas for discussion following the story. For example, Sunderland *et al* (2003a and 2003b) have written a sequence of storybooks for children with particular difficult experiences or behaviours, each with its own guidebook.

A useful one for children in care might be *The Day the Sea Went Out and Never Came Back: A story for children who have lost someone they love* (Sunderland *et al*, 2003b). This story is about Eric the sand dragon who loves the sea very much and watches it going out and coming back every day. When, one day, the sea goes out and does not come back, Eric falls on the sand in terrible pain. It feels to him as if he has lost everything. After a while, Eric is able to save a wild flower by giving it some water. He is encouraged by this and starts to make a beautiful rock pool garden. As he does so, he is able to feel contained enough to experience the full pain of his loss, instead of closing his heart.

The story can be read at a surface level, staying with the metaphor, allowing children to just think about Eric, and allowing the internal world to do its own symbolic work. Children might make the connections themselves, recognising that others have the same kinds of feelings and experiences that they do. Empathically engaging with Eric's experience can allow them to begin to experience their own through the containment of the story. Their worker can support them in these reflections. Workers with more experience, training and access to clinical supervision might actively encourage children to make these connections.

Creative writing

Some children find it easier to communicate their feelings in written form (Yeung *et al*, 2003). As Ahmad *et al* have discussed in their chapter, electronic means of communication are a way of life for most children now, including email, "blogging", and sites such as *MySpace*. This has led to the growth of interactive computer technology to help children to participate more fully in care planning (e.g. Cowan, 2002). Online or email counselling is also becoming increasingly popular with young people (Chui, 2002). It has particular advantages regarding confidentiality and availability, but workers need to be alert to possible miscommunication due to the absence of non-verbal cues that usually provide contextual information in conversation and can influence interpretation of meaning in communication (Hunt, 2002). This is likely to be particularly the case for younger children who are even more dependent on non-verbal gestural cues than older children (Doherty-Sneddon and Kent, 1996).

Written communication by the worker to the child can also have therapeutic benefits. Marner (1995) and Wood (1985) have both written letters to children after meeting with them. In these letters the worker summarises the strengths, insights, actions and intentions that the child had demonstrated or discussed in the session. Rather than this being just a way of communicating a record of progress (in itself of use), it can demonstrate to children that they have been witnessed and understood. A particular advantage of such written communication can be that 'in letters words do not fade away but may be read and re-read' (Marner, 1995, p 171).

Some children may be encouraged to write poetry to express themselves. Again, the focus is not to produce a "good" poem but to enable children to explore their experience in the container of the poem, which gives their thoughts and feelings a shape and structure which they do not otherwise have:

> *If you could say how you felt, you would not write the poem. Writing it is partly exploring an intense experience, coming to terms with it.* (Padel, 2002, p 2)

The worker may need to do no more than give children some help and guidance on how to write, e.g. encouraging them to pick words and phrases which are expressive of what they think and feel and which matter. Some children want the worker to be involved, perhaps even to write down what they say so that it can be shaped into a poem. Other children want to write while on their own but want the worker to hear the poem once written, to witness the personal and intimate expression of the inner experience. As with all artistic and creative work by children, this should be honoured and treated with care and respect.

The first stage of creation of poetry or other creative writing can be particularly cathartic. It is an opportunity for children's unconscious to be given sway, so their internal world can emerge.

The tough, the raw, the uncomfortable and the unresolved can first see the light of day and be given form. (Miles, 1996, p 30)

The initial outpouring is tangible, visible on the page, and can be related to, worked on, organised, clarified and understood over time. The child can return to it again and again to re-experience it in different frames of mind, different stages of life (Bolton, 1999). The stage of re-working the cathartic expression is important, not to turn it into an aesthetically coherent art object, but because it enables the writing to be reflected on and brought closer to what was thought or felt. It is a re-experiencing in order to find the words that most closely evoke the mood or experience that led to the writing. This process enables children to create and recreate themselves and for a new narrative to be developed.

Music

Music is often likened to a language enabling communication about feelings, relationships and internal world experiences (Clynes, 1982; Unkefer, 1990; Di Franco, 1993). Babies, for example, express their feelings and negotiate relationships by altering the pitch, intensity, rhythm and timbre of their own vocalisations to express their feelings to others (Robertson, 1996; Heal and Wigram, 1993). Parents and carers often spontaneously and unconsciously further this communication by singing to the infant to soothe and delight it (Diaz de Chumaceiro, 1995). This expression is rarely direct and conscious but works at the symbolic level when individuals either listen to or actively play music.

Listening to certain kinds of music has been linked to healing (Moreno, 1995) and pain relief (Scovel, 1990; Robertson, 1996). Memories can become connected with particular music and be powerfully and viscerally re-evoked, deliberately or not, when the music is played again, even many years later (Blair, 1964; Berlyne, 1971; Bright, 1993). This can include unconscious, traumatic or pre-verbal experiences (Langer, 1951, 1953; Lehtonen, 1995). Structures and qualities inherent in the music, such as patterns of tension-inhibition-resolution, pitch, tempo and dynamics, may reflect the listener's emotions and provide a contained way for these to be re-experienced and resolved (Meyer, 1956). This has led to the use of guided musical listening (Scovel, 1990) as a therapeutic tool to evoke and contain feelings. However, there is an unresolved debate about whether music can be said to convey absolute and specific meanings which are consistent cross-culturally (see, e.g. Minsky, 1982, and Bright, 1993 for opposing views).

It seems safe to assume that children's responses to guided music listening will not be a simple matter of cause and effect but be influenced by a number of extra-musical influences, such as their mood, the styles of music they are familiar with and prefer (Gfeller, 1990; Lee, 1995), their culture (Meyer, 1956; Thaut and Smeltekop, 1990), social class, education (Alvin, 1966; Lee, 1995) and ethnic origin (Bright, 1993). For example, certain styles selected by the worker might feel culturally or socially alienating to some children, preventing them hearing through this to the underlying musical mood. It is important to be led by the child on this, though, as 'relying on stereotyped notions of what might be acceptable to the child runs the risk of stunting experimentation and patronising or pigeon-holing the child' (Lefevre, 2004, p 340). Encouraging the child to bring their own music for you to listen to together will also be helpful. You don't need to know anything about this style of music or even to like it but simply to convey interest and respect; children will then receive the impression that what is important to them is important to you.

Previous experiences can also influence the child's response to the music, leading to a mismatch of expectations and possible miscommunications. It is possible that the music might even arouse a painful or frightened response in the child, if there are associations with traumatic or abusive experiences, e.g. when the music was last heard (Gaston, 1968). This can also happen for workers and pre-preparation should include exploring their own feelings in relation to different musical styles and sounds. Otherwise, their own counter-transferential reactions might intrude.

The same can be hypothesised for engaging children in direct music-making activity. The child and worker can, though, generate a relationship where a musical idiom is developed which has meaning for both and through which the communication will flow (Gilroy and Lee, 1995). I have previously explored ways in which social workers both with and without musical skills might introduce music as a communicative tool with children (Lefevre, 2004) and refer readers to these for a fuller discussion. Of particular influence will be the theoretical perspective and musical capabilities of the worker, the interests of the child, resources available, and the role, task and the setting for the work (Brandon et al, 1998).

Family centre workers, for example, may have access to a variety of instruments in which they and the child can engage in free, rhythmic improvisation, which enables the child to express feelings in a safe and contained manner. As they create a desired sound with little or no musical skill, percussion offers the opportunity for any child or worker to improvise freely without needing to be constrained by creating melody or harmony (Alvin, 1966). Communication may occur through an interplay of either the child or the worker leading, initiating or responding in a succession of musical statements (Scovel, 1990). A more humanistic approach would be less likely to guide the client in any specific direction, but would rather support, encourage and reflect the client's improvisation both verbally and musically in the belief that the individual's psyche knows best what is needed

(Scovel, 1990). The musically and therapeutically skilled practitioner will find it useful to learn to improvise in a number of different styles in order to mirror, imitate and respond spontaneously using children's "language", enabling them to feel that their expression has been heard and accepted (Robbins, 1993; Kortegaard, 1993).

As with introducing any new techniques, some preparatory work is important.

This could start with attempts by the worker to rhythmically accompany favourite records, perhaps using a drum to first follow, then play with, the beat. A variety of instruments can be experimented with to create diverse sounds and rhythms. It would then be helpful to practise creating one's own rhythms, first alone then with another, using imitation, echoing, contrasting and developing each other's rhythmic motifs. The worker could then move on to explore how moods and atmospheres can be created through using instruments in different ways, including melodic instruments such as pianos, keyboards, recorders, glockenspiels. Once comfortable with playing in this way, these methods could be introduced into the work with the children. (Lefevre, 2004, p 338)

Cook (this volume) describes how she sang songs with the child when taking her on long car journeys between placements and to contact. This is an ideal engagement tool offering 'a safe musical starting point' from which 'the potentially unsafe world' of the new child–worker relationship can begin to be explored – 'rather like having a musical hand to hold' (Flower, 1993, p 42). As Cook suggests, a relationship of trust can develop through building up over time a 'collective memory of feelings and facts which binds you together . . . based on a common emotional experience' (Alvin, 1966, p 132). Such songs become very familiar to the children and appear to provide a 'secure base' (Ainsworth *et al*, 1978; Bowlby, 1988), or act as transitional objects (Winnicott, 1971), being returned to when difficult subjects are under discussion, or when events threaten children's security or well-being. The songs the child chooses may also have a symbolic content deriving from associations with where the song was previously heard, or to the mood or the words (Aldridge, 1993); or as a manifestation of a transference[3] relationship (Diaz de Chumaceiro, 1995). Similarly, songs which the worker spontaneously sings when with, or thinking about, the child may be counter-transferential.

---

[3] See Smallbone, this volume, for a definition of transference.

A word of caution about interpreting children's play

While observing children's play and artwork can help us understand something about their internal experience, there are questions about the extent to which play can be interpreted reliably. Bolton (1999, p 67) stresses that:

There is no one meaning in any image. The image is a window on a whole other world, not a two-dimensional picture.

This suggests that the gaining of understanding from play and imagery should be a process of exploration, of creation, 'of connotation rather than interpretation' (Bolton, op cit, p 66). The image, story or game should be attended to, with respect and care, so that it is allowed to tell its own story. Interpretation suggests the reverse of this, a process of 'denotation', where a specified meaning is attributed by the worker (ibid).

How confident can workers be about such interpretations? There does appear to be correlations between children's play and their attachment experiences as shown by the use of the Narrative Story Stem Technique (NSST). In this method, children are given a number of beginnings to stories and asked to complete them. Their narratives are then analysed and compared with measures of their social behaviour and experience. A review of 11 NSST studies of children aged six or under (Page, 2001) found that those children who had had sufficient experience of sensitive caregiving to enable them to develop security of attachment ended their stories with predictable order and positive outcome. Children without such secure attachment or sufficient experiences of safety and predictability while growing up tended to provide story endings showing violent problem resolutions or tangential responses to problems.

However, Page warns that there is only this level of reliability when the NSST tool is used in a formal and structured way by those trained in its use. More flexible and generalised use of projective tools, such as props and play scenarios, do offer a potential for young children to convey aspects of their experiences and perceptions of social relationships when they lack the verbal language or conceptual structures to indicate this more directly. However, workers are advised to be tentative and cautious in their observations and inferences as there is currently no empirically-validated framework that can explain precisely how children's play reflects their life experience (ibid).

Conclusion

Creative, symbolic and play-based modes are, then, 'the language of communication with the child client' (Webb, 2003, p 405). They enable us to engage children who would otherwise feel uncomfortable talking with us, and facilitate them to express the most important aspects of their experience. If we do not take the time and space to work in these ways, we will not be meeting our statutory obligations; our assessments and care plans will lack the authentic voice of the child who they concern and we risk misunderstanding or ignoring unexpressed feelings and concerns which are significant to children (Dockar-Drysdale 1990; Brandon *et al*, 1998).

It is essential for workers to recognise how powerful these ways of working are (Walton and Smith, 1999). Strong or unexpected reactions may occur. These methods and techniques require sensitive and skilled use and children's artwork must be accorded the utmost respect. They are precious artefacts and must be treated as such. This is one aspect in which practitioners should not take their lead from the child, as some children "trash" their own artwork and will need to be given the message that what they create is important and will be valued.

Self-preparation is essential for workers to begin to appreciate the power of the methods and how to work sensitively and creatively. Experiential learning will be very beneficial, perhaps trying out designing your own genogram or ecomap, free-painting or doing creative writing. It will be helpful to stimulate your own creative and playful self in order to be able to draw upon this readily in your work. It cannot be over-emphasised how this work requires practitioners to understand how children in general, and the child with whom they are working, experience and manage loss, stress, and trauma. They are then better prepared to engage with children on such sensitive matters in ways that do not overwhelm them (Rittner and Wodarski, 1999).

Activity-based play and creative ways of working may have implications for resources, such as needing to purchase toys and arts materials (Hendry, 1988). Kashyap (1989) outlines a range of play materials which could be supplied. It might be helpful for workers always to keep some coloured pens and paper in their bag when visiting children. Pre-prepared props are not mandatory, though. The key can be simply to use what the environment provides where you see the child. This might be the child's own toys in the foster home, schools resources, or the car CD player. The biggest resource practitioners always have is themselves and their capacity to be fun, playful, creative and sensitive with children.

References

Ainsworth M. D. S., Blehar M. C., Waters E. and Wall S. (1978) *Patterns of Attachment*, Hillsdale, NJ: Lawrence Erlbaum

Aldridge D. (1993) 'Music therapy research II: research methods suitable for music therapy', *The Arts in Psychotherapy*, 20:2, pp 117–131

Altshuler S. J. (1999) 'Constructing genograms with children in care: implications for casework practice', *Child Welfare*, 78:6, pp 777–790

Alvin J. (1966) *Music Therapy*, London: Hutchinson

Bannister A. (2003) *Creative Therapies with Traumatized Children*, London: Jessica Kingsley

Barker P. (1985) *Using Metaphors in Psychotherapy*, New York, NY: Brunner/Mazel

Bell M. (2002) 'Promoting children's rights through the use of relationship', *Child and Family Social Work*, 7:1, pp 1–11

Berlyne D. E. (1971) *Aesthetics and Psychobiology*, New York, NY: Appleton-Century-Crofts

Bettelheim B. (1977) *The Uses of Enchantment*, New York, NY: Vintage Books

Bion W. (1962) *Learning from Experience*, London: Heinemann

Blair D. (1964) 'Music therapy', *New Society*, 30 January 1964, 26

Bolton G. (1999) *The Therapeutic Potential of Creative Writing: Writing myself*, London: Jessica Kingsley

Bow J. (1988) 'Treating resistant children', *Child and Adolescent Social Work*, 5:1, pp 3–15

Bowlby J. (1988) *A Secure Base: Clinical applications of attachment theory*, London: Routledge

Brandon M., Schofield G. and Trinder L. (1998) *Social Work with Children*, Basingstoke: Palgrave

Bright R. (1993) 'Cultural aspects of music in therapy', in Heal M. and Wigram T. (eds) *Music Therapy in Health and Education*, London: Jessica Kingsley, pp 193–207

Case C. and Dalley T. (1990) 'Introduction', in Case C. and Dalley T. (eds) *Working With Children in Art Therapy*, London: Routledge

Chui E. (2002) 'Implications of computer-mediated communication on professional counselling in social work practice – a case study of the youth service in Hong Kong', *New Technology in the Human Services*, 14:3, pp 35–46

Clynes M. (ed) (1982) *Music, Mind and Brain: The neuropsychology of music*, New York, NY: Plenum Press

Corcoran J. (1997) 'A solution-oriented approach to working with juvenile offenders', *Child and Adolescent Social Work*, 14:4, pp 277–288

Cowan L. (2002) 'Interactive media for child care and counselling: new resources, new opportunities', *Journal of Technology in Human Services*, 20:1–2, pp 31–48

Diaz de Chumaceiro C. L. (1995) 'Lullabies are transferential transitional songs: further considerations on resistance in music therapy', *The Arts in Psychotherapy*, 22:4, pp 353–357, 20–26

Di Franco G. (1993) 'Music therapy: a methodological approach in the mental health field', in Heal M. and Wigram T. (eds) *Music Therapy in Health and Education*, London: Jessica Kingsley, pp 82–90

Dillenburger K. (1992) 'Communicating with children: the use of art in social work', *Practice*, 6:2, pp 126–134

Dockar-Drysdale B. (1990) *The Provision of Primary Experiences: Winnicottian work with children and adolescents*, London: Free Association Books

Doherty-Sneddon G. and Kent G. (1996) 'Visual signals and the communication abilities of children', *Journal of Child Psychology and Psychiatry*, 37:8, pp 949–959

Doyle C. (2005) *Working With Abused Children: From theory to practice* (3rd edn), Basingstoke: BASW Practical Social Work Series, Macmillan

Dubowski J. (1990) 'Art versus language (separate development during childhood)', in Case C. and Dalley T. (eds) *Working With Children in Art Therapy*, London: Routledge

Edwards C. P., Gandini L. and Forman G. E. (1993). *The Hundred Languages of Childhood: The Reggio Emilia Approach to Early Childhood Education*, Greenwood, CT: Ablex

Fahlberg V. (1994) *A Child's Journey Through Placement*, London: BAAF

Flower C. (1993) 'Control and creativity: music therapy with adolescents in secure care', in Heal M. and Wigram T. (eds) *Music Therapy in Health and Education*, London: Jessica Kingsley, pp 40–45

Gaston E. T. (ed.) (1968) *Music in Therapy*, New York, NY: The Macmillan Company

Gfeller K. E. (1990) 'Cultural context as it relates to music therapy', in Unkefer R. F. (ed.) *Music Therapy and the Treatment of Adults with Mental Disorders*, New York: Schirmer Books, pp 63–69

Gilroy A. and Lee L. (eds) (1995) *Art and Music: Therapy and research*, London: Routledge

Gonski Y. A. (1985) 'The therapeutic utilization of canines in a child welfare setting', *Child and Adolescent Social Work*, 2:2, pp 93–105

Heal M. and Wigram T. (eds) (1993) *Music Therapy in Health and Education*, London: Jessica Kingsley

Hendry E. (1988) 'A case study of play-based work with very young children', *Journal of Social Work Practice*, 3, pp 1–9

Hoelscher K. and Garfat T. (1993) 'Talking to the animal', *Journal of Child and Youth Care*, 8:3, pp 87–92

Holoday R. and Maher S. (1996) 'Using lifebooks with children in family foster care: a here-and-now process model', *Child Welfare*, 75:4, pp 321–34

Horner A. (1984) *Object Relations and the Developing Ego in Therapy*, New York, NY: Aronson

Horner A. J. (1991) *Psychoanalytic Object Relations Therapy*, New Jersey: Jason Aaronson

Howe D. (2005) *Child Abuse and Neglect: Attachment, development and intervention*, Basingstoke: Palgrave Macmillan

Hunt S. (2002) 'In favour of online counselling?', *Australian Social Work*, 55:4, pp 260–267

Kashyap L. (1989) 'Play materials in therapeutic work with children', *The Indian Journal of Social Work*, 50:4, pp 459–468

Klein M. (1989) *The Psycho-Analysis of Children* (trans. Strachey A. and Thorner H. A.), London: Virago

Kortegaard H. M. (1993) 'Music therapy in the treatment of schizophrenia', in Heal M. and Wigram T. (eds) *Music Therapy in Health and Education*, London: Jessica Kingsley, pp 55–65

Langer S. K. (1951) *Philosophy in a New Key*, New York, NY: Mentor Book Co

Langer S. K. (1953) *Feeling and Form: A theory of art developed from "Philosophy in a New Key"*, London: Routledge

Lee C. (1995) 'The analysis of therapeutic improvisatory music', in Gilroy A. and Lee L. (eds) *Art and Music: Therapy and research*, London: Routledge, pp 35–50

Lefevre M. (2004) 'Playing with sound: the therapeutic use of music in direct work with children', *Child and Family Social Work*, 9:4, pp 333–345

Lehtonen K. (1995) 'Is music an archaic way of thinking?', *British Journal of Music Therapy*, 9:2, pp 20–26

Levinge A. (1993) 'Permission to play', in Payne H. (ed.) *One River, Many Currents: Handbook of enquiry in the arts therapies*, London: Jessica Kingsley

Lewis J. M. (1993) 'Childhood play in normality, pathology, and therapy', *American Journal of Orthopsychiatry*, 63:1, pp 6–15

Mahler M. S., Pine F. and Bergman A. (1975) *The Psychological Birth of the Human Infant: Symbiosis and individuation*, New York, NY: Basic Books

Malekoff A. (1994) 'A guideline for group work with adolescents', *Social Work with Groups*, 17:1–2, pp 5–19

Mallon G. P. (1994) 'Cow as co-therapist: utilization of farm animals as therapeutic aides with children in residential treatment', *Child and Adolescent Social Work*, 11:6, pp 455–74

Marner T. (1995) 'Therapeutic letters to, from and between children in family therapy', *Journal of Social Work Practice*, 9:2, pp 169–76

Mattaini M. A. (1995) 'Visualizing practice with children and families', *Early Child Development and Care*, 106, pp 59–74

McGregor I. (1990) 'Unusual drawing development in children: what does it reveal about children's art?', in Case C. and Dalley T. (eds) (1990) *Working With Children in Art Therapy*, London: Routledge

McMahon L. (1992) *The Handbook of Play Therapy*, London: Routledge

McNiff S. (1992) *Art As Medicine: Creating a therapy of the imagination*, London: Shambhala

Meyer L. B. (1956) *Emotion and Meaning in Music*, Chicago: University of Chicago Press

Miles S. (1996) 'Writing as a way of self knowing: creative writing', *Caduceus*, 31, pp 29–32

Minsky M. (1982) 'Music, mind and meaning', in Clynes M (ed.) *Music, Mind and Brain: The neuropsychology of music*, New York: Plenum Press, pp 1–20

Mishne J. M. (1996) 'Therapeutic challenges in clinical work with adolescents', *Clinical Social Work Journal*, 24:2, pp 137–52

Moreno J. J. (1995) 'Ethnomusic therapy: an interdisciplinary approach to music and healing', *The Arts in Psychotherapy*, 20:1, pp 7–21

Moroz K. J. (1996) 'Kids speak out on adoption: a multiage book-writing group for adopted children with special needs', *Child Welfare*, 75:3, pp 235–51

Oaklander V. (1978) *Windows to Our Children: A gestalt therapy approach to children and adolescents'*, Moab, Utah: Real People Press

Padel R. (2002) 'Better than therapy', *The Times*, 10 April 2002

Page T. (2001) 'The social meaning of children's narratives: a review of the attachment-based narrative story stem technique,' *Child and Adolescent Social Work Journal*, 18:3, pp 171–187

Pardeck J. T. and Markward M. J. (1995) 'Bibliotherapy: using books to help children deal with problems', *Early Child Development and Care*, 106, pp 75–90

Pardeck J. T. and Murphy J. W. (1986) 'Micro computer technology in clinical social work practice: benefits and problems', *Arete*, 11:1, pp 35–43

Pardeck J. T. and Pardeck J. A. (1987) 'Bibliotherapy for children in foster care and adoption', *Child Welfare*, 66:3, pp 269–78

Peleg-Oren N. (2002) 'Group intervention for children of drug-addicted parents – using expressive techniques', *Clinical Social Work Journal*, 30:4, pp 403–418

Prior V., Lynch M. A. and Glaser D. (1999) 'Responding to child sexual abuse: an evaluation of social work by children and their carers', *Child and Family Social Work*, 4:2, pp 131–143

Ringel S. (2003) 'Play and impersonation: finding the right intersubjective rhythm', *Clinical Social Work Journal*, 31:4, pp 371–381

Rittner B. and Wodarski J. S. (1999) 'Differential uses for BSW and MSW educated social workers in child welfare services', *Children and Youth Services Review*, 21:3, pp 217–38

Robbins C. (1993) 'The creative processes are universal', in Heal M. and Wigram T. (eds) *Music Therapy in Health and Education*, London: Jessica Kingsley, pp 7–25

Robertson P. (1996) 'Music of the spheres', *The Independent on Sunday*, 5 May 1996, pp 48–49

Scarlett W., Naudeau S., Salonius-Pasternak D. and Pont I. (2005) *Children's Play*, Thousand Oaks, CA: Sage

Schore A. (1994) *Affect Regulation and the Origin of the Self*, Hillsdale, NJ: Lawrence Erlbaum

Scovel M. A. (1990) 'Music therapy within the context of psychotherapeutic models', in Unkefer R. F. (ed.) *Music Therapy and the Treatment of Adults with Mental Disorders*, New York, NY: Schirmer Books, pp 96–108

Striker S. and Kimmel E. (1978) *The Anti-Colouring Book*, New York, NY: Scholastic

Sunderland M. and Armstrong N. (2001) *Using Story Telling as a Therapeutic Tool with Children*, Brackley: Speechmark Publishing Ltd

Sunderland M. and Engelheart P. (1993) *Draw On Your Emotions*, Bicester: Winslow Press

Sunderland M., Hancock N. and Armstrong N. (2003a) *Helping Children with Loss: A guidebook*, Brackley: Speechmark Publishing Ltd

Sunderland M., Hancock N. and Armstrong N. (2003b) *The Day the Sea Went Out and Never Came Back: A story for children who have lost someone they love*, Brackley: Speechmark Publishing Ltd

Thaut M. H. and Smeltekop R. A. (1990) 'Psychosocial and neurophysiological aspects of music therapy intervention', in Unkefer R. F. (ed.) *Music Therapy and the Treatment of Adults with Mental Disorders*, New York, NY: Schirmer Books, pp 85–87

Thomas N. and O'Kane C. (2000) 'Discovering what children think: connections between research and practice', *British Journal of Social Work*, 30:6, pp 819–35

Unkefer R. F. (1990) *Music Therapy and the Treatment of Adults with Mental Disorders*, New York: NY: Schirmer Books

Walton E. and Smith C. (1999) 'The genogram: a tool for assessment and intervention in child welfare', *Journal of Family Social Work*, 3:3, pp 3–20

Webb N. B. (2003) 'Play and expressive therapies to help bereaved children: individual, family and group treatment', *Smith College Studies in Social Work*, 73:3, pp 405–422

Wickham R. E. and West J. (2002) *Therapeutic Work With Sexually Abused Children*, London: Sage

Wilson K. and Ryan V. (1994) 'Working with the sexually abused child: the use of non-directive play therapy and family therapy', *Journal of Social Work Practice*, 8:1, pp 67–74

Winnicott C. (1964) *Child Care and Social Work*, Welwyn: Bookstall Publications, Codicote Press

Winnicott C. (1996) 'Communicating with children', *Smith College Studies in Social Work*, 66:2, pp 117–28

Winnicott D. W. (1971) *Playing and Reality*, London: Tavistock Publications

Wood A. (1985) 'King tiger and the roaring tummies: a novel way of helping young children and their families change', *Dulwich Centre Review*, 4, pp 41–49

Yeung F. K. C., Cheng S. F. and Chau G. Y. (2003) 'Uncle Long Legs' letter box: a letter counseling service for children in Hong Kong', *Child and Adolescent Social Work Journal*, 20:1, pp 37–51

9 Working with disabled children who live away from home some or all of the time

Ruth Marchant

Introduction

> Joshua is eight. He communicates through sounds, movements, facial expressions and some basic signs (mummy, drink, biscuit, car, bus, home). Joshua has lived with a foster family since he was two. All of his review forms record his views as "not applicable" or "not ascertainable".

Disabled children have the same rights and needs as all children. When disabled children live away from home, the same principles, the same guidance and the same laws apply. There is no need to begin from a different place. However, disabled children who are living away from home need social workers who are able to communicate directly with them, involve them in decisions about their lives and make sense of the barriers that they face.

This chapter explores these issues within a clear value base, giving practical suggestions for ways of working, including a range of strategies for communication. These ideas have been strongly influenced by disabled children and young people, particularly through Triangle's consultative groups. All the quotes and examples are from these groups and from other children and young people whom I have worked with.

The chapter considers the social context of childhood disability and the role of social workers, and then follows a likely sequence of work with a child:

At the start:

- communication with disabled children
- gathering information
- making initial contact
- first meetings
- understanding each other

Direct work:
- choice and consent
- working with a third person
- observing children
- representing children's views
- evidentially careful communication

Specific issues:

- attachment and connectedness
- "respite care" and short breaks
- identity and self-esteem
- making sense of impairment

The social context of childhood disability

Work with disabled children takes place within a challenging and confusing social context, and models of disability and impairment are constantly developing (e.g. Shakespeare, 2006). Without doubt, impairment is a very natural and ordinary part of being human (Murray, 2006), yet childhood impairment arouses particularly strong and ambivalent responses. Exploring one's own beliefs around disabled children, their situation and their rights is essential.

There are different ways of understanding and defining disability. The social model uses the term disability not to refer to impairment (functional limitations) but rather to describe the effects of prejudice and discrimination – the social factors which *disable* people (Oliver, 1999). This perspective helpfully makes clear that many of the difficulties faced by disabled children are not caused by their conditions or impairments, but by societal values and structures, service responses and adult behaviour (Shakespeare and Watson, 1998, p 20).

However, the social model has been criticised for denying the reality and pain of impairment (Morris, 1993; Shakespeare, 2006) and others have found difficulties in applying a "pure" social model in practice; for example, Kelly's research with young people with autism found that a social model could not fully account for their experiences: 'for some children, experiences of impairment (such as not being able to understand or desiring to be able to walk) were just as important as disabling structures in society' (2005, p 271).

Working well with disabled children means finding a balance between recognising their humanity as children first, and ensuring their particular needs are met. Approaching disabled children as if they are "just like other children" can be as harmful as assuming that they have needs arising only from their impairments.

Social work with disabled children

Children are as different in their experience of impairment and disability as in all their experiences. However, disabled children are more likely than non-disabled children to be assessed, to use services and to be in touch with professionals. They are also significantly over-represented in the looked after system: disabled children are more than twice as likely to live away from their families of origin.[1] Despite this, information about their needs is limited and they have had 'only a shadowy presence on the research and policy agendas concerned with separated children' (Read and Harrison, 2002).

Disabled children have often been excluded from or marginalised within mainstream services. The Children's Commissioner for England recently described services for disabled children as 'a national scandal'[2] and a major review found a lottery of provision, inadequate strategic planning and confusing eligibility criteria (Audit Commission, 2003).

Given this context, clarity about the social work task with disabled children is crucial. Government policy is designed to enable disabled children to live 'ordinary lives', through effective support in mainstream settings:

Children and young people who are disabled or who have complex health needs [should] receive co-ordinated, high-quality child and family-centred services which are based on assessed needs, which promote social inclusion and, where possible, enable them and their families to live ordinary lives. (Department of Health, 2004)

The well-being outcomes stated in the Children Act 2004 (England and Wales) apply equally to disabled children, whether they are looked after in residential or family settings.

Disabled children and their families seem particularly vulnerable to professional confusion about who is the client. Social work with disabled children has historically often meant social work with parents of disabled children (Middleton, 1996). Working in partnership with parents is important, but it is essential to also work in partnership with children, and where views and needs conflict, clarity becomes crucial.

Communication with disabled children

James communicates through body language and facial expression. His sister describes him well. She says that he 'beams all over' when he is happy and 'screams all over' when he is upset. I think that sums him up really. Perhaps I would add that there are many shades of grey between the beam and the scream. (Parent, quoted by Murray, 2006)

Communication is a basic human need. Social workers who are generally good at child-centred, responsive communication with children are likely also to be good at communicating with disabled children (Marchant and Gordon, 2001). Conversely, social workers who become skilled at communicating with disabled children will improve their practice with all children.

---

[1] Disabled children are disproportionately represented within the looked after children population, making up 10% of all children in care, and only around 5% of the overall population (DWP, 2004-5; DfES, 2005). This is likely to be an underestimate because disabled children who live some or all of the time in residential schools, hospices and link families are not always categorised as "looked after" (Abbott *et al*, 2001).

[2] *Every Disabled Child Matters* website www.edcm.org.uk 2006

Not all disabled children have impairments that affect their communication. However, some impairments affect children's receptive communication: the way they perceive and understand others. Other impairments affect children's expressive communication: the way they send messages and information to others. Some impairments affect both receptive and expressive communication. Many children also have disabling experiences which affect their communication: being talked about as if they are not there, being ignored, being misunderstood, not being taken seriously, not being seen as competent communicators.

There has been significant recent progress in involving disabled children. For example, 85 per cent of short break schemes in England now state that the views of children are sought during the review process. However, as the researchers note, these figures need to be viewed with caution as more detailed information showed that schemes frequently only sought the views of children who used language or could sign; only 16 per cent of schemes mentioned using observation (Carlin and Cramer, forthcoming).

The following sections suggest strategies and approaches where a child does not use spoken language, or has very limited spoken language, or uses language in an unusual way. These children may or may not use formal augmentative or alternative communication methods (AAC) such as sign language, symbols, pictures or electronic communication aids, and you may or may not require help from an interpreter or someone who knows the child well.

Gathering helpful information

Disabled children are likely to have already been assessed, and it makes sense to use information already gathered because children find it frustrating and tiring to tell their story again and again. However, we need to be respectful and careful with children's information. It is useful to ask: 'to whom does this information belong?' and also 'who can check whether this information is accurate?' There is a balance to find between learning from the child, learning from those who know the child well and learning about the likely effects of an impairment or condition before meeting a child. Merry Cross reports a disabled teenager as saying: 'I wish they knew more about disability; I mean, it's sort of embarrassing to have to explain yourself' (1998, p 102).

Learning about a child's condition does not mean becoming an expert. It means knowing enough to fulfil your responsibilities towards the child. There are organisations of and for people with almost all impairments and conditions, and for parents.[3] These are often good sources of accessible and up-to-date information, but it is essential to remember that every child experiences their condition differently. Usually the best source of information will be the child and those who know them well. If possible, ask the child who they think it best to approach:

---

[3] For example, Contact a Family, Tel: 020 7383 3555 http://www.cafamily.org.uk

If I wanted to understand more about how your cerebral palsy affects you, who should I ask?

If I needed to know a bit about your epilepsy, who would be the best person to tell me?

If you are seeking information about a child's communication, the way you approach this is important. Generally, 'Does he talk?' and 'Does she communicate?' are unhelpful questions. A more useful starting point is an assumption that *all* children communicate, and thus the question is '*How* does he communicate?' If the response is that the child doesn't communicate, try asking 'How do you know if he's hungry or tired?', 'How can you tell if she is relaxed or distressed?' Another useful question is 'Can I communicate with this child? And if not, then who can, or who can help me to do so?'

Similarly, written requests for information about a child's communication need to be clear and explicit, for example, 'Please list all the ways s/he communicates (e.g. responds to people; makes requests; shows that s/he wants or doesn't want something; shows his/her feelings)'. Whatever you are told about a child's communication, keep a very open mind and remember that all children use a combination of methods.

Many children communicate best – especially about things that matter deeply – without language: showing, gesturing, playing, drawing, smiling, laughing, crying, making sounds, being quiet, moving, keeping still, hurting themselves or others. Broadening our definition of what is communicative would benefit all children.

Making initial contact

Make direct contact with the child as early on in the process as possible. This can be by letter, text, card, email, phone call or tape; with words, photos, drawings, symbols or objects. Children value being approached directly, and particularly welcome information about who you are, why you will be seeing them and what choices they can make. Photographs are generally popular.

Develop a range of communication resources relevant to your role. These need not be expensive or difficult to produce. Leaflets and brochures can be useful sources of pictures and images. Logos (for shops, buses, restaurants, leisure centres) are freely available and are often recognisable to children. Children's picture books are a good source of colour images. A digital camera makes it possible to develop a large library of photos at little cost.

You will need to match your communication to the systems that children use,[4] for example, here are a range of different symbols for "home":

---

[4] Summary information on a wide range of augmentative and alternative communication methods can be downloaded free from www.triangle-services.co.uk

Be very clear about your role and how you wish this explained to the child. Disabled children and young people meet many adults. Often these adults are going to "do things" to them. The focus of much professional intervention in the lives of disabled children is on "treatment", on the perceived "problems" created by their impairment or condition rather than on their situation.

Be clear and honest about the focus of your involvement: even if you only see a child a few times, your relationship is important and worth attending to. Making direct initial contact, for example, through a letter, also sends important signals to others in the child's life, both parents and professionals. Including a photograph of yourself with the letter is helpful and valued by children of all ages.

Dear Jenny,

My name is Ruth and I am going to be visiting you on Tuesday.

My job is to see how things are for you. The court has asked me to find out

what you think about where you are living.

I will bring some toys with me and some photos of people and places.

I will be happy to meet you,

Ruth

First meetings with children

Think carefully about where you meet children for the first time. Some children need silence and space; others really don't. Schools are often suggested as a neutral place but they may not be conducive to finding out what children think and feel, being notorious for a heavily directive style of communication – mainly teacher-led questioning. This may be particularly true for disabled children (see Millar in Cockerill and Carroll-Few, 2001).

Children should have a say in where you meet, from a limited choice of options if need be. Privacy and comfort are generally important, but keep an open mind about where you do your work. A child or young person may be more relaxed and more able to communicate if engaged in other activities such as play, or art, or going for a walk or drive.

> Mohammed is 15 and has autism and learning difficulties. His social worker is supporting him as he moves from a foster placement into a residential unit. All of the sessions are taking place on buses and in cars: in contained environments where no eye contact is expected or even possible.

All children are different, but these are generally some of the important initial messages to get across; not necessarily in what you say but in how you behave as you arrive.

> *I have come to see* you *(maybe parents, carers or others as well).*
> *I am interested in you and your views.*
> *I don't know what you are thinking or feeling, I need your help.*
> *I'm not in a hurry, but I'll go when you've had enough.*

Say hello and show clearly that you are pleased to be meeting them. Use language carefully to briefly introduce yourself and why you are there, and make it very clear that you value spending time with them. Then take your lead from the child. Follow their interest and agenda rather than expecting them to attend to you. Try to get alongside them instead of in front of them: look where they are looking, follow their attention. It is OK to wait and it is OK to be quiet. Sometimes you can explain, 'I want to be with you, to get to know how things are for you'. Often you have to demonstrate this in your behaviour rather than through language. Calm bafflement is a useful starting point to show that you don't know what's in the child's head.

Understanding each other

Adapt your communication. For example, give time in measures the child can relate to:

I will be here until teatime.
I will see you after Christmas.
You will be staying here for five sleeps.
The review will take as long as Eastenders.

Check frequently whether a child has understood you. Direct check-ing questions like 'Do you understand what I've been telling you?' are rarely helpful because very few young people will answer them with a no.

There is a direct link to how we behave when we don't understand children: it is often hard to say 'Sorry, I'm lost', 'Sorry, I'm stuck', 'I don't understand', 'Can we go back and start again?' But if we pretend to understand children when we don't, we shouldn't be surprised when they pretend to understand us. Here are some other ways to check if a child has understood you:

Can I just check with you what you think is happening tomorrow?
Could you explain to your keyworker/foster carer what I've been telling you about?
Can you tell me what tomorrow's meeting is for?
Can you show me with these photographs who you think is coming to the meeting?

Remember also that children are frequently asked questions by adults who already know the answer, and you may have to work hard to convince children that you don't know what is in their heads.

Working with a third person in the room

Sometimes you will need help to communicate with a child. If the child signs and you don't, you will need an interpreter throughout. With other methods you may need initial help to get going and someone to call on if you get stuck. Choosing who helps is important and you need the child involved in this. If you are doing the choosing, prioritise people who are respectful and responsive in their interactions with the child. It is your job to make clear why the third person is there and the "rules" of the meeting:

Sheila is here because we don't know each other. Her job is to help us understand each other. Sheila doesn't know what you think, and she's not allowed to guess.

Give the child a choice of people as soon as possible: 'Next time I see you, Sheila could help us again, or we could ask Lara or Simon?'

As soon as you and the child are comfortable with each other and understanding each other, offer the opportunity to be alone. Find out which of their support needs a child is willing for you to meet – perhaps wiping noses and mouths, repositioning, helping with a drink, and which not – perhaps eating or going to the toilet. For the child to decide, you need to be honest about your own competence (or lack of).

Choice, consent and control

Given that disabled children have many experiences of having things done to them, we need to be particularly careful about issues of consent and clarity of explanations. We need to remember that we are working in a context in which adults are often economical with the truth, especially with disabled children.

This won't take a minute.
You're going to be just fine.
Now this won't hurt a bit.

Sometimes, it is worse to apparently give choices when the child really has none. Avoid "pretend" choices, make sure that if you are offering a choice you are genuinely prepared to accept refusal as well as agreement. Be careful to say what you mean: be clear about what children can and can't choose.

I'm here to talk with you: where's a good place to sit?
I need to see you again: I can come on Tuesday or Wednesday.
I want to go through your care plan with you – we can do it on my laptop or on paper.

It is hard to make choices if you don't understand what you are being asked about. It is also hard to make choices about big things if you don't get to practice making choices about little things. It helps to approach consent as a process rather than a single event and to recognise that, although children may not understand the full context of why they are being consulted and how the results will be used, they can still be competent to assent or dissent to being with you. This is particularly important when planning to observe children, because the children we most need to observe are those least able to give informed consent.

Assent to your presence might be shown by the child spontaneously initiating positive engagement; coming to you, looking at you, exploring toys or objects that you have brought, initiating activities with you, touching you in a friendly or exploratory way. Dissent to your presence might be shown by the child disengaging from you or avoiding you, turning or moving away from an approach, pushing away people or objects, hiding themselves or their eyes, removing themselves from the activity, or trying to hurt you.

Observing children

For very young children and those with severe cognitive impairments, observation will be a primary source of information. This does not demand specific skills, just the discipline to carefully distinguish between observed events and interpretation of these events.

All children can show their feelings. Here are some observations of two learning disabled children who don't speak or sign or use any formal communication system. How do you think these two children might feel about being away from home?

> As soon as he arrives, Jake races in from the taxi, kisses all the staff and all the children, kisses the TV, the computer game and his bed, and jumps up and down on the sofa laughing at the top of his voice.

> As she arrives, Shelley refuses to leave the taxi. Once carried in, she cries and signs "mummy" and "home", curls up on the floor with her bag and blanket, rocking backwards and forwards and resisting all advances from staff.

Probably, Jake is very pleased to arrive and Shelley isn't, but recording what a child does is usually both safer and more powerful than recording an opinion about what it means.

> A social worker was struggling with a young man who often tried to hit her when she visited. She explained: 'He hits me because I'm not confident, he hits me because he doesn't know me, he hits me because he doesn't like social workers, he hits me because he knows I was involved with the decision to remove him from home.' A short period of observation made clear that the young man was hitting her because she sat too close to him, and when she moved further away he never tried to hit her again.

Periods of observation need not be lengthy to be valuable: for example, a well-planned hour could let you see 15 minutes of playtime, 30 minutes in class and 15 minutes travelling home with the child on the school bus. Sometimes you will need to ask others to observe across longer time periods. If so, you will need to give clear guidance about what you want observed and recorded, for example, 'Please notice and write down what Jonathan does when he first arrives in the building every day this week.' More detailed guidance will be needed where children's behaviour is causing concern, particularly around sexualised behaviour.

In our observations we need to attend carefully to eye gaze, facial expression and gesture, because these are central to children's ability to communicate and understand. This is true for all children (Doherty-Sneddon, 2003), but some disabled children may be particularly reliant on non-verbal communication, while others may not be able to see it or make sense of it. Remember, communication is two-way: children need to be able to make sense of your non-verbal communication, as well as you theirs.

Representing children's views

Existing processes for assessment, planning and reviewing are generally not designed to include disabled children; we need to find ways to change these processes to involve and empower children. Outcomes should as far as possible be made accessible to children and young people. This means that information needs to be analysed and presented in ways that make sense for the child: this can lead to "friendlier" and more meaningful recording systems that are more accessible for everyone.

When writing up, ensure a balance between what (if anything) the child said or signed and what they did (expressions, gestures, behaviour, etc). Use the child or young person's own words/signs/symbols or drawings wherever possible, and check what you have written with the young person if you can.

We need to find ways to make tangible the child's role as a partner in the process of assessment and not its subject (Marchant and Jones, 1999). One approach to child-centred planning is "passports" which belong to the child, and are designed to help people understand their needs, communication and behaviour. Passports are highly personalised and show the child they belong to as human and unique. Passports are a way of ensuring consistency in how different people understand and approach the child. They might include, for example, information about a child's communication, about their behaviour and about their needs (Millar and Aitken, 2004).

The following is taken from the passport of an 11-year-old who was fully involved in its production, including taking more than 100 digital photographs. There are sections about the child, his family, his interests and his needs:

- *Sometimes I get cross and angry, which is OK.*
- *You can tell I am getting cross when I look like this, or shout and throw things, or bite my hand.*
- *I need you to keep me safe, keep other people safe and stop things getting broken.*
- *If I get cross, it is hard for me to hear you.*
- *It is like there are 29 radios on in the room and I don't know which one is you.*
- *I need you to be clear, and not to use too many words. Make sure I can see you.*
- *Move dangerous things out of the way.*
- *I might need you to move me, with your arms through mine, like this.*

If papers are circulated before a meeting, then the views of the child need to be shared at the same time. If evidence is to be presented in video form, then this needs to be viewed either before the meeting or at the beginning of the meeting so that it can be taken into consideration. Children's views should not be presented as an afterthought, when decisions have already been made.

Evidentially careful communication

It is apparently not very safe to be disabled – disabled children face a significantly increased risk of abuse[5] and yet are seriously under-represented in our child protection systems.[6] Given this context, everyone working with disabled children needs to know how to respond when a child may be showing or telling about abuse. Non-directive commentaries on children's play or behaviour are both safe and respectful, gently reflecting back in a confirmatory tone what you see children doing.

Children reliant on closed questions are particularly susceptible to inept adults who may lead children by mistake, for example, framing questions such that the child repeatedly assents:

- *I hear you have been very upset when you need changing? (yes)*
- *Has something happened to make you upset? (yes)*
- *Has someone been touching you down there? (yes)*
- *Was it a man, touching you down there? (yes)*
- *Was it daddy? (yes)*

This is not safe for anyone. A pattern of no/no/no/yes responses is much safer because refuting adult suggestions returns control to the child. The last decade has seen significant forward progress in the development of evidentially safe interviewing strategies for disabled children (Marchant and Page, 1997; Home Office *et al*, 2002); and an increasing recognition that disabled children can be competent witnesses:

> *Agencies should not make assumptions about the inability of a disabled child to give credible evidence, or to withstand the rigours of the court process. Each child should be assessed carefully, and helped and supported to participate in the criminal justice process when this is in the child's best interest and the interests of justice.*
> (DfES, 2006)

Letting children tell in their own words is much safer than asking a sequence of closed questions, even if less clear initially. Absence of vocabulary for private body parts and

---

[5] A retrospective US study of 50,000 children found an unequivocal link between childhood maltreatment and disability, with disabled children being 3.4 times more likely to be abused (a 31% prevalence rate against 9% for non-disabled children) (Sullivan and Knutson, 2000).

[6] 2% of disabled children in need are on the child protection registers in comparison with 8% of the general population of children in need (Cooke, 2000). Concerns about the abuse of disabled children are 50% less likely to be case conferenced (Cooke and Standen, 2002).

abusive acts is a common problem for children whose vocabulary is controlled by adults and attempts have been made to rectify this.[7]

Attachment and connectedness

Disabled children face more separations from their families and research shows that they spend more time with adults and are likely to have fewer friends than non-disabled children. A key social work task with disabled children is thus to value and protect children's positive relationships: with their family, with their friends, and with others involved in their lives. Any intervention should aim to strengthen rather than threaten children's connectedness, which can be particularly fragile.

> Shaheed is nine and has mild learning disabilities. He has been living with his adoptive family for two years. In the park, another family – complete strangers – were getting ready to leave. Shaheed followed them calmly out of the playground and through the gate. It was only when they reached their car that he realised this was not the "right" family.

Links are now being made across the known associations between disability and maltreatment, and between disability and insecure attachments (Howe, 2006), yet relationships between families of disabled children and social services are often dominated by arrangements to separate children from their families through the provision of respite care. At the time of writing, a major campaign, launched by five leading children's charities in the UK, has successfully established the "right" of every family of a disabled child to have short breaks (*Every Disabled Child Matters*, May 2007 – www.edcm.org.uk).

However, there are significant risks in focusing solely on parents' right to a break rather than on children's right to an ordinary life (which would naturally give both children and parents a break from each other). The child's experience of the service can become incidental where its defined purpose is only to give parents "respite". Thus we accept patterns or standards of care for disabled children which would not be tolerated for other children.

> Callum is sleeping in four different places every month: residential school; home; link family and respite care unit. He also has frequent hospital admissions.

---

[7] *How It Is* consists of 384 images for children, designed to fill the common gaps in existing symbol systems about feelings, rights and safety, personal care and sexuality, developed to support children to communicate about a range of important issues. The images are available for free download from the internet at www.howitis.org.uk , or as a booklet with a CD-ROM.

In an average week, Shona has more than 25 adults involved in her everyday support and care: her mum and dad; three home care workers; two community nurses; a taxi driver and escort, a teacher and three classroom assistants, two lunchtime helpers, a physiotherapist and assistant and a team of eight day and night staff at a residential respite care unit. There are another 16 professionals involved on an occasional basis.

Short breaks often take place in a context of widespread adult denial of the impact of these repeated separations on children. Little is understood about how children actually perceive their absence from home and explain their loss to themselves, particularly children with cognitive impairments.

She always clings for the first few days she is back, she likes to see me all the time and even follows me into the toilet, she keeps signing 'no more, no go, no more'.

In a critical study of short breaks, Oswin suggested that all professionals responsible for planning and providing short-term care should start from the assumption that the experience is likely to be traumatic and even harmful, and recognise that homesickness is normal and to be expected. She argued that, for some children, short-term care probably seemed like 'a recurrent bereavement' in which children suffered 'immense grief' (1984, p 167).

To be able to settle into a new placement, whether temporary or permanent, disabled children need to know that they will be safe and well cared for and loved for who they are. They will have the same fears and questions as all children, and often some extra questions arising from their impairment and disability. Part of the social work task is to accurately identify the child's needs and ensure they can be met: 'Yes, your wheelchair will fit through the door'; 'They know how to tube feed and they are used to kids on oxygen'; or, 'Yes, they know how to sign and they know you get really angry and they know how to keep you safe.'

Identity and self-esteem

There are important questions about the ways in which children with impairments identify themselves. As Shakespeare observes, 'the majority of people with impairments have no desire to identify as disabled' (2006, p 198). Our experience suggests that this may be particularly true for children and young people.

Recognising disability as a positive identity is not easy in this society, although research has shown that families are generally more positive about a baby's health problems than medical professionals and as they grow up, disabled children report a more positive outlook than their carers (Nuffield Council on Bioethics, 2006, p 68). However, many disabled children get the message that there is something about them that most people would like to change.

> Hisham was working on a passport about his needs. He was asked to bring some favourite things. He brought a CD by a band called 'Badly Drawn Boy'. He explained that he had brought it because he thought of himself as 'badly drawn' and 'badly put together'.

A teenage girl remembered hearing herself described as 'one of god's little mistakes' and another boy heard someone at a bus stop saying 'if it was mine, I would put a pillow over its head'. Many children pick up the idea that they are somehow wrong, bad, broken, or damaged and that their existence is 'a shame', 'a pity', 'so sad', 'such a tragedy'.

Linked to this, there are significant dangers in the use of a bereavement model where children are not dead, yet this model is endemic in childhood disability (see Middleton, 1996, for further discussion).

To compound this, there is often widespread adult denial of the reality of children's impairments, and some children are offered very little information about their condition. Working with children's understanding of their situation is an important social work task. This is where attention to your own beliefs about impairment and disability is crucial. A child's impairment is an integral part of their identity, not something separate or incidental. It is of course not the only aspect of their identity but should always be considered.

As a first step we need to travel to the child's understanding of their condition: what have they been told, what do they know, what more if anything do they want or need to know? We should not deny the reality of the child's impairment or condition but neither should we assign it unnecessary significance.

Similarly, we should not deny the reality of prejudice and oppression in children's lives:

Because of this, life can be harder and it will be a different life.
But it doesn't have to be a bad life or a sad life.

As they grow up, disabled children will receive negative messages about being disabled, and need a positive identity to counteract these messages. There are some parallels with issues for black children growing up in a racist society but there are also key differences. In terms of family context, black children usually have black families who can provide positive role models whereas disabled children usually have non-disabled parents; in fact, many disabled children rarely meet disabled adults and may assume that they will grow out of their impairments with age. This is a sensible assumption if one meets many disabled children and no disabled adults.

Disabled adults can be important role models for disabled children.

Luke had a spinal injury and was in foster care. At the age of nine he had another Luke living under his bed, who could run about and play football and do all the things that the real Luke couldn't do. Luke had counselling, and became more settled, but the Luke who lived under the bed didn't go away until Luke was introduced to an adult who had a spinal injury like Luke, and used a powered wheelchair like Luke. He also drove a car, and had a job, and was married with children.

Making sense of impairment and disability with children

For many, impairment is not neutral, because it involves intrinsic disadvantage. Disabling barriers make impairment more difficult, but even in the absence of barriers impairment can be problematic. (Shakespeare, 2006, p 43)

Many children can be helpfully supported to disentangle the direct impact of their impairments from the social process of disablement.

You are up against two different things. First, it's hard for you to walk. Second, the world isn't set up very well for people who don't walk.

Disabled children are caught in the dilemmas and stereotypes as much as disabled adults: overcoming the odds, brave, heroic, angelic, special, sick, evil, dangerous.

Our disability frightens people. They don't want to think that this is something which could happen to them. So we become separated from common humanity, treated as fundamentally different and alien . . . it is the assumption that our lives are of such little worth, which we struggle against every day of our lives. (Morris, 1993, p 192)

Children need clear answers to their own questions: 'Will I always be like this? Are there other children like me?' They also need help to find ways to respond to questions from others. Modelling factual, simple, non-judgemental explanations of impairments is helpful.

Tyler can't hear. He uses signs to talk.
Jenny uses a wheelchair to get around.
Gemma eats through a tube into her tummy.

When working with children's understanding of their own condition or situation, it is important to find out what they have already been told, but not to assume that they therefore "know".

Conclusion

It is an exciting time in social work with disabled children, with opportunities to focus direct work in helpful ways. Electronic communication – email, text and live messaging – is opening up new methods to communicate with some disabled children but others will continue to need adults who can observe with skill and caution.

Disabled children more than most need a step change in what happens *after* they have been assessed or consulted; while legislation increasingly requires professionals to listen to children, it does not yet demand that they act upon their views. The point of involving children is to make better decisions about their lives: this means that children's contributions need to be valued and acted on.

References

Abbott D., Morris J. and Ward L. (2001) *The Best Place to be? Policy, practice and the experiences of residential school placements for disabled children*, York: Joseph Rowntree Foundation

Audit Commission (2003) *Services for Disabled Children and their Families*, London: Audit Commission

Carlin J. and Cramer H. (forthcoming) *Creative Responses to Changing Needs? Fourth national survey of short break services for disabled children*, Bristol: Short Breaks UK

Cockerill H. and Carroll-Few L. (2001) *Communication without Speech: Augmentative and alternative communication*, London: MacKeith Press

Cooke P. (2000) *Final Report on Disabled Children and Abuse*, Nottingham: The Ann Craft Trust

Cooke P. and Standon P. (2002) 'Abused and disabled children: hidden needs . . . ?', *Child Abuse Review*, 11:1, pp 1–18

Cross M. (1998) *Proud Child, Safer Child: A handbook for parents and carers of disabled children*, London: The Women's Press

Department for Education and Skills (2005) *Children in Need Census* www.dfes.gov.uk/datastats1/guidelines/children/pdf/CIN2005Ch1rev.pdf

Department for Education and Skills (2006) *Working Together to Safeguard Children*, London: DfES

Department of Health (2004) *National Service Framework for Children, Young People and Maternity Services: Standard 8: Disabled children and young people and those with complex health needs*, London: The Stationery Office

Doherty-Sneddon G. (2003) *Children's Unspoken Language*, London: Jessica Kingsley

Home Office, Crown Prosecution Service, Department of Health (2002) *Achieving Best Evidence in Criminal Proceedings: Guidance for vulnerable or intimidated witnesses, including children*, London: Home Office Communication Directorate

Howe D. (2006) 'Disabled children, maltreatment and attachment', *British Journal of Social Work*, 36:5, pp 743–760

Kelly B. (2005) '"Chocolate . . . makes you autism": impairment, disability and childhood identities', *Disability and Society*, 20:3, pp 261–276

Marchant R. and Gordon R. (2001) *Two Way Street: Communicating with disabled children and young people*, DVD/video and handbook, London: Triangle/NSPCC www.triangle-services.co.uk

Marchant R. and Jones M. (1999) *Assessing Disabled Children and their Families in Practice: Guidance for the framework for the assessment of children in need and their families*, London: Department of Health

Marchant R. and Page M. (1997) 'Interviewing disabled children', in Westcott H. and Jones D. (eds) *Perspectives on the Memorandum*, London: Arena

Middleton L. (1996) *Making a Difference: Social work with disabled children*, Birmingham: Venture Press

Millar S. and Aitken S. (2004) *Personal Communication Passports: Guidelines for good practice*, Edinburgh: The CALL Centre

Morris J. (1993) *Pride Against Prejudice: Transforming attitudes to disability*, London: The Women's Press

Murray P. (2006) *About IBK Initiatives*, www.ibkinitiatives.com/

Nuffield Council on Bioethics (2006) 'Critical care decisions in fetal and neonatal medicine: ethical issues', www.nuffieldbioethics.org/go/ourwork/prolonginglife/introduction

Oliver M. (1999) *Understanding Disability: From theory to practice*, London: Macmillan

Oswin M. (1984) *They Keep Going Away: A critical study of short-term residential care services for children with learning difficulties*, London: Kings Fund

Read J. and Harrison C. (2002) 'Disabled children living away from home in the UK: recognizing hazards and promoting good practice', *Journal of Social Work*, 2: 2, pp 211–231

Shakespeare T. (2006) *Disability Rights and Wrongs*, London: Routledge

Shakespeare T. and Watson N. (1998) 'Theoretical perspectives on research with disabled children', in Robinson C. and Stalker K. (eds) *Growing up with Disability*, London: Jessica Kingsley

Sullivan P. and Knutson J. (2000) 'Maltreatment and disabilities: a population based epidemiological study', *Child Abuse and Neglect*, 24:10, pp 1257–1273

10 Using interactive media in direct practice

Afshan Ahmad, Bridget Betts and Les Cowan

Introduction

As technology has advanced and become more integrated in our everyday lives, so have methods of communicating. Children are growing up in a world of text-messaging and online learning. Gone are the days when children wrote letters to distant pen pals and waited weeks for a reply. Today an email can be typed in a matter of minutes and sent in as many seconds! The challenges that practitioners face are of understanding and utilising this technology, where appropriate, in order to effectively engage and communicate with children and young people today.

> *Communication occurs via a variety of senses. It should not be thought of as limited to verbal interchanges. Adults need to be flexible and willing to try a variety of communication techniques with the goal being to find the ones that a particular child can most easily use to share information.* (Fahlberg, 1994)

This chapter explores the benefits and challenges of using interactive media as an alternative approach to engaging and communicating effectively with children and young people today,

> *. . . we have to acknowledge that the world of the child is not static but changes from one generation to the next. Certainly children's lives still involve imagination, music, role play, dolls, toys and many other media but anyone in contact with children over the last ten years will also appreciate that computer-based activities now attract a lot of attention and are highly valued in youth culture.* (Cowan, 2000)

When we start to use interactive media to engage children in direct work, we are culturally in the young person's own world and approaching them on their own terms. The key point here is the need for professionals to get in touch with the new culture of communication used by children and young people.

What are interactive media?

Technology and computers are an integral part of children and young people's lives today and can be used in a wide variety of ways.

- Games – CD-ROM/console based (e.g. Playstation) or online
- Communication – mobile phones and texting, emailing or "chatting" online
- Sharing – e.g. *YouTube* – a popular free video-sharing website that lets users upload, view and share video clips
- Information storage and retrieval – music, images and video
- Learning, research and shopping online (e.g. music purchase)
- Creativity and manipulation of sounds and images using software, e.g. *Garage Band*, a software application that allows you to create pieces of music and *Google Earth*, which combines Google search with satellite imagery, maps, terrain and 3D buildings. (You can "fly" to your own house by typing in your address and pressing search.)

What is an interactive approach?

By definition, an interactive approach involves both communication and collaboration. Children and young people readily engage with interactive media. The medium itself aids engagement with the process and hence the personal relationship with the practitioner. Interactive games can be a very solitary activity; the point about interactivity is that the computer user is actively involved with the application, not a passive observer or "subject". This is important when talking about the higher level of engagement the use of interactive media can bring to the therapeutic process. The user is also controlling the process, not being controlled by it. The interactive attributes of a computer programme commonly include data or text entry, mouse input, and sounds and visuals that allow a child to become active and involved. Many interactive programmes for children are simply fun, and this element can be exploited in making the interactive therapeutic world a fun place to be.

As Fiske (1990) observes:

Computers are becoming increasingly important as tools for articulating and communicating information and knowledge. At the same time, theories on human learning strengthen the hypothesis that learning is an active process during which knowledge is constructed as opposed to just "received" via some communication channel.

Most children today are comfortable with computers and they are now routinely used in educational settings.

Research findings demonstrate increased motivation and improved engagement by pupils when interactive approaches are used in learning and teaching (Becta, 2003; Pittard *et al*, 2003; Passey *et al*, 2004; Passey, 2005). In a small-scale qualitative study, Sime and Priestley (2005) found that, where interactive computer-based tools (ICT) were used, students engaged more deeply and for longer periods with activities, and took greater pride in the work they produced. Other studies have found evidence that the visual nature of some technologies, particularly animations, simulations and moving imagery, engaged learners and enhanced conceptual understanding (Livingston and Condie, 2003; Passey *et al*, 2004; HMIE, 2005). Research in education demonstrates the potential of interactive approaches to present learning experiences in a range of formats that meets the different learning styles of children and young people.

Facer and Williamson (2004) argue that digital technologies which stimulate "non-linear" working should be developed further and a culture that values and supports creativity and collaboration should be fostered. For example, activities involving animation, sound and digital video offer possibilities for exploitation to create personalised, creative learning materials such as digital narratives and multimedia presentations. These tools potentially can help children to externalise; to share and refine their ideas, thoughts and feelings; and to explore different representations of these. Their work can be easily revisited, adapted and revised using these different media.

The benefits of interactive approaches to teaching and learning are now recognised. However, utilising these resources has been far less common in direct work with children in social work and in the social care field in general (possible reasons for this are explored further on).

Using interactive media tools in social work practice

From a child or young person's perspective

Interactive computer-based tools (resources that have been specifically designed and developed to aid the therapeutic process) can be a particularly appropriate and effective method of communicating with children and young people. They are seen as fun, a familiar medium, engaging and culturally normative. Children can gain a sense of achievement in producing a tangible output – printouts that look good and record what the child put in – the 'I did that' factor, using a high prestige process. Moreover, they are non-threatening and do not need to focus on the first person, i.e. by using third party characters and situations to raise the issues. This shared external focus for attention can be less intimidating for a child than conventional interview methods, thus reducing stress and anxiety.

Young people often have more knowledge and confidence than adults in using interactive resources. They can have more control in taking the lead which can be an empowering experience. This reversal of power dynamics between child and adult can further aid the engagement and communication process. Simply using the mouse puts the child or young person in greater control, boosting their confidence and raising their value. There is also the potential to engage older children by combining other technology that is part of their everyday lives. Safe internet chat rooms, emailing and mobile phone text messaging are familiar and non-judgemental methods of communication for most young people today. Mobile phones can also be used to take pictures, record sound and make mini-movies. These tools do not require a high level of literacy skills. Some computer-based tools have the facility for text to be read out. Such "click to read" facilities need not disadvantage poor readers. There are also options for translation for non-English speakers which might really help workers who are not bilingual.

Interactive media tools can feel safe and confidential to a young person. They can "talk" to it when they want and it won't answer back. They can turn it off when they wish. They can "take back" what they have said, i.e. delete it. It is non-threatening and does not judge.

Within this medium there is a scope for humour and play elements – animations, sound effects, humour in a storyline and the use of cartoon effects (see Appendix A Multimedia tools in social work).

Terry (7) particularly enjoyed the 'Squash your worries' activity in Hopes and Fears. The sound and animation enabled him to communicate his worries and helped him to begin to manage them. He often would "squash" the same worry repeatedly and responded to the sound clip – 'Ah, that's better' – with a smile and a clap after his worry had been squashed. (*My Life Story* interactive CD-ROM)

If the application is a game or adventure, then there is also a sense of achievement in "winning". There is scope for group-based interactions using a board game style application (for example, *Busted* CD-ROM) where group members can play against one another (trying to choose the best behavioural options, etc) and involving consultation and negotiation among team members. All this builds social skills along the way. What the computer "says" often has a higher degree of credibility than what a person says (strangely enough), like seeing something on TV rather than just hearing it from a friend. We can use this to reinforce messages about good and safe behavioural choices, e.g. sexual health and behaviour or offending. Learning from simulations and role-play are well known to be able to influence understanding in ways transferable to "real life" situations. Young people can learn things about behaviour in the safe environment of a therapeutic computer game which they can then take into the real world.

From a professional's perspective

Interactive media resources provide a structure and framework for engaging and communicating with children and young people. Programmes, such as *My Life Story*, *Speak Easy* and *My Life Plan*, provide the flexibility to navigate through and revisit activities in any order, rather than following a set route.

These tools/resources can be used to explore a variety of issues, such as views on contact, relationships, assessing and listening to children's wishes and feelings. Data can be saved and loaded at a later date, avoiding the need to enter information again and again (*SpeakEasy* in particular).

Using interactive media provides controllability of the pace and intensity for both the young person and facilitator. They have a therapeutic use as a "distancing" tool as it is an indirect medium of communication and can be useful in exploring often painful and difficult issues.

Harriet (10) often used the CD (My Life Story) herself, in between sessions, and when she was ready would come back to her carer to talk about what she had been doing. She used the "Baggage" exercise in the Wishes and Dreams section, an activity that allows children to work through their baggage and decide what to do with it, to leave her experience of being sexually abused by her father in the dump truck. This was the first time that Harriet had disclosed these experiences and this activity provided a safe way of beginning to talk about these experiences.

They can provide an overview of progress and changing perspectives.

Jenny (7) used to begin her sessions by sending "Emails" (Past and Present section, My Life Story) to members of her birth family. This not only provided Jenny with the means of expressing her feelings towards family members but provided the facilitator with some indication of how her feelings were changing as they worked through her questions and anxieties as to why she was in care.

There is flexibility to move from one subject to another, returning as and when it suits.

Harjinder (11) used the CD-ROM to revisit her life story book that she had been given when she was placed with her adopters at the age of eight. She had not been actively involved in the production of her life story book and was now beginning to ask questions about herself as a baby and why she was adopted. She was fascinated by the "Facts and Figures" section, and this gave her a framework for asking questions about her origins and birth. The worker discovered that some information that Harjinder wanted was not on her file, so Harjinder wrote a series of questions that she wished her birth mother to answer.

Challenges of this medium

The emergence of new technology can be a daunting prospect for some professionals as it requires new learning and may be perceived as a move away from working directly with people. Access to appropriate training and time to explore the merits and limitations of IT are crucial in developing confidence to facilitate the process. Familiarity with the application or interactive media tool assists in planning sessions, just as one would be familiar with how a genogram works before undertaking an assessment of hereditary patterns within a family.

A common challenge for professionals is keeping up-to-date with contemporary methods of communication and language used by young people, such as text messaging, emailing or chatting on the net (internet). However, this need not be a hindrance.

Acknowledging this lack of understanding and encouraging a young person to take on the role of "teacher" can be an empowering experience which is not only a useful tool in engagement, but can also facilitate a more balanced and perhaps trusting relationship. It also provides the opportunity to explore how these methods of communication and language play a part in the young person's life.

Technical equipment can, and occasionally will, go wrong. Having some basic knowledge about how computers, printers, scanners, etc, function, how they communicate information and connect, can enable the development of trouble-shooting skills so that sessions can run with minimum disruption. These skills and knowledge will also assist in exploring issues of data security, such as who has access to the equipment and whether this should be password protected or saved on an external device, e.g. pen drive or disk (and then saved on file like other confidential information).

Using this approach has resource implications; it is reliant on the use of a computer which is sufficiently equipped with up-to-date software, sound, internet connectivity and other hardware, e.g. a graphics card. It requires agencies to make an investment in hardware and software. In the interim, social workers may need to be creative about accessing the use of equipment, for example, within schools/colleges or carers' homes. However, as technology is progressing, the market is becoming more competitive and affordable – what was once viewed as luxury hardware is already becoming standard (much like air-conditioning in cars today).

The continuing technological advancement of hardware and software can pose a challenge for practitioners in engaging young people with the use of interactive multimedia. There is limited choice of interactive media in social care (which are less frequently updated), and so may be seen as less appealing to young people in comparison to what they may be used to, e.g. Xbox 360, Nintendo Wii and Playstation 3. The software for these consoles tends to have far better graphics (virtual reality type) and sound effects. On a positive note, much of the educational (and social care) software available is relatively basic and does capture the interest of children and young people. This may be due to the absence of competition.

Another challenge is around knowing what IT resources are available and how effective they are in engaging and communicating with children and young people. There is no single source for social work-related IT resources. BAAF and Fostering Network have only limited examples in their catalogues. The internet can be a useful place to start and does not limit choices to UK-developed products.

Digital photography and filming

Photographs are an 'invaluable part of life story work' (Ryan and Walker, 2007). Photography and film help to preserve memories and can be a useful tool in enabling a young person to measure their own progress and growth.

Hamza (5) was adopted for the second time at the age of four. His first adoption had disrupted a year earlier. Initially, he refused to speak of his first adoption or even look at his life story book. His low self-esteem indicated his belief that he was at fault. He began to open up and ask questions about what he was like as a toddler. The adopters found this difficult as they could only respond with the limited information they had. Following some enquiries, it was discovered that the previous adopters had, in fact, filmed him in those early years. On seeing the video footage, Hamza remarked on how much he'd grown and the improvement of his speech. His recollections and/or fantasies of the past had been sad and painful. However, the video enabled him to see a more balanced view of himself.

The emergence of digital technology has meant that photographs can be taken, stored, altered and duplicated with much ease and at little cost. Photos can be scanned and saved on disk, which can substantially reduce the cost of duplication by traditional means.

Kevin (10) was attending weekly therapy following the sudden death of his father. He was becoming increasing distressed as he feared forgetting what his father looked like. It emerged that Kevin's father had avoided having his photo taken. The only photo that existed of him was on his bus pass. This image was scanned, enlarged, and then digitally attached to an image of Kevin, before being printed off as a single photograph. Kevin kept this framed image by his bedside as he said it made him feel close to his father.

One advantage of using a digital camera is that photos can be automatically dated. Another is that photos can be instantly viewed. Many young people now possess their own mobile phone and most mobile phones have a built-in camera. One of the author's daughters regularly uses the camera on her mobile phone to record a photo journal of her life. She records everyday events such as her journey to school, outings with friends and family, even a long journey to Cornwall in the car! She downloads this on to her computer and adds captions to remind her of her thoughts and feelings. These provide opportunities for her and the family to reminisce and reflect. To quote an old cliché, a picture is 'often worth a thousand words'.

Photos can be sent by a variety of ways, e.g. email or blue-tooth, to a PC. Photo-journaling can be a great way to enable a young person to reflect on their experiences, feelings and their relationships with others. Using simple software, such as Microsoft PowerPoint, Word or Publisher, you can import photographs, add text and other images to create a life story film. Windows Movie Maker is another tool for creating a slideshow of images where you can add text and sound. The young person can either record their own voice over the images to "tell their story" or choose other sound/music. Recording the voices of other significant people, such as carers, professionals or birth family members is not only a good way of involving them, but also has the added benefit of portraying different (and sometimes contradictory) perspectives. This can be a particularly productive method for older children or those who do not wish to write, draw or use art materials. Being able to use functions such as spell check can make a young person feel less self-conscious and more in control.

Where photographs are limited or not available, other images can be imported. This can provide an indication of how the young person feels.

Kirsty (14) found it difficult to describe the birth family home. She did not want to draw so we did a search for clipart images. She chose two images; the first she said was the home that people saw. This was a drawing of a set of terraced houses. The second image was a lone castle-like building, set in the night. This image, she stated, was how she viewed the home.

There are many software packages available for editing film, such as Nero or Pinnacle Studio. By connecting your camcorder to the computer you can "capture" (save) the film to your hard drive and then edit, add images, sound and text. Again, this method has the benefits of being able to record and distinguish multiple perspectives and, used creatively, can have additional therapeutic value.

Dominic (15) decided he wanted to "interview" his carers, social worker and grandparents. He had worked through and planned the questions he wanted to ask. Speaking in the third person, he was able to use the camera as a distancing tool. He was able to ask questions such as why he (Dominic) was in care and why his grandparents had not taken him into their home. The answers were not different to what he understood, but he had needed to hear them say it, to feel the sadness and regret they felt. The editing process meant that he reviewed the film many times and, in doing so, talked openly about his own feelings. The process enabled him to come to terms with his sense of rejection and to move towards developing a positive relationship.

Conclusion

In practice, it is essential to see the IT application as an aid to practice and not a substitute. Interactive resources work best where they are used as a platform to aid consultation and participation, to stimulate discussion, pose alternatives and act as a prompt to thinking and talking. They can also provide a map for what needs to be covered and what issues need to be addressed, hence providing a supportive training resource for the worker as well. IT data applications are more easily updateable than conventional records, and issues around storage, access and duplication are minimised.

The use of interactive media in social work provides an alternative, contemporary and familiar medium in engaging and communicating with children and young people. It is a "child-centred" approach that can be fun for both worker and child. It gives children and young people some control over the process and also provides them with opportunities for reflection and to work some issues out for themselves. It is therefore important for us as professionals and carers to keep up to date and to familiarise ourselves with the ways in which children and young people communicate today, and to consider how we can creatively utilise these tools alongside more traditional approaches in social work. We perhaps need to ask ourselves the question, 'If you're not using an interactive media of some sort – why not?'

Appendix A

Multimedia tools in social work
A review of current materials

*All resources marked ** come from Information Plus, which is a leading UK developer of interactive media in social care*

Billy Breaks the Rules is an animated decision-making adventure game. Starting from an initial dilemma, by choosing how Billy will react to his problems, players can make up their own storylines. Specific issues include: rules, sanctions, relationships and responsibility in a family setting.

Billy and the Big D-cision sees Billy back in bother having to decide how to cope with being offered drugs at school. Includes not only the animated adventure game but sources of help and advice for Billy, printable worksheets and a unique drugs database, all accessible from Billy's mobile phone

Billy and the Break In finds Billy yet again faced with a difficult dilemma. His pals want to break into the off-licence and steal some money and drink. What's he going to do? It tackles issues of youth crime, peer pressure and responsible decision-making in an adventure game format.

Bridget's taking a long time is a unique resource for helping children in adopting families come to terms with a new arrival. Illustrations, animation and a talking story all help children think and talk about hopes, fears and anxieties in adoption. Includes video interviews with birth children and printable worksheets.

Bruce's Multimedia Story is an interactive version of a best-selling children's counselling book. Following Bruce's adventures helps children to talk about disruptions and anxieties in their own lives.

BUSTED is a monopoly-style computer board game for up to four players or teams. Instead of properties, players land on squares about family, friends, school, work, fun, action, etc. Depending on their choices, players can gain or lose points and learn about social skills.

FCA Welcome CD-ROM is an interactive tool for young people's introduction to Foster Care Associates, an independent fostering agency. It seeks to complement the agency's written children's guides by providing a colourful, visual and audio interactive alternative, particularly for those young people who may have difficulty with reading. It was produced in consultation with young people and has a combination of fun- and fact-based activities. Video footage, such as a young people's forum discussion, prompt and encourage young people to question issues that affect them. It also contains a glossary of terms in a child-friendly format.

Lifeball takes the lottery ball machine to new heights as a social learning device. Instead of numbers, this machine has colours relating to social skills. Every turn has a problem to solve, an impact on scores and a discussion topic.

My Life Story uses a menu based on a treasure island map and includes over 750 data entry items, 45 interactive activities, 30 printable worksheets and 60 pages of professional training material. It provides the opportunity to move from the intense to the light and fun, but without losing focus. It also allows the young person to maintain some control over this.

My Life Plan is a new resource for person-centred planning for adults with learning disabilities. Using the metaphor of a town map, users can link to buildings representing all the key issues such as health, work, learning and home. The programme includes a photo import facility.

Problematic is a new format for social learning for 14–18-year-olds. Using a simulation of a radio phone-in show, players can give advice to callers in relation to their problems and on the way consider their own issues and choices.

Speakeasy addresses the problem of helping looked after young people contribute to plans for their future. Sections include: "My Review", "Keeping in Touch" and "Future Plans". As well as printable screens, *Speak Easy* also produces a compact report for child care reviews.

In My Shoes

In My Shoes is a computer package that helps professionals communicate with children and learning disabled adults about their experiences, views, wishes and feelings, includ-

ing potentially distressing experiences such as illness and abuse in home, educational and other settings. The interviewer sits alongside the child and assists, guides and interacts with them through a structured interview process. In My Shoes has a sound research base and has been sponsored by the Department of Health/DfES and others. It is useful for psychologists, social workers, child psychiatrists, other mental health staff, health workers, educational workers and specialists in forensic services.
www.inmyshoes.org.uk/

Appendix B

Useful websites
www.incentiveplus.co.uk
The UK's largest online catalogue of resources for the promotion of social and emotional competence and positive behaviour in children and young people.

www.information-plus.co.uk
Information PLUS is a specialist developer of social learning software. Their aim is to produce a unique range of resources to tackle real personal, social and behavioural issues through a non-threatening, enjoyable software environment.

www.innovativeresources.org
St Luke's Innovative Resources publishes and sells card packs, books, stickers and posters. Their original, high-quality resources have grown out of the strengths-based social work services offered by St Luke's, Australia.

www.husita.org
HUSITA (Human Services Information Technology Applications) is an international virtual association dedicated to promoting the ethical and effective use of IT to better serve humanity.

http://dmoz.org/Computers/Internet/WWW/Web_Logs/
(for a list of blogging sites)

www.lifecard.org.uk
Lifecard is an interactive multimedia application for use by looked after children and their carers. It seeks to provide an alternative method of undertaking life story work. On connecting to a secure database via the internet, information in the form of text, images and film can be uploaded to a child's file. *Lifecard* provides a guided format to preserve information and can be used as a therapeutic tool in exploring feelings and issues. Additionally, there is a facility whereby information can be stored but not viewed by the young person until they reach 18 years.

References

Becta (2003) *What the research says about ICT and home school links*, Coventry: Becta. becta.org.uk/page_documents/research/wtrs_icthome.pdf

Betts B. and Ahmad A. (2003) *My Life Story*, Orkney: Information Plus

Betts B. (2004) *Speakeasy*, Orkney: Information Plus

Cowan L. (2000) 'Interactive media for child care and counselling', in Resnick H. (ed) *New Opportunities, New Resources: Electronic technology for social work education and practice* (2nd edn), Orkney: Information Plus

Facer K. and Williamson B. (2004) *Designing Technologies to Support Creativity and Collaboration*, NESTA Futurelab. www.nestafuturelab.org/download/pdfs/research/handbooks /handbook_01.pdf

Fahlberg V. (1994) *A Child's Journey through Placement*, London: BAAF

Fiske J. (1990) *Introduction to Communication Studies*, London: Routledge

HMIE (2005) *Improving Achievement in Science in Primary and Secondary Schools*, Livingston: HMIE

Information Plus (2001) *Billy and the Big D-cision*, Orkney: Information Plus

Livingston K. and Condie R. (2003) *Evaluation of the SCHOLAR Programme: Final report for the Scottish Executive Education Department*, Edinburgh: Scottish Executive. www.flatprojects.org. uk/evaluations/evaluationreports/scholarreport.asp

Passey D. and Rogers C. with Machell J. and McHugh G. (2004) *The Motivational Effect of ICT on Pupils*, DfES/University of Lancaster, www.dfes.gov.uk/research/data/uploadfiles/RR523new.pdf

Passey D. (2005) *E-learning: An evaluation review of practice across the West Midlands Regional Broadband Consortium*, WMNet www.wmnet.org.uk/wmnet/custom/files_uploaded/uploaded_ resources/874/2005report.pdf

Pittard V., Bannister P. and Dunn J. (2003) *The Big PICTure: The impact of ICT on attainment, motivation and learning*, London: DfES (3rd edn), www.dfes.gov.uk/research/data/uploadfiles/The bigpICTure.pdf

Ryan T. and Walker R. (2007) *Life Story Work* (3rd edn), London: BAAF

Sime D. and Priestley M. (2005) 'Student teachers' first reflections on information and communications technology and classroom learning: implications for initial teacher education', *Journal of Computer Assisted Learning*, 21:2, pp 130–142

11 Opportunity-led work with children

Adrian Ward

Introduction

Where and when does communication with children happen? In the planned meeting or "interview" when a social worker undertakes a scheduled task? Possibly, if things run according to plan – but things do not always turn out as we had hoped and the formal session may sometimes be the *least* likely setting for useful communication, just because it is planned and scheduled and the child's natural defences and anxieties may be especially high, or just because "the time isn't right". For the sort of communication where young people can really start to reflect on what hurts or worries them most, or can get in touch with half-hidden feelings and free-floating memories, we may also have to be ready to respond to whatever hints and prompts may come from them at unexpected moments, the in-between times or during some other activity such as a car journey or visit to a school.

In the direct care context, such moments arise all the time, as residential and foster carers live alongside the young people in their care through everyday life, or as family centre staff interact with children in informal interactions through the day; even in the fieldwork or "office-based" practice of social workers, there may be many possibilities for communication which arise in the most unexpected ways. There may also be times when an interview intended to cover one area suddenly reveals a whole other potential area or level of concern which may need to be responded to and acted upon there and then. When these opportunities do arise, however, we may feel unprepared for them because they are not "in the script" and we may therefore be unsure how to respond to and capitalise upon them, apart from relying on our instinct and intuition, which *may* help us but which may not be sufficient for the responsibility we have.

What we need is the ability to notice such opportunities when they do arise, the skill to respond to whatever hints and clues the child may indicate and to develop useful communication out of what may be uncertain, ambiguous or unpromising beginnings, as well as to judge when this may or may not be helpful to the child. This chapter briefly out-lines an approach to this sort of work, which I have called "opportunity-led work" (Ward, 1995, 1996, 2006; Ward *et al*, 2003), because the focus is on these opportunities for useful and even therapeutic communication which may arise out of everyday interactions. This is an approach which focuses on the "micro-skills" involved in making skilful responses to opportunities for communication, including developing the ability to make on-the-spot decisions about what to do or say next, and the confidence to respond effectively and creatively to unexpected events and comments. The aim of this approach is to enable workers to handle such moments and incidents purposefully, i.e. to make clear connections between the detail of these interactions and the overall aim and objectives of their work.

Case example

Let us start with a simple scenario:

> Imagine yourself as a social worker approaching the house where you are due to visit a child in foster care. The child, Naomi, is 12 years old, and she has been living here for three months with Jackie, her foster carer, and Jackie's daughter, Peta. This is Naomi's third placement, and the previous two only lasted a few weeks each. As you approach the house, Jackie calls out 'Hi!' from the kitchen through the open front door, but meanwhile Naomi is sitting hunched up on the pavement near the gate and she calls to you: 'And you needn't believe a word she fucking tells you either!'

Now consider what you would do or say in this scenario, and more importantly, how you would *decide* what to do or say? What options do you have, how do you choose between them, and what opportunities may this situation offer?

There is an almost infinite range of possibilities, of course, including (a) a direct response to Naomi asking her what is worrying her, (b) a brief "hello" to Jackie and a pause beside Naomi inviting further comment, or perhaps (c) positioning yourself between the two and hoping to encourage dialogue. Any of these responses may or may not have the effect of opening up communication in what may be a fairly tense and even critical moment, and if it is handled right, this might be the beginning of something very productive. There is, of course, no single "right" answer to the scenario, because the details of such incidents vary so much, but there may be some "wrong" answers, in the form of responses which might *not* help to promote useful communication, or which may actively inhibit it. We do not know at the moment, for example, what lies behind Naomi's apparent anxiety about whatever Jackie might say about her. All we know is that she has very effectively drawn our attention to this anxiety. We might view our task at this moment as one of trying to take up this challenge – or we might feel it was better not to rise to the bait straight away, and risk provoking further verbal or possibly physical aggression.

Although situations such as this – moments where you are faced with a critical decision as to what to do or say next – are very common, they are not very commonly thought about. We often feel unsure about the best response in the heat of the moment, and it may only be later in the day when we have had more time to think about it, and when the moment has passed, that we can come up with an appropriate comment. In the moment itself it can feel as if we don't have enough time to think. In fact, there is almost always more time to think than we may realise, and skilled practitioners can condense this sort of thinking into the briefest of spaces, just as skilled sports players often appear to have much more time to decide which shot to play than do less able players.

The aim of the "opportunity-led work" model is to encourage workers to become more familiar with the process of thinking and responding in such circumstances, and thus more confident in spotting and using opportunities for communication when they arise. In essence, it is a very simple model, based on the familiar concept of the social work "process", although it is also fluid enough to allow for the considerable complexities that can develop in rapidly changing interactions.

Opportunity-led work: the social work process in miniature

The concept of the social work "process" – from assessment, engagement, intervention and sustaining the intervention, through to closure and ultimately evaluation – underpins many of the theories and models of social work practice. It is usually applied to a "case" or other substantial piece of work, but it turns out to be a helpful temporal and sequential framework for analysing interventions at the micro as well as the macro level. Even in the brief interaction that we envisaged with Naomi and Jackie, for instance, we can identify a process or sequence in the work. Just as in a larger-scale piece of work, here too the worker will first:

- *observe* what is said and done, then
- *assess* it,
- *decide* about how to respond,
- *intervene* or try out that response and maybe modify or develop it as the communication either flourishes or dries up, and eventually bring the piece of communication to an
- *ending*, before hopefully
- *reviewing* and *evaluating* it.

In some cases, all of this sequence may happen within a few seconds and the interaction may remain of low significance, but in other cases, the interaction may develop into an especially useful and significant communication. There will be many factors which will influence the way in which such moments develop, including the mood, receptiveness and abilities of the young person, but among these factors will also be the skill and perceptiveness of the worker. The real skill lies in spotting the "window" (cf Oaklander, 1978) which may allow for useful and productive communication and knowing how to develop this into a fuller conversation.

We now consider the stages in the process of opportunity-led work, with brief illustrations from the scenario – although it may also be helpful in using this material if you also keep in mind some situation or opportunity for communication which may have arisen in your own practice.

Observation and assessment

We consider the two functions of observation and assessment together, although each is really a full topic on its own. The first essential is that the worker attends to every detail in the situation: who says (or doesn't say) what; what their body language may suggest; what the interactions between the key players appears to be and perhaps who is missing? (in the above incident, for example, does the absence of Peta have any significance?); the presence of any other clues in the physical environment such as objects which are broken, damaged or scribbled on, photographs torn up, etc. The worker will need to observe and assess emotions, his or her own as well as those of others, and to weigh up any contradictory signs, such as angry statements said with a smile, or sad statements in a deadpan tone. He or she will already perhaps be asking him/herself, 'what is my initial/instinctive reaction, and is there any good reason to override this?'

He or she will also start asking further questions such as 'why is this happening or being said *now* and by *this* individual? Has it happened before, perhaps at this time of day or year, or at a similar stage in a placement?' We know something of the history of Naomi's previous placements – how does that affect our assessment of this situation? We are beginning to move from immediate observation to assessment, looking for meanings and patterns, contradictions or paradoxes. This also involves weighing up some of the intangibles in a situation such as gauging the "atmosphere" in the home, which in this case may be hard to judge as you approach the gate. What may have happened during or perhaps just after your previous visit? We would also need to keep in mind the whole network of relationships and what the strains or "pinch-points" may be – what else is going on in Naomi's life and what does it mean to her, or what else may be happening for Jackie, or between Naomi and Peta? Do they appear to be in reasonable communication with each other, and if not, why may that be?

Assessing the situation will also involve taking account of the key issues of power, prejudice and dependency which permeate all practice. For example, who feels (or appears) power*ful* or power*less* in this situation and why? How may the arrival of a "powerful" social worker affect or even trigger the feelings being expressed, or might the social worker be perceived by one or both of the individuals as a potential "rescuer"? Is there a "victim/persecutor/rescuer" triangle (Woodhouse and Pengelly, 1991) being played out or proposed? Who is experiencing what sorts of prejudice in their lives either indirectly or directly, perhaps in the form of harassment or bullying, and how might that relate to this moment? It may also be helpful to think in terms of the concept of "difference" and how this may be affecting the situation, for example, whether feelings about aspects of social class, ethnicity or sexual orientation may have arisen in the placement and whether Naomi may be hinting at difficulty in discussing or resolving such feelings either with her foster carer or with her social worker.

Finally, we also need to think in terms of dependency or attachment; for example, who is expressing what sorts of strong emotion here, and how might these relate directly or indirectly to their emotional and inter-personal needs and whether or not these are being met? Does the strength of expressed emotion appear to "fit" with the circumstances or might other factors be influencing this? What quality of relationship is suggested by the situation?

Observation and assessment in this sort of situation are complicated tasks, which often have to be completed rapidly but also flexibly, because situations evolve and develop, and workers need to keep their ears and eyes open as well as cultivate the more intuitive capacity which enables them to anticipate possible developments.

Decision-making

Observing and assessing are not the same thing as making a decision about what to do, but they do provide the evidence on which that decision can be made. Making the decision itself is complicated, even though it will sometimes have to be made in an instant. The emphasis in what follows will be on *how* the decision will be made, and I focus especially on the priorities and aims involved.

Being clear about priorities may involve three main considerations: urgency, feasibility and ethics.

- Firstly, what is most **urgent**: for example, if Naomi is being dangerous to herself or others, we will probably respond on these grounds although still maybe inviting reflection and communication. The judgement here may therefore include deciding what must or can be done *now* and what can wait or would be better done later, elsewhere or by someone else.
- Secondly, we must decide what is **feasible**: in terms of the available resources of time, space and personnel, but also in terms of our own abilities, confidence and energy level, *and* in terms of the quality of our relationship with the individual and with the others involved. This decision will lead us into the detailed consideration of tactics and methods, some of which are outlined below.
- Thirdly, we must consider the **ethics** of the situation, including the legal requirements and constraints upon us. This will involve being aware of the rights and needs both of the young people (and their families) and of those caring for them and others, as well as considering issues such as privacy and confidentiality. This may raise delicate issues in a situation such as Naomi's, in which feelings about what is private or confidential, and who is saying what about whom, may be very strong.

Aims

It may be useful to think in terms of what *sort* of results we want our intervention to achieve (e.g. calming a storm in a teacup, or promoting the expression of pent-up feelings by a troubled child) and secondly, to think about *how* we propose to achieve that result. In the example given, this might involve focusing our response primarily either on Naomi or on Jackie *or* perhaps on the quality of communication between the two, and concentrating on either coaxing, reflecting back, interpreting or active listening, among the many options. We will therefore need to think in terms of tasks, timescales, and tactics:

- *Task*: How will our proposed action connect with the agreed tasks with this particular young person and the aim of the work, for example, maintaining a successful placement for Naomi, retaining Jackie as a valued foster carer, keeping the peace in the neighbourhood, etc? Note that these aims may conflict at times!
- *Timescales*: For example, what do we want to have achieved in the next two minutes, what by the end of the visit and what by the end of this placement? For each of these, our intervention should be based upon our judgement about what is happening and why, and on a hypothesis as to what difference our actions might make. Sometimes we may not be able to anticipate far ahead, of course, and we often have to adjust our aims as events unfold.
- *Tactics*: In relation to each combination of task, timescale and priority, there will be a range of possible tactics open to us in planning our response, and it is this range which we will consider in the next section. One of my assumptions in mapping out this framework has been that we should always assume that we have a *choice* as to what to do or say, even though it may not always feel like this. Indeed, the mark of an experienced practitioner is that, rather than being driven to *react* unthinkingly to situations, he or she is able, upon reflection, to select an appropriate *response* from their (and their team's) repertoire to any given situation. This does not mean, of course that we will not sometimes take calculated risks or trust our intuition where we are uncertain, but that even in these scenarios we will be making a conscious choice as to how to respond – and of course, the decision-making may not stop at this point, as we may have to make many subsequent decisions as the situation unfolds.

Lest the impression be created that this is all just a matter of picking out a suitable rational response from a bag of ready-made interventions, I want to emphasise again here that, as creative and reflective practitioners, we all learn as we go along, reviewing our actions and discovering our mistakes along the way. This is what Schon meant by 'reflection in action' (1987).

Action

We come now to the "action" phase of this process, in which we consider some of the specific types of response from which the worker may select. As we have already seen, the range of potential responses is almost infinite, so for the sake of mapping out this framework I concentrate simply on *types* of intervention rather than listing each possible action or formulation of words. I hope it will also be clear that I am not advocating the type of formulaic or "scripted" typical responses to incidents which sometimes appear in procedural manuals, but an authentic and personalised response.

One broad distinction to be made is between those interventions with a short-term or "behavioural" aims and those with a longer-term focus on the child's needs, although these need not be mutually exclusive of course.

Short-term/behavioural/"first aid" interventions

I discuss these first, because it is safer to assume that most everyday incidents require an everyday response, rather than always leading into deep and meaningful communication. In many situations, what is appropriate is to give a "normalising" response to the unexpected ('Any chance of a cup of tea, Jackie?'), or to accept a challenge such as that from Naomi, but to do so in a matter-of-fact way which plays down the anger implied in her tone, perhaps acknowledging that an issue has been hinted at, but at the same time not "rising to the bait" (e.g. 'Hi Naomi, good to see you. Something cooking?'). Equally, the worker might give a "holding" response by saying to either Naomi or Jackie, 'I'll be with you in a minute', while responding in more depth or detail to the other.

These short-term responses might be summarised as variations on the theme of "managing the situation", rather than seeking to open up communication (although communication will still be the means towards the end).

In other situations, the challenge may be experienced as one of managing tension or conflict. Even here a short-term response may be preferable to seeking to open up communication (and risk being seen as "rewarding attention-seeking behaviour"). Tactics here might include: offering people alternatives where possible ('Shall we talk out here or inside?'); defusing the tension in the situation; and allowing people to climb down from conflict, e.g. making a brief tactical retreat or pausing for reflection. Some workers might seek to use humour with Naomi, hoping to lighten a possibly threatening atmosphere, while others might counter Naomi's opening gambit with an equally unexpected response such as offering her a piece of chewing gum. The wider your repertoire the better, and it can often be helpful when reviewing and evaluating such episodes to "quick-think" as many possible responses as you can think of.

The above is only a small selection from the possible range, and for other suggestions see Redl and Wineman (1957), Redl (1966), Trieschman (1969), Fahlberg (1990) and Ward (1996).

Longer-term/therapeutic interventions

While many incidents just need the sort of short-term handling outlined above, there are many others in which something more is required. Here, the appropriate response may be to take up the opportunities for communication which the situation offers, and to use the ensuing communication with the young people to promote insight, learning or other positive change for individuals and/or for a group or family. This is skilled and intricate work, which we can only summarise here. One main distinction to be made within the possible responses is in terms of whether to concentrate on an individual or group/family focus – whichever focus is selected, certain key questions will arise.

Individual discussion

An individual approach may be preferable where there is only one child apparently involved, or where it is primarily an individual concern for this child which has been signalled. Even where several individuals are involved, it may still be preferable tactically to focus initially on one key individual, or to deal with each individual's concerns first, before progressing to group or family discussion or bringing in outsiders or external issues. If the individual mode does seem preferable, the questions which arise will include: should the discussion be held right now, or immediately afterwards or perhaps at a later time? Should the discussion be held here on the spot, close by, or somewhere away from the immediate surroundings? It may be helpful to ask Naomi what she would find easier: 'Shall we go down the road a bit?' If it does seem appropriate to move away and talk with Naomi, we may need to "clear the ground" with Jackie, so that she won't feel too threatened by this separate discussion, and perhaps promise to rejoin her for a three-way discussion when that seems right.

The actual techniques which may be used in such a conversation with a child would again require a separate chapter in their own right, but, briefly, include:

- *Active listening*: engaging fully in listening to what is being said and encouraging further communication. 'Can you say a bit more, Naomi? You sound worried/really fed up/pissed off.' Sometimes a period of patient waiting and "engaged silence" on the part of the worker (either with or without eye contact) can allow the child space to start to talk, conveying the message, 'I'm here to listen rather than to preach'.
- *Reflecting back*: helping the young person to articulate their feelings more fully or accurately, by conveying an interest in them and checking out their exact meaning and message, perhaps including some interpretative comment, such as: 'You're saying you don't want me to listen to Jackie. Are you saying that you feel "got at" or that you don't feel safe, or that she knows something which you don't want me to hear?'
- *Making links*: Helping the young person to explore the possible connections between this situation and other events, such as issues from their own family

life/earlier difficulties/current concerns: 'Does this remind you of how it was at home/in your last placement?'

The use of approaches such as these depends, to some extent, on the social worker's existing relationship with Naomi, and there is always some risk of closing down the communication if we "force the pace". This is where ongoing re-assessment helps in constantly reading the unfolding dialogue. These techniques also only refer to the start of the conversation, and many more steps may emerge if the child feels able to take those steps, including, if appropriate, some thoughts about what sort of further action may need to be taken in connection with what has been discussed.

Group/family discussion

Similar questions will arise in relation to decisions about a broader-based response to an incident, and the main question will be as to whether it would be better to talk with all those involved rather than focusing just on a key individual. In the scenario given, the best option might be to bring Naomi and Jackie together as soon as possible to explore what is happening – and perhaps also to involve Peta if this seems helpful. Naomi is a member of this family, albeit a new one, and her opening gambit certainly suggests strong feelings about her interactions with at least one key member of that family. It may be, for example, that Naomi feels she is being expected to become a member of this family whereas she doesn't feel much like one at all, or equally it may be that Naomi feels that Jackie is actually getting through to her and showing some real care, but that this is too much for Naomi to cope with at the moment and she feels panicked at how much Jackie seems to understand her. Family systems theory suggests that the most productive response may be to address the issue where it belongs, i.e. in the context of family-wide communication. Perhaps in this case, Naomi and Jackie – and Peta – could be invited to reflect together on how each of them feels in relation to this recently re-formulated family and how they each may imagine the other to be feeling.

In a group context, such as a residential home, many individual expressions of strong feeling emerge from informal group interactions (Brown and Clough, 1989), and it is often most helpful to address the issues in the group, either informally by involving those who happen to be present or more formally by calling a meeting. Here, the worker may need to remember the "systems" principle that in a group care unit everyone is a member of a large group and they will be affected whether we plan for this or not, so it is often better to involve the whole group even if only a sub-group appears to have been involved in the original communication (Ward, 1993, 2006). There will nevertheless also be an ethical question: in what sense does the communication really "belong" with the rest of the group, or in what sense may it be confidential for an individual?

Again the range of groupwork techniques is large and readers should turn to other sources for the full range. Here, I simply highlight some key functions of therapeutic groupwork in this context. These include the following:

- providing "containment" for troubled individuals and groups, by helping them to recognise and think about their anxieties, fears or other difficult feelings (Worthington, 2003a);
- providing a forum in which issues of personal and social power within the group may be safely raised and learned from, rather than being re-enacted in destructive ways, e.g. racist comments, bullying (Worthington, 2003b);
- pnabling young people to understand themselves and each other, by talking about their family situations and thinking about how such factors may be affecting their state of mind and their current behaviour (Pooley, 2003).

Sustaining the intervention

The discussion so far might appear to imply that opportunity-led work involves a single decision or set of decisions, after which the situation either closes quickly or evolves along a predictable path of interactions. In reality, of course, nothing could be further from the truth: while some events do require only the simplest of responses, many others require a much more complex and evolving sequence of interactions, with the worker needing to re-assess and re-evaluate at regular intervals. For example, an initial short-term response may have to give way rapidly to something quite different as the situation unfolds – and vice versa, opportunities for communication occasionally melt away unexpectedly or have to be cut short prematurely in order to prevent further difficulties.

In one sense, the daily life of a busy family or residential unit consists of a virtually seamless flow of such events, one merging into or overlapping with another, one situation influencing the handling of the next, and so on. To separate out one hypothetical "opportunity" from this mêlée might be seen as wholly artificial, were it not for the fact that for the child and the worker involved, each incident does have its own significance and does require the same attention to detail: this is one reason why the work is so challenging but also so potentially rewarding. The task of "sustaining the intervention", therefore, begins almost as soon as the "action" phase has begun, and may continue for some considerable time.

In the context of the situation with Naomi, sustaining the intervention might involve supporting the child in making the transition from "sounding off" individually to engaging in a deeper dialogue with her foster carer, or it might also involve helping Jackie to move from feeling threatened by an angry young person to recognising her own needs for support and validation in her challenging task.

We should also note that, if the intervention is to be sustained, then the worker, too, may need to be sustained: he or she will certainly need to stay in touch with other staff or managers as the situation unfolds, and may need the availability of ongoing support in the form of "live supervision". Such supervision may not be immediately available for Naomi's social worker during the visit to this family, but he or she will need to remain reflective and aware of his or her own feelings during and after the intense communication which such an episode can entail, and perhaps seek support and supervision on return to the office.

Closing and evaluation

There are three main things to consider in the "closure" phase of an intervention, whether it has been a brief exchange of words, a sustained dialogue between the worker and the young person, or a more substantial family- or group-meeting.

Firstly, it is obviously important to bring the situation to an agreed and clear ending so that those involved can resume their other activities and responsibilities, but also to minimise any risk of the situation being misunderstood or misrepresented at a later stage. This can be thought of in terms of closing down the communication – making sure that no loose ends have been left, so that people are not left unsure what has been said to them or unclear about or dissatisfied with the response which they have had. It may be important for the worker to actually say something like 'Well, that's finished with now', or 'Let's leave it there for the moment'. It will not always be clear as to when this can be said, and the worker may need to check with the child or group, e.g. 'Are you ready to leave it there?' or 'How do you think we should finish this off?'

Clearly, this process will be more delicate where a situation has developed into some deeper or more painful communication. For example, if Naomi's situation were to have developed into a family discussion about how each member was feeling, it may be helpful to acknowledge that the air has been to some extent cleared, but that this may not be the last time such discussions will need to take place. It might even be validating for Naomi to acknowledge her role in drawing attention (however awkwardly) to the feelings in the first place.

Secondly, decisions may need to be made as to what else has to be done in connection with the facts and feelings of the situation. For example, information may need to be conveyed to other people, or strong feelings may need to be allowed for during the ensuing period and may need to be raised again later elsewhere – in either case, this will need to have been discussed during the conversation itself. Sometimes the worker may need to close the incident by giving a firm undertaking as to how it will be followed up, either with this individual or with other people. The written recording of significant communications is essential, so questions will arise as to who records what and why.

Thirdly, after the communication has been concluded, there is the need for review and evaluation – to evaluate our ways of working and to improve our understanding, incorporating any changes into our policies and procedures. Individuals (both workers and children) may need supervision, catharsis, free time, relief, etc. If the situation has been an especially difficult one to handle, other people may not realise how strong the worker's feelings were, and (as we saw above) he or she may need to seek out a supervisor or an appropriate team member and ask for immediate support. Moreover, if *the worker* has strong feelings, it is likely that the children and others involved will also have equivalent feelings, and somebody (not necessarily this same worker) may need to offer them some further support. The period immediately following a sustained piece of opportunity-led communication may be an especially sensitive time for some of those involved – including those only apparently involved at the fringes of the communication. It is not uncommon for other young people (either in foster or residential care) who witness such communication to find that they start to feel more in touch with their own needs to be heard and understood and to seek out opportunities for themselves, which may be unfortunate timing for the worker who by now is ready for a coffee break.

The above discussion also brings us back to "context": not only, as we saw under "assessment", do the workers have to be aware of their organisational context, but the context has to be aware of *them*. In other words, staff can only provide opportunities for children if they, too, have opportunities for communication and reflection. This way of working therefore requires regular and supportive supervision and staff development. For residential workers, this will include a programme of staff meetings and consultancy. An atmosphere of trust and respect within a residential team working under these pressures is essential but not easy to sustain: staff need to be able to reflect on their uncertainties and acknowledge their mistakes so that they can learn from them. A useful paper by Andrew Collie (2002) offers some examples of ways in which staff training and development can be offered on an opportunity-led basis, in addition to any planned programmes. In this way, the learning is likely to be maximised since there will be a "felt" connection or matching between the mode of learning and the mode of practice (see also Ward and McMahon, 1998). For all teams, field or residential, it may also be helpful to set aside time to discuss how this type of incident or potential communication can be handled, and for team members to pool their wisdom and share their concerns.

Conclusion

This chapter has outlined the main elements of an approach to responding to opportunities for communication with young people. Although the range of possible situations and responses is infinite, the model itself is a simple one, involving observation and assessment, decision-making, action and review, and the emphasis is mainly on identifying and using those opportunities for deeper communication with children which will sometimes arise out of such situations. The skill lies firstly in spotting the opportunities, and secondly in making the best use of them. It is an approach which requires attentiveness, responsiveness and creativity (and the working through of one fictional example is not intended to provide a blueprint or script for any particular responses in other situations), but for the approach to be used well in a team, it also requires support and encouragement within the team itself. In this sort of work, all interactions need to be seen within the broader contexts of the group, the staff team and the work as a whole.

References

Brown A. and Clough R. (1989) *Groups and Groupings: Life and work in day and residential centres*, London and New York, NY: Tavistock/Routledge

Collie A. (2002) 'Opportunistic staff development strategies in therapeutic communities', *Therapeutic Communities*, 23:2, pp 125–132

Fahlberg V. (ed.) (1990) *Residential Treatment: A tapestry of many therapies*, Indianapolis, IN: Perspectives Press

Oaklander V. (1978) *Windows to our Children: A Gestalt therapy approach to children and adolescents*, Moab, UT: Real People Press

Pooley J. (2003) 'Keeping families in mind', in Ward A., Kasinski K., Pooley J. and Worthington A. (eds) *Therapeutic Communities for Children and Young People*, London, Jessica Kingsley Publishers

Redl F. (1966) *When we Deal with Children*, New York, NY: Free Press

Redl F. and Wineman D. (1957) *The Aggressive Child*, New York, NY: Free Press

Schon D. (1987) *Educating the Reflective Practitioner*, San Francisco, CA: Jossey Bass

Trieschman A. E. (1969) 'Understanding the stages of a typical temper tantrum', in Trieschman A. E., Whittaker J. K. and Brendtro L. K. (eds) *The Other 23 Hours: Child-care work with emotionally-disturbed children in a therapeutic milieu*, New York, NY: Aldine

Ward A. (1993) 'The large group: the heart of the system in group care', *Groupwork*, 6:1, pp 63–77

Ward A. (1995) 'Opportunity-led work: 1. Introducing the concept', *Social Work Education*, 14:4, pp 89–105

Ward A. (1996) 'Opportunity-led work: 2. The framework', *Social Work Education*, 15:3, pp 40–59

Ward A. (2006) *Working in Group Care: Social work in residential and day care settings*, (2nd edn), Bristol: Policy Press

Ward A., Kasinski K., Pooley J. and Worthington A. (eds) (2003) *Therapeutic Communities for Children and Young People*, London: Jessica Kingsley Publishers

Ward A. and McMahon L. (eds) (1998) *Intuition is not Enough: Matching learning with practice in therapeutic child care*, London: Routledge

Woodhouse D. and Pengelly P. (1991) *Anxiety and the Dynamics of Collaboration*, Aberdeen: Aberdeen University Press

Worthington A. (2003a) 'Relationships and the therapeutic setting', in Ward A., Kasinski K., Pooley J. and Worthington A. (eds) (2003) *Therapeutic Communities for Children and Young People*, London: Jessica Kingsley Publishers

Worthington A. (2003b) 'Structured work: the space to think', in Ward A., Kasinski K., Pooley J. and Worthington A. (eds) (2003) *Therapeutic Communities for Children and Young People*, London: Jessica Kingsley Publishers

12 Ascertaining the wishes and feelings of children in the children's guardian role

Anna Gupta

Introduction

Over the past three decades, there has been increasing recognition of the importance of involving children who are looked after in the decisions that affect them personally. A child's right to participate in decision-making is encapsulated in Article 12 of the United Nations Convention on the Rights of the Child (1989), as well as in domestic legislation. In England and Wales, the Children Act 1989 requires that the court, when making any order, shall have regard to 'the ascertainable wishes and feelings of the child concerned (considered in light of his age and understanding)'(s1(3)(a)). Amendments to the Children Act 1989, included in the Children Act 2004, widened the requirement to ascertain children's wishes and feelings to include assessments of children in need (s17), children accommodated under section 20 and children subject to child protection enquiries (s47). Similar requirements are included in the welfare checklist of the Adoption and Children Act 2002, as well as the Children (Scotland) Act 1995 and Children (Northern Ireland) Order 1995.

In addition to being a legal requirement, there is also increasing evidence that the participation of children can improve decision-making and help promote positive developmental outcomes. Sinclair and Franklin (2000) argue that children's participation leads to more accurate, relevant and better-informed decisions and plans, which are more likely to be implemented. Gilligan (1998, p 90) explains that one of the three 'building blocks of resilience' is a sense of self-efficacy and there are 'many opportunities where child welfare professionals can consciously help young people in care to develop a sense of self-efficacy, not least by involving them in the planning process'.

A review of the implementation of the Children Act 1989 concluded that: 'Given the right support, many children are capable of participating fully in decision-making. To enable them to take part, they need skilled, direct work and adults who are reliable and will champion their needs' (Department of Health, 2001, p 94). This chapter examines the work of the children's guardians, who provide independent representation for children in public law family court proceedings in England and Wales, and whose role includes ascertaining their wishes and feelings and ensuring the court is made aware of these. In this chapter I consider the literature and draw upon my experience as a children's guardian.

A brief history of the emergence of the children's guardian service

The need for separate representation for children in proceedings that concerned them was highlighted by the report into the death of Maria Colwell (Department of Health and Social Security, 1974). The Children Act 1975 made it possible for courts to appoint guardians *ad litem* to investigate the child's interests and report the child's wishes to the court. However, this provision was largely unimplemented until 1984, when local authorities were obliged to set up panels of guardians *ad litem* to provide separate representation for children involved in care proceedings and contested adoption applications. Head (1998, p 192) suggests that: 'dissatisfaction with the level of protection afforded to children and past failure to listen to the child's voice created a climate of opinion which allowed the role of the guardian ad litem to come into being'.

Following the implementation of the Children Act 1989, the role of guardians *ad litem* was expanded. The appointment of a guardian *ad litem* was made mandatory in public law cases unless the court was satisfied that this was not necessary (s41(6)). In April 2001, the panels were disbanded and the responsibility for the service was taken over by the Child and Family Court Advisory and Support Service (CAFCASS), a quasi-government organisation with responsibility for advising the family courts in both public and private law proceedings. At this time the term "guardian *ad litem*" was changed to "children's guardian".

Direct work with children

The role of the children's guardian is to safeguard and promote the interests and rights of children in public family law proceedings. Their purpose is two-fold as it involves providing the court with as full and accurate an assessment of the child's life and functioning as possible, as well as ascertaining the child's wishes and feelings and ensuring that the court is aware of them in making any decision about the child's future (Timms, 1992). The key focus is on the child and guardians undertake a variety of tasks, including interviewing parents and family members, observing contact, reading file records and providing a report for the court. When working directly with the child, their tasks involve giving information about the court process, ascertaining the wishes and feelings of the child, assessing the child's needs and explaining the court's recommendations and the outcome of the proceedings.

As the guardian is appointed for the purpose of specific court proceedings, their task is time limited and their role is 'essentially information-gathering, not therapeutic' (Timms, 1992, p 65). However, clearly attention must be paid to the process of the work and how the guardian can build rapport, gain a child's trust, and convey to the child that they are being listened to and their perspective valued. A particular challenge for a guardian is to strike the right balance when developing a relationship with the child. As

Timms (1992, p 65) explains, 'throughout the process the guardian . . . is seeking to acquire enough information to represent the child effectively, without becoming over-involved, and to establish a rapport with the child without raising unreal expectations of an ongoing relationship'.

Introductions

Guardians should be appointed at the commencement of the court proceedings. Although there will be limited time to plan the first visit, as much information as possible should be gained from the written reports and discussions with professionals, parents and carers. Key issues that need to be considered prior to the first visit and reviewed in light of ongoing work include:

- What is the child's age and stage of development – are there any disabilities that need to be considered? If so, do additional arrangements need to be made to facilitate communication?
- What is the child's ethnic, cultural and religious background? What impact may the guardian's ethnicity and gender have on the child? What is the child's first language and is an interpreter required?
- What is the child's emotional state? What information is available on experiences of harm, separation and loss? If separated from parents, under what circumstances and what is known about the child's views?
- What information does the child already have about the court proceedings and role of the children's guardian?
- Given the above, what written information, toys and play equipment does the guardian need to take to the first visit? How are sibling groups with children of different ages and stages of development going to be managed?

The first visit will usually take place where the child is living, with some negotiation taking place with the carer and the child as to where in the house the conversation should take place. A balance needs to be struck between the child feeling safe and some privacy being offered to the child and the guardian. In Ruegger's (2001b, p 36) study of children's experiences of guardians, one child reported that she felt safe 'knowing that her foster carers were in the kitchen when she was talking to her guardian'. Several other children identified the presence of siblings as being a comfort when they first met their guardian. One seven-year-old boy agreed to talk to me in private on my first visit as long as the foster carer's dog was also present.

An important part of this first session will be building rapport with the child and in the process explaining to the child the role of the guardian, the roles of other professionals, including the child's solicitor, and the workings of the court in ways accessible to that individual child. There are a number of leaflets and guides available from CAFCASS which explain the role of the guardian and the process of court proceedings. Key issues to convey to the child are the independence of the guardian and that their role is to find out what the child thinks about what has happened and what they would like to happen in the future, so that this can be conveyed to the judge. Limits of confidentiality and the time-limited nature of the role must also be explained. This can be a particularly challenging task, particularly if the plans proposed involve removal of the child from their home. Brophy's (2006) review suggests that the consistent provision of adequate information by guardians is an area warranting improvement.

For younger children it may be more helpful to use toys to explain the court process, for example, using soft toys to set up a court and having a wise animal as the judge. This can then be reconstructed later to help the child express what they want to say to the wise animal (Norris, 2001). Important throughout this session is to not make assumptions and to clarify the child's understanding of various terms, including that of "court". A child I was working with thought I was referring to the Court Hotel down the road! It is also important to clarify the difference between civil and criminal proceedings in order to dispel ideas that court is where people go when they have done something wrong. Children who have recently arrived in Britain, including those who have come as asylum-seekers, may have particularly limited, and sometimes fearful, understanding of professionals and court services.

A challenge for guardians in this first interview is to give and gain enough information without overloading the child, which requires professional judgement based on the child's age, level of understanding, concentration and engagement. Much of this information will need to be revisited in future meetings (Ruegger, 2001a). As a guardian, I have often been surprised how often information, including the time-limited nature of my role, needs to be repeated. Like Ruegger (2001a), I have found it useful to use pictorial material, such as calendars to help children understand the timescales of the court process.

Work with the child during proceedings

As the case progresses, the guardian will need to continue to maintain contact with the child, in order to gain further understanding of the child's world, wishes and feelings, and keep the child informed of the court proceedings. Studies involving children have indicated very different views about the locations of the meetings with their guardians. For example, some described school as being a good place to meet, while others expressed strong negative feelings about meetings at school (Ruegger, 2001b). Clark and Sinclair (1999) highlight the importance of giving the children some choice and control over where they would like to meet their guardian. The need to have some degree of control over the process of the work was vividly illustrated by a 14-year-old boy with whom I worked. He was a young person who frequently absconded from his placements and was difficult for professionals to engage with. He would only agree to meet with me if I took him out to a restaurant of his choice. During the course of the proceedings we worked our way through the major cuisines of the world.

Hunt *et al* (2003) found considerable variation in the amount of time guardians spent with children. There was a statistically significant association between time spent and the age of the child, duration of the case and number of placements. Guardians also reported spending more time where there were difficulties in communicating or establishing a trusting relationship, or when compensating for inadequate social work input. Developing a trusting relationship can take time, particularly with children who have experiences of being let down by adults and have had to form numerous relationships with professionals. I was the guardian for a young person from Sierra Leone, who was pregnant by sexual abuse, and extremely confused and traumatised. Initially, she could not make eye contact or speak to me apart from monosyllabic answers. I visited her each week for the first month to try to sensitively and gently convey to her that I was an adult who was interested in her perspective and well-being. Eventually she opened up to me and together with her solicitor we argued successfully that both she and her child should remain within the extended family, which was her wish.

With regard to issues of trust, it is crucial to make clear who would be given the information discussed in the sessions with the guardian. Several children in Ruegger's (2001b) study were unaware that their parents would have access to the guardian's report and felt distressed and betrayed when this occurred. Other studies similarly highlight the importance of guardians paying careful attention to informing the children about what will happen to the information they give and involving them in thinking about how the information can be shared (Clark and Sinclair, 1999; Masson and Oakley, 1999).

A key role for the guardian is to assist the court in making final decisions about where a child lives, whom they have contact with and under what legal framework. However, during the course of the proceedings they need to be kept informed about the child's progress. If the guardian is unhappy about issues relating to the welfare of the child or management of the case, she can, following negotiation with the other parties, refer the matter back to court. Frequently, in my experience, these issues will revolve around sibling placements and contact. Ruegger (2001a) describes the work of a guardian who gave notice of her intention to oppose the renewal of an interim care order, not because she felt the children should return to their parents' care but because it forced the local authority to explain their care plan, about which the children were very unhappy due to their separation from and lack of contact with each other.

Ascertaining wishes and feelings and reporting to court

When ascertaining the wishes and feelings of the child, the level of the child's understanding is crucial for the guardian to explore. Children will need information on the choices available and the likely consequences of each option (Head, 1998). This requires skilful intervention and can take time. When working with younger children, guardians can use creative techniques to help children express their wishes and feelings, including a "what I want to happen ladder", drawings or play equipment. Norris (2001) describes a piece of work she undertook with a six-year-old child using a toy rabbit, asking her to "help" the rabbit think about going to live with its mother and how it felt about this. For an older child, a more straightforward conversation may be more appropriate.

Some children will be able to answer honestly and clearly direct questions about where they want to live and whom they wish to see. One eight-year-old boy I worked with, for whom the plan was adoption, but who wanted to remain with his foster carers and in contact with his mother, was well able to inform me of his views. He said, 'I don't know why the social worker keeps telling me she is going to find a new mummy and daddy for me. I already have two mummies, one who I live with and one who I like seeing. I don't need any more.' Other children will find this process distressing, confusing and some questions too difficult to answer. Children involved in care proceedings will have experienced loss and disrupted attachment relationships. Many will have also experienced abuse and neglect. These children may have feelings of ambivalence or conflicts of loyalty to parents and carers. It is particularly important to convey to a child in these situations that, while their wishes and feeling will be given serious consideration, the judge has the responsibility for making the final decision. Head (1998, p 194) argues that the guardian 'who listens carefully to what the child says, both in words and in actions, should be in a position to judge how difficult it is for the child to express views in the face of fear or family loyalties'. The quality of the *listening* is crucial and needs to involve observation and attention to the way in which the child expresses their views, as well reflection on professionals' own responses to the child's statements (Aldgate and Seden, 2006).

Guardians have a duty to give their own views of what is in the interests of the child, as well as representing the child's wishes and feelings. As Mr Justice Wall explains, 'the dilemma of the guardian's role is that he or she has to represent the best interests of the child – and what is in the best interests of the child is not necessarily what the child wants' (Wall, 1997, p 24, quoted in Head, 1998). The guardian, when deciding what weight to give to a child's views, will clearly need to consider the child's age, understanding, emotional state and impact of the decision to support or not support the child's wishes. Frequently, this decision is far from straightforward and guardians must critically reflect upon the impact of their own and others' values and attitudes on their work. Thomas (2000) presents a typology of adult attitudes to children's involvement and advocates for a *value-based* approach, which regards children's involvement in decision-making as a positive process, that is consistent with their rights and good practice, and can lead to better outcomes.

A guardian would normally work with the child's solicitor, who represents their views in the court arena. However, when a child's view differs from that of their guardian, the child's competence to instruct their solicitor independently will have to be established. Whilst it is ultimately for the court to decide, the duty is placed on the solicitor to assess competence, in consultation with the guardian. Although there is no absolute demarcation based on age, Stevens (2001) found little evidence of separate representation of children aged ten and under. Other factors for consideration include the child's understanding of the issues at stake and the clarity and consistency of their instructions (Stevens, 2001). Whilst this right of a competent child to have their views presented on an equal footing in the court arena exists in law, there is some evidence to suggest that the paternalistic attitudes of professionals and avoidance of conflict may be resulting in limited use of this provision (Masson and Oakley, 1999; James *et al*, 2004). The one issue that children do have a veto on is whether they see an expert appointed in the proceedings, although Ruegger's (2001b) study found that children across the age range in general felt they had no choice about seeing the expert.

Thomas (2000, p 49) suggests that professionals are faced with particular challenges when working with children in their middle childhood where 'the competing demands of self-determination and "best interests" can often be evenly matched'. As a guardian I have found this to be a particularly complex issue when it comes to contact in permanent placements. For example, what weight should be given to the wishes of an eight-year-old to see her birth family when her adopters and social worker are not supporting this? Balancing the needs and wishes of siblings for contact, particularly when some siblings remain in contact with birth families and others do not, is also an extremely challenging task which may, on rare occasions, require the appointment of two guardians. If a guardian does decide to recommend courses of action different from that which the child wants, it is essential that reasons for this be carefully explained. If the child is old enough and not separately represented, discussion should take place about how the child's views can be explained to the judge. The guardian could include verbatim accounts in her report or help the child write a letter to the judge.

As part of their work with children, guardians need also to consider the child's attendance at court. When ascertaining their views on this, it needs to be made clear that the judge is the final arbiter of this decision. Timms and Thoburn's (2003) study of children involved in a range of court proceedings found that the majority did not attend court. However, there were children involved in family proceedings who would have liked to be able to attend court, but did not have the opportunity to do so. A few of the older children with whom I have worked have had strong views about 'talking to the judge' even when we are in agreement. One 15-year-old boy sat through a two-day hearing and was actively involved in the negotiations about his return home to his mother. Another young person, a 14-year-old girl, just came to court to speak to the judge directly about her unhappiness at the plan of sibling separation. When it may be too difficult for children to sit through lengthy and often distressing court proceedings, Ruegger (2001a) suggests giving consideration to bringing them to court when it is not in session as this can help them feel more involved and informed. However, this will depend on the individual child, and some children in Masson and Oakley's (1999) study found that this was not enough.

Explaining outcomes and endings

The guardian needs to ensure the child is made aware of the outcome of the court proceedings, and Ruegger (2001a) suggests asking the child beforehand from whom they would like to hear the decision and trying to ensure that this happens. Irrespective of whether this is done by the guardian or not, the guardian must arrange a final visit to the child to say good-bye, and, if age appropriate, ensure they are given information about how to contact their solicitor. Consideration needs to be given to providing the child with written information about the court proceedings, or another tangible reminder, for example, photographs for life story work or a letter. Norris (2001) explains that handing over to the children a folder of the work they had done together symbolised the completion of the task and enabled them to say good-bye.

Conclusion

Children's guardians have a central role in ensuring that children's wishes and feelings are given due consideration in court proceedings. The task can be very challenging and children require skilful guardians who are willing and able to grapple with the complexities of ensuring a child's right to be listened to, as well as decisions to be made in their best interests. After the court proceedings are over, looked after children will also continue to need the other professionals involved in their lives to be willing to take seriously their participation in decision-making processes.

References

Aldgate J. and Seden J. (2006) 'Direct work with children', in Aldgate J., Jones D., Rose W. and Jeffrey C. (eds) *The Developing World of the Child*, London: Jessica Kingsley

Brophy J. (2006) *Research Review: Child care proceedings under the Children Act 1989*, London: Department for Constitutional Affairs

Clarke A. and Sinclair R. (1999) *The Child in Focus: The evolving role of the guardian ad litem*, London: National Children's Bureau

Department of Health and Social Security (1974) *Report of the Committee of Inquiry into the Care and Supervision Provided in Relation to Maria Colwell*, London: HMSO

Department of Health (2001) *Children Act Now: Messages from research*, London: The Stationery Office

Gilligan R. (1998) 'Beyond permanence? The importance of resilience in child placement practice and planning', in Hill M. and Shaw M. (eds) *Signposts in Adoption: Policy, practice and research issues*, London: BAAF

Head A. (1998) 'The child's voice in child and family social work decision making: the perspective of the guardian *ad litem*', *Child and Family Social Work*, 3:3, pp 189–196

Hunt J., Head A. and Drucker N. (2003) *Capturing Guardian Practice Prior to CAFCASS*, Oxford: Centre for Family Law and Policy

James A. L., James A. and McNamee S. (2004) 'Turn down the volume? Not hearing children in family proceedings', *Child and Family Law Quarterly*, 16:2, pp 189–202

Masson J. and Oakley M. (1999) *Out of Hearing: The representation by guardians and solicitors in public law proceedings*, Chichester: Wiley

Norris G. (2001) 'Direct work with children', in Ruegger M. (ed) *Hearing the Voice of the Child: The representation of children's interests in public law proceedings*, Lyme Regis: Russell House Publishing

Ruegger M. (2001a) 'The role of the guardian ad litem: a personal view', in Ruegger M. (ed.) *Hearing the Voice of the Child: The representation of children's interests in public law proceedings*, Lyme Regis: Russell House Publishing

Ruegger M. (2001b) 'Children's experiences of the guardian ad litem: service and public law proceedings', in Ruegger M. (ed.) *Hearing the Voice of the Child: The representation of children's interests in public law proceedings*, Lyme Regis: Russell House Publishing

Sinclair I. and Franklin A. (2000) *Young People's Participation*, Quality Protects Briefings No. 3, www.rip.org.uk/openaccess.html

Stevens S. (2001) 'Assessing the competence of the child to give instructions: the solicitor's role', in Ruegger M. (ed.) *Hearing the Voice of the Child: The representation of children's interests in public law proceedings*, Lyme Regis: Russell House Publishing

Thomas N. (2000) *Children, Family and the State*, Basingstoke: Macmillan

Timms J. (1992) *The Manual of Practice Guidance for Guardians ad litem and Reporting Officers*, London: HMSO

Timms J. and Thoburn J. (2003) *Your Shout! A survey of the views of 706 children and young people in care*, London: NSPCC

Wall Mr Justice (1997) *Strengthening Interagency Links and Keeping Children in Focus*, Workshop Papers, London: Department of Health

13 Unaccompanied asylum-seeking and refugee children and their transition into care

Ravi KS Kohli

Transitions for asylum-seeking and refugee children are dangerous and complex, and throw up a host of psychosocial challenges for them as they move from harmful environments into relatively safer ones (Loughry and Eyber, 2003). The purpose of this chapter is to describe what is known about the experiences of children and young people on journeys in politically volatile circumstances, and to propose ways that allow those helping them to get a fix on the movement they represent. Here, three dimensions of the care of unaccompanied minors are considered:

- firstly, the ways in which they experience safety after arrival in a host country, given the many dangers they are exposed to, and what others do that makes them feel safe;
- secondly, the ways in which they regenerate a sense of belonging with and to other people following the rupture or decay of established relationships, and the frames of friendship and solidarity that can be grown around them to allow new stable relationships to emerge;
- thirdly, how they define and achieve success and the ways helpers can assist them in feeling accomplished in their new lives.

In all, unaccompanied minors are seldom a homogenous group, undifferentiated in their suffering (Richman, 1998). The emerging picture we have of them through research shows them to be survivors as well as victims of the particular circumstances that have removed them from their roots. In that sense it would be inaccurate to perpetuate a simple image of them all as damaged people needing aid from skilled helpers in wealthy contexts. Yet among their capacities to survive skilfully in different ways and to drive their lives forward, specific vulnerabilities emerge, associated with war and its aftermath, which need to be managed in an informed and coherent way. This chapter considers how practitioners and carers for unaccompanied minors can see their lives in a three-dimensional way, identify where their strengths and vulnerabilities lie, maintain what Kerr (1995) refers to as '*a tender, optimistic stance*' towards them, and co-construct a map for moving beyond the label of "asylum seeker" to the territory of ordinary living again.

A transition to the asylum country

As these children arrive at ports of entry in Western industrialised nations, they carry many experiences into their new world. Some of these experiences are bad, some good and some are hopeful. Often, because of their dramatic nature, bad experiences are the ones that receive attention, most notably the circumstances of becoming a refugee and the psychosocial needs that stem from these (McCallin, 1996). These needs are then allied to the challenges they face within the asylum context, and in the UK a number of writers have highlighted the suffering they continue to endure after arrival (Stanley, 2001).

To some degree, unaccompanied minors carry resonances with social workers and other helpers, which are simultaneously familiar and unfamiliar. Unaccompanied minors, like their indigenous counterparts who move in and out of care, come from backgrounds where they have faced danger, sudden or enduring harm, and materially and psychologically dishevelled prospects. Their family of origin is likely to have fragmented under the weight of pressure exerted by powerful forces. Equally, research confirms that their civic lives lose their shape, rhythm and pattern, so that they can no longer grow evenly within a frame that is predictable and nurturing (Petty and Jareg, 1998). But whereas indigenous children move into care from families that are fragmented and sometimes dangerous (Fisher *et al*, 1986), unaccompanied minors appear to be expelled by families that care for and invest in them. This rather paradoxical act by families – of loving a child sufficiently to send them to the care of unknown strangers – provides the pulse of movement for unaccompanied minors. In order for them to reach their destination countries, agents have to be secured, documents manufactured, transit fees paid, all wrapped in differing levels of risk (Robinson and Seagrott, 2002). Once they reach a port of entry, there are people there to question them, and these people have to be convinced that their stories are sufficiently credible to allow them to enter. If an agent has abandoned them just after arrival, then the port authorities or the police are obliged to contact social services to make a referral of a child in need of care and protection under the Children Act 1989. It is at that point that unaccompanied minors come face to face with internal borders, where they have to convince a different set of people that their past lives combined with their present circumstances make them credible candidates for care under s20 of the Children Act 1989 (Dennis, 2007).

> Zelda, aged 17, is an unaccompanied asylum-seeking young woman from a West African country, who arrived in the UK seeking asylum when she was aged 14. Her father and mother died during a period of civil war, and she was helped to escape by an aunt. Zelda did not know which country she was being sent to. She brought no mementos, photographs or keepsakes with her, just some clothing and false papers. She was brought into the UK by an agent who left her at the port of entry after getting her through customs. The port authorities contacted the local social services department,

which accommodated Zelda under s20 of the Children Act 1989. She has lived with an African-Caribbean foster mother for three years, and is said to be resettled comfortably within the extended family. She has periods of intense sadness, which she manages by spending time alone. She does not want therapy. She wants to be a doctor, and is studying hard and is determined to succeed educationally. The social worker describes her as 'clean, well-groomed, bright, capable and assertive'. Her asylum status is still not finalised, although it is likely she will be allowed to remain in the UK on humanitarian grounds.

A transition into care

Research studies that specifically consider the needs of unaccompanied minors in industrialised nations are few, but they yield some important facts about what they may need when moving into care in such contexts. Perhaps unsurprisingly, given established findings in relation to indigenous children (Bilton, 2003), several studies point out the need for a trusting relationship with significant adults as being the foundation of recovery for unaccompanied minors in substitute care (Jockenhövel-Schiecke, 1990; Steinbock, 1996; Kidane and Amerena, 2004; Hek, 2007; Kohli, 2007). Wade *et al* (2005), in the only study in the UK to provide depth and detail of social work services to unaccompanied minors, steadily revealed a complex picture of the variables that impact on the transition into care. They looked at the trajectories of 212 asylum-seeking children in three local authorities in England, and the ways their resettlement was shaped by services within those authorities. The study confirmed that about half the young people were found a placement on the same day as the referral, and that where they ended up depended on their age, their circumstances at the time, the ways workers used agency policies and procedures for responding to unaccompanied minors, and the level and type of placement resources available. Overall, their results suggested that kinship care could provide stable and familiar attachments, that foster care for younger children was advisable, that cross-cultural placements involved a difficult period of readjustment, and that isolation could be lessened by the judicious use of independent visitors, community links and support workers who were part of packages of care tailored to individual children and young people, depending on their specific needs. Finally, Wade *et al* (2005) summarised the resettlement needs of unaccompanied minors entering care into four key areas:

- a safe and supportive place to live;
- continuities with past relationships, customs and cultures, and opportunities to create new ones;
- access to purposeful education and training;
- opportunities to move forward from troubling experiences, re-centre their lives and find new purpose in everyday routines and activities.

This simple and important list of features chimes perfectly with the observations by Daniel *et al*, (1999) who identified six "domains" within which interventions into the lives of all vulnerable children could be framed – namely, the promotion of a secure base, educational success, friendships that have a positive impact, nurturing talents and interests, promoting "positive values" including empathy for others, and being and becoming socially competent. In turn, these domains provide the scaffolding around which issues of safety, belonging and success can be grown for unaccompanied minors (Kohli and Mather, 2003). Yet, to some degree, the simplicity of the list hides a level of complexity in each of its elements, and it is to this complexity that I now turn, picking up a few examples to illuminate a broader picture of the challenges faced by unaccompanied minors in their transition into care.

Safety

Asylum-seeking and refugee children may be hemmed in by deep and persistent fears about catastrophe, through knowing their losses, and not knowing who they will find in the new context to shelter them from harm. In a minority of circumstances, children will have been in danger themselves before departure, or witnessed violence, or been violent in order to escape. Current evidence suggests that the impact of war on children varies considerably, depending on a mixture of disposition and circumstance (Boyden and de Berry, 2004). Not all asylum-seeking children are traumatised, but the majority may be very fearful, uncertain and disorientated at the beginning of their asylum lives (Richman, 1998). In these circumstances, they may require regular reassurance by their key worker that they will come to no physical harm in the placement, and that the daily routines of finding shelter, food, medical care, education and friends in an environment that is nurturing, are achievable. Given the substantial levels of uncertainty – for example, whether the people they have left are dead or alive, the people they are with are trustworthy, whether their asylum application will be successful – fear may contort their ordinary ways of being into silence, and an unspoken watchfulness (Kohli, 2006). As with indigenous children in care, there is some evidence to suggest that people who are experienced as kind, honest, realistic, practically helpful and reliable, and who make an effort to understand the world of unaccompanied minors, offer some key building blocks towards establishing a sense of safety over time (Williamson, 1998). Unaccompanied minors can begin to unfurl the maps of their hidden worlds more readily with workers who understand that there is a purpose to silence and secrets (Bertrand, 2000). Equally, a sense of safety is not just a psychological state, but also a legal fact. For those minors who do not know about their final immigration status, getting leave to remain in the asylum country is a cornerstone of establishing stability and, on the basis of that stability, drawing out a durable map of the future. So carers and others, who work actively to pursue a favourable decision, are valued by unaccompanied children as buffers and stabilisers in uncertain and hostile circumstances.

Belonging

Moving from the edge of belonging to the centre is part of a journey for many economic or political migrants (Aciman, 1997), often with the explicit intent of gaining citizenship within the host country. Asylum-seeking and refugee children face the prospects of moving without the help of familiar adults, and have to depend on the skills of strangers to secure both legal and psychosocial aspects of belonging over time. As they engage in this journey of belonging, two matters require their attention. Firstly, how to carry over a sense of solidarity and kinship from the past to the present. Secondly, how to trust people from the country of origin, as well as the people in the asylum country, so that they can feel at ease over time. Elsewhere, I have said that:

> An unaccompanied young person may well experience integration into the host community alongside disintegration from the community of origin. The pace, focus and pattern of these shifting and fluid affiliations will vary according to individuals' personal choices and their capacities to manage changes that are thrust upon them. The choices may be mediated, for example, by sensing safety in the anonymity of an unfamiliar culture and locality, or they may, conversely, be signalled by re-creating a strong affiliation with others from similar cultural backgrounds. Both similarity and difference may offer dangers and opportunities in relation to belonging, but neither will in itself provide a complete "one size fits all" guide to the well-being of each individual. (Kohli and Mather, 2003, p 205)

So while it is important to assert that unaccompanied children find the comfort of belonging in various ways with people with whom they are familiar (particularly in siblings being placed together – see Wade *et al*, 2005, p 159 *et passim*), there is unlikely to be a simple correlation between similarity bringing concord and difference resulting in discord. Williamson's (1998) study of the wishes and feelings of unaccompanied minors emphasised that being connected to networks which are sustaining is not the same as being connected to networks which are resurrected from the past, although it is valuable to keep up cultural affiliations in the ways in which the children themselves choose to. Preparing, cooking and eating home food, using a place of worship if they wanted to, having a prayer mat, having a short wave radio to listen to home news and access to the internet to contact scattered family members all contribute to a sense of being able to carry the past over in manageable ways into the present. Faiges-Hijon (2005, p 2) emphasises that this carry over is not just a part of a sentimental transportation, but an active and malleable ingredient in making a new life as they 'create meaning around themselves'. As part of this refurbishment of belonging, people from the asylum country who act as cultural guides, assist with the practicalities of daily life, introduce unaccompanied children to social activities which can take their minds off their day-today struggles and come to be experienced as guardians and protectors, appear to be valued. Belonging, therefore, becomes over time an amalgamation of the old and new, the roots and shoots, and a multiplicity of meanings and possibilities of embedding themselves in the host community emerge as a consequence. Overall, unaccompanied minors appear to strive for a sense of recreating a capacious sense of "home" where they can live their new, evolving lives, and where security leads to a sustainable web of friendship and care, and then on to success.

Success

In addition to the wish to move from the edge to the centre, is the will that unaccompanied minors appear to show in moving from the bottom towards the top in terms of educational and material success (Rutter and Jones, 1998; Wade *et al*, 2005). There is some evidence to confirm that the majority of refugee children fare well within educational systems in host countries so long as the conditions of support are attuned to the diversity of educational needs they present (Wilkinson, 2002; Rutter, 2006). Unaccompanied children may have been sent from the homeland to keep a part of the family alive, and also to rescue it from poverty (Christiansen and Foighel, 1990; Robinson and Seagrott, 2002). In this respect, the act of seeking sanctuary is a blended strategy, partly based on survival as well as a longing for success, and economic and political reasons for departure co-exist in many resettlement stories. However, at times, asylum-seeking children can be caught holding the political reasons up to the light of immigration inspection, and letting the economic reasons lie in the shadows created by that light (McFadyean, 2006).

Practitioners and carers report many attempts by unaccompanied minors to make something of themselves and to 'be something in the future' (Wade *et al*, 2005, p 110), while attempting to make sense of their past and present. In that context, educational provisions can provide rhythm and predictability through regular attendance, a chance to focus on potential gain rather than loss, and an opportunity to redeem and rebuild. Unaccompanied children themselves report that entering the new territory of a school, after having been through several other borders, requires confidence and skills in using the right language in the class and in the playground (Minority Rights Group International, 1998; Kohli and Mather, 2003), and that stability, based on safety and belonging within the school, increases the chances of academic success. However, while there is some evidence of comparatively good progress for refugee children, depending on the quality of pre-flight educational experiences allied to sensitive help in transition into school (Ofsted, 2003), the forces that contort their day-to-day lives appear large in comparison to the processes and people that defend them from those forces. In the meantime, the research base that informs best practice in relation to sustained success for refugee children is at a relatively modest level of maturity, both nationally and internationally.

Conclusion

After considerable risk-taking and multiple losses, unaccompanied minors have much to gain from, and much to give to, the societies they move towards (Hopkin and Hill, 2006). What they find helpful is becoming clearer and can give useful guidance to practitioners. To some degree, the three dimensions of safety, belonging and success represent the DNA of helping all vulnerable children, even though they have a particular flavour within the twists and turns of a refugee child's journey. As with all transitions, many unaccompanied children plough their own resolute paths towards resettlement. In doing so, some prosper and others fail in their attempts to resuscitate ordinary life. Some may disappear into the common folds of citizenship, if allowed to attain the goal of unremarkable and predictable lives. They are, after all, not extraordinary children, but children in extraordinary circumstances. Overall, there is plenty of scope for applying what we already know about the care of vulnerable children to the transitions that these children make, as well as in finding out more about what creates and sustains durable solutions in the asylum country.

References

Aciman A. (ed.) (1997) *Letters of Transit: Reflections on exile, identity, language and loss*, New York, New York: The New Press

Bertrand D. (2000) 'The autobiographical method of investigating the psychosocial wellness of refugees', in Ahern F. L. (ed.) *Psychosocial Wellness of Refugees: Issues of qualitative and quantitative research*, New York, New York: Berghahn Books

Bilton K. (2003) *Be my Social Worker: The role of the child's social worker*, Birmingham: British Association of Social Workers/Venture Press

Boyden J. and de Berry J. (2004) *Children and Youth on the Front Line: Ethnography, armed conflict and displacement*, New York, New York: Berghahn Books

Christiansen L. K. and Foighel N. (1990) 'Trauma treatment for unaccompanied minor refugees: experience from the work in OASIS in Copenhagen', in Jockenhövel-Schiecke H. (ed.) *Unaccompanied Refugee Children in Europe: Experience with protection, placement and education*, Frankfurt: International Social Service, German Branch

Daniel B., Wassell S. and Gilligan R. (1999) 'It's just common sense isn't it?' Exploring ways of putting the theory of resilience into action', *Adoption & Fostering*, 23:3, pp 6–15

Dennis, J. (2007) 'The legal and policy frameworks that govern social work with unaccompanied asylum seeking and refugee children in the UK', in Kohli R. and Mitchell F. (eds) *Working with Unaccompanied Asylum Seeking Children: Issues for policy and practice*, Basingstoke: Palgrave Macmillan

Faiges-Hijon A. (2005) *The Concept and Recreation of Home Amongst Unaccompanied Asylum Seeking and Refugee Young People in Britain*, Oxford: Oxford Brooks University

Fisher M., Marsh P. and Phillips D. with Sainsbury E. (1986) *In and Out of Care: The experiences of children, parents and social workers*, London: BT Batsford

Hek R. (2007) 'Using foster placements for the care and resettlement of unaccompanied children', in Kohli R. and Mitchell F. (eds) *Working with Unaccompanied Asylum Seeking Children: Issues for policy and practice*, Basingstoke: Palgrave Macmillan

Hopkin P. and Hill M. (2006) *This is a Good Place to Live and Think about the Future: The needs and experiences of unaccompanied asylum-seeking children in Scotland*, Glasgow: The Glasgow Centre for the Study of Child and Society/ Scottish Refugee Council

Jockenhövel-Schiecke H. (ed.) (1990) *Unaccompanied Refugee Children in Europe: Experience with protection, placement and education*, Frankfurt: International Social Service, German Branch

Kerr A. (1995) 'A psychoanalytic approach to the work of the guardian ad litem', in Trowell J. and Bower M. (eds) *The Emotional Needs of Young Children and their Families: Using psychoanalytic ideas in the community*, London: Routledge

Kidane S. and Amerena P. (2004) *Fostering Unaccompanied Asylum Seeking and Refugee Children: A training course for foster carers*, London: BAAF

Kohli R. (2006) 'The sound of silence: listening to what unaccompanied children say and do not say', *British Journal of Social Work*, 36:5, pp 707–721

Kohli R. (2007) *Social Work with Unaccompanied Asylum Seeking Children*, Basingstoke: Palgrave Macmillan

Kohli R. and Mather R. (2003) 'Promoting psychosocial well-being in unaccompanied asylum-seeking people in the United Kingdom', *Child and Family Social Work*, 8:3, pp 201–212

Loughry M. and Eyber C. (2003) *Psychosocial Concepts in Humanitarian Work with Children: A review of the concepts and related literature*, Washington DC: The National Academies Press

McCallin M. (ed.) (1996) *The Psychological Well-Being of Refugee Children: Research, practice and policy issues*, Geneva: International Catholic Child Bureau

McFadyean M. (2006) 'A lapse of humanity: child asylum seekers are cast as liars or economic migrants in a leaked government document', *The Guardian*, Thursday November 16

Minority Rights Group International (eds) (1998) *Forging New Identities: Young refugee and minority students tell their stories*, London: Minority Rights Group

Ofsted (2003) 'The education of asylum-seeker pupils', HMI 453, Office for Standards in Education. www.ofsted.gov.uk/assets/3418.pdf (accessed 10.1.2007)

Petty C. and Jareg E. (1998) 'Conflict, poverty and family separation: the problem of institutional care', in Bracken P. J. and Petty C. (eds) *Rethinking the Trauma of War*, London: Save the Children

Richman N. (1998) *In the Midst of the Whirlwind: A manual for helping refugee children*, London: Save the Children

Robinson V. and Sagrott J. (2002) *Understanding the Decision Making of Asylum Seekers: Finding 172, Research, Development and Statistics*, London: Directorate, Home Office

Rutter J. (2006) *Refugee Children in the UK*, Maidenhead: Open University Press

Rutter J. and Jones C. (eds) (1998) *Refugee Education: Mapping the field*, Stoke on Trent: Trentham Books

Stanley K. (2001) *Cold Comfort: Young separated refugees in England*, London: Save the Children

Steinbock D. J. (1996) 'Unaccompanied refugee children in host country foster families', *International Journal of Refugee Law*, 8:2, pp 6–48

Wade J., Mitchell F. and Baylis G. (2005) *Unaccompanied Asylum Seeking Children: The response of social work services*, London: BAAF

Wilkinson L. (2002) 'Factors influencing the Academic Success of Refugee Youth in Canada', *Journal of Youth Studies*, 5:2, pp 173–193

Williamson L. (1998) 'Unaccompanied – but not unsupported', in Rutter J. and Jones C. (eds) *Refugee Education: Mapping the field*, Stoke on Trent: Trentham Books

Section 4

Direct work in context

14 Knowing the child: the importance of developing a relationship

Andy Cook

Often the phrase "direct work" is used to refer to a discrete piece of work with a child such as producing a life story book or ascertaining the child's wishes and feelings in order to inform the court of these. Direct work is much more than this. Direct work is what occurs during all face-to-face contact between worker and family members. Direct work can occur in any situation and can take place over any time span; it relies upon the skills of the worker to utilise situations as and when they occur. It forms the basis of the relationship created between worker and child. Such a relationship is crucial to understanding the child's perception and experience. In turn, developing such an understanding is essential in ensuring that decisions regarding the child's future are fully informed and most likely to achieve best possible child development outcomes.

The most critical decisions for social workers concern issues of risk and safety. These include consideration of where children should live for the duration of their childhood and what form of contact they should have with birth families if unable to live with them. Despite numerous texts outlining the process of risk assessment and guidelines regarding setting the type and level of contact, there is no set formula which can be applied to all cases without making sense of individual experience through the relationship built with the client. This premise lies at the heart of social work practice and I will attempt to bring this alive by examination of a particular case. My work with Tandara was a journey for both of us; one to safety and security for her and one of learning for me. It was an emotional and cognitive journey punctuated by many actual physical journeys which we undertook together.

I removed Tandara from the care of her aunt and uncle, under police protection, when she was five years old. She had several bruises on her face which the paediatrician judged had been deliberately inflicted. Tandara told the doctor that she did not know where the bruises had come from. I had only met Tandara once previously, two days prior to this, and she had refused to speak to me. She had stayed physically close to her aunt and avoided eye contact with me when I talked to her although did nod to indicate that she understood what I was saying. I knew from the school that although English had not been Tandara's first language, her English language skills were now on a par with those of her peers. I was very aware of being a white worker visiting a black family who had emigrated to England and I wondered how they interpreted my position of power and authority. I felt uncertain about my ability to make sense of the social interactions within a family which might have different social norms to mine. I was at a loss as to how to communicate more effectively with Tandara on that visit, and felt awkward and inadequate. I was therefore left feeling dissatisfied regarding the thoroughness of my initial assessment. Time and again, child abuse tragedies have illustrated that ethical and safe practice must include not only "seeing the child" as a minimum requirement but also communicating with the child in a meaningful way. I did not have any sense of why Tandara chose not to communicate with me at that stage and could only guess at many possible reasons. I hoped she understood that I was there to help her. I had told her that no one was allowed to hurt her; that hurting children is against the law; and now she had very obviously been hurt by someone. Perhaps she felt betrayed by me already. Or perhaps she knew that she had a better understanding of her own world than I did, and knew that her world involved children being hurt.

It was difficult for me to judge how Tandara might experience being removed from her home and taken to a strange family for the weekend. Our relationship had barely begun and I had little understanding, or even guesswork, of her life experience and viewpoint. It could have been a very traumatic experience for her. However, the extent of Tandara's injuries and the lack of any obvious protective factors in the home led to the decision to remove her and I found myself driving Tandara across the county to an emergency foster placement late on a Friday evening. Tandara said little to me on that first journey, although what she did say has stayed with me. I explained to her that we were worried that she had been hurt and that I was taking her somewhere safe for the weekend. Tandara's response sent shivers down my spine. She threw her arms in the air and said, 'Andy's taking me to stay with a nice lady.' It was such a clear statement from a child I hardly knew and who had no reason to trust me. This was the first communication from Tandara which I felt certain I understood and it did much to reassure me that we had weighted factors correctly when deciding to remove her from home. Our relationship had really begun.

Later in the journey, when I was talking about the foster carers, Tandara said, 'They won't make me eat nasty things, will they?' This question seemed easy to answer and to give reassurances to. It was only months later that the significance of this question became vividly clear when Tandara disclosed having been force-fed her own faeces, urine and vomit. It would have been impossible to interpret the meaning behind Tandara's question at the time but the message is clear; take time to listen to what a child is saying to you, no matter how trivial it appears on the surface, and be prepared to consider the almost unimaginable, as some of the children we work with have experienced the almost unimaginable. This is no easy task as we all instinctively attempt to view our world as both controllable and comprehensible, in order to maintain a sense of stability, safety and purpose. The trauma victim knows that her sense of invulnerability was an illusion and has experienced total helplessness. This was certainly true for Tandara. As I gained a greater knowledge of her life experience, I found I had to confront some of my own illusions regarding human behaviour and the safety and predictability of life.

Tandara's family were angry and distressed by her removal from their care. They handed over very few possessions for her to take with her for the weekend and told me nothing of Tandara's routines. This meant that the emergency foster carers and I were left to do the best we could to support Tandara through this separation and loss. Tandara displayed little grief reaction, and with hindsight I believe she was actually relieved to have been removed from a dangerous and traumatising environment. Before I left her for the weekend, I talked with Tandara about visiting her again on Monday and told her that she would be able to see her family after the weekend. I assumed that this would be reassuring for her to hear. My assumption was wrong. Tandara made no response to my comments but when I did see her on the Monday, she was able to tell me that she did not want to see her aunt or uncle.

The issue of Tandara's contact with her family quickly became an area of dispute in the court arena. The local authority has a duty to promote contact between children in care and their family members unless this duty is dispensed with by the court. Tandara's family members were requesting contact with her but Tandara continued to state that she did not want to see them. Some professionals argued that contact should be "tried out" whereas I believed that we should progress at Tandara's pace and continue to explore the origins of her wish not to see her family. I argued that in the short term we would be fulfilling our legal duty to promote contact through ongoing discussions with Tandara. I believed that it was too soon to make long-term decisions regarding contact, as Tandara's experience and views were not yet fully understood. This position was accepted by the court and Tandara was given time to adjust to her new circumstances and think about and express what she wanted. She did begin regular good-quality contact with her cousin after being in care for several weeks. She also decided that she wanted to see her uncle once but did not see her aunt again during the year that I was her key worker. Her reasons for this gradually became clear over the course of many months.

Tandara had been born in Africa and moved to England aged three after having had several different carers while still in Africa. I was aware that when Tandara entered the care system in England she lost contact with anyone from her own culture, and not only this, her world was suddenly predominantly filled with white people, including myself. I attempted to redress this balance by arranging an independent visitor for Tandara who shared her cultural heritage. However, Tandara refused to see this woman, perhaps because she reminded her of her aunt, and she began to tell me 'Africa is cancelled'. Tandara was happy not to be living with her birth family and to be feeling safe, but it seemed that safety was becoming associated with white adults. Obviously Tandara's safety was of priority but I began to get worried about the long-term negative impact on her identity if she continued to reject all things and people from her country and continent of birth. When good-quality regular contact was established between Tandara and her cousin,

I felt relief. I hoped that she could be helped to separate her experience with her aunt from her sense of cultural identity.

The journey to the emergency foster placement was the first of many journeys Tandara and I took together. Our relationship greatly benefited from the necessity of travelling to hospital appointments, ABE interviews[1] and new placements. Going on car journeys together gave us a reason to spend time together. Initially, conversation did not flow freely and it was my responsibility to judge how best to use the time and at what pace and intensity to attempt communication. I used the first journey to talk to Tandara about what a foster carer is and what a social worker is and also spent periods with little being said. My main aim was to keep Tandara fully informed about what was happening, as her experience had taught her that the world was a potentially dangerous place and I wanted to alleviate any worries she might have. On subsequent journeys, as we grew to know each other more, Tandara played a more active role in directing the conversation and she proved to be a delightful companion. Journeys together gave us the opportunity to have serious conversations but also the opportunity to sing at the top of our voices, to play I-spy and to have fun with words such as changing each other's names (I was obviously Andy Pandy). Car journeys provided continual distractions in the form of changing landscapes; they allowed for avoidance of eye contact when eye contact was too daunting and were, for us, a perfect forum for getting to know each other.

Tandara's second foster placement broke down, as the foster carer found Tandara to be very demanding, following her around the house, needy of attention, and also challenging to the point that the carer found herself shouting at Tandara and also frightened by her. Tandara's internal working model of other people as unavailable, herself as unloved and the world as a dangerous and unpredictable place was confirmed in this placement. Gilligan (2001) discusses how foster carers can facilitate a turning point in a child's life through the re-aligning and re-learning of attachments by providing an alternative experience of being cared for.

My growing knowledge of Tandara's experience and perspective allowed me to offer the new carers support in understanding Tandara's experience and worldview. They needed to maintain a consistent approach which neither avoided conflict nor engaged in it in an angry fashion, unlike the previous carer who became involved in power struggles with Tandara. They needed to repeatedly behave in ways that disconfirmed Tandara's mental represent-ations of other people, herself and the world. Tandara was faced with the double task of both resolving the immediate effects of the trauma of physical abuse and developing internal working models of self and others that allowed for a positive experience of self and a sense of trust in her primary caregiver's nurturance and commitment.

---

[1] The Achieving Best Evidence interview is a video interview conducted according to Home Office guidelines with a view to being submitted as evidence to court in criminal proceedings.

My relationship with Tandara allowed me to provide her with some sense of containment and continuity as she made her transition to her third placement. Again, I undertook the actual physical journey with her as well as offering her emotional support and information throughout the transition. Again, Tandara displayed little emotional reaction to the separation and loss. My sense was that this was a coping mechanism and that Winnicott's notion of 'false self' (Winnicott, 1960) could account for Tandara's cheerful presentation upon leaving the placement. I talked with Tandara about the sense of fear, loss and sadness that some children feel on moving. This technique of discussing a situation at a position once removed, allowed the conversation to be less threatening to her as it was not directly about her, and it also avoided telling her what she was feeling. I talked about the different feelings that Tandara might be experiencing inside and she listened carefully but did not own any sad feelings until yet another move occurred, from her third foster placement to a permanent foster placement.

It was in Tandara's third foster placement that she experienced the safety and containment necessary for her to disclose the abuse that she had suffered at the hands of her aunt. She talked about the beatings she had received, being given cold baths and being force-fed her own faeces, urine and vomit. She made initial disclosures both to the foster mother and to the foster carer's daughter, who was a couple of years older than herself. She also made a major disclosure regarding past physical abuse to a peer at school. This happened to be overheard by a teacher who understood the significance of what was being said, despite Tandara's very off-hand matter-of-fact manner in attributing blame for an old injury to her aunt. These disclosures were passed on to me and I worked with Tandara to help prepare her for ABE interviews. Tandara told me that she thought her aunt should go to prison. We spent much time discussing this and what it might mean for her. When her aunt received a two-year conditional discharge, I helped Tandara understand what this meant and to also come to terms with it as, at the time, she did not feel it was a fitting punishment. We also talked much about families, Tandara's memories of other family members and her wishes regarding a future family.

There are many ways of undertaking direct work with children and each practitioner will have preferred mediums, as well as each child being more comfortable communicating in particular ways. It may be necessary to try a variety of methods before achieving a "good fit" and it may be necessary to go beyond comfort zones in order to establish good rapport with a child. Certainly, Tandara is the only child to have heard me sing and appeared to experience this as a positive shared activity despite my initial discomfort! I am more comfortable with using spoken communication with children or pens and paper. When I visited Tandara in placement or sat in various waiting rooms with her, she knew that I always had felt tip pens and paper in my bag and she enjoyed playing with them. It soon became apparent to me that it was words that she enjoyed rather than drawing pictures so we often played written word games as well as the verbal ones in the car. Sometimes when I wanted to discuss difficult things with her or check out her understanding of an issue, I wrote half a sentence and asked if she could finish it. When I wrote 'I have a social worker because', she completed it with 'so then I don't get hurt'. In the same way, she was able to tell me that she did not like me being bossy, did like me being funny and that my job was to look after her, explain things to her, find her places to live and arrange for her to see her cousin. Such communication enabled a clarity between us that was both humbling and facilitative of my doing a good job.

The importance of having a coherent narrative, which gives meaning to your life, is becoming increasingly recognised. I was able to work with Tandara at producing an account of her life linking the past with the present and the future in an understandable way. This included both "life story" work and "wishes and feelings" work and I struggle to imagine how either could have been effectively achieved as a stand-alone piece of work outside of the relationship which we had built together. There were some difficult decisions to be made regarding what to include in Tandara's life story book and our relationship enabled us to talk together about whether to include documents such as police photographs of her injuries and details of her aunt's criminal conviction for injuring her. I was keen for Tandara to contribute to her life story book and she was eager to do so. She wrote about her recent memories of being removed from her family and her time in different foster placements. By this point in our relationship she was also willing to talk with me about her memories of living in Africa and she also wrote some of these down to go in her book. Prior to this she had refused to talk about her birth country.

Understanding Tandara's wishes and feelings both in respect of her birth family and potential permanent foster or adoptive families was an ongoing process made all the more complex by Tandara's disowning of her cultural heritage. She associated her culture with abandonment and abuse. In contrast, she was in receipt of positive nurturing influences from white carers and professionals. She appeared to embrace white British culture to a point that was self-destructive. I am sure that my relationship with Tandara was aided by her wish to identify with all things white British but this made me, to some extent, part of the problem. There was a danger that Tandara would not feel safe with any permanent family that she was matched with purely on the basis of ethnicity. She was strong-willed, knew her own mind and was certainly capable of doing her best to disrupt any placement that she was not satisfied with. She wanted a permanent family but for a period would not contemplate the idea of living with a black family. We spent considerable amounts of time talking about what she wanted and needed from a permanent family, and her views on this did shift over time. I was fortunate in having access to consultation with a child and adolescent psychotherapist over these and other challenges which Tandara presented. It was imperative that I understood Tandara's emotional journey as it took place in order to make decisions about how best to meet her therapeutic needs, the appropriate timings of interventions and which alternative family provided a best match to meet her need for a safe, secure and loving family.

Developing a relationship with a child is essential when care planning in a key worker role. Developing such a relationship cannot be forced or rushed. The relationship develops over time and through shared experience, and has to overcome breaches of trust that the child has experienced in other relationships. In the case of an abused child these are likely to be substantial. Initially, every time Tandara and I went on a car journey together, Tandara was fearful that I was returning her to her aunt, and would regularly check that I knew where I was going, and would say, 'Don't take me to aunty's'. After a period of weeks, Tandara no longer needed to do this, and appeared to trust that I would do as I said. I worked towards this by always explaining events in advance, making them as predictable as possible. I also attempted to give Tandara some sense of control in her life by listening to and heeding her views. For example, in making contact arrangements between Tandara and her family, I was guided predominantly by Tandara's wishes and feelings, and moved at her pace in exploring these issues. I provided her with accurate information and was careful to explain things in concrete terms appropriate to her developmental stage. Thus, the relationship fulfils many functions and can both aid the care planning process and be reparative for the child. I attempted to model a secure base for Tandara through her moves in foster care, and I aimed to give her a sense of "felt security" while her future remained uncertain. In assuming responsibility for her safety in my role of corporate parent, I hoped that Tandara felt a sense of containment as described by Bion (1962), similar to the 'holding environment' described by Winnicott (1963).

In the key worker role there are numerous opportunities for building a trusting relationship, many of which could be lost in a bureaucratic world of increasing paperwork and focus on timescales. It is important not to underestimate the impact of just "being there" as a stable and reliable presence, providing clear information through the uncertainty and change that accompanies statutory intervention into family life. We are *in loco parentis* for looked after children and this carries an ethical obligation, as well as a legal duty, to act as a good parent, and a good parent should certainly know their child. A good parent also has times of receiving huge satisfaction and joy from being with their children, as well as sharing in their hurt and fears, and this was certainly true for me in my relationship with Tandara.

References

Bion W. R. (1962) *Learning From Experience*, London: Heinemann

Gilligan R. (2001) *Promoting Resilience*, London: BAAF

Winnicott D. W. (1960) 'Ego distortions in terms of true and false self', in *The Maturational Processes and the Facilitating Environment*, New York, New York: International Universities Press, Inc

Winnicott D. W. (1963) 'Communicating and not communicating leading to a study of certain opposites', in *The Maturational Processes and the Facilitating Environment*, New York, New York: International Universities Press Inc, pp 93–105

15 Remembering never to forget and forgetting never to remember: re-thinking life story work

Alan Burnell and Jay Vaughan

Remembering: then and now

Over the past nine years, as part of the Family Futures[1] assessment process, we have reviewed the histories of over 300 children. What is striking about these chronologies is that in the Form E[2] the child's early experience in the birth family is usually summarised quite briefly, and generic terms such as "neglect" and "abuse" are used frequently. As a consequence, such chronologies do not convey the true nature of the traumatic experiences that the children have endured. When children are in our treatment programme, we go back to the original family files in order to gather more detailed information. We also interview relevant people, for example, social workers and birth relatives, in order to get first-hand accounts of a child's early life. The detailed information discovered paints a more powerful and distressing picture. When this information is placed within a developmental framework, the impact of those early experiences on the child's development becomes very clear. When considering this information in the context of the given child and their development, parents and therapy team members will often be moved to tears. This is an important point in preparing to talk to a child about their past, because the adults involved have truly understood what life must have been like for the child in their early formative years.

This process of acquiring detailed histories, understanding the impact on the child's development and the effect it has had on the child then and now, is at the heart of life story work (LSW). If the information gathered is superficial or clichéd, and if it is not understood through a developmental framework, then it loses its therapeutic potential and potency.

Children in foster care are often confused about their identities, their families, and their pasts. This confusion is the result of changing caretakers, a scarcity of accurate information, and inadequate preparation for moves. Foster children do not live with people who can verify their pasts, and so their confusion continues.

---

[1] Family Futures is a registered Adoption Support Agency offering an integrated multi-disciplinary assessment and treatment service for children who have experienced developmental trauma and are now fostered or adopted.

[2] Form E is a BAAF child placement form which provides basic biographical and historical information about a child who was accommodated. It has been replaced by the Child Placement Report in England.

Making life story books is one way to reduce confusion. A life story book is a collection of information about a child's life that includes historical data, recollections, memorabilia, and stories by and about a foster child. This organized presentation of the family background and problems, foster care placements, and other life experiences provides a child with a clearer picture of his/her life. (Beste and Richardson, 1981, pp 529–560)

The above extract from Beste and Richardson encapsulates the traditional approach to LSW and clearly shows that the original purpose of life story books was to help children have a clear understanding of their life story in order to confirm their sense of identity. Life story books were, therefore, developed in the USA in the 1970s for children in public care and this practice was taken on board by social workers in the UK.

The theme of identity remained prevalent in the literature on children who were adopted or fostered from the 1970s through to this decade (Brodzinsky, 1987; Triseliotis, 1997; Ryan and Walker, 2007. Life story books and life story work were useful ways of addressing the issue of identity for children in care. However, our recent practice experience has raised other issues for us in our direct work with children. Fifteen years ago, in attempting to work with children on their life story books, we became aware the children were often resistant to the work or became distressed and acted out. They would become either disinterested or withdrawn, or agitated and aggressive, sometimes wanting to destroy the pictures or pages that were being worked on.

We now understand the reason for this, which is that the content of the history of most children who have been removed from their birth families is very distressing, and that the very process of doing the work invokes unresolved traumatic memories. Because of this, we now see it as impossible to separate the task of compiling a life story book from engaging with a child in a broader piece of therapeutic work. It is inevitable that, when talking to a child about their "life story", conscious and unconscious memories from the past will be triggered. It is most common that children will not articulate these memories, but will go into a "feeling state" associated with the memory and begin to act out. This not only makes it difficult to continue with the life story book but is also an indication that the child is still traumatised by these early memories. These memories are suppressed or disconnected from the child's normal sense of themselves. The aim of a therapeutic approach to the child's traumatic memories would be to help integrate these memories into the child's conscious beliefs about themselves and their past and to remove the traumatic distress associated with these memories. We will go on to discuss how this can be done.

There is now recognition in the USA and a growing awareness in the UK that children in the public system are highly traumatised as a result of their earlier life experiences (van der Kolk, 2005). So profound is the impact of repeated traumatic experiences on infant development (van der Kolk, 2005) that a new diagnostic category is being suggested in the US called "Developmental Trauma Disorder" (van der Kolk, 2005). The rationale for a new diagnostic category being proposed for the *Diagnostic and Statistical Manual of Mental Disorders* (DSMV) is that although children coming into the public care system have clearly had significant traumas in their infancy, they do not display the typical symptoms of Post Traumatic Stress Disorder (PTSD). This has perplexed many clinicians in the USA and the UK. The National Child's Traumatic Stress Network's Complex Trauma Task Force (2003) has presented the view in their report that the diagnosis of PTSD is still applicable for children who have experienced normal development prior to being the victims of single trauma events. However, children who have had traumatic experiences in utero and in early infancy suffer a more globally pervasive impact on their neuro-physiological development.

We also have a better understanding of how preverbal memories are organised, thanks to recent developments in neuro-developmental research (Perry, 1999; Schore, 2001), which highlights that, rather than forgetting traumatic experiences, we remember them very deeply in our minds and in our bodies. Memories attached to emotional states are therefore deeply embedded and not forgotten. An example of this is a young girl now aged nine who had a fear of the shower and of having her hair washed and brushed. This perplexed her adoptive parents despite every effort on their part to carry out this essential grooming as sensitively as they could. When we carried out a file search and looked at a paediatric report of the injuries that the girl had when taken to casualty by the social worker and police, one of the injuries described were what appeared to be 40–50 tiny pin pricks on each side of her head. What we deduced from this was that she had been hit about the head with a hairbrush. This could have been in the shower. We can only speculate about this. However, it enabled the therapist and the parents to talk further to the girl, who was then able to recall the incident, which she described as very painful and very frightening. Until this conversation, she was unaware of the reason for feeling so fearful when she was in the shower with wet hair. This has implications for helping children to remember the things that they would rather forget, but cannot.

Our programme of psychological therapy at Family Futures is based on attachment theory, research into early childhood trauma and the principle that achieving therapeutic engagement with children who are fostered or adopted requires that the worker first explore with the child their early traumatic experiences. Only then is it possible for a child to begin to form a secure attachment to a carer or parent and only then is it possible to develop a positive and integrated identity. This is not a simple linear progression from desensitising the child from their early traumatic memories to the development of secure attachment formation and a positive identity and sense of self. There is a circularity about the process which means that therapeutic work with a child often goes in stages with one aspect of the child's early traumatic experience being looked at by the child's therapist and parents. The attachment consequences of these early experiences are then reflected upon.

The effect that this early experience had on the child's self-esteem is considered with the child by the therapist and the parents or carers, before the next traumatic experience in the child's history is tackled.

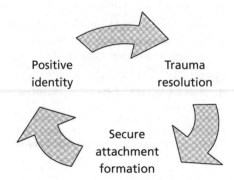

Positive
identity

Trauma
resolution

Secure
attachment
formation

Central to attachment theory is the concept of the narrative, as originally conceived by Bowlby. This idea was linked to another key concept in attachment theory, "internal working models", first described by Bowlby (1979).

> *The work of therapy, according to Holmes (1998) involves story making and story breaking. The therapist helps the patients at once to tell a story coherently, and also to allow for the story to be told in a different, and perhaps, more healing light.* (Fonagy, 2001)

Children who have experienced multiple separations and poor parenting do not have a coherent narrative and have fragmented rather than integrated internal working models of primary carers. The aim, therefore, of direct work with children is to help the child form a more coherent narrative. However, what we have learnt is that the trauma of early childhood abuse and neglect leads to an incoherent narrative that militates against both attachment and the development of a sense of self. It is for these reasons that we believe that early childhood traumas need to be addressed in the direct work with children. A recent publication by a practising social worker, *Life Story Books for Adoptive Children* (Rees, 2006), is an innovative approach to life story work, which takes as its starting point, the early childhood trauma and attachment difficulties of childhood trauma.

How can we help children understand their lives?

We touch now on the debate about who should do this work, given that we are redefining it as a therapeutic process as well as a means of helping with identity. Ryan and Walker (2007) continue to insist that therapy is separate from LSW and should not be undertaken by social workers under the guise of LSW. We suggest, however, that LSW does not only need to be undertaken as part of an intensive process, as at specialist resources such as Family Futures, but also can be undertaken with therapeutic understanding in mind from the outset of the child's time in care and by carers/social workers as part of their normal work. The focus of this chapter is more on the intensive centre-based approach to LSW. However, the principles also underly work done directly by social workers and foster carers.

It is never too soon to begin

One important question to consider is when to begin life story work. It has been argued that life story books and life story work cannot be started until a child feels secure and is in a permanent placement. In our view, life story work should begin the moment that children enter care. Children placed in foster care are usually highly distressed by the separation from their normal environment. They are often confused and bemused as to why this has happened. Foster carers and social workers can play a vital role in helping children to make sense of their experience while it is happening, or soon after. This can be done simply by talking to children in an honest and age-appropriate way. As in all life story work, a chronology of events is helpful for the child to have, but more important is adult recognition of the feelings of distress, fear and anxiety that these events have engendered in the child.

At any point in a child's placement history, parents, carers and social workers together engaging with the child in a creative process of helping them to make sense of their life is vital for their adjustment and future mental health.

Researching the child's history

Whether LSW is carried out as an intensive and focused intervention or as an aspect of the key social work role, it is advisable to carry out comprehensive file research. This should include reading childcare files, court reports and adoption files. In addition to this, medical records and any information from the police about call-outs, etc, for domestic violence or other suspected criminal activity or disturbance that did not lead to a prosecution, can flesh out the picture of a child's early experiences. In addition to collating paper sources of information about a child's history, it is invaluable to obtain first-hand accounts from birth relatives, foster carers and social workers who have known the child at any point in their life. The purpose of this exercise is to compile as comprehensive and detailed a picture of the child's early life as possible. With this information it is possible to begin the work of explaining their history and life experience to the child in an age-appropriate way.

Preparing parents and carers

Before engaging with the child, the social worker or therapist should process the child's history with the parent or carer. This is not only to ensure that they have the correct chronology but to ensure that their own emotional reaction to the information has been explored. Constructing a history with a child is not just a process of conveying information but a way of helping the child to feel that their experience is understood and validated, and they are absolved of responsibility for what has been perpetrated on them. During the process of building a history which is coherent and true, parents and carers need to help the child understand and reflect upon their feelings about these events, in the past and in the present. Preparing parents and carers for this task is an exercise in parent education. Many parents and carers may not be aware of the extent of the child's early traumatic experience or the impact it may have had on their subsequent development. Sharing this information and discussing it with the parents can also be a therapeutic experience for them, such that it will give them insight into their child and a greater sense of empathy.

The task of sharing information with parents can, however, be difficult and distressing for both parents and professionals. Many reports are written using jargon and are possibly sanitised, in order to protect the reader from the true horror of the child's experience. It is important, if this process of sharing information with the child is to be meaningful, that the true extent of their early suffering is fully faced. For this reason, it is important that the parents and professionals involved with the child have done this themselves first, before endeavouring to share the information with the child.

To give an example of this process, the adoptive parents of an eight-year-old child had the information which was recorded on the Form E. This contained statements such as 'John, in his early years, suffered from neglect as his mother struggled to parent three young children.' When the social worker looked at the original family file, there was a health visitor's report documenting a filthy, fly-infested kitchen with dog excrement on the floor, and devoid of food. John, who was 18 months old at the time, was found in his playpen. He had obviously been left there without toys for a long period of time and he had also started to pull apart his nappy and eat it. This first-hand account sheds a more shocking light on John's formative years. When this and other information was shared with the parents, they had a mixture of emotional responses. Firstly, disbelief that such conditions could be found today, then anger both at the birth mother and at the failure of services to protect John. The adoptive parents were both moved to tears when thinking about the circumstances that John had endured. This reaction was made more complicated because, of late, they had resented John for his challenging behaviour. They were left feeling guilty for their sometimes harsh over-reactions to John's behaviour. This complexity of reaction demonstrates the need to help parents process their own reactions to such distressing information before they are able to help the child come to terms with it.

Piecing the past together

Having reviewed the child's history with the parents and carers, the next task is to go through the child's history with the child. In the past this process has centred on putting together a life story book, which may have been prepared by the social worker and shared with the child, or put together by the social worker with the child and or carer or parent. This process often seems ad hoc. We would advocate that the process of exploring the child's history with them should be done always in the presence of their parents or foster carer. The rationale for this is that the literature on trauma resolution for children (van der Kolk, 2005) shows that children can only approach these difficult memories when they feel safe. It is the parents' or carers' role to provide that safety and by doing so enhance the quality of the child's attachment to them. Further, the literature on the psychological impact of trauma suggests that children who have experienced early childhood trauma have very strong shame reactions to past experiences (Hughes, 2005; Schore, 2001). The presence of the parent or carer enables the child to feel that they and their past are accepted and they are not "bad" or unlovable because of the things that have happened to them. At some point during the course of any disclosure work, a child may show physical signs of distress or emotional dysregulation as the physical and bodily expressions of repressed memories manifest themselves. If the child is not to be re-traumatised by the process of remembering, then the parent or carer needs to be on hand in order to reassure, comfort and empathise with the child. This inter-subjective experience is at the heart of the attachment formation.

Pacing the process

Because of the depth and the complexity of life story work, it is not possible or desirable to embark upon this work within a narrow time frame. It is hard to predict at the outset how long the process will take as it will depend upon the ability of the child to engage, their age, the time period that will need to be covered, and what new disclosures the child might make during the work. One of the key tasks for the social worker or therapist is to pace the work. Children are most receptive to new information and reflecting upon their past when they are in a state of "quiet alert". Babies and children reach this state when their physical needs have been met; they are relaxed and not hyper-aroused and are attending to the parent or carer in a reciprocal way. Such attention states can be short-lived and, for some children, hard to reach. However, it is in this state that children are receptive and reflective and able to engage.

During life story work, children need to be receptive to the process, but not aroused, because this would mean that they are not able to process or helpfully integrate the information. It is essential to "micro-track" the child's autonomic nervous system response, to assess whether a child is becoming frightened or having a fight, flight or freeze response. If they are being activated into having a trauma response, for example, this would indicate that the life story work is going too fast or is being presented in a way that is re-traumatising the child rather than helping them resolve their traumas.

Choosing your medium

Depending on the developmental age of the child and their preference for different activities, the life story work can take many different forms. There are a number of factors to bear in mind.

In order not to re-traumatise a child, it is crucial to pick an arts medium that allows the child to have the correct aesthetic distance (Landy, 1986) to the life story work. In general terms there are art techniques such as sand tray work and puppets, which are literally at arms length and are probably particularly appropriate for both younger children and children who are feeling especially overwhelmed by their history. The small size of the toys, the distance of the puppet at the end of an arm, and the ability of a toy or puppet to survive anything is, for such children, an essential prerequisite. For other children who find it hard to connect with their early experiences, more powerful and evocative techniques, such as mask work or psychodrama, are possible but always to be used with caution. Mask work means that the child is literally able to enact parts of their life, while psychodrama enables them to bring to life their past. All of this is very exciting and potentially very disturbing, unless extremely carefully managed. Alongside these two opposite ends of the spectrum rests the perhaps more familiar and manageable large roll of paper on which a timeline can be created; this can begin as one-dimensional and then become three-dimensional or sculpted with objects being placed on the timeline. There are variants of this with journeys being created from one home to the next spread around the room.

In many ways, the possibilities of how to map out a child's life story are endless; what is important, however, is to never underestimate the power of the arts and the impact of such work. There is never any harm in beginning cautiously and working gradually towards coherence for the child, bearing in mind that the end objective is not to complete the task, but to enable the child to approach their story in a way that feels safe and manageable. The ultimate aim is to help the child reflect on their experience and in almost unimaginably small steps begin to see the connection between their past experiences and the difficulties with which they struggle in the present. Small is definitely beautiful. Work with children using these creative approaches has been well described and documented in recent literature (e.g. Bannister, 2003; Archer and Burnell, 2003; Rose and Philpot, 2005).

Another important consideration is the child's capacity to make sense of the information. Some children find it easier to understand when concrete rather than abstract or metaphorical ways of relaying information are used.

Another connected consideration is the need to understand the particular difficulties the child may have, such as dyslexia, which might affect their wish to participate in a written account of their history. Or, for example, children who find auditory information hard to process and fare better with visual information may need an approach which involves a non-language medium. This clearly demonstrates that really knowing that child is the first step in deciding how to work with them. The responsibility for effective communication lies with the practitioner.

Working with a child – a life story work case example

Tina sat curled on the sofa clutching a little plastic baby doll about the size of her big thumb. Tina was ten years old and this was the first time she had been able to bear thinking about what had happened to her in her birth family. It was also the first time she had acknowledged how much she remembered. For years, Tina had held fiercely onto the view that her birth mother had loved her and been good to her. She would say it was all social services' fault. Tina's behaviour and hatred of "mothers" had always left her adoptive mother feeling rejected by Tina.

Tina now sat between her adoptive parents and began to very quietly ask questions of the therapists. Her breathing was calm and deep as she asked 'why did she leave me alone in the house?' There was quiet as the answer seemed to flash across Tina's face. Tina talked of her mother's behaviour: 'When she came back she would get out little pieces of tin foil and lay all this stuff out on the table. Afterwards she would go all funny and flop. I was always scared when the tin foil was on the table. I knew what it meant.' Tina frowned and put her head slightly to one side. She said, 'I hate tin foil'. Her adoptive mother smiled at her and everyone, without speaking, remembered the recent incident in the kitchen at home when Tina had started hitting her adoptive mother with a roll of kitchen foil.

Tina had lots of questions. One of the therapy team wrote down all the questions and placed the list beside the sand tray. The sand tray showed a baby's cot and sofa with a huge monster sitting on it. In front of the monster was a table. On the table were little pieces of torn up tissue. No one had quite understood what these pieces were until Tina had just spoken. One of the therapists asked Tina what the baby in the cot might have said to the mother if it had been able to speak. Tina slipped off the sofa and placed the small plastic baby doll back in the cot. In a small voice she whispered 'Don't do it, Mummy, don't do it – please, Mummy, please'. She sounded so scared, small and completely alone. Tina's adoptive mother slid off the sofa to sit beside her and put her hand gently on Tina's shoulder. Tina looked at her and said, 'why did she do it?' Her mother answered, 'Don't know darling. I don't think she knew how to do it differently. Poor baby Tina. I wish I had been there to look after you. I am so sorry I wasn't there.' Tina very slowly picked up the little baby from the cot and held it for a while in the palm of her hand before slowly handing it to her mother and closing her fingers around the figure. No one spoke as her adoptive father also slipped to the floor, holding in his arms his wife and daughter as they cried.

Conclusion

For those of us who have engaged with children who are fostered or adopted and their carers and parents, it is both exciting and scary, sad and rewarding. We believe that life story work should move away from the narrow confines of books and photos designed to preserve a sense of continuity and identity for the child, to a more profound and funda-mental process of healing, repair and recovery from traumatic experiences which have shaped the whole being of a child. The role of the social worker is critical to this process. Social workers, in our experience, often feel anxious or deskilled when engaging in direct work with children. Therapy with children has become the province of the therapist. However, we need to recognise the therapeutic role that life story work can play in helping children recover and develop a coherent story about their lives. It is important that we also acknowledge the centrality of the social worker's role as working in partnership with parents and carers in this process.

We, professionals and parents, can achieve this by helping children to remember not to forget, in order that early trauma experiences can be integrated into a coherent narrative of their life.

References

Archer C. and Burnell A. (2003) 'Trauma, attachment and family permanence', London: Jessica Kingsley

Bannister A. (2003) 'Creative therapies with traumatized children', London: Jessica Kingsley

Beste H. M. and Richardson R. G. (1981) 'Developing a life story book program for foster children', *Child Welfare*, 60:8, pp 529–534

Bowlby J. (1979) *The Making and Breaking of Affectional Bonds*, London: Tavistock Publications

Brodzinsky D. (1987) 'Adjustment to adoption: a psychosocial perspective', *Clinical Psychological Review*, 7:1, pp 25–47

Fonagy P. (2001) *Attachment Theory and Psychoanalysis*, New York, New York: Other Press

Holmes J. (1998) 'Defensive and creative use of narrative in psycho-therapy: an attachment perspective', in Roberts G. and Holmes J. (eds) *Narrative and Psychotherapy and Psychiatry*, Oxford: Oxford University Press

Hughes D. A. (2005) 'An attachment-focused treatment for foster and adoptive families', *British Psychological Society Service and Practice Update*, 4:4, London: British Psychological Society

Landy J. (1986) *Drama Therapy: Concepts and practices*, Springfield, Illinois: Charles C. Thomas Publishers

National Child's Traumatic Stress Network's Complex Trauma Task Force (2003) *White Paper on Complex Trauma on Children and Adolescents*, Los Angeles, California: US Department of Health and Human Services.

Perry B. D. (1999) *Splintered Reflections: Images of the body in trauma*, New York, New York: Basic Books

Rees J. (2006) *Life Story Books for Adoptive Children: A family friendly approach*, London: Bite Size/Family Futures Publications

Rose R. and Philpot T. (2005) *The Child's Own Story*, London: Jessica Kingsley

Rowe J. (1973) *Children Who Wait*, London: BAAF

Ryan T. and Walker R. (2007) *Life Story Work* (3rd edn), London: BAAF

Schore A. N. (2001) 'The effects of early relational trauma on right brain development, affect regulation and infant mental health', *Infant Mental Health Journal*, 22:1-2, pp 201–269

Selwyn J., Sturgess W., Quinton D. and Baxter C. (2006) *Costs and Outcomes in Non-Infant Adoptions*, London: BAAF

Triseliotis J. (1997) *Adoption: Theory, Policy and Practice*, London: Continuum International Publishing

van der Kolk B. (2005) 'Developmental trauma disorder: towards a rational diagnosis for children with complex trauma histories', *Psychiatric Annals*, 35:5, pp 401–408

16 Real-time communication in residential care

Adrian Ward

Working with young people in residential settings can feel quite different to other forms of social work, partly because things may be much less structured and formal than working in an office or using official meeting-rooms, and partly because there is so much more time available in which to work alongside the young people and gradually build up a relationship.

Much of the most valuable work arises "on the hoof", in the midst of everyday activities such as watching TV or eating supper, or it may develop out of conflicts or moments of sadness or anxiety in "real time", perhaps straight after a difficult phone call or on the way to a visit home, rather than being recalled or anticipated in a planned meeting. Sometimes the pattern of communication will develop slowly, and piecemeal, over a number of hours or days, with comments or reflections being added or reminders put in as the situation moves on. It is therefore important for workers to develop an awareness of how communication may build up over time but also how it may "erupt" in heated moments, often triggered by very minor incidents. They also need the ability to hold in mind the different levels at which young people may communicate both directly (verbally) and indirectly through actions, silences, physicality and symbolism. The advantage of the residential setting (likewise of foster care) is that the potential for this real-time communication is immense, but using this potential does depend on the sensitivity and skill of the workers.

Inter-relationships and group dynamics

Communicating in residential care also relies critically upon an awareness of the group and how it operates, as well as on the workers' ability to capitalise on the opportunities for mutual support and understanding which may arise in the group. The "group", in this context, means not only the group of young people and their relationships with each other, but also the group or team of staff – as well as the *whole* group of staff and young people together (Brown and Clough, 1989). There is a constant ebb and flow of feeling and awareness across the whole group in relation not only to the ongoing dramas of children's lives, but also to their relationships both with each other and with their families and friends, as well as the interplay between all of these elements and the dynamics of the staff group and their own networks and relationships (Emond, 2002, 2005). These complex interrelationships and large-group dynamics are there whether we choose to acknowledge them or not (Ward, 1993), and indeed they may not always be immediately apparent in each dialogue between worker and child, although they are the texture within which everything else is woven, and often the individual conversations may make little sense without a full awareness of the whole pattern. Workers therefore need to develop the ability to work within and across groups, picking up on the subtleties of interaction at every level, and keeping all of this in mind even when they are engaged in a one-to-one conversation (Stokoe, 2003).

These group interactions are happening all the time and require monitoring and intervention throughout any day's work, but the best way to capitalise on them is for the residential unit to evolve a pattern of group meetings both for the young people themselves and for the whole group of staff and children, drawing on the traditions of the "community meeting" in therapeutic communities (Worthington, 2003a). These meetings can be used to promote a culture of open and honest communication, and to allow for the expression of those strong feelings which inevitably arise in everyday life in such settings. An essential component in promoting good communication with young people in residential care is therefore to establish and sustain a pattern of regular "open" meetings between staff and young people, in which matters of concern can be safely raised. It takes time and patience to establish such meetings (Ward, 1995) because it involves building an atmosphere of trust and mutual respect and enabling both staff and children to develop the confidence to work in this way, but once they are established they can become the "hub" around which much of the work of the place revolves.

One-to-one relationships

In addition to these aspects of communication, residential care also provides the opportunities for intensive one-to-one relationships in which a worker can offer a combination of practical and emotional support to an individual child, often focused on the child's ongoing concerns about their future as well as their past (Worthington, 2003b). In some cases these "key" relationships may be centred on a sequence of planned meetings, although again much of the work will arise from the opportunities which develop in the course of everyday life and its challenges (see my earlier chapter in this book). For many young people it is this key relationship which can provide a means of unlocking the anxieties and even despair within which they may feel trapped, providing a consistent and reliable relationship in the midst of the turmoil into which they may have been thrown by their circumstances, and offering the hope that, with the help of a trusted figure, things may begin to improve and even be resolved (Anglin, 2004). These may begin to sound like high hopes, and the challenge is certainly great, but the possibilities are genuinely there if they are understood and fully used, though always within the professional structures of supervision and accountability for the worker.

In this chapter we explore one small example of such communication between a child and a worker, mostly focused on the key relationship between the two of them, but also drawing on the "texture" of group and team relationships as described above. It is a fictional example drawing upon elements of actual events, edited here to draw attention to certain key factors. After we leave this story we will return to some further reflections on the nature of the work.

Gary and Linda

Gary felt sad; he was warm, but he was not happy. He lay on his bed, thumb in mouth, eyes shut, rocking gently from side to side, side to side. He couldn't understand why it had happened again: everyone seemed to hate him, everybody knew how bad he was and hated him for it. Everything he said just made people angry. Even saying nothing seemed to make them angry. He swallowed hard, rocked again, clamped his other hand around the one with its thumb in his mouth and tried not to cry. It was late on Friday evening and the rest of the house was quiet; some of the others were out still but he couldn't face it. He couldn't really face anything, even himself.

At 12, Gary was on his own, or that was how it felt. His mum had had enough of him, his dad had gone years ago, his step-dad was always so violent, and his sisters too little to understand. He did see his mum and sisters sometimes, when he went home for a weekend, but it never seemed to work out and he always came back feeling worse. This time he was more worried, because he just knew something bad was going to happen at the weekend.

Someone was in the doorway. Gary kept on rocking, eyes shut although he knew someone was there, but he listened. It was Linda – he knew it, she would always come up quietly like this and wait there by the door. Sometimes she would just say nothing for a long time, just like him. This time she said his name quietly, and he stopped rocking for a minute, then started again. He knew it was her and he made a sort of mumbling sound, not saying anything, just being himself inside, secretly hoping that she might guess how he felt. A tiny pulse of relief touched him at the thought that at last someone had come to talk to him rather than ignoring him or shouting him down as everyone else seemed to.

This went on for ages. She was still standing there. Why didn't she go? She always did this, like she knew what was happening, as if she could read his mind. In fact he liked this idea, but he couldn't tell her that, in case it broke the spell.

He rocked himself in something more like a rhythm now, to and fro, side to side, almost comfortable in his sadness. He grew tired and lay still, his eyes still shut. Linda must have moved closer and sat down, because this time when she spoke his name the voice was much closer and he could almost feel the warmth of her breathing. In the distance someone was washing up and the telly was on: maybe the others had come back. He liked hearing these sounds in the background too – it made the house feel a bit more open, like there was always someone around, someone else in case he didn't get on with Linda. And he liked hearing his name, almost as if it proved to him that he really was Gary and that it was worth somebody calling him by his real name, instead of some of the abuse he got from the others.

'I thought I'd just come and sit with you,' said Linda, and Gary listened intently, then rocked again. His mind was upside down and his heart was racing. He was a bit out of breath now from the rocking – he was big for his age and it took a lot of energy to keep rocking like that, but he needed to do it. They had put an extra mattress by the side of his bed so that he wouldn't bang his head or make too much noise if he did need to rock, and that made it feel almost cosy, which he liked. At least if he was warm there he could feel a bit special in himself. Now Linda was listening – she hadn't said she was, but he knew that she listened and he liked that too. He didn't know how to say anything, but it was good to know that somebody might be ready to listen, just in case he could say something one day.

'Are you worried about tomorrow?' asked Linda.

'No!' said Gary, although he knew she wouldn't believe that. He rocked again, eyes still shut.

'I just wondered,' she said, 'I noticed you coming upstairs after that argument and I heard you rocking. I thought you sounded worried.'

'I didn't say I was worried, did I?' Gary replied quickly, then rocked again.

'You didn't need to,' said Linda.

Then Gary stopped rocking and went very quiet; he held his eyes very slightly open for a moment – just the width of half an eyelash – then closed them tight again. Still she just sat there, not looking at him now, just gazing past him at the wall, as if she was thinking something to herself.

'You never come with me when I go home!' he said, then wondered where that had come from.

'I did come with you at first', she replied, 'But then I thought you wanted to go there yourself on the bus. To make your own way there.'

He couldn't answer that, because he knew it was true, and in any case he didn't want to be seen with a care worker walking up to his house: that would only land him in more trouble with the kids down the road. He kept quiet, but now rocked his head just slightly, keeping his body still and thoughtful. 'Full up of stuff,' he thought to himself, 'full up of stuff, nobody listens, even Linda doesn't really understand. Nobody really knows.'

'You're never here on a Saturday anyway', he said, again surprising himself at speaking his mind so clearly, because he knew he was really shy inside.

'Yes I am,' she replied, a bit hurt about that, because it seemed to her that she was always working weekends. She let that go, but said, 'I will be here in the morning, if you do want me to come along'.

Gary said nothing. His eyes were shut again, but he was glad, because he'd got a promise out of her, and he knew she kept her promises. One time she had even come back in when she was off duty, just to take him to the doctor's. He held on to his sheet with one hand, thumb still in mouth, and pulled the pillow close to his ear with the other as if he didn't want to hear what she was saying.

'Is it just too difficult at home at the moment?' she asked him, but this time there was no reply. She sat there for a while longer, thinking that she had perhaps pushed a bit too far now, and decided to retreat for a few minutes. 'Would you like a hot chocolate?' she tried.

'All right,' he replied, 'But not too hot, you know how I like it.'

'I do,' she said, 'I'll be back.'

She went downstairs and made the drink, grabbing a quick word with Aysha, her colleague, explaining to her what she thought was happening with Gary.

'I noticed how jumpy he was when he came in from school,' said Aysha. Gary was just coming to the end of his first year in high school, and things were not easy for him, but he had held himself together through most of this term, keeping his more troubled behaviour for the children's home. Aysha had noticed that he had talked enthusiastically this afternoon about his "WRM" classes.

'What's that?' asked Linda.

'Working with Resistant Materials,' said Aysha, 'It's what they used to call woodwork.'

'I should think Gary's a real expert,' observed Linda, and they smiled.

Linda went back upstairs with the drink, but Gary was asleep now, so she set it down beside his bed and stroked his head then gently closed the door. Linda and Aysha together managed the return of the remaining young people from their evening out, sitting with one of them in the kitchen for half an hour while the others dispersed to their rooms.

Linda wrote up some notes on Gary's evening in his records, and reflected that even the little that he had communicated directly was a real step forwards: he was usually so shut away in himself, angry, withdrawn or both, that it was often very hard to reach him. She had sometimes had to sit with him for half an hour before he would say anything at all, whereas this time he had at least indicated that he needed more support with his home visits, even if he couldn't say much more. She had noticed him opening his eyes slightly to check that she was still there, and took this as a sign that he was looking for more communication. She had been his key-worker for several months now, and felt that he was possibly just starting to trust her and value his times with her. Trust was a difficult thing with these kids, though, and no sooner did you think you'd achieved it than they would rip it apart and rip you apart too if you weren't careful.

Linda wondered whether she had pushed too hard in asking the direct question about how hard things were at home, or whether he would have said more if she hadn't gone to fetch the drink, but nothing was certain in this work, and she decided on balance that she had at least given him the opportunity to make a clear statement about feeling too anxious to go home if he had needed to.

She also realised that she had not followed up with Gary on the argument downstairs which had provoked him into seeking refuge in his bedroom, but she judged that this had just been a "trigger" for him, and although the argument would need to be acknowledged and resolved with the child in question, it would be unhelpful to make too much of it.

Linda decided that she would offer to go part of the way home with Gary in the morning, perhaps walking as far as the bus stop or maybe driving him most of the way home, in the hope of offering him a bit more time to talk, and to confirm that she recognised his need for support. She had found that he could sometimes talk more openly about himself in a more neutral or safe setting than in the residential home. She thought she might also give him some small token or reminder of herself to take with him, so that even if she could not be there at home with him, he could maybe keep her more clearly in mind. Perhaps she would give him a packet of chewing gum or maybe something a bit more permanent – a button or buckle – something which suggested fastening – the ability to attach? The trick would be to offer him something in a way which would be acceptable to him and allow him to acknowledge (at least to himself) that it might help. To another child, Terry, an older girl, she had given a tiny Lego figure in a baseball cap and carrying a little bag, after Terry had been fiddling with this figure when she came across it in Linda's car as she was getting a lift to school. Terry had kept hold of this figure for months while she lived at the home and now that she was living in a hostel, she had it glued to her key-ring.

Linda realised that Gary was quite worried about this week's visit home, but after conferring with Aysha and re-reading his notes, she judged that there was no reason to question this visit or intervene directly in it, despite Gary's increasingly tense relation-ship with his step-father. She felt rather that he should be monitored on return and she decided that she would suggest to her manager that there should be a meeting with Gary's social worker soon to review his home visits, discuss them with him and exam-ine how he could be more fully supported towards his eventual return home, which was clearly causing some anxiety all round. In any case, she also knew that the social worker would not be available to discuss this with over the weekend even if she had wanted to.

The above scenario will perhaps be familiar to many residential workers – and probably to foster carers too. The need to stay in good communication with each of the young people, despite their many individual difficulties, and to set this against the need to keep everyday life going on as "normal" as possible, involves aiming for some balance between the "ordinary" events of everyday life and the "special" needs of each individual (Ward, 2006). Linda saw beyond Gary's apparently reluctant manner and difficult – even aggressive – behaviour, which might be off-putting in "ordinary" life, and she recognised some of his underlying emotional and physical needs. She could acknowledge his need for comfort and self-comfort, accepting some element of regression in his rocking and thumb-sucking, and offering him an acceptable form of physical support by sitting close to him and offering him a warm drink – even remembering how he liked this drink. These small practical details in everyday life, including warmth and comfort, food and drink, are of real significance in helping young people feel valued enough to take the bigger steps of attempting verbal communication about what really matters to them (Carter, 2003).

Meanwhile, Linda could try to move forward the direct verbal communication by asking Gary direct questions in a way which seemed to enable him to speak his mind, even though he found this very hard and she eventually decided it was best to "back off" a bit. She could also offer him some symbolic communication in terms of some little object which might help him to hold himself together by keeping it in mind that she would be thinking about him. She had noticed that this sort of thing could mean a lot to children in such turmoil, even though they might seem "hard" on the surface, and reluctant to acknowledge their "softer" needs. She believed it was better if this sort of symbolic object evolved naturally out of the time she spent with the child (Dockar-Drysdale, 1990), and it would often be something which might appear trivial to anyone else but which had come to mean something to this child. And occasionally she had decided just to offer some spontaneous little gift if she felt that would help. Linda also knew that at the "house meeting" the next morning, it would be important to acknowledge the argument that had provoked Gary's anger, and that this might just provide the opportunity for the young people to share with each other some of the distress and anxiety about home contacts which several of them had in common. She was aware that some of them talked about such matters when the adults were not around (Emond, 2002) but felt that they could gain much from being able to talk more in the meetings about this.

Linda felt positive about Gary and genuinely wanted to help him, but she also tried to keep their relationship well within the appropriate boundaries, by sharing all her discussions with him with her colleagues and writing up her notes in his records, as well as by conferring with the manager and with Gary's social worker from the Looked After Children's team. She would go out of her way to help and support him, but not to the extent of letting her concern override her other responsibilities. She found this sort of close direct relationship with young people rewarding as well as challenging, and had found that she especially valued the chance in supervision to reflect on what was developing in her work with the children. If ever supervision was cancelled or interrupted, she felt a real loss to the quality of her work and her understanding of where she was going in it – it was like the tiller which she used to control her professional "rudder". At times she could feel quite overwhelmed herself by the awful sadness or bleakness of the children's lives, and then feel that she was useless to really help them – whereas in fact this was often because she was "picking up" the children's despair and experiencing it as if it was her own (Shohet, 1999). Supervision would help her to regain her balance and direction so that she could somehow be both a real person to them as well as being an employed professional who had chosen to do this work to make her living – as well as having a life of her own!

Reflecting on the challenges

At this point, we leave the story of Gary and Linda, although of course the story would continue right through the weekend, and when Gary returned to the home on Sunday night, whoever was on duty would need to be sensitive to his anxieties. Linda would need to pick up the threads with him when she was next on duty, and the whole episode would need to be integrated into the pattern of his care.

It is worth reflecting further on the complex challenge of Linda's work and on the skills which she is called upon to use. She certainly has a lot of "multi-tasking" to do, as she keeps Gary in mind while also working with the whole group of young people. She has to combine close personal care and attention for the young people on an everyday and sometimes mundane basis with retaining a sense of the professional task with which she is engaged, ensuring that all of her work with the young people is geared towards support-ing them in their journey through placement and into their future (Hill, 2000; Milligan and Stevens, 2006). She also has to work with a lot of uncertainty and negativity – accepting rejection by young people who have been themselves rejected so many times, but staying available to them when they are ready to seek more help. She has to rely on her intuition at times – like gauging when to withdraw for a moment to allow a child space to reflect, without at the same time creating a feeling of abandonment at a critical moment.

In this sense, communicating with troubled young people is very much an art rather than a science. You can use all sorts of knowledge and even "techniques" at times, but at the heart of it all is an innate sensitivity to the variations in children's moods and in their ability to express themselves, plus the ability to monitor your own emotions and under-stand your complicated reactions to the many twists and turns which you will encounter (Crompton, 1980, 1990). For this reason, among the most useful knowledge you will need is self-knowledge: understanding more about what it is in your own life which has led you to choose this sort of work, as well as thinking about what sorts of things may have helped you most in your own darker times – such as talking with friends, seeking physical comfort or exercise, activity or a sense of escape – and reflecting upon how you may be able to provide some of this for the young people you are working with (Winnicott, 2004). At the same time, of course, you have to be careful not to seek to re-live your own traumas through the young people. Thus, having experienced difficulties in your own life is not a disqualification (nor, it should be noted, is it a qualification!): what is important is to have learned from your difficulties and reflected on what they have taught you, not only about yourself but also about how people in difficulty can be helped (Smith, 2006).

Working towards this sort of self-knowledge is not a one-off activity or simply the product of an "experiential" weekend, but an ongoing and even lifelong commitment to learn more, develop more and thus be able to offer more while still preserving and even enhancing your own personal sense of self. These are qualities which need to be learned, although they cannot easily be taught! We have mentioned supervision and the use of staff support meetings: many of the most successful child care workers also seek their own experience of counselling or psychotherapy as a means of understanding and nurturing what is, after all, the most important and precious "tool of the trade": yourself. Some specialised training courses include an explicit element of self-development (Ward and McMahon, 1998), although this is probably more common these days in counselling courses than in social work courses. Without such a component there is a risk that the training, and the work, will remain hollow and shallow, and will ultimately help neither the young people nor their families. It is also the responsibility of managers and training departments to ensure that their staff have access to appropriate support and development in this area just as in the more pragmatic aspects of their work.

In conclusion, my aim in this chapter has been to create an impression of what is involved in supporting and communicating with children in residential settings, looking in particular at the role of the key worker in the context of a team and set within the overall framework of the larger group of children and their carers. We have seen the importance of patience, of listening and attending to physical comfort, of offering and accepting symbolic communication as well as direct verbal engagement, and of understanding how communication patterns need to be monitored and attended to as they build up over a period of weeks and even months. I have called this "real-time communication" because much of it relates to current and immediate anxieties ongoing in the child's life, even though the feelings which are triggered off often relate to the child's deeper and more long-running concerns. Some of the most helpful interventions may be made at the unlikeliest times and in surprising places. We have also seen the value of intuition, self-knowledge and supervision as the core of the discipline and the need for an ongoing commitment to such self-knowledge on the part of both the staff and their managers.

References

Anglin J. P. (2004) *Pain, Normality and the Struggle for Congruence: Reinterpreting residential care for children and youth*, New York, New York: Haworth

Brown A. and Clough R. (ed.) (1989) *Groups and Groupings: Life and work in day and residential settings*, London: Tavistock

Carter J. (2003) 'The meaning of good experience', in Ward A., Kasinski K., Pooley J. and Worthington A. (eds) *Therapeutic Communities for Children and Young People*, London: Jessica Kingsley

Crompton M. (1980) *Respecting Children: Social work with young people*, London: Edward Arnold

Crompton M. (1990) *Attending to Children: Direct work in social and health care*, Sevenoaks: Edward Arnold

Dockar-Drysdale B. (1990) *The Provision of Primary Experience: Winnicottian work with children and adolescents*, London: Free Association Books

Emond R. (2002) 'Understanding the Resident Group', *Scottish Journal of Residential Child Care*, 1, pp 30–40

Emond R. (2005) 'An outsider's view of the inside', in Crimmens D. and Milligan I. (eds) *Facing Forward. Residential Child Care in the 21st Century*, Lyme Regis: Russell House Publishing

Hill M. (2000) 'Inclusiveness in residential child care', in Chakrabarti M. and Hill M. (eds) *Residential Child Care: International perspectives on links with families and peers*, London: Jessica Kingsley

Milligan I. and Stevens I. (2006) *Residential Child Care: Collaborative Practice*, London: Sage

Shohet R. (1999) 'Whose feelings am I feeling? Using the concept of projective identification', in Hardwick A. and Woodhead J. (eds) *Loving, Hating and Survival: A handbook for all who work with troubled children and young people*, Aldershot: Ashgate

Smith M. (2006) 'Act justly, love tenderly, walk humbly', *Relational Child and Youth Care Practice*, 19:4, pp 5–16

Stokoe P. (2003) 'Group thinking', in Ward A., Kasinski K., Pooley J. and Worthington A. (eds) *Therapeutic Communities for Children and Young People*, London: Jessica Kingsley

Ward A. (1993) 'The large group: the heart of the system in group care', *Groupwork*, 6:1, pp 63–77

Ward A. (1995) 'Establishing community meetings in a children's home', *Groupwork*, 8:1, pp 67–78

Ward A. (2006) 'Models of "ordinary" and "special" daily living: matching residential care to the mental heath needs of looked-after children', *Child and Family Social Work*, 11:4, pp 336–346

Ward A. and McMahon L. (eds) (1998) *Intuition is not Enough: Matching learning with practice in therapeutic child care*, London: Routledge

Ward A. Kasinski K., Pooley J. and Worthington A. (eds) (2003) *Therapeutic Communities for Children and Young People*, London: Jessica Kingsley

Winnicott C. (2004) 'Development towards self-awareness', in Kanter J. (ed.) *Face to Face with Children: The life and work of Clare Winnicott*, London: Karnac

Worthington A. (2003a) 'Structured work: the space to think', in Ward A., Kasinski K., Pooley J. and Worthington A. (eds) *Therapeutic Communities for Children and Young People*, London: Jessica Kingsley

Worthington A. (2003b) 'Relationships and the therapeutic setting', in Ward A., Kasinski K., Pooley J. and Worthington A. (eds) *Therapeutic Communities for Children and Young People*, London: Jessica Kingsley

243

17 Incorporating principles from social pedagogy into direct work with children in care

Pat Petrie

The government White Paper, *Care Matters: Time for Change* (Department for Education and Skills (DfES), 2007) is the latest attempt to address the state of child care in England. As many of the chapters in this book make clear, the position of children in care is one of great disadvantage and inequality, compared with the rest of the population. For children whose history includes public care, poor social outcomes are too often the norm (e.g. Corlyon and McGuire, 1997; McCann *et al*, 1998; Buchanan, 1999; Department of Health (DH), 2000; Richardson and Joughin, 2000; Social Services Inspectorate, 2001; Bhabra and Ghate, 2002; Chase *et al*, 2002; Ward *et al*, 2002; Meltzer *et al*, 2003; Jackson *et al*, 2006). But there is much evidence that their everyday experience of care is also not a happy one (Morgan 2005, 2006a). The proposals set out in *Care Matters* aim to give looked after children a better and more equal start in life.

Care Matters: Transforming the lives of children and young people in care (DfES, 2006) proposed that work with children should 'incorporate the principles of social pedagogy' (p 48), a philosophy and profession of working with children which can be found in some European countries. The subsequent White Paper *Care Matters: Time for Change* (DfES, 2007) announced a pilot scheme by which pedagogues, qualified abroad, would be employed in English residential homes.

This chapter sets out some of the key principles, practice and qualifications framework of social pedagogy and compares these with the system in England and Wales, and, in particular, considers how social pedagogy differs from social work and care work. In doing so, the chapter draws on findings from research conducted by this author and her colleagues at the Thomas Coram Research Unit (TCRU) (Petrie *et al*, 2006, 2007). The chapter concludes by discussing the feasibility of introducing pedagogic principles into the training and education of staff in England.

What is social pedagogy?

In English, the term "pedagogy" is rather unused outside the theory and practice of formal education, where it refers to the science of teaching and learning. For much of continental Europe, the term has a wider application. It is a system of policy, theory, practice and training that supports the overall development of the child. From this perspective, pedagogy is to do with children's upbringing, with their "education" in the broadest sense of the word: it is not reserved narrowly for schooling. However, there are signs that the usefulness of the wider definition and its applicability to work with children are being taken up in England also.

In the countries included in our various studies – Denmark, France, Germany, Flanders, the Netherlands and Sweden – it has been possible to identify a pedagogic system. This consists of policy and practice, theory and research, and the training and education of the workforce, with each component feeding into and drawing from the others.

"Pedagogy" and "social pedagogy" (which are sometimes used interchangeably) are still unfamiliar territory for English speakers, although they are recognised in much of Europe as the basis for work with children.

Social pedagogy refers to the whole domain of social responsibility for children, encompassing many types of provision. Historically, social as opposed to parental responsibility for children and young people came to the fore in the nineteenth century when the state began to be involved in the well-being and education of the children of the labouring classes. Social and economic forces had brought poor people into the towns, where they were visible and threatening to the affluent classes. New ways were found by which the problem of poverty could be addressed. In Germany these became known as social pedagogy. The term *sozialpädagogik* was first defined in 1844 by Karl Mager, the editor of the *Pädogische Revue*, as the 'theory of all the personal, social and moral education in a given society, including the description of what has happened in practice' (Winkler, 1988, p 41, as translated by Gabriel Thomas, one of our German colleagues). In 1852, an English writer, although not using the term, listed examples of what Mager referred to as 'what has happened in practice':

> *There is a Scriptural instruction as the foundation, then secular instruction, industrial classes, street employments, refuges, the feeding schools, adults, mothers and infant classes, clothing and sick funds, saving banks, libraries and reading rooms, magazines and periodicals, prayer meetings, lectures, ragged churches and emigration.*
> (J. MacGregor, 1852, p 22, quoted in Cowie, 1973, p 37)

Today, while the home is sometimes described as the first site for pedagogy, and parents as the first pedagogues, society continues to play a part in providing pedagogic institutions, alongside or instead of parents. With European eyes, the agenda of *Every Child Matters* (DfES, 2003) may be seen as a pedagogic document relating to the whole population of children and providing for their well-being. *Care Matters* is similarly "pedagogic", although it relates to a special group of children rather than the whole population. Similarly, positioning the local authority as "corporate parent" for looked after children can be viewed as a pedagogic policy. *Care Matters* is about the local authority's responsibility to maintain and promote children's overall well-being: their physical and mental health and their formal education: in short, everything that is contained in the term "social inclusion".

A final note on terms is necessary, before moving on to consider the training and practice of pedagogues and their direct work with children. In French, and some other Romance languages, *l'éducation* conveys a meaning similar to "pedagogy" as the term is used in Northern Europe. Crimmens (1998, p 310) cites Tuggener (1986), who suggests that the commonality of *l'éducation* and pedagogy may be assumed on the grounds of the similarities in their origins, historical development and the similar forms of training which are characteristic of pedagogy across Europe. In what follows, the term "pedagogy" should be taken as covering the French term *l'éducation*, and allied terms in other Romance languages.

Pedagogic principles

Pedagogues work with all age groups and in a range of settings, including residential care for young people, fostering support and adult services. In many countries, they are the main practitioners employed in early childhood education. Mostly, they work directly with children. Although they work in different settings, the principles for practice in the various settings remain the same. In the course of interviews with pedagogues themselves, with managers of residential homes, foster care support workers, pedagogue trainers and policy-makers in local and central government, some of the core aims of pedagogy were identified.

First, the practice of pedagogy is based on the intention to respect others as fellow human beings: children and the people who are important to them, such as family and friends, and colleagues in the same establishment as well as those in outside agencies. Pedagogues work with an understanding of children's rights that is not limited to procedural or legislated requirements.

In group settings, such as residential homes or out-of-school services, children and staff are seen as sharing the same "life space". Pedagogues do not see themselves as divided from the children, in a superior hierarchical domain; they are part of the group. They share many aspects of children's daily lives and activities and the group's associative life is an important resource. Pedagogues also value the individual, their unique identity and their contribution to the group, so that pedagogues and children are seen as building the "living space" together.

The pedagogue's work is conducted through their personal relationship with the child. The relationship is built around listening to, and communicating with, children, respecting their views and identifying and working with individual talents as well as problems. "Everyday" activities, such as play, eating together, homework, creative activities and holidays are seen as meaningful, not a matter of routine.

In pedagogy, the construction given to the child is that of the child as a whole person, with mind, intellect, physicality, creativity and sociability interconnected. Pedagogues often speak of their work as involving the whole human person: head, hands and heart and they aim to relate to children, similarly, in the round. In other professions, such as teaching or health work, the professional may be concerned with one of these aspects of the child, more than others. For their part, pedagogues work to support the child's overall development, in the course of everyday life together.

The strong personal basis of the work is not at the expense of professionalism; the personal and the professional form the two sides of the pedagogy coin. While pedagogy involves each worker's own strengths and personality, personal qualities are not seen as a sufficient basis for working with children. Both initial and ongoing training aim to produce a habit of reflection that draws on theoretical understandings *and* on self-knowledge. Group and staff meetings are also framed as opportunities for reflection. The professional basis of pedagogy is seen as permitting the pedagogue to stand back, to take stock of challenges and to act in the best interests of children, and of themselves.

Nothing has been said, in the above, about protecting children. This is not because pedagogues see child protection as insignificant. Rather, it is taken for granted that children's safety is paramount and that working on the basis of both the personal and the professional, and addressing the welfare of the whole child, will work to secure their safety.

So how does pedagogy differ from social work? Possible tensions between the two professions have often been raised by participants in seminars and conferences, where the research described throughout this chapter has been presented. It may be that such tensions are more apparent than real.

Perhaps the biggest difference between pedagogy and social work (as understood in England) is the extent to which pedagogues and social workers are employed in settings where they have ongoing interaction with children and young people, sharing their daily lives. For most social pedagogues this is the normative experience, the work for which they receive their initial training. But spending their working days with the same group of children is less normative for most people trained as social workers. For example, most residential care workers in the UK tend not to be social work trained. Social work and European social pedagogy, then, do not appear to be in competition; they relate to different working contexts and both may have a place as distinct professions.

For field social workers, the introduction of qualified pedagogues to work directly with children has potential benefits. Pedagogic training stresses the necessity for team work and multi-agency cooperation. Pedagogues should be well placed to share with social workers their own expertise, including their informed perspectives on children and on plans for their care. Social pedagogy and social work, although different, are not alien to each other. Indeed, social pedagogy is sometimes seen as one type of social work (Payne, 2005). For example, in Sweden, modules in pedagogy are offered on some social work courses. A recent report (Cameron *et al*, 2007) suggests a framework linking qualifications in social pedagogy to those of other disciplines, including social work.

We turn now to the training and education of pedagogues, and how they are prepared for work on the basis of these principles.

What is the training for pedagogues?

Pedagogic theory is an academic field in its own right and the basis for education and training for staff working with children and young people. The education of fully qualified pedagogues lasts usually for three years, culminating in a degree-level qualification. There are also examples of lower-level courses, for example, for two years, full time, that do not provide a full qualification, but allow employment in roles such as pedagogic assistant. There are also masters degrees and doctorates in pedagogy.

To an outsider, there appeared to be great similarities between the main pedagogy courses in the different countries we visited for our research (see also Courtioux *et al*, 1986). Courses provide students with a broad theoretical base for their work drawing on, for example, psychology, sociology and relevant theories such as attachment theory and theories of group dynamics. Practical and professional skills and knowledge are also covered, during practice placements and at college. These include, for example, relevant legal frameworks, conflict management, working with challenging behaviour, group work and so on. How these skills and knowledge are used within practice is the subject of reflection within the student group and with course tutors.

A distinctive feature of pedagogy training is support in the creative and practical everyday skills that will be a necessary part of their work. Students undertake one or more activities such as sport, art, music making, drama, car mechanics or gardening, at their own level. These are often the basis for group projects. In a training college in Copenhagen, for example, students undertake several joint projects, each lasting around six weeks, based on specific creative activities, like puppetry or music making. These projects have three main aims. One is to increase students' own skills in the area. Another is to consider how the activities could be adapted for use with children, whether for recreation or for more therapeutic purposes, often with reference to particular practice placements. A further intention, applied to all group projects, is for students to reflect, individually and together, on group processes and their own contribution, linking this to relevant theory.

Practice placements play a large part in students' training and education. There can also be an expectation that students undertake practice placements in other countries. This is seen as challenging the students, to some extent, and widening their perspective, especially with regard to their own work and the assumptions on which it is based.

The more theoretical, higher-level, pedagogic degrees may also provide practice placements. However, these degrees are seen mainly as a preparation for work in administration, research and development in the public and voluntary children's sector. Thus, practitioners and those employed in policy development and administration should be able to operate within the same knowledge framework and with something of a common mind.

Comparisons between pedagogy courses and English social work and care qualifications

On the basis of entry requirements and curricula, English social work degrees are of a rather similar standard to those for the fully qualified pedagogue. For both professions, many practitioners qualify at first degree level, while others obtain a qualification at a level similar to that of a masters degree. The main differences are of content and emphasis. In particular, social work training in England and Wales is generic. Social workers qualify to be competent in both direct practice and case management with the full range of service users and contexts for practice. By comparison, the main focus of pedagogue training is to work directly with the same group of service users, often children, on a daily basis.

The NVQs in social care, the standard qualification for residential care workers, are of a different order from these degree-level qualifications. The NVQ system has no requirement for related training or education, although short courses may sometimes be provided and undertaken. Neither does the NVQ usually have an entry requirement. NVQ candidates must provide evidence that they fulfil the role for which they are already employed, in the light of national occupational standards. The NVQ provides a process of assessment, not of education, and the NVQ assessor's role is not primarily educational. Also, NVQs are based on the assessment of a multiplicity of items relating to the social care of children. While many of these items would be seen as relevant for pedagogy, pedagogy courses have more integrated aims and processes: the approach does not lend itself to division and itemisation. In addition, with the NVQ, the level of theoretical knowledge expected is lower and the opportunities for safe supported reflection are less. It is not altogether fair to the NVQ system, therefore, to compare it with the education and training represented by the pedagogue's qualification: they are categorically different.

With regard to specific subject areas, one large difference between pedagogy and the English qualifications is that while child development theory is one of a number of important topics for social work training it occupies a lesser place than it does in the pedagogy qualifications; and while child development theory has some place in the NVQ in children's health and social care, it is at a low level. A further difference is that the pedagogy qualification prepares students, as we have seen, for working in and with groups, group processes and teamwork. Pedagogues usually work with and in groups of service users. They are trained to be conscious of the dynamics and conditions of living in groups, which will be the main context for their work. Group considerations are less central for social work degrees – or indeed for the practice of social work. They have no substantial role in social care NVQs, where the focus is more strongly on the individual. A further major difference is that the creative and practical subjects which form a substantial part of the pedagogue's training (see above) are not to be found in English social work training and have little or no part in social care NVQs.

Pedagogues in children's residential and fostering services

We turn now to some of the research findings from our studies of residential and foster care and the part played by pedagogy. We start by looking at a comparison of residential care in England, Denmark and Germany. We conducted interviews with 56 heads of establishment, 144 staff and 302 young people, overall (Petrie *et al*, 2006). In these countries, residential care had a more prominent status than in England. It had provoked less concern regarding the quality of care provided to children, and employed more highly qualified staff, specifically educated and trained as "pedagogues". We asked managers questions about the qualifications of all staff employed in the services studied. Nearly all the pedagogues in Denmark held a qualification at degree level, including, predominantly, pedagogy, but also social work and psychology. Half of those employed in the German establishments had such a qualification, with the other half qualified at a lower level after a full-time, three- to four-year course that was somewhat less theoretical than the degree in pedagogy. By comparison, just one-fifth of staff in England had a degree in a relevant subject. Around one-third of the English workers held a qualification such as the NVQ Level 3, and a further third had no qualification for their work. These figures are broadly comparable with those found in other English studies (McQuail, 2001; Brannen *et al*, 2007).

So, it appeared that the status of staff in residential homes in Germany and Denmark was higher than in England, although there was little difference, on average, in staff pay in the three countries. Staff turnover, recruitment and retention, caused greater concern in England, with higher turnover, more difficulties reported in recruiting and retaining staff, and disquiet about poor working conditions and the low status of residential care work. Danish establishments reported fewest problems with the recruitment and retention of staff.

How does pedagogy inform staff practice?

We found that pedagogic education and training made a difference to practice and to staff's understanding of practice options in residential care. Workers in Denmark most frequently reported that they responded to young people's difficulties by listening to them. In England, staff reported listening least frequently. Compared to staff in Denmark and Germany, English workers relied more heavily on talking and discussing, rather than listening and empathising. We asked staff about the last time that they had provided emotional support for a young person who had approached them with a problem. In answer, few staff in England said that they had provided physical comfort through cuddling the young person (8 per cent, compared to 20 per cent in Germany and 32 per cent in Denmark).

Asked if staff showed him respect, a young man in a German home replied that they did. As an example, he said:

Maybe, if I'm coming in, in a bad mood, then they don't ask immediately what happened [they give me space]. *They take me as a person, not only as an adolescent. They don't think they are something special. If she says* [promises] *something, then she is there. If I want something, then she listens. She keeps things to herself, if I want that . . . She is there for me, if I need her.*

Another said:

If I have problems and ask them 'Do you have some time?', then they listen to me and don't interrupt me.

Educators in colleges of pedagogy speak in terms of the pedagogue being "present" and "a presence" for the child; the above examples show the realisation of this principle, from the trials perspective. As Roger Morgan (2006b), speaking of his consultations with young people in care, has pointed out:

Their views are simple – they just want help with personal problems, to be listened to and included in the decisions made about them, treated with respect and to be able to liaise with a social worker who shows empathy.

This approach is central to the education of pedagogues.

We presented staff with vignettes about children in various sorts of difficulties (for example, a child crying in the night and having difficulties at home, children having problems at school, drug-related behaviour). In response, workers in Denmark, all of them fully qualified pedagogues, reported more and more varied responses than other workers, and indicated a more reflective approach. In answer to various questions, English staff referred more frequently to procedural or organisational matters and to short-term behaviour management, indicating a less personal professional role than that adopted by pedagogues.

We found, also, that there were between-country differences in the young people's experience of residential care. The English young people, whose current placements were, to date, of shorter duration than those of young people in Germany and Denmark, were rather less inclined than young people in the other countries to advise a new resident to approach staff for advice. They reported less involvement and less satisfaction regarding the ways in which decisions were made about day-to-day activities. They reported less frequent holidays, and were far more likely to report that they had not been on holiday at all during the last year, compared to the children in the other countries. They said that they enjoyed group activities and activities with members of staff slightly more frequently than the children interviewed in Germany, but less than those interviewed in Denmark. In England, outside friends visited young people less often and having a friend to stay overnight was very rare, compared to the other two countries.

Young people in Denmark consistently offered more positive replies about their experience in care than those in Germany and England. The accounts of the young people in Germany mostly fell between those of the other two countries, echoing the different levels of qualification across the three countries, with Denmark having most highly qualified staff, England having least and Germany in an intermediate position.

Pedagogy and foster care

A further study, also for the DfES, reviewed foster care and fostering services in Denmark, France, Germany and Sweden (Petrie *et al*, 2007). The study covered a range of issues, including the role of pedagogues in fostering services. In general, foster carers were not qualified as pedagogues in any of the countries visited. Exceptions were found in the professional foster care provided by a few agencies in East Germany, where, compared to West Germany, there were more difficulties in recruiting foster carers, and some formal employment of pedagogues for fostering hard-to-place children. In Denmark also, people with appropriate qualifications, including pedagogues, were sometimes specifically recruited to accept two or three such children, in their homes.

In all of the countries studied, although pedagogues were not for the most part working as foster carers, the principles of pedagogy were apparent in the training and support of foster carers. Pedagogues were often employed specifically to support the placement of children and sometimes to work directly with them during the placement. With the exception of Sweden, the training and support of foster carers was often the work of qualified pedagogues. For example, in France, with a requirement for foster carers to complete 240 hours of training, training was often delivered by the schools of social work which trained social pedagogues among other types of social workers.

Pedagogy was seen as having a good fit with fostering services. The perceived strengths of the pedagogic approach for foster care included that it was action-oriented, that it provided a "normal" way of thinking about children and their upbringing, and that it focused on children's strengths and their everyday activities. The trainers and support workers involved with foster carers were able to draw on their own pedagogic theory and knowledge of child development. Importantly, pedagogues' own professional experience and training could provide insights into working with "the head, the hands and the heart", all of which are required in fostering. The work of the pedagogue is both professional *and* personal, based on relationships. Like the foster carer, the pedagogue is "there" for the child both emotionally and practically, while also bringing reflection and judgement to the task.

Within the sometimes demanding personal relationships of foster care, the carer, just like the pedagogue, has to be able to access a more "professional" perspective, in order to judge what is best for the child and to act accordingly.

A senior civil servant in Germany commented on the important part played by pedagogues in public and voluntary sector fostering agencies:

Families have to be properly chosen and prepared and that costs money. If you build up this professional [pedagogic] support for fostering properly, it is not the cheap option. While it can be better for children from a development, success and social pedagogical point of view to be in families [rather than residential care], it is not cheaper.

In conclusion

Care Matters (DfES, 2006) proposes a national qualifications framework for foster and residential carers, which would 'incorporate the principles of social pedagogy' (p 48). As has been noted, there is no tradition of pedagogy within the UK. How, then, might such principles be embedded in education for practitioners to work with children in care contexts?

Research at TCRU continues to explore the potential to introduce pedagogy in England (Cameron *et al*, 2007). A briefing paper (Petrie *et al*, 2005) and an exploratory study (Cameron, 2007) funded by the Esmée Fairbairn Foundation identified some possibilities for consideration.

First, there is some evidence that pedagogues are already working successfully in England. A UK agency specialising in recruitment of German pedagogues has placed some 200 qualified practitioners in local authorities and other agencies, on permanent contracts (Ladbroke, 2007). With the harmonisation of qualifications across Europe, pedagogues from the new member states of the EU are said to be increasingly employed in this country in social work and children's services. Also, pedagogy students sometimes undertake practice placements in England. Danish pedagogy students on six-month full-time placements were highly praised by their English supervisors (Cameron, 2007). Reportedly, they fitted in well to existing modes of practice, they developed excellent relationships with children and staff, and they were creative. They were seen as trustworthy, such that they were frequently allowed to undertake responsibilities beyond the normal remit of placement students (whether this is desirable is another question).

Second, there already exist British qualifications which, in broad terms, are based on the pedagogic approach. These include the BA in Curative Education at the University of Aberdeen, the BA in European Social Work at the University of Portsmouth, and degrees in Youth and Community Work such as those to be found at the University of Durham, and the YMCA George Williams College in Canning Town (Canterbury Christchurch University). There are also some foundation degrees in development, which are building on pedagogic curricula and methods, such as Working with Children at the Institute of Education and at the University of Portsmouth.

There remains the question of social pedagogy as a difficult concept for English speakers.

> *In the English language, there is no single word that can stand for "education-in-its-broadest sense" to distinguish it from "education-associated-with-the academic-curriculum". But it is "education-in-its-broadest sense" that many continental Europeans mean when they talk about pedagogy.* (Petrie *et al*, 2006)

An alternative to "pedagogy" that is sometimes used is "social education". The term may sound more familiar, but it has the problem that it sounds like part of the formal educational curriculum, for example, relating to citizenship.

Cecchin and Røn Larsen (2006), introducing their book, *From a Pedagogical Point of View: Pictures and narratives from Danish day-care centers*, observe:

> *When we choose to maintain the notion of pedagogic, however hard it is to say in English, it is because we fear that something is being lost in (its) translation to either care or education. Something that has a great deal to do with the way we, as a society, raise our children to be tolerant and democratic citizens, with a grounded feeling of their own culture, but with an open mind to the ideas of others. We figure that this is a societal need that we cannot afford to ignore.* (Cecchin and Røn Larsen, 2006, p 2)

The relative strangeness of the term "pedagogy" or "social pedagogy" could be one of its strengths. It invites enquiry and it could encourage new ways of thinking and suggest new opportunities – not least with reference to the well-being of looked-after children.

Acknowledgements

The research that this chapter draws upon was carried out at the Thomas Coram Research Unit by the author, and by Dr Janet Boddy, Dr Claire Cameron, Ellen Heptinstall, Susan McQuail, Antonia Simon and Charlie Owen. It was funded by the DfES and the DH. I would like to thank the Departments for their support, mentioning particularly Carolyn Davies, Helen Jones and Caroline Thomas. The following research officers and research associates were involved in the studies reported in the chapter: Christine Bon, at I.R.T.S., Paris, Ile de France; Professor Dr. Herbert Colla, Dr. Thomas Gabriel, Rouven Meier, Tim Tausendfreund, Michael Tetzer at the University of Lıneburg; Professor Marie Bie and Dr. Filip Coussée at the University of Ghent; Inge Danielsen at the Københavns Socialpædagogiske Seminarium; Jytte Juul Jensen of the Jydsk Paedagog Seminarium, Århus; Dr. Ingrid Höjer, in the Department of Social Work at the University of Göteborg; Professors J. Van der Ploeg and E. Scholte, University of Leiden; M. Guy Dréano, formerly of Buc Ressources.

References

Bhabra S. and Ghate D. with Brazier L. (2002) *Consultation Analysis: Raising the educational attainment of children in care, Final report to the Social Exclusion Unit*, March 2002, London: Policy Research Bureau

Brannen J., Statham J., Mooney A. and Brockmann M. (2007) *Coming to Care: The work and family lives of workers caring for vulnerable children*, Bristol: Polity Press

Buchanan A. (1999) 'Are care leavers significantly dissatisfied and depressed in adult life?', *Adoption & Fostering*, 23:4, pp 35–40

Cameron C. (2007) *New Ways of Educating: Pedagogy and Children's Services: Final report to Esmée Fairbairn Foundation*, London: Esmée Fairbairn Foundation

Cameron C., McQuail S. and Petrie P. (2007) *Report to DfES: Implementing a pedagogic framework: a feasibility study*, London: DfES

Cecchin D. and Røn Larsen M. (2006) *From a Pedagogical Point of View: Pictures and narratives from Danish day-care centers: A photo book, poster presentation*, Reykjavik: ECEERA Conference

Chase E., Douglas N., Knight A., Rivers K. and Aggleton P. (2002) *Teenage Pregnancy among Young People Looked After by Local Authorities: Determinants and support for the mother, father and child – a review of the literature* (unpublished report for the Department of Health), London: Thomas Coram Research Unit, Institute of Education

Corlyon J. and McGuire C. (1997) *Young Parents in Public Care: Pregnancy and parenthood among young people looked after by local authorities*, London: National Children's Bureau

Courtioux M., Davies H., Jones J., Kalcher W., Steinhauser H., Tuggener H. and Waaldijk K. (1986) *The Social Pedagogue in Europe: Living with other as profession*, Zurich: FICE

Cowie E. (1973) *Education*, London: Methuen

Crimmens D. (1998) 'Training for residential child care workers in Europe: comparing approaches in the Netherlands, Ireland and the United Kingdom', *Social Work Education*, 17:3, pp 309–319

Department for Education and Skills (2003) *Every Child Matters*, London: DfES

Department for Education and Skills (2006) *Care Matters: Transforming the lives of children and young people in care*, London: DfES

Department for Education and Skills (2007) *Care Matters: Time for change*, London: DfES

Department of Health (2000) *The Children Act Report 1995–1999*, London: The Stationery Office

Jackson S., Simon A. and Owen C. (2006) 'Outcomes for children in care', in Chase E., Simon A. and Jackson S. (eds) *In Care and After: A positive perspective*, London: Routledge

Ladbroke A. (2007) *Children Webmag*, 26 May 2007, University of Nottingham
www.childrenwebmag.com/content/view/369

McCann J., James A., Wilson S. and Dunn G. (1998) *Caring for Children Away from Home*, Chichester: John Wiley & Sons

McQuail S. (2001) *Working with Children: European Models of Pedagogy and Residential Care: Germany, unpublished report*, London: Thomas Coram Research Unit, Institute of Education, University of London

Meltzer H., Corbin T., Gatward R., Goodman R. and Ford T. (2003) *The Mental Health of Young People Looked After by Local Authorities in England*, London:ONS

Morgan R. (2005) *Being Fostered: A national survey of views of foster children, foster carers and birth parents about foster care*, London: Commission for Social Care Inspection
www.csci.org.uk/publications/childrens_rights_director_reportsbeing_fostered.pdf

Morgan R. (2006a) *Placements, Decisions and Reviews: A children's views report*, Newcastle: Commission for Social Care Inspection. Accessed online 25 September 2006
www.csci.gov.uk/PDF/placements_decisions_reviews_(tagged).pdf

Morgan R. (2006b) Press release: 'Children put social workers under the microscope'
www.csci.org.uk/about_csci/press_releases/children_put_social_workers_un.aspx

Payne M. (2005) *Theories of Social Work* (third edition), Basingstoke: Palgrave Macmillan

Petrie P., Boddy J., Cameron C., Heptinstall E., McQuail S., Simon A. and Wigfall V. (2005) *Pedagogy: A holistic personal approach to work with children and young people across services*, Briefing paper, Thomas Coram Research Unit
www.ioe.ac.uk/tcru/Ped_BRIEFING_PAPER.pdf

Petrie P., Boddy J., Cameron C., Simon A. and Wigfall V. (2006) *Working with Children in Care: European perspectives*, Maidenhead: Open University Press

Petrie P., Boddy J., Cameron C. and Wigfall V. (2007) *Foster Care in Denmark, France, Germany and Sweden*, unpublished research report, London: Thomas Coran Research Unit
www.ioe.ac.uk/tcnu/Ped_BRIEFING_PAPER.pdf

Richardson J. and Joughin C. (2000) *The Mental Health Needs of Looked After Children*, London: Gaskell

Social Services Inspectorate (2001) *Fostering for the Future*, London: Department of Health/SSI

Tuggener H. (1986) 'Social pedagogy as a profession: a historical survey', in Courtioux M., Davies H., Jones J., Kalcher W., Steinhauser H., Tuggener H. and Waaldijk K. (eds) *The Social Pedagogue in Europe: Living with other as profession*, Zurich: FICE

Ward H., Macdonald I., Pinnock M. and Skuse T. (2002) 'Monitoring and improving outcomes for children in out of home care', in Kufeldt K. and McKenzie B. (eds) *Child Welfare: Connecting research, policy and practice*, Waterloo, Ontario: Wilfrid Laurier Press

Winkler M. (1988) *Eine Theorie der Sozialpädagogik*, Stuttgart: Klett-Cotta

18 **We're all human beings, aren't we?** Working with lesbian, gay, bisexual and transgender young people in care

Ane Freed-Kernis

Introduction

The developmental issues for lesbian, gay, bisexual and transgender (hereafter lgbt) young people in care present specific and unique challenges to those working with them. This chapter combines a review of the current research into these issues with the voices of lgbt young people to provide some guidance for professionals working with this group. After setting up the distinctions between various terms, the chapter then moves on to exploring the process of "coming out" so central in shaping the experiences of lgbt young people. The following sections look at the generic issues faced by lgbt young people in education, health care and staying safe before going on to examine those specific to lgbt young people in care. Throughout, the emphasis is on best professional practice in working with these young people. The chapter ends by looking at the steps required to broaden individual professional practice to encompass organisational traits and structures that best empower lgbt young people in care.

In order to illustrate issues with firsthand experience, a number of young people who have been or are cared for by the Albert Kennedy Trust contributed to this chapter.[1] Where quoted, their names have been changed.

A note on terminology

Before starting, it seems helpful to define a few of the commonly used concepts: "Sex" refers to the chromosomal, physical characteristics a person is born with, either male, female or intersex. "Gender" is a self definition expressing how the person views themselves in terms of preferred gender role (usually male, female, trans or intersex,

---

[1] AKT was set up in 1989 following the death of 16 year old Albert Kennedy. He fell to his death from the top of a car park in Manchester whilst trying to escape a group of "queerbashers" in a car. Manchester's gay community was moved into action and AKT was formed as a result; in 1990 it became a registered charity. AKT supports young lgbt people by: (a) providing appropriate homes through supported lodgings, fostering and other specialist housing schemes, (b) enabling young people to manage independent living successfully, and (c) improving attitudes within society towards lgbt young people. This is achieved through placing/pairing lgbt young people with lgbt carers, mentors and befrienders.

though there are other self-definitions), and "sexuality" is the expression of sexual feelings, for example, bisexual, gay, heterosexual, lesbian.

"Gay" is used to describe men who are attracted to or have sex with men. "Lesbian" is used to describe women who are attracted to or have sex with women. "Bisexual" or "bi" is used to describe people who are attracted to or have sex with either men or women. "Transgender" or "trans" describes a wide group of people ranging from people who occasionally cross-dress to people who undergo gender reassignment surgery (Department of Health, 2007b).

The issues of gender identity, sex and sexuality are not the same, but a number of the prejudices and therefore effects are shared, hence the combination of all these issues in this chapter. There are, however, significant differences and, where relevant, these have been elucidated.

It is important to remember that sexuality is not fixed, and that people can change how they define their sexuality. For example, a young person may define themselves as bisexual, and then later as gay or lesbian or they may initially self-identify as gay or lesbian, and later identify as trans and heterosexual; many permutations are possible (Mallon, 1998). As sexuality is fluid (Fish, 2006), and young people often come out incrementally, it can be difficult to separate the issues for lgbt people. 'Throughout the "coming out" period, there tends to be a shifting of sexual orientation and self-identification, and the pressure of a stigmatised sexual identity forces some GLB adolescents to go to great lengths to prove to themselves and others that they are not gay' (Blake *et al*, 2001, p 944). It should also be remembered that lgbt people can be disabled, of any class, religion or ethnicity, and that those identities will influence and interact with aspects of the lgbt identity.

Identity formation and "coming out"

One of the major tasks of adolescence is to experiment socially and form a sense of identity. This tends to be done by young people acting or presenting themselves in a variety of ways, and shaping their identity based on the responses received. For lgbt young people, this identity formation must integrate aspects of gender and/or sexuality in addition to those that their heterosexual counterparts need to consider (Ragg *et al*, 2006; Mallon, 1999a).

One such aspect is the process of "coming out", the voluntary announcement of sexuality or gender identity. Arey (1995) suggests four stages of coming out for lesbian and gay young people, which are refined by Cooley (1998). These are:

1. sensitisation (pre-coming out);
2. identity confusion (coming out);
3. identity assumption (exploration);
4. commitment (first relationship).

Whilst these stages were originally perceived as linear and sequential, not all young lesbian and gay people follow the same pattern, and the process can be halted, reversed, and can occur at different rates for different people (Mosher, 2001). Reactions to the announcement play a key role in shaping the dynamics of what can be a lifelong process of coming out (Anderson, 1998).

> Alex, on coming out: *Inside I had always known, but didn't want to admit it. People started calling me "dyke" at college. I tried to pretend it was not happening. At 17, I accepted it properly, but I told no-one for ages. A teacher realised that I had problems; he was gay and wanted to support me. I went for counselling, was still confused, but started to get involved in LGBT groups, make friends and accept myself and be accepted... Eventually I told my friends. A few were negative, but most accepted. At this stage I had still not told my family, my mum and sister.*

The process for young bisexual people is relatively unknown, and it is unclear to what extent bisexual identity is consolidated during adolescence (Ryan and Rivers, 2003). It seems to have some similarities with lesbian and gay young people in terms of the process, but can be complicated by the reactions of others, for example, the notion that they are gay or lesbian, but hiding it, or that they are wanting the best of both worlds. Bisexual young people can thus feel rejected by both the heterosexual and gay and lesbian communities. It may also be that bisexuality is seen by young people as less stigmatising than being lesbian or gay (Mallon, 1998).

The process of coming out as transgender as described by young people is similar to the one for lesbian, gay and bisexual young people, as are the reactions they encounter (Department of Health, 2007c). However, the process is also uniquely challenging in that it often involves changing name and pronoun (Department of Health, 2007c) as well as behaviour ("passing" as the other sex, using other toilets, etc), and may include a reappraisal of sexuality as well.

For lgbt young people, the difficulties of building their identities are exacerbated by homophobia, biphobia, transphobia and heterosexism, and they are keenly aware of the social disapproval, stereotyping, jokes, abuse and public debate on the issue. This environment can hinder the exploratory processes of young lgbt people coming out, as they may feel inhibited about sharing their identities or they may try to "pass" as heterosexuals. Research suggests that some young bisexual people "pass" as hetero-sexuals in the child welfare system, as the homophobia there induces them to live in the "heterosexual" part of their identities (Mallon, 1998).

The increasing legislative equality and visibility enjoyed by the lgbt communities (e.g. equal age of consent, civil partnerships, TV soap characters) have affected the issues for lgbt young people, in particular, the issue of coming out (Maguen *et al*, 2002; Waldo *et al*, 1998; Fish, 2006). A culture of greater visibility and tolerance tends to mean earlier coming out, sometimes with unexpected or unintended consequences, which younger people may be less well equipped to deal with. The effects on young people can be devastating as coming out can lead to a deterioration in family relationships. It is not uncommon for these young people to be evicted from the family home or face living in an abusive or hostile environment. In a study of 375 adolescent homeless people aged 13 to 21, Cochran *et al* (2002) found that 14.3 per cent of lgbt young people left home because of conflicts with their parents over their sexual orientation.

> Miles: *I first thought I was gay when I was 12 years old. I asked a friend if it meant that you were gay if you liked boys, and the friend told my mum, who hit me, punched me in the face and shouted at me. I ran away at this point.* (Miles later identified as a trans, heterosexual woman)

At the point of coming out, lgbt young people need support, but 'rather than focusing on the developmental needs of the youth, parents and other caregivers can divert energy into their own coping and adaptation to the disclosure' (Ragg *et al*, 2006, p 245). This has the effect of isolating the young person at a time when they need support the most, a process often bolstered by rejection from the extended family and friends.

> Alex: *After I left home I came out to my sister. At the time she went silent and told me to "go now". She phoned a few days later and said that I was not the person she thought I was, and that she cannot accept me. That is the last I heard from her.*

The issues faced by transgender young people are complicated by the implicit questioning of gender identity as opposed to sexual orientation. Burgess (1999) suggests that the issues for transgender young people are that external factors induce internal stress, for example, the physiological changes associated with the onset of puberty are likely to invoke shame and repulsion. Also, defying expectations can lead to confusion and isolation as well as mental health issues. School and family issues are likely to be even more difficult for young transgender people, as they are less likely to find help in forming their identities than lgb young people.

Role models are important to young lgbt people (Mallon, 1999b; Burgess, 1999; Wilber *et al*, 2006). As they may have lost their families, or have no lgbt adults in their families, other role models for how to be an adult lgbt person become more important.

> Alex: *When Fame Academy was won by Alex Parks, a lesbian, I had a positive role model. I'd always had negative views on homosexuality. I felt frightened, as I found her attractive, but having a role model helped me to accept myself.*

If the natural supports for young lgbt people have been eroded, they are more reliant on professional support such as counsellors or social workers. Thus they need professionals to be competent to deal with the particular developmental issues for them. Sensitivity to issues surrounding the coming out process can go a long way to building this competence. The next section looks at some key issues faced by lgbt young people before going on to look at issues specific to those in care.

Key issues for lgbt young people

This section seeks to summarise key research findings on the issues faced by lgbt young people so as to give the practitioner a sense of the range and scale of the challenges faced in three key areas: education, health and personal security.

Education

While there is no evidence that lgbt young people are inherently more or less academically able than their heterosexual counterparts, there is a great deal of evidence that they have a very different experience in school (Tuttle and Pillard, 1991). Homophobic bullying is startlingly common and research shows that up to 65 per cent of young lgb people have experienced this (Hunt and Jensen, 2006; Warwick *et al*, 2006; Poteat and Espelage, 2007). In a survey of 1,177 students at university from 2002, EachAction (2007) reports that 43 per cent of students believed their school was unsafe for gay pupils, whereas only 6 per cent thought it unsafe for minority ethnic pupils. One of the more disturbing elements of homophobic bullying in schools is that research points to the key role of school staff in perpetrating this. The issues seem to be particularly stark in faith schools (Hunt and Jensen, 2006). The effects of homophobic bullying on the individuals concerned can be grave. Isolation and depression are common with increased truancy rates a frequent response (Poteat and Espelage, 2007). Experience in AKT shows that a number of lgbt young people simply stay away from school in response to bullying. While lesbian, gay and bi-sensitive school policy can mitigate many of these effects, the effects of this school experience is that academic results suffer, thus affecting the life chances of lgb pupils (Blake *et al*, 2001; Hunt and Jensen, 2006). While the studies have examined the experiences of lgb pupils, there is little exploration of the experiences of transgender young people in care.

Health

The oppression and stresses experienced by lgbt young people have important repercussions for physical and mental health. Lesbian, gay and bisexual young people have increased risk of a number of mental health issues, including suicide, depression and self-harm (Ferguson *et al*, 1999; D'Augelli and Hershberger, 1993). While lesbian and gay young people are four times more likely to suffer major depression than their straight counterparts, bisexual young people have poorer mental health still (Dobinson *et al*, 2003–4). The suicide rate among young gay and bisexual men is particularly high

(Remfadi *et al*, 1998). For transgender people, self-harm and suicide rates are high (34% of all adult transgender people have attempted suicide (Department of Health, 2007b)). Typical risk factors for suicide amongst lesbian, gay and bisexual young people include being younger, gender non-conformity, conflicts with parents over sexual orientation, not coming out, being told it is "just a phase", and leaving home because of negative attitudes towards sexual orientation (Department of Health, 2007a). Research indicates that: 'Seventeen per cent [of trans people] were refused (non-trans related) healthcare treatment by a doctor or a nurse because they did not approve of gender reassignment' (Department of Health, 2007b, p 5). In addition to this sobering list, substance misuse rates for alcohol, drugs and tobacco are higher for lgb young people than those of their heterosexual counterparts (Beautrais, 2000; Uk.gay.com, 2005; Austin *et al*, 2004), with lesbian and bisexual girls more likely to smoke and consume alcohol, and gay and bisexual young men more likely to use illicit drugs (Department of Health, 2007a).

Violence and abuse

Regardless of actual sexuality or gender identity, gender-atypicality is a major risk factor for being physically or verbally attacked (D'Augelli *et al*, 2006; Ryan and Rivers, 2003; Waldo *et al*, 1998; Young and Sweeting, 2004). In particular, research shows that 'those perceived as too effeminate or too butch [are] at the greatest risk of violence' (Mallon, 1998, p 107). Physical and verbal attacks directed at lgbt young people of either gender in care are common, with attacks both by young people and staff (Mallon, 1998). Generally, young men were more often threatened with violence than young women (D'Augelli, 2002), and transgender women more than transgender men (Department of Health, 2007b). Survey findings show that violence and intimidation towards lgbt individuals is prevalent; 80 per cent of young lgb people had been verbally intimidated, 11 per cent had been physically attacked, and 9 per cent had been sexually attacked (D'Augelli *et al*, 2006). The risk of attack increased for the younger gay and bisexual men, with higher rates of attack for bisexual than gay young men (Huebner *et al*, 2004). As young lgbt people are more likely to be homeless, they are also at risk of sexual exploitation; in AKT's experience often going home with older people in order to have somewhere to stay for the night.

The list of threats and issues faced by lgbt young people is formidable but far from insurmountable. The following section looks at further issues faced by lgbt young people in care with a focus on the professional competences these issues necessitate.

Specific issues for young lgbt people who are in care

The experience at AKT highlights how the point of coming into contact with social services or homelessness organisations has been a traumatic time for a number of the young people we work with. Recent negative experience of what happens when they reveal their sexuality/identity means that young people are often more reluctant to do so a second time and the circumstances behind their distress and/or homelessness are often hidden from social care professionals. What young people need at this stage is acceptance, and what they fear most is further rejection, either of themselves or their identity. There is often an assumption that being lgbt is less normal and less preferable (Mallon, 1999b).

> Alex: *Initially on leaving home, I went to a hostel for two months. At the hostel I was not out, and when a young woman in her mid-twenties guessed, I had a negative reaction from a friend, who told me to stay away from her children, and instructed the children to stay away from me. This was very hurtful, as I thought we were friends. I was 18 at the time.*

This section considers three core themes, originally developed by Ragg *et al* (2006), which are central in determining the quality of care received by young lgbt people.

Vulnerability – empowerment

The vulnerability – empowerment theme was evident with the young people who contributed to this chapter. They were worried about the information held about them, and also worried that they might be "outed" to people they might not choose to be out to. Confidentiality was a core issue. One young person said:

> *This needs to be a biggie. Who is gonna know? It was the biggest issue in the home, where they kept a log book, so everyone knew your business.*

Information and advice was seen as empowering. Most of the advice young lgbt people need will be no different to that which other young people need, but what is important is that it is delivered in an inclusive way, which does not assume the gender of sexual partners, uses the correct personal pronoun, etc. (Department of Health, 2007a; Department of Health, 2007c). Some aspects of advice, however, will need to be of a specialist nature. In the case of transgender young people, this might be information on the transgender community, sex reassignment surgery and hormone treatment. In particular, Burgess (1999) suggests that transgender young people need hope in order to deter them from misusing hormones or altering their bodies using harmful or unsafe techniques. For lgbt young people, the need for specialist information may be on sexual health around HIV/AIDS, and general health as well as mental health issues, as these are particularly prevalent in the lgbt community (Beautrais, 2000).

Safety is always an issue for young lgbt people, and is even more of an issue when they enter care. In a US study, many (89%) lgbt young people were rejected by care establishments at intake, and many moved because of homophobia in the placement (Mallon, 1998). The young people described the restraint used as violent, use of the police to back up staff, and also that nights were less safe due to there being less staff. Many young people were in fear of rape, particularly young lesbians in care, who were raped by men attempting to "cure" them (Mallon, 1998). Issues of safety need to be addressed carefully with all lgbt young people in care. They are particularly vulnerable in all settings.

Ragg *et al* (2006) suggest three competences/values relevant to the vulnerability – empowerment theme:

1. *Tuning in* – sensitising oneself to the plight of the young person;
2. *Working through* – helping young people to deal with value-free facts, not anxieties;
3. *Advocacy* – using safe language, respecting diversity, and challenging when others breach diversity protocols to establish a safe, accountable culture.

Stigmatisation – validation

In terms of the stigmatisation – validation theme, the young people at AKT told of how they felt stigma acutely. They had the double jeopardy of being in care as well as being lgbt. Most of them had feelings of internalised homophobia, and stigmatisation fed into this, triggering feelings of self-hate or of being unlovable. Some of their workers had generalised or stereotyped views, which were seen as unhelpful and inhibiting to their positive identity development. Some young people also had experience of not being believed, or assumptions made that this was just a phase, with professionals often looking for causation of the perceived abnormality in childhood trauma or family dysfunction (Mallon, 1999b).

One young person described being in psychiatric care where the staff were 'obsessed with my sexuality' when this was not an issue for the young person. Another commented on staff in a young people's hostel:

They asked you to talk about the past 24/7 which would do your head in. They seemed to concentrate so much on the past that they never asked what you wanted to do with your future.

Validation tended to come from being with other lgbt young people and developing pride (Ragg *et al*, 2006), as well as from workers who validated young lgbt people. Mentoring systems, like those in place at AKT, can be an effective support for this validation.

Four values/competences were suggested in relation to the stigmatisation – validation theme (Ragg *et al*, 2006):

1. *Individualising* – recognising young people as separate from their sexuality group and unique, with positive traits;
2. *Strength finding* – building resilience to help balance the negative elements in young people's lives;
3. *Affirming* – seeing young people's struggles as important, which in turn allows them to integrate their experiences into their identity;

4. *Normalising* – validating feelings as natural and normal, even if others have views opposed to this. For example, being helped to mix with other lgbt people, find books, films, etc, of lgbt stories.

Rejection – acceptance

On the rejection – acceptance continuum, the young people had experienced a great deal of rejection, both open and subtle. The experience of rejection motivated young people to try to avoid it on other occasions, for example, by trying to "pass" as heterosexual, or by testing out professionals carefully before coming out to them. If young people had once been rejected by others due to being lgbt, there was a tendency to try to minimise rejection by withholding the lgbt identity in the belief that 'if they really knew me they would reject me'. However, the effect of this is to ensure that the young person only receives qualified support, not the unconditional support to which they are entitled.

A number of young people had experienced more subtle rejections of being compared to others and found not to measure up, or being dismissed, which seemed more difficult to deal with, due to their subtlety.

Acceptance is powerfully reparative for young people after rejection by their families. Alex described how helpful her carer's extended family has been, as they have accepted her as part of the family. At her first Christmas with them she was unsure of what to expect, and was surprised that they all bought her presents, and that she was clearly seen as part of the family. She quoted her carer's mother as saying: 'You are part of our family now, you can't get rid of us now'.

The competences/values (Ragg *et al*, 2006) which relate to the acceptance–rejection theme are:

1. *Remaining open* – helping young people explore without stereotyping or jumping to conclusions;
2. *Supportive engagement* – engaging with young people in a real and caring fashion – one young person advised, *'Don't be horrible to young lgbt people'*;
3. *Responsive exploration* – asking questions which allow the young person to discover their own feelings.

All of the above competences and attitudes will enhance work with all vulnerable groups, and would be a welcome addition in any setting.

Creating inclusivity – the lgbt-sensitive organisation

Developing personal and professional competencies are a must for all professionals seeking to effectively support lgbt young people. However, to truly stand any chance of consistently meeting the needs of lgbt young people, some level of institutional realignment is necessary. To this end, this final section develops six areas (derived from the work of Wilber *et al* (2006)) in which action can be taken for services looking to improve on their inclusiveness.

Creating an inclusive organisational culture

The young people commented on this at length. They picked up subtle cues as to whether they were welcome in the organisation by such means as posters in the waiting rooms, leaflets, as well as staff attitudes. They were very skilled at picking out which members of staff were likely to help them and which were not. The following is a list of things which professionals can do individually.

- Remember that your job is to assist young lgbt people to become well-functioning adults with an integrated identity.
- Assume that all young people whom you come into contact with have issues of sexuality or gender identity. That way, you will allow all young people to explore these issues and young lgbt people will be included within this.
- Educate yourself about lgbt young people – do not wait until you have a young lgbt person in your office. Also, be sure to identify resources for young lgbt people when your own expertise runs out (adapted from Mallon, 1999b).
- Help parents/carers/teachers resist the wish to "treat" the young person to become non-lgbt.
- Provide access to role models (how many people do you know from public life, outside of the arts, who are lgbt?) Use specialist organisations, some of which are listed below.
- Worker turnover is an important issue. Whilst this affects all young people in care, the additional issue of trust when coming out is important to lgbt young people, who need to explore their identities (Ragg *et al*, 2006). Building trust takes time. Ensure good introductions of new workers.
- Address isolation and persecution. Homophobic attacks are common (Outright, 2006; Ragg *et al*, 2006; Burgess, 1999).
- Use the strengths of young lgbt people (Anderson, 1998). Many equal opportunities policies operate on the unspoken assumption of minorities as victims as opposed to people with additional qualities, that is, deficit models. On this point, some of our young people were proud to have given talks in schools, and helped in recruiting and training staff. What all the activities had in common was that they treated the young lgbt people as people with something to add, because of their diversity, as opposed to people with something missing.
- Use consultancy and supervision. It is necessary to process the issues raised by work with lgbt young people: 'Social workers need, at a minimum, close supervision and consultation to process these issues' (Mallon, 1999b, p 5).

- Use correct pronouns, don't ask for "real" name, don't be critical of dress, avoid medical words such as disorder/disease.

Recruiting and supporting competent caregivers and staff

Recruiting and training staff to the competences above would be a good start. However, professionals also need to deal with their personal issues about this. As one young person put it: 'If it is an issue for you, don't take it out on young people. It could push them back into the closet.' Staff training which includes lgbt young people would also help in developing the skills needed.

Promoting healthy adolescent development

This means being informed about what constitutes healthy development not just in heterosexual young people, but ensuring that you are knowledgeable about different or additional developmental issues for lgbt young people. This may include providing specific health information, e.g. on sexual health, gender reassignment and hormonal treatment, and ensuring that young people know that there are others who share their issues. With all lgbt young people in care, the issue of safety needs to be addressed. They will need help and advice on staying safe more than other young people in care.

Respecting privacy and confidentiality

This is a major issue for lgbt young people who want to decide for themselves if, how and when to come out to others. The recording policies of agencies need to be examined, so that this information is not routinely recorded in open sections of files, and that young people maintain control of the information. Openness and accountability are key issues to consider, along with the empowerment of young people. Remember that you cannot un-tell people!

Providing appropriate placements

This is a difficult issue, as many young people may not be open about their sexuality or gender identity. Issues such as room sharing can be tricky (where do you put transgender young people? Which bathroom do they use?) There are no easy answers to these questions, but awareness and sensitive negotiation can resolve most situations. The issue of staff who behaved in homophobic ways was an issue for young people, who had found that those staff made the whole placement unsafe, as their behaviour gave implicit permission for other young people to bully them (Burgess, 1999; Wilber *et al*, 2006).

Providing sensitive support services

The young people contributing to this chapter had all sought specialist services via AKT, so may have been an unrepresentative sample. However, most of the literature suggests this is of major importance to young lgbt people. The young people wanted support services to give messages like the following.

- 'You are not on your own.'
- 'We are here for you.'
- 'Life will not always be like this.'
- 'Treat young lgbt people as you would anyone else; give them as much support as everyone else.'
- 'Give choices of what young people can do.'

It was clear that what they sought was encouragement, belief in their future and support to achieve. Whilst most of the young people had poor experiences of social workers, they commented on lgbt staff positively. One reflected that:

The difference was that they saw my potential, and concentrated on my doing well in the future. They see what you can become more than your past.

Conclusion

This chapter has outlined some of the particular developmental challenges faced by young lgbt people. The widespread abuse, oppression, isolation, rejection and marginalisation experienced by lgbt young people makes for harrowing reading. Yet the aim here is not to depress or shock, but to highlight the ways in which their experience is shaped by their sexual preferences which generate a diverse set of specific issues in the face of prejudice and ignorance. The focus here has been on looking at how these specificities demand a core set of competences from practitioners working with lgbt young people. The competences suggested are essentially good practice with any vulnerable client group, and could be used in both qualifying and in-house training. Whilst the competences are important, they need to be combined with an attitude of openness, respect and acceptance. Competence and attitude will go a long way towards meeting the needs of young people, *all* young people. In seeking to understand this often misunderstood marginalised group, the specificities of lgbt young people have been highlighted. Yet this was not the way the young people interviewed for this chapter wished to be understood. They did not wish to be seen as 'special' or 'different', rather, at heart, theirs was a simple request for equality:

After all, we're all human beings, aren't we?

References

Anderson A. L. (1998) 'Strengths of gay male youth: An untold story', *Child and Adolescent Social Work Journal*, 15, pp 55–71

Arey D. (1995) 'Gay males and child sexual abuse', in Fontes L. A. (ed.) *Sexual abuse in nine north American cultures*, California: Sage

Austin S., Ziyadeh N., Fisher L. B., Kahn J. A. and Colditz G. A. F., Lindsay A. (2004) 'Sexual orientation and tobacco use in a cohort study of US adolescent girls and boys', *Archives of Pediatrics and Adolescent Medicine*, 158, pp 317–322

Beautrais A. L. (2000) 'Risk factors for suicide and attempted suicide among young people', *Australian and New Zealand Journal of Psychiatry*, 34, pp 420–436

Blake S., Ledsky R., Lehman T., Goodenow C., Sawyer R. and Hack T. (2001) 'Preventing sexual risk behaviors among gay, lesbian, and bisexual adolescents: the benefits of gay-sensitive HIV instruction in schools', *American Journal of Public Health*, 91, pp 940–946

Burgess C. (1999) 'Internal and external stress factors associated with identity development of transgendered youth', in Mallon G. P. (ed.) *Social Services with Transgendered Youth*, New York, Howard Press

Cochran B. N., Stewart A. J., Ginzler J. A. and Cauce A. M. (2002) 'Challenges faced by homeless sexual minorities: comparisons of gay, lesbian, bisexual and transgender homeless adolescents with their heterosexual counterparts', *American Journal of Public Health*, 92:5, pp 773–777

Cooley J. J. (1998) 'Gay and lesbian adolescents: Presenting problems and the counsellor's role', *Professional school counseling*, 1, pp 30–34

D'Augelli, A. R. (2002) 'Mental health problems among lesbian, gay, and bisexual youths ages 14–21', *Clinical Child Psychology and Psychiatry*, 7, pp 433–456

D'Augelli, A. R., Grossman A. H. and Starks M. T. (2006) 'Childhood gender atypicality, victimization, and PTSD among lesbian, gay and bisexual youth', *Journal of Interpersonal Violence*, 21, pp 1462–1482

D'Augelli, A. R. and Hershberger S. L. (1993) 'Lesbian, gay, and bisexual youth in community settings: personal challenges and mental health problems', *American Journal of Community Psychology*, v21, p 421(28)

Department of Health (2007a) 'Briefing 3: Young lesbian, gay and bisexual (LGB) people', in Health D. O. (ed.), http://www.dh.gov.uk/en/Publicationsandstatistics/Publications/Publications PolicyAndGuidance/DH_078347 accessed 18.9.07

Department of Health (2007b) 'Briefing 11, Trans people's health', in Health D. O. (ed.), http://www.dh.gov.uk/en/Publicationsandstatistics/Publications/PublicationsPolicyAndGuidance/D H_078347 accessed 18.9.07.

Department of Health (2007c) 'A guide for young trans people in the UK', in Health D. O. (ed.), http://www.dh.gov.uk/en/Publicationsandstatistics/Publications/PublicationsPolicyAndGuidance/D H_074258 accessed 18.9.07

Dobinson C., Macdonnell J., Hampson E., Clipsham J. and Chow, C. (2003–4) 'Improving the access and quality of public health services for bisexuals'. Ontario Public Health Association, http://www.opha.on.ca/ppres/2003-04_pp.pdf accessed 1.11.07

Eachaction (2007) 'Is homophobia a major issue?', www.eachaction.org.uk/html/ishomophobia amajorissue.html. Accessed 23.1.07

Ferguson D. M., Harwood, L. J. and Beautrais A. L. (1999) 'Is sexual orientation related to mental health problems and suicidality in young people?' *Archives of General Psychiatry*, 56, pp 876–880

Fish J. (2006) *Heterosexism in Health and Social Care*, Basingstoke: Palgrave Macmillan

Huebner D. M., Rebchook G. M. and Kegeles S. M. (2004) 'Experiences of harassment, discrimination, and physical violence among young gay and bisexual men', *American Journal of Public Health*, 94, pp 1200–1203

Hunt R. and Jensen J. (2006) *The School Report: The experiences of young gay people in Britain's schools*, London: Stonewall

Mageuen S., Floyd F. J., Bakeman R. and Armistead L. (2002) 'Developmental milestones and disclosure of sexual orientation among gay, lesbian and bisexual youths', *Applied Developmental Psychology*, 23, pp 219–233

Mallon G. P. (1998) *We Don't Exactly Get the Welcome Wagon. The experiences of Gay and Lesbian Adolescents in Child Welfare Systems*, New York: Columbia University Press

Mallon G. P. (1999a) *Let's Get it Straight. A Gay- and Lesbian-Affirming Approach to Child Welfare*, New York: Columbia University Press

Mallon G. P. (1999b) *Social Services with Transgendered Youth*, New York: London: Harrington Park Press

Mosher C. M. (2001) 'The social implications of sexual identity formation and the coming-out process: a review of the theoretical and empirical literature', *The Family Journal: Counseling and Therapy for Couples and Families*, 9, pp 164–173

Outright (2006) *Survey of 18,000 Gay & Lesbian people commissioned by Channel 4*, OMD & gaydar radio, http://www.gaytoz.com/bResearch.asp Accessed 24.1.07

Poteat V. P. and Espelage D. L. (2007) 'Predicting psychosocial consequences of homophobic victimization in middle school students', *Journal of Early Adolescence*, 27, pp 175–191

Ragg D. M., Patrick D. and Ziefert M. (2006) 'Slamming the closet door: working with gay and lesbian youth in care', *Child Welfare*, 85, pp 243–265

Remfadi G., French S., Story M., Resnick M. D. and Blum R. (1998) 'The relationship between suicide risk and sexual orientation: results of a population-based study', *American Journal of Public Health*, 88:1, pp 57–60

Ryan C. & Rivers I. (2003) 'Lesbian, gay, bisexual and transgender youth: victimization and its correlates in the USA and UK', *Culture, Health & Sexuality*, 5:2, pp 103–119

Tuttle G. E. and Pillard R. C. (1991) 'Sexual orientation and cognitive abilities', *Archives of Sexual Behaviour*, 20, pp 307–318

UK.GAY.COM (2005) *Gay youth smoke more, study finds*, http://uk.gay.com/headlines/7030, Accessed 8.2.05

Waldo C. R., Hesson-McInnis M. S. and D'augelli A. R. (1998) 'Antecedents and consequences of victimization of lesbian, gay, and bisexual young people: a structural model comparing rural university and urban samples', *American Journal of Community Psychology*, v26, p 307(28)

Warwick I., Chase E., Aggleton P. and Sanders S. (2006) *Homophobia, Sexual orientation and Schools: A review and implications for action*, London: Department for Education and Skills

Wilber S., Andreyes C. and Marksamer J. (2006) 'The model standards project: creating inclusive systems for LGBT youth in out-of-home care', *Child Welfare*, 85, pp 133–149

Young R. and Sweeting H. (2004) 'Adolescent bullying, relationships, psychological well-being, and gender-atypical behavior: a gender diagnosticity approach', *Sex Roles*, 50, pp 525–537

Resources:

www.akt.org.uk Albert Kennedy's website. Provides housing, mentoring and advice for lgbt young people under 25

www.bisexual.org National website for bisexual people

www.eachaction.org.uk Works with homophobic bullying in schools.

www.innerenigma.org.uk Provides information to trans or intersexed people, their partners and families

www.lgf.org.uk Lesbian and gay foundation. Provides advice and help for lesbian, gay, bisexual and trans people

www.mermaids.freeuk.com Offers support and information to children and young people who are trying to cope with gender identity issues and their families and carers

www.queery.org.uk Directory of lgbt activities

www.regard.dircon.co.uk National organisation of disabled lgbt people

www.tht.org.uk Provides information and services to people affected by HIV

19 Group work with adopted children

Lorraine Wallis

Introduction

The approach to group work with adopted children and young people discussed in this chapter was heavily influenced by the organisation we originally belonged to, The Children's Society, whose values and practice emphasised the importance of children and young people's participation.

In 2000, my colleagues and I began a consultation with adopted children and young people who had been placed for adoption through our project. Our aim was to find out which services they wanted us to provide. The consultation was important as little was known at the time about the views and experiences of adopted children and young people (Thomas *et al*, 1999; Department of Health (DH), 2000). A key message arising from the consultation was the need to develop opportunities for adopted children and young people to meet together on a regular basis to enable them to share experiences and build relationships. These opportunities were felt to be valuable in counteracting potential feelings of isolation and to promote the sense of belonging to a wider community of adopted children and young people (Wallis, 2001). Our starting point was to listen to what adopted children and young people wanted and needed rather than addressing issues and problems they presented. Our approach is in contrast to previous provision for adopted children and young people which had tended to focus on short-term therapeutic groups either before or after they were placed for adoption (Triseliotis, 1988).

As a result of the consultation, we began running groups with these children and young people in June 2001. We have since worked with over 40 adopted children and young people, aged from 4 to 21, who regularly attend our groups. In 2005, we joined Coram Family and our work with adopted children and young people has continued to grow and develop. Since January 2006, local authorities have been required under Regulations to provide opportunities for adopted children to meet together (HMSO, 2005, Reg. 3.1a). This then is an appropriate time to share the key messages arising from our consultation, and the experiences, themes and issues which have arisen from our group work. This chapter explores the journey we have undertaken with the children and young people and focuses on the aims of our work. We particularly hope to convey young people's enthusiasm for this approach to inclusive practice.

The consultation

In 2000, we carried out a consultation with young people who had previously been placed for adoption through our project. Using group discussions and questionnaires we gained the views of 17 young people aged 13–20 (a third of the young people placed for adoption through the project). A clear message arising from the consultation was the importance of providing groups.

It is a good idea, it would help a lot, so you know you're not alone.

The groups is a brilliant idea because it is a good chance for children to chat about being adopted.

During the consultation process, it became clear that children and young people were a vital source of support for one another.

Young children can talk to other young children better than they can talk to adults.

When you don't know how you should feel, another adopted young person can help you.

You can have a friend like you who understands what you are going through.

So, over the following two years, we began to develop groups for the under sevens, 7–10-year-olds, 11–13-year-olds, and those aged 14 plus.

The groups and their aims

The groups have three main purposes, to help adopted children and young people to:

- network;
- access support;
- participate in the development and delivery of adoption services.

In working towards these aims we found that, firstly, it was important to think about how the groups are staffed. During the consultation, young people requested that adoptees help out at the groups. To this end we encouraged members of the teenage group to volunteer to help in the groups for younger children. Their presence has been very popular – younger children are often in awe of the fact that these teenagers share in their experience – and an important element of developing a network for adopted children and young people.

A second important need identified by the consultation, which was confirmed by our group work practice, was offering direct support for adopted children and young people.

The consultation indicated that the majority of young people felt that the project social worker was an active source of support for them.

[The social workers] help us through difficult patches at home. Comes and talks to us but the main thing is they're always here to help you in any situation.

In contrast, around a quarter of the young people felt unclear about the role of the project social worker; they were more of a distant figure to them.

I have not been in touch with them for a long time. I know someone contacted my mum to see how my sister and I were doing.

There were clearly times when adopted children and young people wanted direct support, which they had not been able to access.

The hardest time was when my brother just wanted to leave me and my adopted parents, which was very hard for me.

When I first met my new family I didn't know them and I thought why am I going with strangers who I don't know?

In our groups we aim to give children and young people permission to talk about adoption but do not force discussion. Bringing young people together with the sole focus of talking about adoption can be an emotional and exhausting experience and is not sustainable in long-term group work. Throughout the year we will have some planned sessions which focus on their views and feelings about adoption, but we find issues arise and are discussed during regular activities. For example, young people will share with one another their experience of contact with birth family, children will talk about how many mummies they have or describe their brothers and sisters who do not live with them. They can talk about visiting their old foster carers in school holidays or their worries about the safety of their birth mother who was a victim of domestic violence. They can express how unfair they feel it is that they cannot see their birth mother when their birth brother in foster care can. These are conversations that would not naturally occur at school or youth club but have become very much part of our long-term group work and enable us to provide direct support to children and young people when issues arise. For example, a young man who wanted contact with his birth father asked us to approach his adoptive mother because he did not know how to raise the issue with his adoptive parents.

This groupwork may stimulate the children to go home with lots of questions about their adoption. This may feel uncomfortable for some adoptive parents and may even leave them with some concerns about the group undermining their adopted child's transition into their family. Some parents might also be concerned that at these groups their child is in danger of mixing with children who are severely damaged. All these views have implications for the success of group work. To prepare adopters we have found that it is important to introduce the idea of groups to them as early as possible and to present this as a service they and their child have a right to access, highlighting the benefits and warning of the possible consequences, e.g. provoking questions for children. To this end a presentation about the groups has become a regular slot at the preparation groups for prospective adopters.

The third aim of the group work has been to promote children and young people's participation in service development at a national, regional and project level by helping to disseminate their views to service providers and ensuring they have their say in decisions that affect their lives. For example, at a national level our adopted children and young people were involved in consultation exercises for the Children and Adoption Bill. On a project level the children and young people have taken part in the recruitment and selection of staff and volunteers.

In contrast to therapeutic group work, the participatory approach to working with children and young people does not always sit easily with adoption. Unlike the promotion of young people's participation in decision-making in public arenas such as school or even in the looked after system, adoption is very much seen as part of the private sphere of the family. There has been a symbolic shift from the public world of social work and family courts to the private sphere of their new family. Adopted children, and their adoptive parents, want to be seen as part of a "normal" family and group work that focuses on their adoption identity and encourages them as a group to have their say about adoption and adoption services may be seen to oppose this process. However, it is clear from our initial and subsequent consultations with adopted children and young people that questions and issues about adoption are always present, but adopted children and young people do not always have the forum, medium or permission to express them.

The impact of long-term, participatory group work

In a snapshot survey of teenagers' views on the groups, two key themes emerged: the groups provided a chance for them to meet others in the same situation and share their experiences, and it was also an opportunity to gain confidence. They felt that having regular, fairly lengthy meetings (we usually meet for six hours because of the distances young people have to travel to attend) with the chance to do an activity together was crucial in securing these benefits. They felt the activities enabled them to get to know each other better and become more comfortable about sharing their feelings with one another. They also felt that mutual respect between staff and young people was an important element of the groups.

> It is different to any other group because you can speak to someone like an adult and not feel like a kid.

What has been so surprising about the groups is the way they bring together young people who would not naturally form friendships in the playground at school but who are able to bond and accommodate one another through the shared experience of adoption. Children and young people who may have struggled to become part of other groups are successful, often popular, members of these groups, as this young woman, an adoptee, describes.

A lot of children out there are psychologically scared and groups like this help the children work through their fears and their phobias and help them gain an understanding of who they are and why they are so special and help them gain confidence in what they have grown through.

The identity children and young people are forging in their new families and the complex relationships children have with social workers have implications for their willingness to join a group. For some young people it became important that they had what they regarded as their "own" worker and we have learned from the young people that group workers can provide crucial support, for example, when there is disruption of an adoption placement. For others, it is not so. It is important to note that all but one of the teenagers who attend groups have memories of their birth family life and are open about their adoption status in their day-to-day lives. In contrast, young people who are about to move to secondary school who are choosing not to tell people they are adopted may find groups for adopted children less attractive. When children are first placed with their adoptive family, no longer having a social worker can be a symbolic element of becoming part of a "normal" family. Past experiences can lead some children and young people to be suspicious of social workers. These children may also be reluctant to join a group they associate with being "social worked".

While adopted children have been shown to experience better outcomes than children who remain looked after (Triseliotis *et al*, 1997; Rushton, 2003), we have still found a significant number live independently or become parents earlier than most of their peers and are often less well prepared to cope. Some young people have demonstrated challenging behaviours, which has meant their adoptive families are struggling to support their child when they move out of the family home. This combination of factors has highlighted the important role that group workers can have in supporting these young people to access the support they need and help to support parents in the process. Providing support and continuity to children and young people during these isolating and vulnerable times has been enabled by the long-term group work and has become a key element of our work. Thus, we have been able to mediate between teenagers and parents when relationships have been strained, direct young people to services and support when they have moved out of the family home, and provide some continuity to young people who have moved back to the looked after system when their adoptive placement has broken down.

Long-term group work has not been simply about helping individual children and young people but about listening to their views on adoption and enabling them to share these views with the people who can make a difference. To this end, young people were involved in a regional project to disseminate their views to adoption teams in the statutory and voluntary sectors. This piece of work, called "Adopted young people: our messages", emerged out of partnership work with two other agencies which have also been running groups for adopted young people over the last five years: Adoption Support and St Francis Children's Society. We decided to bring our young people together, giving them an important chance to meet a wider range of adopted young people, maybe someone who shared their views and experiences, and to begin to explore the issues they felt it was important to tackle.

The young people chose to focus on three key areas: education, contact with birth family, and running groups for adopted children and young people. At the end of the day, their feedback indicated that they wanted to use a range of mediums to record their views in order to share them with those running services for adopted children and young people. Working in partnership with two other agencies was invaluable. As workers, we had an opportunity to share our views and experiences of group work and share resources, enabling us to be more ambitious and motivated in what we attempted to achieve in our participation work. Together we secured a grant from Y Speak to run a weekend away for 25 adopted young people.[1]

During the weekend, art proved to be a very powerful vehicle for the adopted young people to express their views (Hopkins, 2007; Howells, 2006). One young man with mild learning difficulties who took part in the art workshop had never previously used the groups to express his feelings about adoption. At home his mother commented that he never talked about adoption. Yet at the art workshop he was able to express the confusion he felt about adoption and how difficult he felt it was to seek help. He painted on his canvas intertwining tubes which he felt symbolically resembled DNA. The background offered a contrast painted in green, the colour of the bedroom walls of his first foster home. He wrote:

My art is about adopted people being confused and not knowing which way to go for help. The lines going everywhere show their confusion. I used green paint and white lines because green makes me feel safe, it's quite a safe colour.

Choice and control have been important approaches to developing groups where children and young people can express their views. We have learnt that acknowledging potential

---

[1] The Y SPEAK Consultation Fund is a scheme which awards grants to help young people take their views to decision-makers. The Fund was run by Change Makers, who provide a platform and process for young people to get actively involved in their communities.

differences within the group before and during discussions is vital to ensuring that members are not left feeling further isolated, for example, as the only person who does not want to trace their birth family or as the only person who has no memory of their birth family. This was vividly demonstrated to us by a young woman keen to meet other adopted young people, but who created a painting which demonstrated how she felt different from the other adopted young people. The canvas was black with a number of over-lapping and brightly painted rectangles of different sizes. In the bottom left corner was her fingerprint. Here is what she wrote about the piece of work.

> *The idea behind this painting is that the shapes represent adopted children everywhere. They are all geometrically similar due to the fact that they have one thing in common, adoption. However, they are all different colours, shapes and sizes, showing how each person is different. They are surrounded by a black background, which represents the rest of society. They are separated, yet part of it. I have also put my thumb print at the bottom left hand corner, as it is a part of who I am, and I wanted to include a part of myself in the painting.*

Acknowledging difference and giving young people clear permission to opt out of discussions is vital to this work. In the consultation, we had also observed that the one young person who was adopted from birth was quite shocked at the account of another young person's troubled teenage years. How to manage this blend of experiences has always been a key issue for group work with adopted young people.

The artwork was shared with local adoption teams in the region and some young people took part in presenting the work. The medium proved an effective way of enabling social workers to access young people's experiences and views.

> *Food for thought, such a wonderful idea.*

> *Your work really made me think and understand adoption from a child's perspective. Thanks.*

> *The pictures are very powerful, as are the words – a reminder of some of the tensions you experience and this will help me in the work I do with adopted children. Many thanks.*

Conclusion

There are two key messages arising from our experiences: the importance of children and young people's participation and the value of long-term group work in developing relationships. We feel that the starting point for the development of group work with adopted children and young people is the children and young people themselves. We have always been impressed by the ideas and insights they have shared, along with the support they have shown one another. Their message to us is clear. They want to build long-term relationships with other adopted children and young people. They want a safe space where they can express their views on adoption with people who would understand and could offer help. They want a chance to have their say about adoption to help adopters, prospective adopters and service providers understand the issues that affect adopted children and young people. Their work has had a powerful impact. The starting point is not always what we can do for adopted children and young people but what they can do for each other and for others.

References

Department of Health (2000) *Adoption: A new approach – a White Paper*, London: HMSO

HMSO (2005) *The Adoption Support Services Regulations 2005*, Statutory Instrument 2005 No. 691, London: HMSO

Hopkins G. (2007) 'Drawing on feelings', *Community Care*, 8–14 February 2007

Howells G. (2006) *Report on the Role of Art in Group Work with Adopted Children and Young People*, Unpublished, Shepshed: Coram Adoption East Midlands

Rushton A. (2003) *The Adoption of Looked After Children: A scoping review of research*, London: Social Care Institute for Excellence/The Policy Press

Thomas C., Beckford V., Lowe N. and Murch M. (1999) *Adopted Children Speaking*, London: BAAF

Triseliotis J. (1988) *Groupwork in Adoption and Foster Care*, London: BAAF

Triseliotis J., Shireman J. and Hundleby M. (1997) *Adoption: Theory, policy and practice*, London: Cassell

Wallis L. (2001) *Adopted Young People: Having our say* (unpublished), London: The Children's Society

Section 5

Supporting the practitioner

Difficulties with reflective thinking in direct work: the role of supervision and consultation

Leslie Ironside

Even when I was little I always used to blame the social worker for everything that happened. John, a 12-year-old child in care

Introduction

Reflective practice is foundational to effective direct work with children, enabling practitioners to think about and understand not only the children with whom they are working but also themselves and their own motivations and responses. However, this is not easy or straightforward to achieve. Practitioners often find themselves struggling with difficult feelings (their own, the children's and those of the child's parents or carers) and unable to untangle complex interpersonal dynamics. They often find their thinking capacity deserting them at such times. This chapter will consider why and how this occurs and discuss how supervision and consultation can have a role in enabling practitioners to recapture their reflective thinking.

Interruptions to reflection

The capacity to establish and sustain a reflective state of mind is the foundation of effective parenting. It provides the basis for the development by the child of resilience in the face of adversity. Peter Fonagy and colleagues (1994) describe the mother's capacity to 'envisage the infant as a mental entity, a human being with intentions, feelings and desires' (p 247). They go on to say that: 'This can form the basis of her ability mentally to contain the baby and correctly to understand and appropriately react to her infant's need in vocal or gestural communications as well as in the provision of her physical care . . . it requires the mother to *reflect* upon the mental state of another human being, and in this way goes beyond demonstration of affection and concern' (p 247, my italics).

The development of this capacity is equally as important in substitute caretaking and professional practice with children who are looked after in public care (see Smallbone and Ruch, this volume). It underpins direct social work relationships with children and the professional agency response as a whole. However, such a reflective state of mind can be difficult to maintain in the face of the often strenuous and challenging nature of this work.

The children themselves will, by definition, have experienced things as having gone very wrong in their lives and are likely to have been traumatised by this. They will have experienced, when leaving their birth parents, a breakdown in this reflective process, if indeed it ever existed, and a breakdown in the basic need for the continuing and conclusive assurance of the cycle of love between children and their parents (Fairburn, 1952). The practical management of the very difficult behaviour that is often a child's response to this sense of abandonment is in itself a great challenge for carers and professionals. Carrying responsibility for working with, caring for and living beside such traumatised minds is also likely to be emotionally testing.

A compassionate approach, where the practitioner is able to reflect upon and sustain the impact of the child's state of mind, leading to deep and profound contact, thought and decision making, is one response to the kind of emotionally raw experience inherent in this work, and the preferred one, but it is not the only one which occurs. There is often something intrinsically disturbing about such a contact which leads some practitioners to seek ways of avoiding the emotional impact of being "in touch" with a child. This leaves them less emotionally available to children and disrupts their capacity to contain them. Others feel compassion but this on its own is not enough and carries its own risks. Instead, the task is to be able to be close enough to the child to experience the often traumatic emotional charge of such a relationship, whilst also maintaining a boundary, and sense of self, and so be distant enough not to be overwhelmed by the emotional affect of the relationship.

This is not an easy undertaking. The emotionally disturbing nature of the contact may cause the worker to seek ways of avoiding the poignant affect which is provoked. His or her capacity to be reflective may come under attack, disrupting the ability to reflect upon, understand and contain the presenting emotional and behavioural state of the child. In the extreme, this might influence decision-making processes in both the individual worker and the system designed to help the child in care. Systems can of themselves become 'trauma-organised' (Bentovim, 1992) and it can at times seem as though the difficult states of mind that the children find themselves in can become quite "contagious". Foster carers, in particular, can find themselves in states that feel quite alien to themselves (Ironside, 2004) and social workers and other professionals trying to think through and respond appropriately to very difficult situations can be thrust into emotional turmoil that can test their internal resources to the extreme.

However, as painful and difficult as the work is, if the complex understanding advised in this chapter is maintained, the worker will be able to take a step back and reflect upon what is happening. This will ensure that his or her practice is in touch with the child's traumatised mind and not disrupted and deflected by it. He or she can come to an understanding of how many children in care have had their internal resources tested to breaking point and beyond. In this sense, the worker's untoward emotional experience can be viewed as an asset as it enables him or her to be in touch with and reflect upon the child's state of mind. Supervision, both internal (Casement, 2006) and external, can enable children's states of mind to be thought about and worked with, rather than shunned. The internal membrane between the self and the experience that is so often perforated by trauma can begin to be re-established and the experience may be integrated and thought about rather than acted upon inappropriately or avoided.

In order to illustrate these themes, I turn to four examples from my work as a child and adolescent psychotherapist. In the first example, I focus on my work with an individual child. This sets the scene and illustrates the child's own struggle to maintain a reflective capacity and complexity in her thinking as well as highlighting how emotionally difficult it can be, as a practitioner, to witness, be reflective and usefully available to a child in an extreme state of distress. In the second example, I discuss consultation work with foster carers (illustrating an "internal supervision model"). This example illustrates their struggle with the child in their care and the parallel processes that were alive in the consulting room. In the third example, I discuss consultation work with a social worker. This highlights the use of an external consultative model and illustrates how a practitioner may be thrust into a particular role that denudes their reflective capacity and may lead to hasty, if not avoidant, case management decisions. In the fourth example, I discuss the evaluation of a pilot training course for social workers aimed towards further developing a reflective capacity within their work and highlight the importance of integrating this approach into ordinary supervisory and managerial processes.

Working with an individual child

Jane, a young girl of eight, was attending weekly therapy with me. She was very guarded in her presentation but attended willingly and regularly. Gradually she seemed able to drop her guard a little. She was a girl who idealised her mother and denigrated social workers, spitting with anger and rage that she had been taken into care. She spoke of hating the social services and totally holding them to account for what she felt was a great miscarriage of justice. There was no doubt in the professional network that on the grounds of neglect and physical abuse she needed to be in care. She, however, argued otherwise and continued to have contact with her mother and father.

In one session, just after a holiday break, she very tentatively began to explore something quite new that was both frightening and exciting to witness. I could barely catch my breath as she spoke of how strange it felt – her foster carers were beginning to feel like her parents! She tentatively spoke of how peculiar this was and how she did not know what to do with the feeling. She liked it but then, with rage in her voice, added, 'They are not my parents! What about my mum?'

We tried to talk things through whilst her mind shifted from one paradigm to another. If she began to care for her foster parents, did that mean she was betraying her birth parents or her affection for them? Could her foster parents be like her parents without being her parents? Her divided loyalties left her feeling totally confused and vulnerable. I found myself feeling not only deeply humbled but frightened by the experience. Could I bear to contain and reflect upon this material and the feelings it provoked in me?

Jane had felt able to let me know about such precious and precarious matters, matters which for the moment she could not talk about with her foster parents or with her social worker. She had allowed herself to allow me to reflect upon her mental state as another human being (Fonagy et al, 1994) in a most profound way and it was emotionally very painful for her. In the external world she was beginning to wrestle with groundbreaking feelings towards her foster carers and her parents and in parallel to this, in the session with me, she, for the moment, was able to allow me to be in the role of "the parent" at this deeply, deeply intimate level. And it felt very fragile.

Reflections

I have chosen this example from my work as it illustrates a very particular issue that may arise when "being beside" a child in care. On the face of it, one can but only applaud the child's presentation and the use she was making of therapy, and yet it is crucially important to note that, as a practitioner, being in touch with such an emotional experience was, in parallel to Jane's own experience, also very testing and almost "too hot to handle" and reflect upon.

I was in the privileged position of being her therapist and charged with trying to help her make sense of her life. Unlike her carers, social worker, teacher and so on, I did not have to deal with a hundred and one other things at the same time. Extrapolating from this, we can imagine how a child may quickly feel that the "other" is too "busy" or distracted to listen or how in other circumstances the emotionally painful tone of the interaction may have swayed the worker to inadvertently be too "busy" too listen.

In our meeting, however, we see a tentative and difficult move in this child's mind and a shift in what might best be described as her mourning processes. What also became apparent was that Jane was beginning to hold a much more complex picture of things in her mind and begin to reflect upon her experience. This was not a straightforward process. In some ways she became more difficult to live with, the inconsistency and unpredictability more difficult to manage than the belligerent but consistent attitude she had previously held. Nobody quite knew where they were with her and in the professional network meetings we could think about, discuss and joke about how mad it was that in part we wanted the "old" Jane back – at least then we had known where we stood!

Consultation work with some foster carers

Foster carers, Mr and Mrs Smith, were referred to me for some consultation work by their social worker because of concerns about their 13-year-old foster child, Lucy. At the time I was employed within a fostering team to specifically work with foster carers to help them think about and best manage the children in their care. My role was to act as someone who could be there to see the world through the carers' eyes and, whilst being part of a professional team, I was also outside that team and able to help the carers reflect on and develop their relationship with the social services department.

I needed to begin this work by thinking of what issues may commonly be raised for the carers of an adolescent. Many of the ordinary anxieties of parenting are present in parenting young people in care but they can take on an exaggerated form and an intensity that is far from ordinary. Each stage of a child's development takes on its own shape but the process of adolescence is particularly tempestuous, especially if it comes on the back of a prior history of traumatic loss and separation. The pleasure of witnessing children's development can run alongside a mourning process; the loss of the younger child and the replacement of that child with one that at times parents may hardly recognise. Alongside this is the decrease of parental control that is appropriate to earlier childhood.

Parents have to struggle with the anxiety this process can evoke and this may stir up uncomfortable feelings and fuel the fires of a desire for omnipotence. Any child may feel, to the parents, as though he/she is moving out of 'parental control' (Waddell, 2002). However, negotiating such *ordinary* processes alongside a history of trauma and neglect (Bentovim, 1992) can be extremely complex and *extraordinary*.

Lucy was one of three siblings who had been living in the Smiths' care for many years. Lucy's birth mother was a drug addict, involved in violent relationships and not able to look after her children. The foster carers knew the mother well and contact was maintained.

I was puzzled about why these carers had been referred as Lucy's behaviour, as recounted, did not seem extreme, certainly in comparison with other referrals. In part, these carers seemed to be struggling with the ordinary process of separation and individuation, and yet the social worker's referral letter had led me to believe that the carers were quite at the end of their tether and finding it very difficult to cope.

At the meetings, I heard how Lucy was going to school but would occasionally bunk off, and did not really seem interested in things. She would take the bus into school and then just stay on it and not get off at the right stop. The carers really struggled with how to punish her. They kept her in for excessive periods of time and seemed to double up on the detentions she was receiving at school. To me this seemed a bit extreme, in the light of the presenting behaviour. As we talked, the understandable parental fear that Lucy was going down the same path as her mother seemed paramount and the anxiety this stirred up did seem to lead to a particular attitude towards Lucy and her behaviour. In part the "keeping her in" seemed more to do with "keeping her safe", i.e. off the streets and away from the possibility of meeting drug dealers, rather than to do with her misbehaviour. In this sense the foster carers were serving a different master and, as such, it was little wonder that they were feeling ineffectual in terms of disciplinary issues.

Their response was perhaps understandable in the context of the contact between Lucy and her mother but, seemingly, it had tipped into a panic where they had become more and more controlling of her. Parts of themselves could see how different Lucy was from her mother but the terror of repetition had taken over. They felt stuck and confused and they were certainly not talking about their concerns with Lucy for fear that, if they did so, this would add to the likelihood of these worries becoming a reality.

At this point in time, these caring foster parents were struggling to reflect upon Lucy's mental state as another human being in a holistic way as they were so preoccupied with the terror that she would be like her mother. Mr and Mrs Smith themselves seemed in the grip of a very anxious style of attachment, preoccupied with "keeping Lucy safe" rather than allowing there to be room for thought and exploration. They had become unable to follow that essential, but anxiety-provoking, parental task of "exposing our children to danger". They had become quite obsessed by her behaviour and could think of little else.

A note on technique

My approach to this type of work is modelled on the importance of the development of the reflective space (Fonagy *et al*, 1994) described above. I seek to bring a 'mentalising' (Fonagy *et al*, 2004) approach to my encounters with carers, and provide them with an experience of their minds being reflected upon such that they can develop, or in some extreme cases, begin to regain, their own capacity for self-organising, reflective thinking. Such meetings are initially often filled with anxiety. The mere fact that carers are at my door can engender relief for them but also fuel an anxiety that they have not done things well enough. My approach is to ask 'what is the matter', endeavour to contain anxiety, promote a 'let's think about this together' approach, and try to find some pointers as a way forward in the situation. My task then with Mr and Mrs Smith was to establish an effective partnership in which we could think about things together.

These caring foster parents seemed to make very good use of the initial sessions, to "offload" and think through their worries and anxieties. I realised that this was the first time that they had been able to verbalise their fears; they had managed to alert their social worker to their concerns but had also been worried about how much to tell him for fear that they would be judged in a negative way and the children removed from their care. We were able to think about this and how the social worker was cast in a particular light, again based upon fear. At later joint meetings with the social worker, these fears could be thought about and discussed but, at this point in time, the observation also allowed us to speculate about a potential parallel process: might Lucy also be worried about how much she can talk about things for fear of some catastrophe happening?

Matters seemed to be progressing fairly well and I wondered about drawing the sessions to a close, feeling that I had, perhaps, done all I could for the time being. I was under a lot of pressure in terms of workload and things seemed to be more settled. I felt a bit useless and rather at a loss as to how to proceed. Mulling things over to myself, I wondered about Lucy and her perhaps too feeling useless or at a loss in this situation. I also wondered about the foster parents' reaction and how perhaps they may also have been feeling an anxiety similar to my own, struggling to make meaningful contact with this child. My queries about further "parallel processes" between us led me to make a small and tentative "questioning" intervention at our next meeting.

Intervention

Technically, I felt it was important to respect the traumatised mind that continued to be in the ascendancy, to suggest ideas and to be aware that I might be seen to be talking a lot of nonsense, as well as having the humility to be aware that this might indeed also be true! I spoke to them about how I had been unsure how to take things forward, my feeling of being at a bit of a loss, and whether this might help us in our thinking about Lucy's feelings. Both the foster parents seemed to really light upon this; they took the idea up and expanded upon it in a very useful way. They began to think about how they might really have turned a blind eye to Lucy's needs as an individual. Interestingly, the tone of the sessions now *felt* completely different, I now felt engaged and useful! They in turn were galvanized into a different mindset in which they felt much less persecuted by Lucy's relatively minor misdemeanours and this made for a radical change in their relationship with her. They began to engage with her in a different way, doing more things with her in a pleasurable way *and* allowing her more independence.

Reflections on the consultation role

Judging and timing such interventions is crucial and we do not always get it right! Workers will need to feel confident to acknowledge their feelings if they are to use them to assist in the work. It is essential not to be seduced into drawing work to a close too early when the practitioner feels uncertain or at a loss. Of course, there are times when resources are very scarce and it would be foolish to ignore the reality of such pressures. But, as in this case, it is important not to confuse the external resource issue with internal dynamics that can be so informative in terms of understanding a particular communication and a particular decision-making process.

Consultation work with a social worker

A social worker, Paul, whom I meet with for regular consultations about the children on his caseload, began a meeting by asking, almost before he had sat down, whether I knew of a good residential placement for a child. I had a great deal of respect for Paul's work and realised through the tone of the request that this question carried with it a great deal of anxiety and his style of presentation felt quite out of character. I began to ask about the child and was initially told that it was not really something that he needed to explore as there were a lot of other things he wanted to discuss. He paused, though, and added that a decision had been made for the child to leave the foster placement and it was really felt that the child would be best placed in a unit. I replied that I would be very happy to think this through with him and think about a suitable residential unit but that I was also puzzled by the nature of the request, that I was being asked about a unit without any knowledge about the child and felt I needed a bit more information. (It is important to add in relation to my internal feelings, and my concurrent internal supervision, that I felt I had to hold fast to my own thinking. I felt as if I was going against a fast moving tide and that probably the last thing Paul wanted to hear from me was that we should complicate matters, pause and think about things.)

Paul then explained that he had been at a regular professional network meeting about a child, John. The foster carers had been finding his behaviour really difficult. They really loved John but did not feel they could cope any more. Paul then explained how he had been under a great deal of pressure at the meeting to identify a suitable unit with immediacy and agreed that he would look into it. He then added, 'It is interesting, I am not even sure it should be my job . . . and the meeting was meant to be there to discuss matters but I was just presented with the decision. I felt really fed up . . . bullied'. The parallel process in terms of Paul's approach to our meeting were now becoming apparent and I suggested to Paul that perhaps for that very reason this was a case we should think about. Paul laughed and said, 'Yes, you're right'.

We then went on to discuss the case and think about what he might do next. We felt that the best thing might be to get back to the foster carers and think things through with them a bit more, to learn how to best understand what they were saying at the meeting; were they "letting off steam", wanting people to know how dreadful things were, and/or did they really feel that the placement should end? Paul realised he had not really addressed these issues in the meeting, John's presentation raising such anxiety that there was, it seems, no room for thought. We began to think about why it was that, in this particular case, there had been what seemed a rapid and no-questions-asked move towards an immediate residential placement that, for the moment, we had to acknowledge may or may not be appropriate. Paul also now added that he felt that in a large measure even the idea of another foster family had been leap-frogged over and thought this might be due to the carers' undoubted loving feelings towards the child and how painful they would find it to see him in another family. He believed that they would understandably find this really difficult to address but then with increasing confidence felt that he could begin to approach this with them and with the network. He thought he could go back and address the way in which the emotional pain of the situation may have led to them all avoiding some painful issues.

We further discussed how it may be right that a residential placement was the most appropriate way forward, and some thought would be given to identifying one but that, in addition, some further work was needed. This would include both thinking about whether or not the placement could continue and, if so, what additional resources may be needed for this, and, also to think about what, if any, other placements may be suitable and available.

This consultation meeting had begun with an off-hand request for some information and a dismissal that the case did not need discussion but had ended with Paul using the full consultation time to talk about John's situation. He commented on how he knew at the back of his mind that things were not right and, in acknowledgement of the apparent increased amount of work ahead of him, joked good humouredly as he left that that was the last time he was going to raise something in passing with me as it had left him with so much work to do!

Reflections

In the early stages of the meeting, I as the consultant took what might be described as a robust "parental" line towards a "dismissive child" but as the meeting progressed, this moved much more towards that of a model of a parental couple talking together in a child's – John's – best interests. This is an interesting parallel with my work with Mr and Mrs Smith. There, the internal process of self-reflection had helped us move (metaphorically) from it seeming like a "robust containing parent and dismissive child" towards being more like a "parental couple talking together in the child's/client's best interests".

A model for group reflection

The following model is one way of facilitating the development and integration of reflective practice into the busy day-to-day activity inherent in social work practice. I met with a group of six social workers engaged in working with children in care for two hours a fortnight for eight sessions. This allowed for an introductory session, six sessions in which each participant presented, in turn, a case study for discussion, and a concluding session. Participants were asked to write a process recording each week of half an hour of a meeting with a client in order to develop their observational skills. These process recordings, including the social workers' feelings about the interaction, provided the main focus of each consultation.

This methodology draws upon principles from psychoanalytic thinking and the Tavistock Clinic's method of infant observation (Miller *et al*, 1989; Turney, this volume). The aim was that the similar exercise of asking the participants to systematically record their interactions with a client would increase their observational skills and ability to reflect upon their emotional responses to their "turbulent environments".

Evaluation

The following examples from the evaluation forms indicate the ways in which the participants viewed the experience and highlight the ways in which this approach can be integrated into daily practice.

I feel more grounded again, not just problem focused, and able to recognise and credit my own work. I am thinking more about transference and counter transference these days.

The course acted as a reminder to look at cases in a more holistic way. Often social work supervision is based upon facts, dates and planning in practical terms. I feel the course was an opportunity to remind myself and my manager that it is important to look at the dynamic between myself and the clients I am working with. It is important to reflect on this – this can sometimes provide the space to look at a case with fresh input and insight.

More often than not, social work has become about solution-focused work with families and individuals. It is important to make the time and space to look at our work in relation to our interactions with clients and the relationship we develop with that particular client. To me it is a vital piece of the jigsaw.

It was reassuring that we were given examples of how to avoid getting caught up in the right and wrong ways to respond to a situation but to help the client reflect on their thinking and help them find the right way for themselves with our guidance. Often our role is so pressurised, working with foster carers and adopters who often contact us in crisis expecting immediate answers to their difficulties. This can make workers feel deskilled or feel a reluctance to work with particular clients whereas we all have a lot of skills to draw upon.

Apart from a difficulty in finding time to write up process recordings as part of the training, it is important to note that there was not a feeling that this style of work meant a necessary increase in workload. There was, rather, a recognition of how sometimes the feeling of being too busy to follow this approach may also be an avoidance of the painful dynamics intrinsic in the work. The reflective approach seemed to help with the feeling of demoralisation which can also be endemic in this work. It helped the practitioners not to feel so isolated and alone and seemed to bolster their own sense of resilience and confidence in their own capacity to practice. To echo one of the responses, this approach seemed to help the participants to reflect on their thinking and help them find the right way for themselves both in their contact with clients and in the different use they might make of supervisory structures.

Conclusion

The robustness and resilience of the practitioner to be reflective in his or her decision-making process is going to be mitigated by many factors, external and internal to that worker. How well workers *feel* supported in their private and professional world is of extreme importance. Pressure of workload, managerial and supervisory structure, the nature of personal relationships and life experiences all influence effective working practice.

The practitioner of whatever discipline will, when engaged in this work, encounter problematic emotional states in the minds of the children in care, in the minds of carers and colleagues and, indeed, in his or her own responses to this turbulent work which will deeply affect practice. The practitioner may also become the container for various projections (see Smallbone, this volume) and may well be disturbed by the process. The ability to hold a reflective state of mind and contain and think may itself then be in need of some containment and thought. Where this capacity is difficult to maintain, a process of consultation, at an internal and/or external, and at a group and/or an individual level can help to maintain a reflective approach to the work and aid decision-making processes.

Many thanks to Marcus Page, Barry Luckock and Michelle Lefevre for their thoughtful comments on earlier drafts of this paper and many thanks to the children, foster carers and social workers who have worked with me but must, for reasons of confidentiality, remain anonymous.

References

Bentovim A. (1992) *Trauma Organised Systems*, London: Karnac Books

Casement P. (2006) *Learning from Life*, Hove: Routledge

Fairbairn W. R. D. (1952) *Psychoanalytic Studies of the Personality*, New York: Brunner-Routledge

Fonagy P., Steel M., Steele H., Higgitt A. and Target M. (1994) 'The Emanuel Miller Memorial

Lecture 1992. The Theory and Practice of Resilience', *Journal of Child Psychology and Psychiatry*, 35:2, pp 231–257

Fonagy P., Gergely G., Jurist E. and Target M. (2004) *Affect Regulation, Mentalization, and the Development of the Self*, London: Karnac Books

Ironside L. (2004) 'Living a provisional existence: thinking about foster carers and the emotional containment of children placed in their care', *Adoption & Fostering*, 28:4, pp 39–48

Miller L., Rustin M. E., Rustin M. J. and Shuttleworth J. (1989) *Closely Observed Infants*, London: Duckworth Books

Waddell M. (2002) *Inside Lives: Psychoanalysis and the growth of the personality* (second edition) London: Karnac Books

21 Developing "containing contexts" for the promotion of effective direct work: the challenge for organisations

Gillian Ruch

Introduction

There is no doubt, as is attested to by the earlier chapters in this book, that undertaking direct work with children is an extremely emotionally charged and challenging social work activity. And yet, paradoxically, direct work is often the aspect of social work which many students on qualifying programmes are entranced by and drawn to. A partial explanation for this level of interest might be found in the tendency to portray direct work activities, such as life story book work or ecomaps, in what can appear to be a "rose-tinted" manner – one which fails to fully recognise the life experiences that children and young people have encountered that necessitate them engaging in such activities. All too often, accounts of direct work in the social work literature detail "successful" work, with little reference to the emotional intensity and complexity that it inevitably encompasses (Ruch, 1998). Direct work is rewarding and can be fun, but, as Luckock and Lefevre recognise in the opening chapter, to portray it in this "rose-tinted" way without acknowledging its challenges is to do a disservice to both the children concerned and those undertaking the work.

It is not my intention in this chapter to deter students or practitioners from doing direct work but to enable them to engage in this aspect of social work with "their eyes open", knowing what to expect and what sorts of support they need to do it effectively. Helping someone to have "their eyes open" is not always an easy task. I am not sure any social work lecturer or team manager wants to recommend books entitled *Surviving Fears in Health and Social Care* (Smith, 2005) or book chapters entitled 'Containing anxiety in work with damaged children' (Pawson, 1994) for fear of putting off students or practitioners before they've begun! Yet, social work educators and managers who are responsible for equipping students and qualified practitioners to function as competent, ethical and effective social work practitioners must ensure that they understand the realities of social work practice.

This chapter seeks to assist in the process of "opening the eyes" of practitioners to the impact of direct work and to outline for managers and practitioners the characteristics of organisations and support systems which enable practitioners to "keep their eyes open", to "survive" the fears they encounter and to continue to do the work. Whilst running the risk of restating comments made earlier in the book (e.g. by Lefevre, Smallbone and Ironside), the chapter starts with a brief overview of the role of anxiety, emotional defences and containment in social work practice. I consider it a risk worth taking, given the enormous part they play in the effectiveness (or not) of direct work with children. The chapter then moves on to explore a conceptual model of containment which, when used to inform the creation of support structures, provides organisational contexts that promote and sustain good practice in direct work with children and young people.

Children's lives, anxiety and containment

My definition of direct work includes both formal and time-limited pieces of work, such as that undertaken with Jenny (below), and the informal, spontaneous interventions that can arise at any time when engaged with a child or young person, what Ward (this volume) refers to as "opportunity-led work".

> Jenny was a ten-year-old girl with whom I undertook some direct work to help her understand the physically, emotionally and sexually abusive experiences inflicted by her father and his friends. In the course of our meetings, Jenny would engage in enacting stories which involved her adopting powerful, superior and intrusive positions and putting me in a subordinate, powerless role. On one occasion, I was made to lie on the floor, ostensibly ill, and was subjected to Jenny thrusting injections into my arm, telling me it was 'all right' and that 'I would be "OK".'

> Unsurprisingly, these sessions with Jenny had a powerful impact on me. It is not difficult to see how Jenny was replicating, in the safety of a therapeutic setting, her own abusive experiences and experimenting with being in the more powerful position of the abuser. I relied heavily on clinical supervision with a child psychotherapist to help me understand both the meaning of Jenny's play and my part in it. At times in the sessions I felt acutely uncomfortable – as if I was condoning Jenny's "abusive" playacting behaviours. Finding my own professional boundaries was a delicate task and one for which I needed experienced help.

The example of work undertaken with Jenny graphically illustrates the powerful nature of the material that children bring to direct work sessions. Whilst the unstructured format of these sessions might have facilitated a freer exploration of emotions, structured paper and pen-based activities, such as drawing ecomaps and life maps, or spontaneous, unplanned "opportunistic" interactions, can elicit equally powerful and unexpected emotional responses. What most practitioners engaged in any type of direct work would testify to is that, if a child feels they have a safe relationship with a social worker, powerful emotions will sooner or later be expressed in more or less unexpected ways and places. Rarely does direct work "go to plan" (Ruch, 1998). Given the potential for this to happen, practitioners need to be equipped to deal with the unexpected and have access to a regular forum where they can reflect on and make sense of what has happened. Only by doing so can they continue to be emotionally available to the child. One way of developing direct work skills and learning to cope with the "unexpected" is to become more familiar with how children's emotional behaviours are invariably associated with anxiety.

In the case of my work with Jenny, I became aware that, while she was emotionally expressive in the sessions, often displaying powerful feelings of anger and hate, my predominant feeling prior to and during sessions was one of anxiety – what would happen, and how would I deal with it? As a result, I found it difficult to think about what Jenny was expressing in the session and would be pre-occupied with my own safety and whether what I was doing was considered professionally appropriate. Through supervision, I began to understand how I was experiencing Jenny's anxiety-ridden feelings about what had happened to her and how people had perceived her behaviour.

Primitive feelings of fear, anger, envy, etc. are inextricably bound up with anxiety (Trowell, 1995; Carroll, 1998; Hunter, 2001). By finding ways of managing, or "containing" the anxiety, the other emotional responses can be thoughtfully addressed. In a seminal paper on the professional experiences of nurses, Menzies-Lyth (1988) identified how social systems or behaviours become established as defences against individual and institutional anxiety. Two of the defensive behaviours that Menzies-Lyth identified were, firstly, the tendency of the nurses to de-personalise patients, for example, by referring to a patient as 'the liver in bed nine', and detaching themselves from the affective responses a patient's circumstances might arouse in them; and secondly, the extent to which nurses engaged in routine tasks to an unnecessarily repetitive extent, for example, cleaning equipment and counting supplies, tasks which kept them from relating too closely to the patients under their care.

It is not difficult to identify situations where social workers engage in avoidant defensive behaviours, for similar reasons (Beckett *et al*, 2006). The proliferation and prioritisation of paperwork within social work settings and the decline in opportunities for statutory social workers to undertake direct work with children and young people are pertinent examples of depersonalising and distancing practices. Yet the emotional content of the professional task and the anxiety it provokes does not go away. What happens is it gets denied and displaced, with the associated risk of it being expressed in more dysfunctional and potentially dangerous ways, such as burn-out and stress-related staff absences. If practitioners are to be encouraged to fully grasp and engage with the emotional complexities of direct work, how can the anxiety generated be most effectively managed?

Multi-faceted containment – a conceptual model

Bion's (1962) notion of containment offers a helpful conceptual framework for thinking about anxiety and its management. For Bion, containment, or more specifically *emotional* containment, can be understood in the context of the relationship between the mother/primary carer and her baby – the mother/carer is "the container", the baby is "the contained" – and refers to the capacity of the mother/carer to "contain" a baby's emotional responses. Containment involves the mother/carer responding to her baby's powerful anxiety-ridden feelings – or what Bion refers to as the 'nameless dread' associated with such primitive feelings – and returning them to her baby in a manageable form (Shuttleworth, 1989; Trowell, 1995). Recent research (Ruch, 2004) that I undertook into practitioners' experiences of working with children and families developed Bion's thinking and identified three different types of containment necessary for reflective and effective practice. The research found that Bion's emotional containment was only one type of containment that practitioners required to sustain good practice. Alongside emotional or "feeling" containment, practitioners needed organisational or "doing" containment and epistemological or "thinking" containment.

Emotional or "feeling" containment

Emotional containment is an important aspect of direct work, as it affords practitioners a space where the unthinkable experiences, such as those expressed by Jenny, can be thought about, processed and made bearable. Supervision (discussed further below) is the obvious, although not the only, forum in which emotional containment can be made available. If practitioners do not experience emotional containment, there is a serious risk of false or insecure professional autonomy emerging. False or insecure professional autonomy, arising from insufficiently containing experiences equates, in Bion's terms, to a practitioner's impaired functioning and limited ability to cope with anxiety-provoking situations. In the case of my work with Jenny, without emotionally containing supervision, my impaired ability to listen to Jenny (a form of depersonalised and detached defensive practice) would have become entrenched and affected the quality of the work done. Conversely, positive professional autonomy is associated with emotionally containing contexts that, paradoxically, enable practitioners to acknowledge their professional dependency needs. By providing appropriately containing support mechanisms, practitioners do not have to focus on their professional survival but can acknowledge their professional vulnerability and dependency, thereby allowing them to direct their intellectual and emotional energies to thinking about the concerns of the child with whom they are working. Although emotional containment is essential for effective direct work, its own effectiveness, however, is reduced if the other two types of containment – organisational and epistemological – are not available to practitioners.

Organisational or "doing" containment

Within social work practice there is always the risk of polarising its different components. As Luckock and Lefevre (Chapters 1 and 2, this volume) acknowledge, practitioners, in statutory childcare contexts in particular, struggle to ensure that their capacity to undertake direct work is not undermined by other demands on their time. Social workers are required to juggle the competing need to do, think and feel if they are to effectively undertake their work. The current climate tends to emphasise the "doing" dimension, and the thinking and feeling dimensions of the work have become increasingly marginalised (Ferguson, 2005). Direct work, however, should not be prioritised at the expense of other aspects of practice, e.g. efficient procedures and paperwork; rather a "both and" approach is vital if the effectiveness of direct work is to be fully realised. Organisationally containing work contexts can make this realisable.

Organisational containment focuses on issues of professional and managerial clarity but equates to something more than simply procedurally informed practice. Practice that is primarily procedurally driven runs the risk of the procedures becoming institutional defence mechanisms against the uncertainty and anxieties of practice (Menzies-Lyth, 1988). The recurrence throughout the 1990s and into the 21st century of childcare tragedies (Reder and Duncan, 1993, 2004; Department of Health, 2003), in spite of major organisational restructuring, policy innovations and procedural revisions, provides confirmatory evidence that organisational and procedural responses per se may be necessary but are not a sufficient form of containment for effective and reflective social work practice. Stevenson's (1999, p 96) acknowledgement of 'the extraordinarily pervasive nature of what has become the unbalanced search for certainty and safety through procedures, in practice and in training' highlights the extent to which organisational containment is sought after but misconceived. Narrowly understood and operationalised forms of organisational containment, as outlined above, generate risk-averse, defensive and restrictive practice; they become institutional defences as opposed to dynamic relationships and are ineffective as a consequence. They engender a false belief that risk can be extinguished, provided the prescribed procedures and practices are followed.

Crucial to the effectiveness of organisational containment is the existence of managers and management structures which can act as containers for the anxieties that direct work and the competing organisational demands generate. One of the childcare teams involved in the research referred to earlier (Ruch, 2004), experienced negligible organisational containment and lacked a "containing" manager. The absence of a "containing" manager was exacerbated by the organisational uncertainty experienced by the team, which was soon to be subjected to a local authority-wide re-structuring. Most team meetings were spent enmeshed in discussions about the team's future, at the expense of taking time to think carefully about new referrals and how work could be undertaken with distressed children and their families.

For these practitioners, the team manager was unable to contain the anxiety generated by the organisational uncertainties they were facing or the work they were required to undertake. In Bion's terms, the "containing manager" becomes the container for the unprocessed experiences of practitioners. Through clear management strategies and effective manager–practitioner relationships, the manager can contain organisationally generated and practice-related anxiety. Without a thoughtful, containing context in which practitioners can process the feelings aroused by their organisational context and professional practice, their capacity to engage in emotionally complex and demanding work is diminished.

In my work with Jenny, it would have been all too easy to adopt a procedurally prescribed approach and to restrict my involvement with her to the bare minimum, i.e statutory visits and reviews. My capacity to engage in the direct work can be attributed, in part, to my team manager, Faye. By clarifying the nature of my remit with Jenny and supporting my consultation sessions, Faye afforded me organisational containment which enabled me to manage the potentially overwhelming anxiety associated with the work.

Epistemological or "thinking" containment

Epistemological containment is the third facet of containment which, when facilitated along with emotional and organisational containment, creates a holistically containing environment that maximises the potential for ethical and effective practice. No two practitioners will experience a piece of direct work in the same way and direct work never turns out to be what the practitioner plans or expects. This capacity to cope with the unexpected and uncertainty, to be able to "not know" (Daniels, 2005) and to continue to engage in direct work sessions when it is not clear what is being achieved or where it is heading, is an integral component of good practice. Epistemology refers to the diverse range of knowledge that informs practice. Epistemological containment, then, in the context of direct work, represents the capacity for individuals to be "open-minded" in their response to a child's circumstances and to think creatively and in diverse ways around the issues raised. Such containment is fostered in four important ways:

- by work contexts which embrace and value the diverse sources of knowledge informing practice, e.g different theoretical frameworks, research, policy, intuition and practice wisdom;
- by contexts which promote communicative and collaborative forums, and practices which encourage discussion and debate about the uncertain, contentious and complex issues that direct work raises;
- through well-developed collegial and team relationships, which are invariably generated by the existence of the communicative and collaborative forums referred to above;

- by team managers who are able to encourage the previous two team characteristics – diverse reflective forums and collegial relationships.

In most teams, opportunities to discuss work-related issues are restricted to three forums: supervision, team meetings and informal discussions. Whilst none of these should be dismissed as unimportant, the extent to which more detailed reflective discussions happen in these forums is limited. Epistemologically containing contexts require a team manager, such as I experienced with Faye, who facilitates practitioners having access to a broader range of reflective spaces, e.g. co-working relationships, formal case discussions, group supervision and regular individual or group consultation with external "experts" (child psychotherapists, play therapists, etc). What this might look like in practice is discussed below.

Holistic containment

This combination of emotional, organisational and epistemological containment creates an overarching form of containment – holistic containment. Holistically containing settings acknowledge the inter-dependence of the diverse contexts and types of containment and provide the optimal conditions for the development of the reflective practice which is required for effective direct work. How then might these different types of containment be operationalised? What might the structures look like which can help promote containment and containing practice contexts?

Containing organisational structures and systems

Supervision for practitioners and managers

Historically, supervision has been the primary support system that has existed to support practitioners and offer emotional containment. Contemporary trends in practice, however, have begun to erode the established tripartite models of supervision that traditionally have addressed the management, education and development needs of practitioners. Supervision is increasingly reduced to a workload management tool. This reality, however, need not be a negative one, provided that the systemic principle of adopting a "both and" stance, referred to above, is adhered to. What this means is that the narrower version of supervision which focuses on management issues must be valued for the organisational containment it offers practitioners, but it must be complemented with alternative support mechanisms that address the emotional and epistemological needs of practitioners. In some contexts this might be referred to as clinical supervision and generally be offered on an individual basis. Other types of collective supervisory forums, however, such as co-working and case discussion, also exist and it is these collective forums that are discussed below.

It is the responsibility of team managers to ensure that adequate supervisory arrangements are in place. For team managers to take on this responsibility effectively, they need to be sufficiently secure in their own professional position so that they can, firstly, tolerate practitioners having considerable autonomy in the different reflective forums that should exist to supplement supervision and promote good practice and, secondly, be prepared to abdicate some control, albeit not their line management responsibilities, to other professionals, for example, therapists acting in consultancy capacities to teams. Encouraging the development of team managers who can understand their role in terms of devolving and dispersing control and nurturing autonomous practitioners is not always straightforward.

One of the biggest obstacles to the development of open-minded and facilitative managers is the paucity of supervision available to them and it is rare, certainly within the social work literature, for supervision of managers to be given much attention. Frontline managers are located in a demanding and invidious position within their organisation – having to be responsive to the needs of practitioners, while being constrained by the expectations of the organisation (Kearney, 2004). Despite their operational management positions, frontline managers receive almost exclusively managerial supervision and all too quickly can become subsumed by the demands of the organisation and become distanced from the emotional realities of practice and the needs of practitioners. The support needs of frontline managers are greatly under-addressed. Organisations which seek to promote good practice and containing work contexts would do well to attend to the containment needs of this tier of the organisation as well as those at practitioner level.

Communicative and collaborative team practices

Despite the fact that almost all social work practitioners are located in teams, it is remarkable how little literature exists on the significance of teams and team working for good practice. In contrast, the conceptual framework of containment discussed above places a heavy emphasis on the potential of communicative and collaborative team practices to promote good practice. Two examples of such practices are co-working and case discussions.

a) Co-working

Conventional conceptions of direct work are based on an individual practitioner working with a child or young person. Any difficulties or issues raised by the work would primarily be discussed individually and confidentially in supervision or possibly informally with a colleague. In the context of direct work, co-working could involve a number of permutations, for example, two workers, one whose responsibility is to work with the child, the other to work with the parents/carers (a model commonly used in clinical settings, such as CAMHS teams) or two or three workers with responsibility for working with individual siblings and parents/carers from one family. However the co-working is configured, what it encourages is more transparent thinking and communication about what is happening for a child or family. Co-working practices necessitate practitioners arranging formal sessions to discuss how the work is progressing and, by definition, involve an exchange of experiences, thoughts, feelings and ideas for future work. Through these discussions, difficulties can be explored, assumptions can be challenged and hypotheses formulated and tested.

b) Case discussions

Case discussion can happen in a number of different reflective contexts. It can be integrated into team or allocation meetings, be part of group supervision or be a designated forum in its own right. Other ways in which case discussions can be configured include group supervision facilitated by the team manager or senior practitioner, where practitioners present cases for the team to think about together or in team consultation sessions using external consultants. Given the pressurised nature of practice contexts and the resistance to thinking about practice that can be encountered (Ruch, 2007), finding ways in which case discussion can be synergised with existing activities is likely to meet with more success than inviting teams to adopt a completely new forum dedicated to case discussion.

Allocation meetings offer an ideal space for case discussions. Such forums often get reduced to a bureaucratic mechanism for managing the workload, but an alternative way of conceptualising these forums, one which incorporates case discussion into them, is as a place where collective reflective thinking is done which informs to whom a case is allocated and the choice of intervention. When thinking about the needs of a child or young person, such forums can challenge what otherwise might be a premature decision to undertake direct work as opposed to family work, for example, or equally could highlight direct work approaches which might be very appropriate to the child's circumstances and inform how the sessions might be structured.

Such collaborative and communicative mechanisms reduce the individual responsibility carried by one practitioner and emphasise the shared nature of the task and collective expertise within any one team. They open up possibilities in practice and enable practitioners to cope with uncertainty and "not knowing" (Daniels, 2005). As such they are fundamentally empowering, as they challenge hidden assumptions and privileged thinking and allow everyone a voice. Furthermore, if practice is modelled on collaborative and communicative approaches, it enhances the likelihood of similar practices being adopted in the work itself. Practitioners can engage in direct work in more transparent, reflective and empowering ways that recognise the expertise of the child or young person concerned.

Holistic containment – obstacles and opportunities

Supervision, case discussions and co-working practices create the conditions in which practitioners can feel organisationally, emotionally and epistemologically contained and, by implication, contribute to the promotion of reflective, effective and ethical practice. The obstacles that can exist to practitioners either having these opportunities available to them or being willing to engage in them when they are, however, must not be underestimated (Ruch, 2007). For many, this is unfamiliar territory and requires sensitive handling by those responsible for facilitating the sessions. To fully benefit from containing, collaborative and communicative forums, practitioners need to be willing to admit their vulnerabilities and be open to the inter-dependent, reciprocal relationships that they generate. The potential of such forums is considerable and by engaging in them practitioners can discover what it means not simply to survive but to thrive in demanding, but potentially rewarding, practice contexts.

Over time, the impact on professional practice of exposure to containing contexts, forums and practices can be internalised by practitioners. As a consequence of this exposure, practitioners can more readily draw on an internal model of reflection/ supervision (Bower, 2003) which complements external reflective forums where they exist and substitutes for them where they are absent. The capacity of practitioners to utilise external sources of support, facilitated by team managers, and to develop their own internal support structures contributes to the development of holistically containing and, by implication, I would suggest, effective practice contexts. These "containing contexts" empower the practitioners who work within them and thereby, through the processes of mirroring (Mattinson, 1992), increase the likelihood of empowering practice taking place with children and young people.

Conclusion

My own experiences of working with children such as Jenny, my research activities and my exposure, through teaching on post-qualification childcare programmes, to the practice dilemmas of practitioners working with children and young people in complex, emotionally charged and risk-laden circumstances are the foundation on which the ideas introduced in this chapter are built. I am convinced that attending to the needs of practitioners and team managers is pivotal for effective direct work with children and young people. I hope that this chapter has achieved its two-fold objectives: firstly, to encourage practitioners to seek the support they need to sustain good practice by "opening their eyes" to the realities of direct work with children and young people and removing the "rose-tinted spectacles" that can distort how direct work is viewed; secondly, to make organisations aware of the conditions required for "containing contexts" to flourish, by acknowledging, in particular, that effective direct work requires support being available, not only for practitioners, but for frontline managers too. With such clarity of vision existing at all levels of the organisations – from practitioners to senior managers – the future of direct work looks bright.

(All names used in case studies have been changed to preserve anonymity)

References

Beckett C., McKeigue B. and Taylor H. (2007) 'Coming to conclusions: social workers' perceptions of the decision-making proces in care proceedings', *Child and Family Social Work*, 12:1, pp 54–63

Bion W. (1962) *Learning from Experience*, London: Heinemann

Bower M. (2003) 'Broken and twisted', *Journal of Social Work Practice*, 17:2, pp 143–152

Carroll J. (1998) *Introduction to Therapeutic Play*, Oxford: Blackwell Science

Daniels G. (2005) 'Thinking in and out of the frame: applying systemic ideas to social work with children', in Bower M. (ed.) *Psycho-Analytic Theory for Social Work: Thinking under fire*, London: Routledge, pp 59–71

Department of Health (2003) *The Victoria Climbié Inquiry: Report of an inquiry*, London: HMSO

Ferguson H. (2005) 'Working with violence, the emotions and the psycho-social dimensions of child protection: reflections on the Victoria Climbié case', *Social Work Education*, 24:7, pp 781–795

Hunter M. (2001) *Psychotherapy with Young People in Care: Lost and found*, Hove: Brunner Routledge

Kearney P. (2004) 'Firstline managers: the mediators of standards and the quality of practice', in Statham D. (ed.) *Managing Frontline Practice in Social Care*, London: Jessica Kingsley, pp 103–115

Mattinson J. (1992) *The Reflective Process in Social Work Supervision* (2nd edn), London: Tavistock Institute of Marital Studies

Menzies-Lyth I. (1988) *Containing Anxiety in Institutions: Selected essays, Volume One*, London: Free Association Books

Pawson C. (1994) 'Containing anxiety in work with damaged children', in Obholzer A. and Zagier Roberts V. (eds) *The Unconscious at Work: Individual and organisational stress in the human services*, London: Routledge

Reder P. and Duncan S. (1993) *Beyond Blame: Child abuse tragedies revisited*, London: Routledge

Reder P. and Duncan S. (2004) 'Making the most of the Victoria Climbié inquiry', *Child Abuse Review*, 13, pp 95–114

Ruch G. (1998) 'Direct work with children: the practitioner's perspective', *Practice*, 10:1, pp 37–44

Ruch G. (2004) *Reflective Practice in Contemporary Child Care Social Work*, unpublished PhD Thesis, University of Southampton

Ruch G. (2007) 'Reflective practice in childcare social work: the role of containment', *British Journal of Social Work*, 37, pp 659–680

Shuttleworth J. (1989) 'Psychoanalytic theory and infant development', in Miller L., Rustin M., Rustin M. and Shuttleworth J. (eds) *Closely Observed Infants*, London: Duckworth

Smith M. (2005) *Surviving Fears in Health and Social Care: The terrors of night and the arrows of day*, London: Jessica Kingsley

Stevenson O. (1999) 'Social work with children and families', in Stevenson O. (ed.) *Child Welfare in the United Kingdom*, Oxford: Blackwell Science, pp 79–100

Trowell J. (1995) 'Key psychoanalytic concepts', in Trowell J. and Bower M. (eds) *The Emotional Needs of Children and Their Families: Using psychoanalytic ideas in the community*, London: Routledge

Notes about the contributors

Afshan Ahmad

Afshan Ahmad began her social work career in 1989. She joined the Foster Care Associates in July 1998, having completed a DipSW and DipHE. She is currently working as national life story co-ordinator for FCA, and is involved in direct work with children in placement, including the completion of life story work, alongside training other professionals.

Bridget Betts

Bridget Betts is an independent social worker and also an adopted person. She has been involved in training and preparing carers, and preparing children for permanence and adoption, including life story work.

Alan Burnell

Alan Burnell is one of the Co-Directors of Family Futures, and the Co-ordinator of the Family Futures MA Level Course on Adoption and Attachment. Being adopted as a baby has had a profound impact on his personal and professional life. Following his degree and social work training, he was privileged to work with some very inspired practitioners, who led him to believe that it is always possible to improve services for each generation of children. His commitment to adoptive families stems from his own adoptive parents, who embodied the spirit of adoption at its best, and from the adoptive families with whom he has worked over the past few years.

Andy Cook

Andy Cook's chapter in this book is based upon her experience as a duty and assessment social worker. She is now employed as a Senior Practitioner Consultant at the Clermont Child Protection Unit where she undertakes a range of risk assessments both in and out of the court arena. She is a member of the solution-focused family therapy team and also co-facilitates a group treatment programme for male perpetrators of domestic violence.

Ane Freed-Kernis

Ane Freed-Kernis has been working with young people in care for over 30 years. A qualified child care social worker and trainer of over 30 years of professional experience, she currently works as inter-agency training co-ordinator for an LSCB in north-west

England as well as a social worker for a local authority. Having been involved in lesbian, gay, bisexual and transsexual organisations since 1980, Ane has developed a keen interest in the issues faced by young LGBT children in care. This interest has led to her working as mentor, trustee and trainer volunteer for the Albert Kennedy Trust in Manchester for the last seven years and formed the research focus of her recently completed MSc in Child Care and Child Mental Health.

Anna Gupta

Anna Gupta is a Senior Lecturer in Social Work at Royal Holloway, University of London. She is the Director of Social Work Education in the Department of Health and Social Care. She has been the Director of the successful London Post-Qualifying Child Care Award at Royal Holloway for the past seven years. She is a qualified social worker with extensive experience of child care social work and management, including as a children's guardian and expert witness in public law family court proceedings. She has published work on various aspects of child welfare, including on working with families living in poverty, childhood neglect and black African children and the child protection system. She is currently involved in an evaluation of family group conferences for black and minority ethnic families.

Alex Hillman

Alex Hillman is a Research Associate at Cardiff University, working in the qualitative research node of the Economic and Social Research Council National Centre for Research Methods. She is currently working in a participatory research project with looked after young people. She has previously conducted ethnographic research in health settings.

Sally Holland

Sally Holland is a Senior Lecturer at Cardiff University and Course Director of the MA Social Work. She is currently working in a participatory research project with looked after young people within the qualitative research node of the Economic and Social Research Council National Centre for Research Methods. She has previously researched and written about assessment of parenting, family group conferences, family support, child protection and children's national identities. She has worked as a social worker with children in local authority and voluntary sector settings.

Margaret Hunter Smallbone

Margaret Hunter Smallbone is the author of *Psychotherapy with Young People in Care* (2001) and has contributed chapters and articles to several publications, including *The Handbook of Child and Adolescent Psychotherapy* (1999). She is Consultant Child Psychotherapist for CAMHS in Hertfordshire, having worked for South London and

Maudsley Trust for 15 years, where she established a dedicated mental health team for looked after children. Margaret was trained at the Tavistock Clinic and began her professional life as a psychotherapist in a local authority children's home. She has retained a connection with looked after children and currently contributes to a specialist fostering service, Integrated Services Programme, in Chesham and Enfield.

Leslie Ironside

Leslie completed his training as a Child and Adolescent Psychotherapist in 1989. After working in Croydon and Worthing CAMHS, he took up the post of Consultant Child and Adolescent Psychotherapist in Brighton in 1995. He has had a long-term interest in working with children in care, and developed a service for looked after children and for children with attachment difficulties. He also worked in private practice and developed the Centre for Emotional Development, which aims to provide high quality educational conferences and lectures in the field of child and adolescent mental health and development. He left the NHS in 2004 and now works full-time as Director for the Centre and as a freelance practitioner and consultant. He has published a number of articles and chapters in journals and books.

Ravi KS Kohli

Ravi KS Kohli is Head of Applied Social Studies at the University of Bedfordshire. He migrated to the UK in the 1960s, and qualified as a social worker in 1984. His research and writing are primarily related to refugees. He is the author of *Social Work with Unaccompanied Asylum Seeking Children*, and co-editor, with Fiona Mitchell, of *Working with Unaccompanied Asylum Seeking Children: Issues for policy and practice*, both published by Palgrave in 2007.

Michelle Lefevre

Michelle Lefevre is a Lecturer in Social Work and Social Care and Director of Postqualifying Programmes for social workers in children's services at the University of Sussex. After gaining her social work qualification, Michelle worked first in local authority field social work, including keyworking with children in care, and then as a senior practitioner/consultant in a nationally recognised clinic setting with children and families where there were issues of significant harm and trauma. Since qualifying as an arts psychotherapist, Michelle has worked independently as a therapist with adults and children and as an expert witness, alongside her academic post. Michelle's recent publications include research reports and articles on social workers' communication skills in work with children, the social care needs of children with complex health care needs, and relationship-based practice.

Barry Luckock

Barry Luckock is a Senior Lecturer in Social Work and Social Policy and Director of the MA in Social Work at the University of Sussex. Having trained first as a teacher and then as a social worker, he has practice experience with children and families in schools, residential care, local authority field social work and as a guardian *ad litem*. His current research interest is in family policy and practice, including adoption, and integrated children's services. His recent publications include co-authored books on adoption support and the teaching, learning and assessment of communication skills with children in social work education. Barry spent some of his own childhood in care.

Ruth Marchant

Ruth Marchant co-directs Triangle, an independent organisation working with disabled children and young people across the UK. Ruth works directly with children, both consulting about general issues and assessing concerns about maltreatment. Most of her work is with children who communicate without speech; representing their views and evidence in contested situations, including court. Ruth's background is in psychology and play work. Ruth is a registered intermediary with the Home Office.

Pat Petrie

Pat Petrie's main research and theoretical interests are in social pedagogy, foster and residential care in continental Europe; services for families with disabled children; out-of-school play and care; and the extending role of the school. Much of her work has been conducted in continental Europe. Books include: *Out-of-School Lives, Out-of-School Services; From Children's Services to Children's Spaces; A New Deal for Children? Reforming education and care in England, Scotland and Sweden*, and *Working with Children in Care: European perspectives*. Her professional background has included teaching young people with emotional, social and behavioural difficulties in residential settings. She has four children and three grandchildren.

Emma Renold

Emma Renold is a Senior Lecturer in Childhood Studies at the School of Social Sciences, Cardiff University. Her teaching and research interests pivot around young masculinities, femininities and sexualities; gendered and sexualised bullying; and participatory research methods with children and young people. Key publications include: *Girls, Boys and Junior Sexualities* (Routledge, 2005) and *Peer Violence in Children's Residential Care* (Palgrave, 2004).

Nicola Ross

Nicola Ross is a research associate, based in QUALITI, the Cardiff University node of the Economic and Social Research Council National Centre for Research Methods. She is currently conducting participatory research with looked after children and young people involved in a multi-media research project. She has worked in academic and voluntary sectors for a number of years, conducting research with children, young people and families.

Gillian Ruch

Gillian worked as a Senior Social Worker in statutory child care teams before moving into social work education and research. Her research and practice interests lie in practitioner well-being and therapeutic approaches to work with children and families. Whilst undertaking doctoral research, she became aware of the complex inter-play between reflective and relationship-based practice and the organisational contexts of child care social work and their impact on the well-being of both practitioners and the children and families with whom they work. Recent publications exploring these themes include: 'Reflective practice in child care social work: the role of containment', *British Journal of Social Work*, 37, pp 659–680; 'Relationship-based and reflective practice: holistic approaches to contemporary child care social work', *Child and Family Social Work*, 10, pp 111–123; and 'Thoughtful practice: child care social work and the role of case discussion', *Child and Family Social Work*, 12:4, pp 370–379.

Gillian Schofield

Gillian Schofield is Professor of Child and Family Social Work and Co-Director of the Centre for Research on the Child and Family at the University of East Anglia. An experienced social work practitioner, guardian, researcher and lecturer, she has a special interest in developmental attachment theory and its application to understanding and helping children who have experienced abuse and neglect, children's pathways in foster care and adoption and social work with children. She has published widely in these fields and her work is used nationally and internationally in developing social work practice.

John Simmonds

John Simmonds is Director of Policy, Research and Development at the British Association for Adoption and Fostering. Before coming to BAAF, he was Head of the Social Work Programmes at Goldsmiths College, University of London. He is a qualified social worker and has substantial experience in child protection, family placement and residential care settings. He has published widely, including co-editing the first *Direct Work with Children* with Jane Aldgate in 1988. He is the adoptive father of two children.

311

Nigel Thomas

Nigel Thomas is Professor of Childhood and Youth Research at the University of Central Lancashire. He was a social work practitioner and manager in Derbyshire and Oxfordshire for 20 years, after which he taught and researched in child welfare and childhood studies at Swansea University. His publications include *Children, Family and the State: Decision-making and child participation* (Policy Press, 2002) and *Social Work with Young People in Care* (Palgrave, 2005). He is co-editor of the journal, *Children & Society*.

Danielle Turney

Danielle Turney is a Senior Lecturer in Social Work and Director of the Post-Qualifying Specialist Award in Social Work with Children and Young People at the University of Bristol. She is a qualified social worker and has worked in local authority children and families social work. After PhD research exploring anti-racist practice, she moved into social work education, focusing on work with children and families and on child observation. Her main research interests are in child neglect and broader issues of child welfare and protection. Recent publications have addressed different aspects of social work practice with child neglect.

Jay Vaughan

Jay Vaughan is one of the Co-Directors of Family Futures, which specialises in offering intensive therapy and support to families who have fostered or adopted traumatised children. Jay completed her postgraduate qualification in Dramatherapy in 1989 and then completed two years of post-qualifying supervised practice. Since that time she has trained with Dr Daniel Hughes on his style of attachment therapy as well as training with the Theraplay Institute on the use of Theraplay principles. Jay has been working with traumatised children for many years and believes passionately in the use of the arts in therapy for children and their families. Jay has also trained on the work at Family Futures around the UK and teaches at the Institute for the Arts in Therapy and Education.

Lorraine Wallis

Lorraine Wallis has worked as a Research and Development worker at Coram Adoption East Midlands for the last eight years. During this time she developed groups for adopted children and young people and helped create a number of participation projects to ensure that the views of adopted children and young people are heard. Her work has also involved the development of a community-based recruitment project for black adopters, which was inspired by the findings of her research on why people do not pursue their adoption enquiry. Prior to this post, she worked in universities conducting research, latterly focusing on looked after children and young runaways.

Adrian Ward
Adrian Ward is Consultant Social Worker at the Tavistock Clinic in London. He has an extensive background in the practice and leadership of residential child care, and his work now includes teaching, research and consultancy in group care issues and therapeutic practice. He is especially interested in working with staff teams and managers on exploring and improving their practice. He is the author of many articles and book chapters in this field, co-editor of several books, and author of *Working in Group Care* (2nd edn, Policy Press, 2006), and former editor of the journal, *Therapeutic Communities*.